THOR
FOR ASGARD

WRITER: **ROBERT RODI** PENCILER: **SIMONE BIANCHI**

INKS AND INKWASH: **SIMONE BIANCHI & ANDREA SILVESTRI** (ISSUES # 3-6)

COLOR ARTIST: **SIMONE PERUZZI**

ASSISTANT EDITOR: **SEBASTIAN GIRNER** EDITOR: **AXEL ALONSO**

COLLECTION EDITOR: **CORY LEVINE**

EDITORIAL ASSISTANTS:
JAMES EMMETT & JOE HOCHSTEIN

ASSISTANT EDITORS: **MATT MASDEU,
ALEX STARBUCK & NELSON RIBEIRO**

EDITORS, SPECIAL PROJECTS:
**JENNIFER GRÜNWALD
& MARK D. BEAZLEY**

SENIOR EDITOR, SPECIAL PROJECTS:
JEFF YOUNGQUIST

SENIOR VICE PRESIDENT OF SALES: **DAVID GABRIEL**

BOOK DESIGNER: **RODOLFO MURAGUCHI**

MATERIAL FROM *THOR SPOTLIGHT*
WRITER: **MIKE CONROY**
DESIGNER: **MICHAEL KRONENBERG**
EDITOR: **JOHN RHETT THOMAS**

EDITOR IN CHIEF: **AXEL ALONSO**
CHIEF CREATIVE OFFICER: **JOE QUESADA**
PUBLISHER: **DAN BUCKLEY**
EXECUTIVE PRODUCER: **ALAN FINE**

THOR: FOR ASGARD. Contains material originally published in magazine form as THOR: FOR ASGARD #1-6. First printing 2011. ISBN# 978-0-7851-4445-8. Published by MARVEL WORLDWIDE, INC., a subsidiary of MARVEL ENTERTAINMENT, LLC. OFFICE OF PUBLICATION: 135 West 50th Street, New York, NY 10020. Copyright © 2010 and 2011 Marvel Characters, Inc. All rights reserved. $24.99 per copy in the U.S. and $27.99 in Canada (GST #R127032852); Canadian Agreement #40668537. All characters featured in this issue and the distinctive names and likenesses thereof, and all related indicia are trademarks of Marvel Characters, Inc. No similarity between any of the names, characters, persons, and/or institutions in this magazine with those of any living or dead person or institution is intended, and any such similarity which may exist is purely coincidental. **Printed in the U.S.A.** ALAN FINE, EVP - Office of the President, Marvel Worldwide, Inc. and EVP & CMO Marvel Characters B.V.; DAN BUCKLEY, Publisher & President - Print, Animation & Digital Divisions; JOE QUESADA, Chief Creative Officer; JIM SOKOLOWSKI, Chief Operating Officer; DAVID BOGART, SVP of Business Affairs & Talent Management; TOM BREVOORT, SVP of Publishing; C.B. CEBULSKI, SVP of Creator & Content Development; DAVID GABRIEL, SVP of Publishing Sales & Circulation; MICHAEL PASCIULLO, SVP of Brand Planning & Communications; JIM O'KEEFE, VP of Operations & Logistics; DAN CARR, Executive Director of Publishing Technology; JUSTIN F. GABRIE, Director of Publishing & Editorial Operations; SUSAN CRESPI, Editorial Operations Manager; ALEX MORALES, Publishing Operations Manager; STAN LEE, Chairman Emeritus. For information regarding advertising in Marvel Comics or on Marvel.com, please contact Ron Stern, VP of Business Development, at rstern@marvel.com. For Marvel subscription inquiries, please call 800-217-9158. **Manufactured between 2/28/2011 and 3/28/2011 by QUAD/GRAPHICS, VERSAILLES, KY, USA.**

10 9 8 7 6 5 4 3 2 1

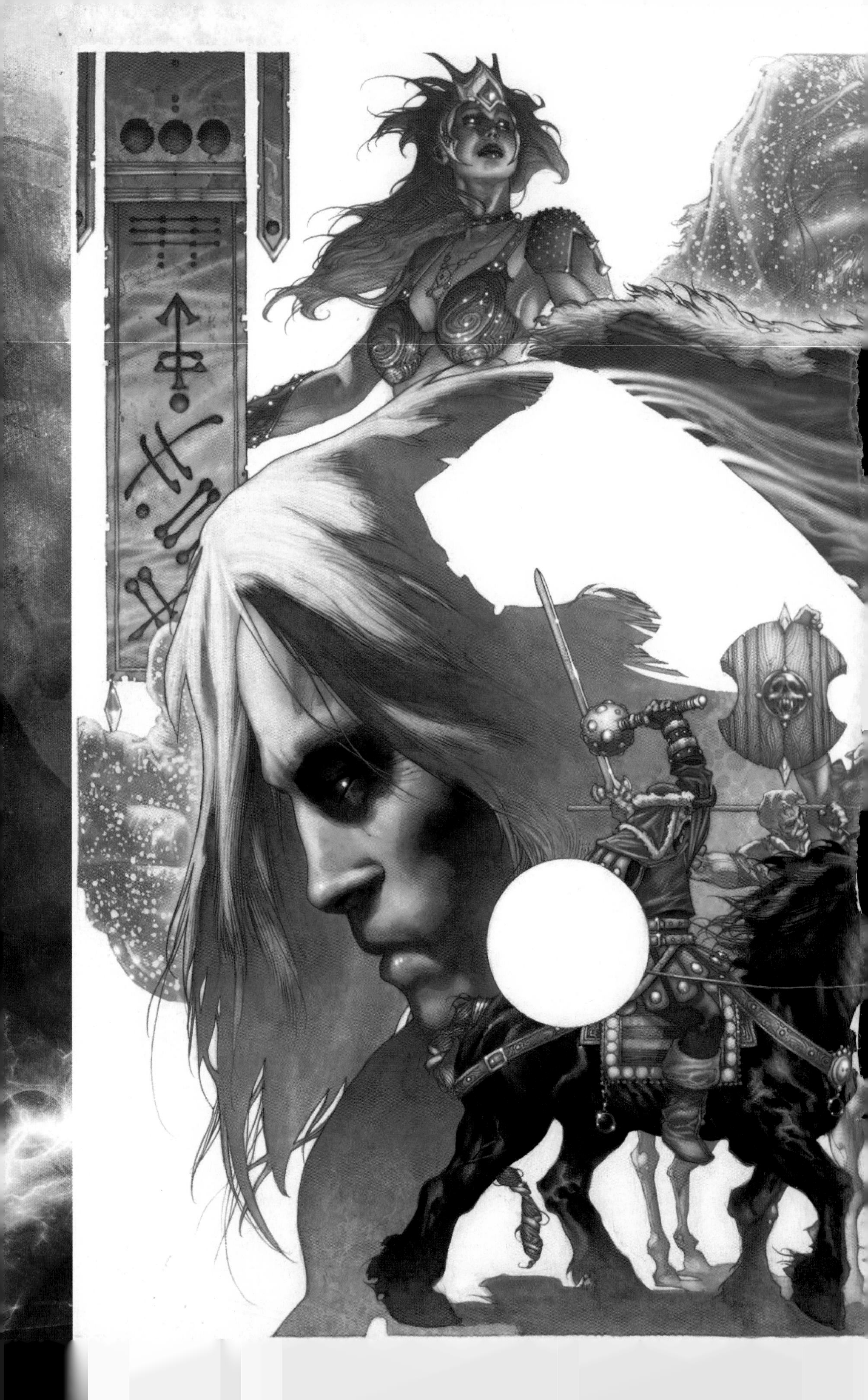

1

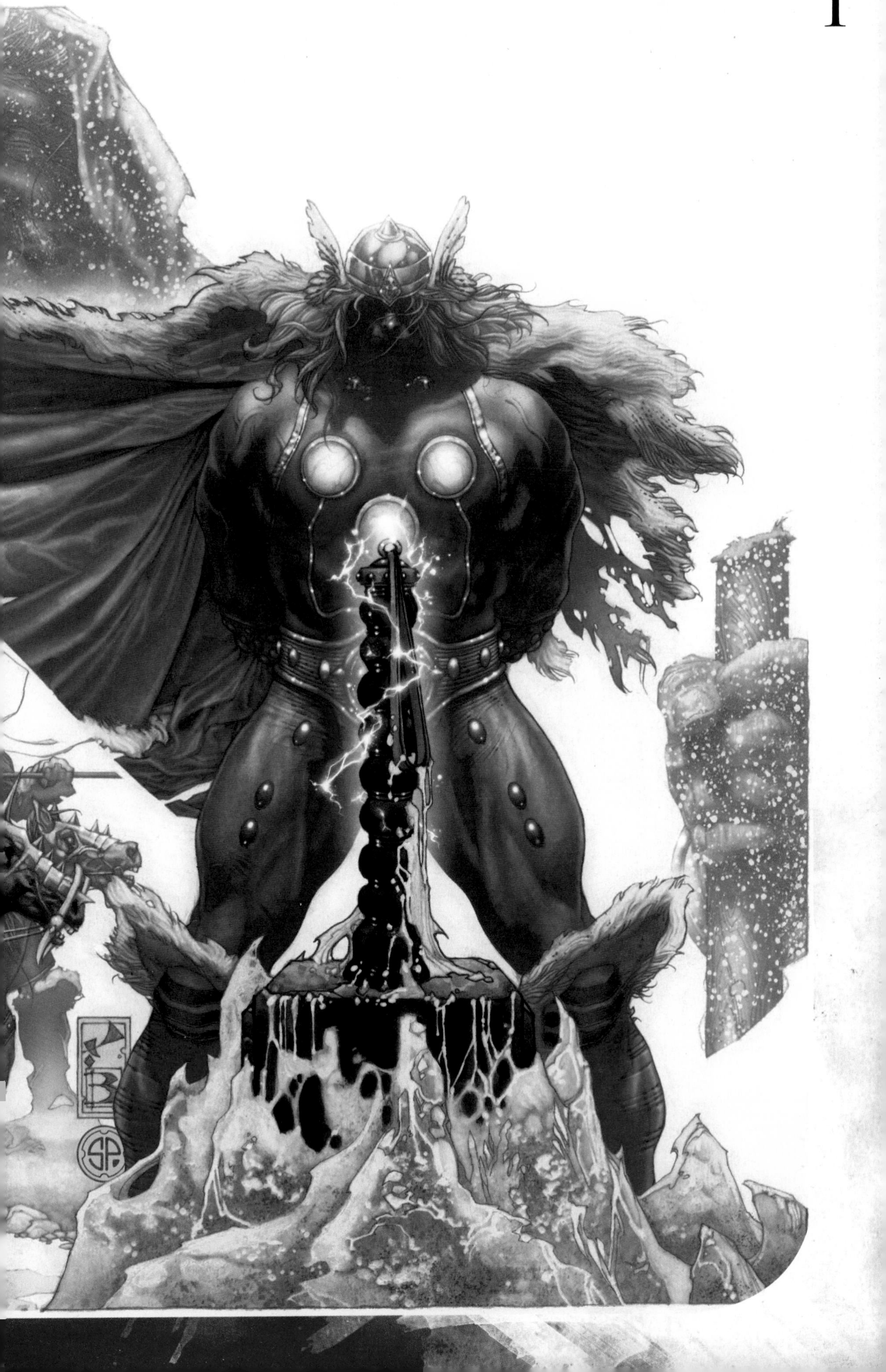

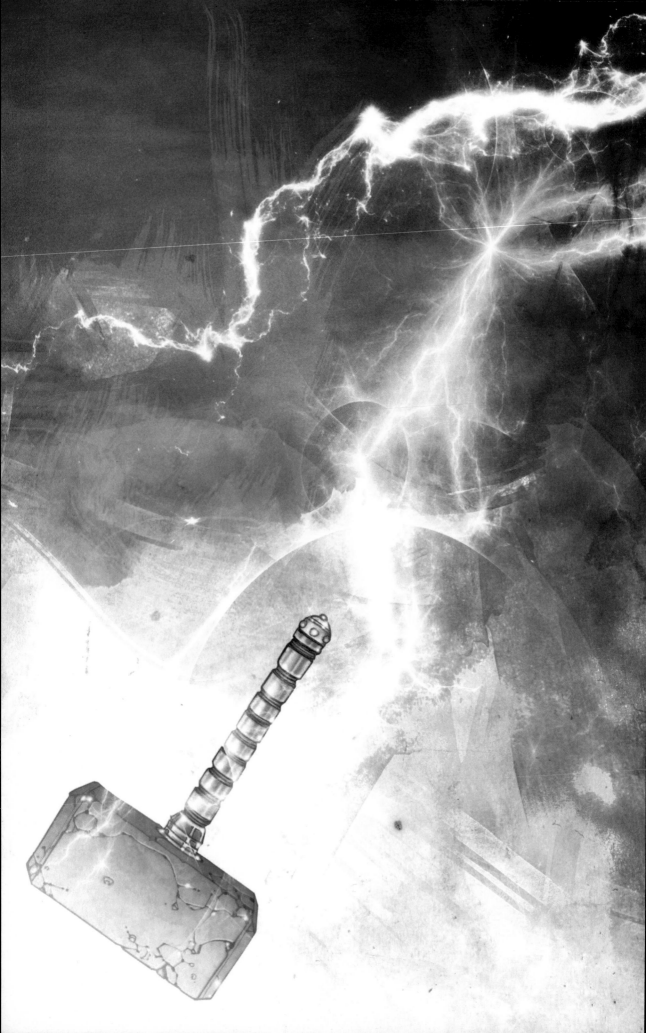

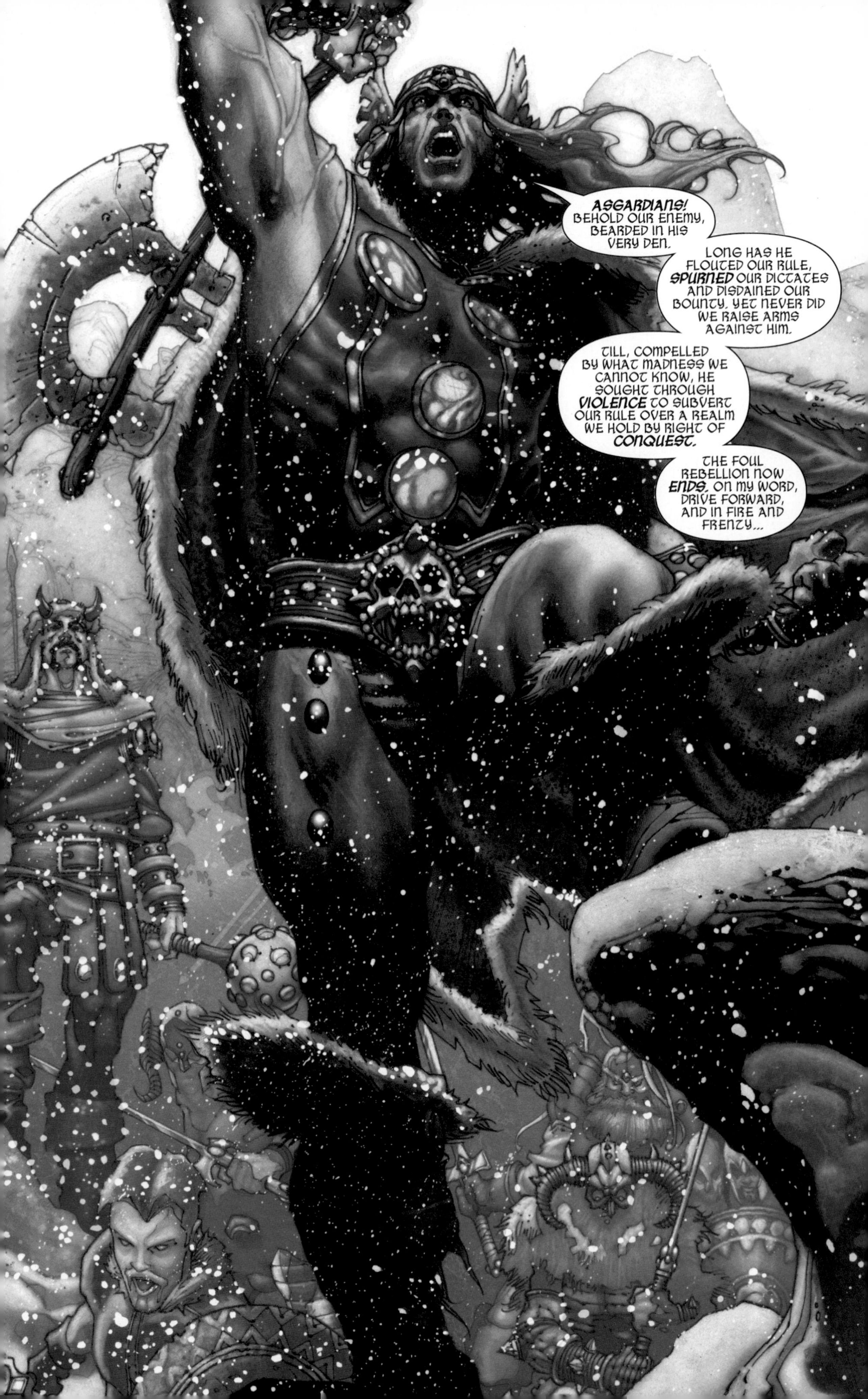
ASGARDIANS! BEHOLD OUR ENEMY, BEARDED IN HIS VERY DEN.
LONG HAS HE FLOUTED OUR RULE, SPURNED OUR DICTATES AND DISDAINED OUR BOUNTY. YET NEVER DID WE RAISE ARMS AGAINST HIM.
TILL, COMPELLED BY WHAT MADNESS WE CANNOT KNOW, HE SOUGHT THROUGH VIOLENCE TO SUBVERT OUR RULE OVER A REALM WE HOLD BY RIGHT OF CONQUEST.
THE FOUL REBELLION NOW ENDS, ON MY WORD. DRIVE FORWARD, AND IN FIRE AND FRENZY...

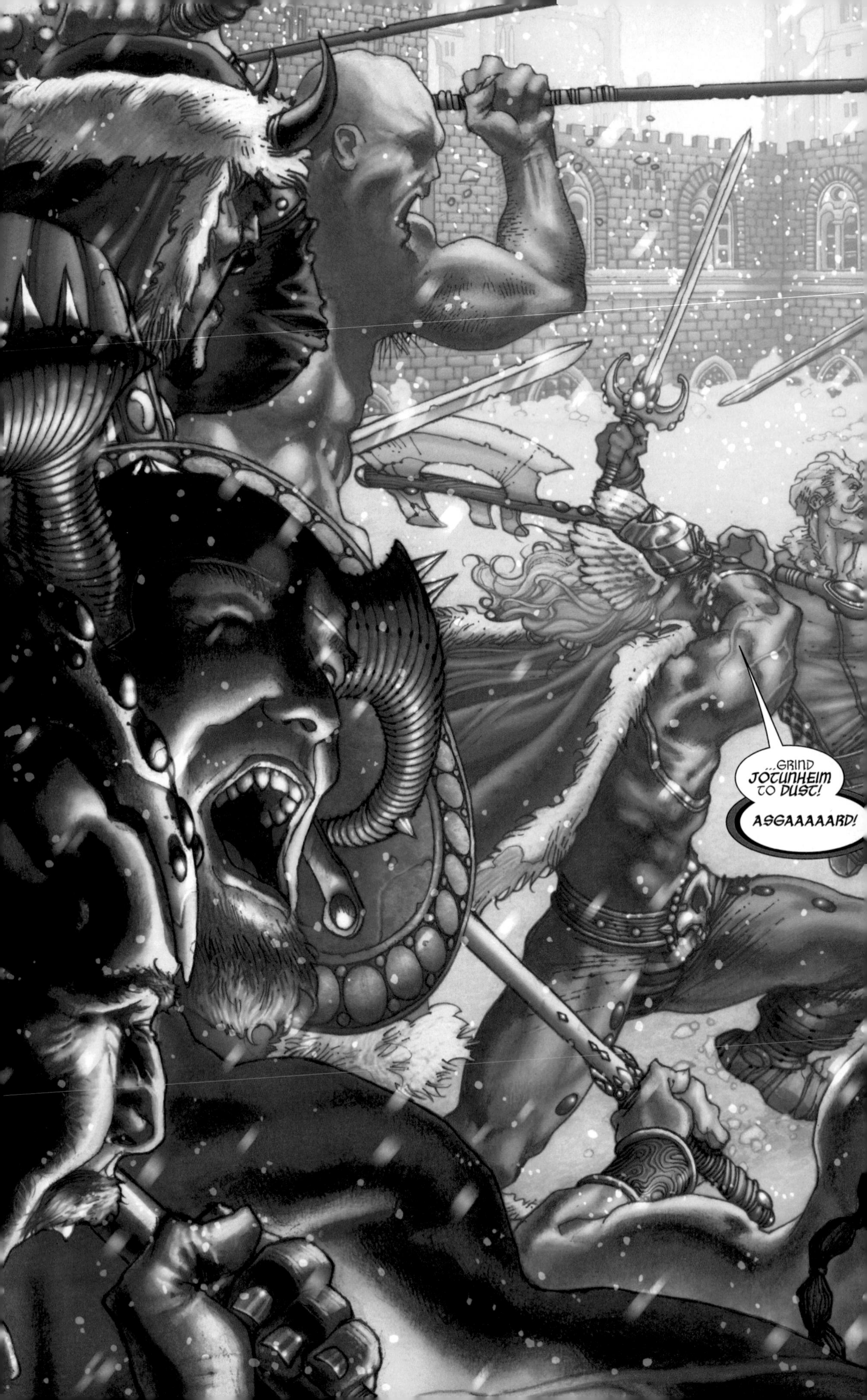
...GRIND JÖTUNHEIM TO DUST!
ASGAAAAARD!

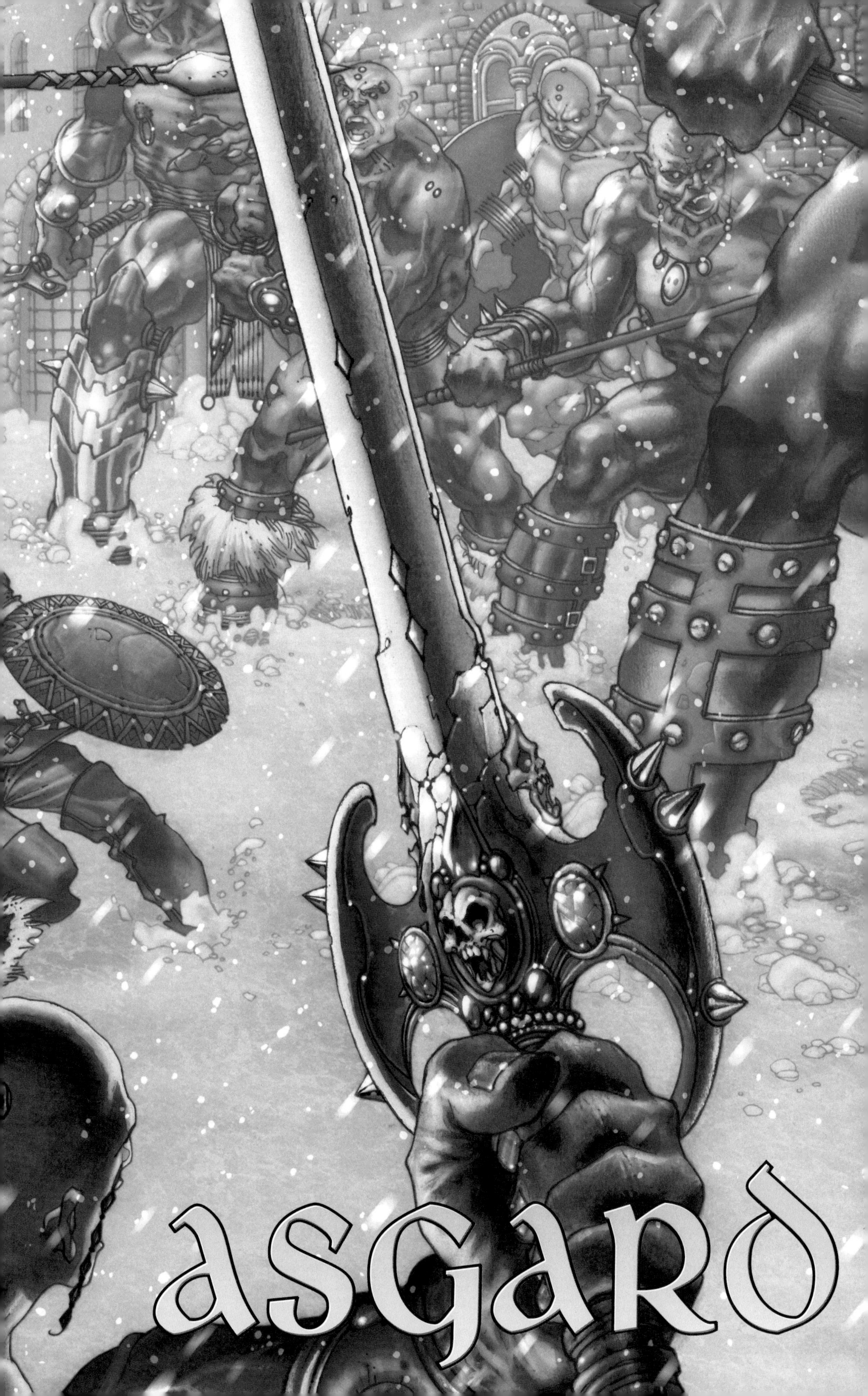
Asgard

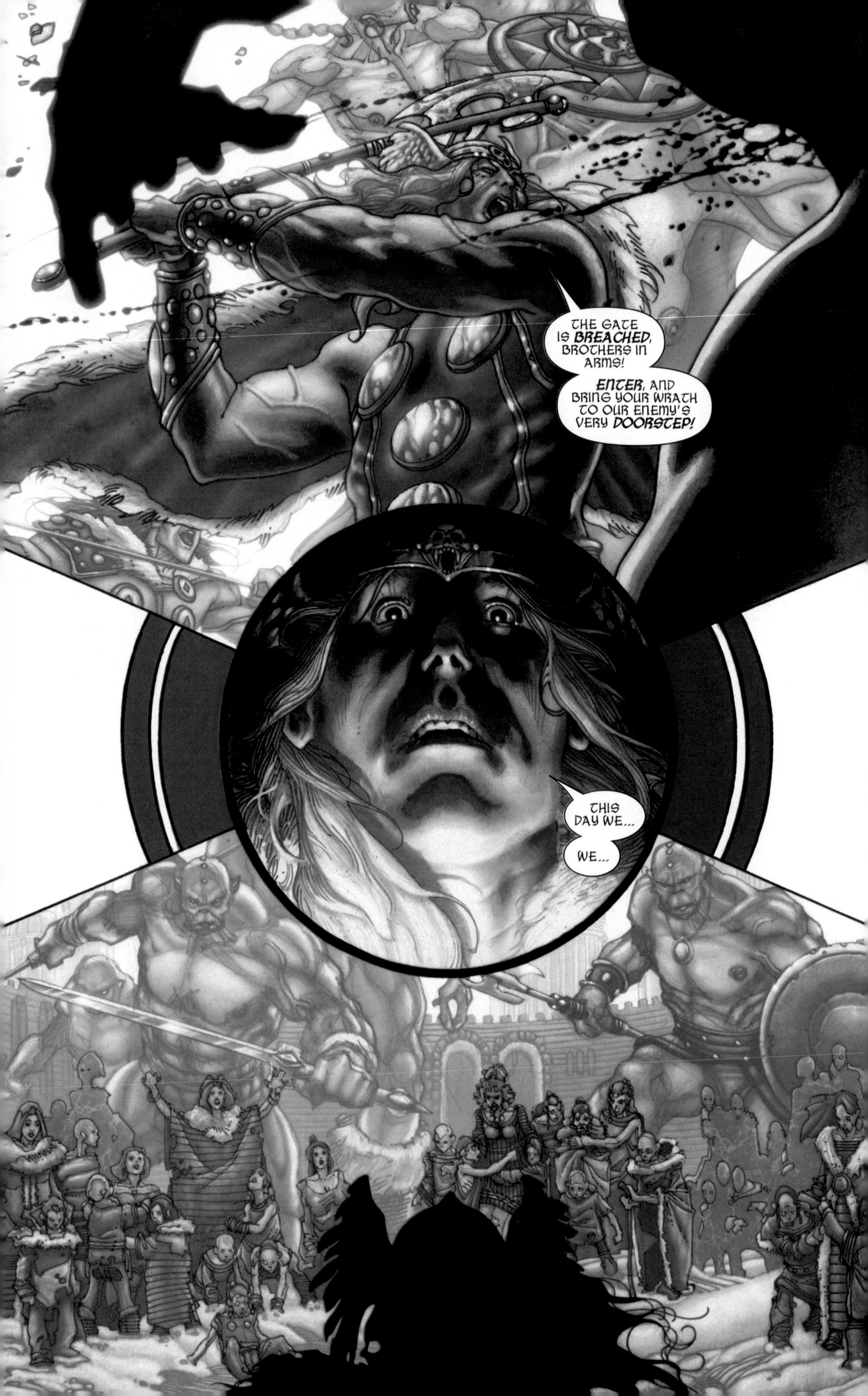
THE GATE IS *BREACHED*, BROTHERS IN ARMS!
ENTER, AND BRING YOUR WRATH TO OUR ENEMY'S VERY *DOORSTEP!*
THIS DAY WE...
WE...

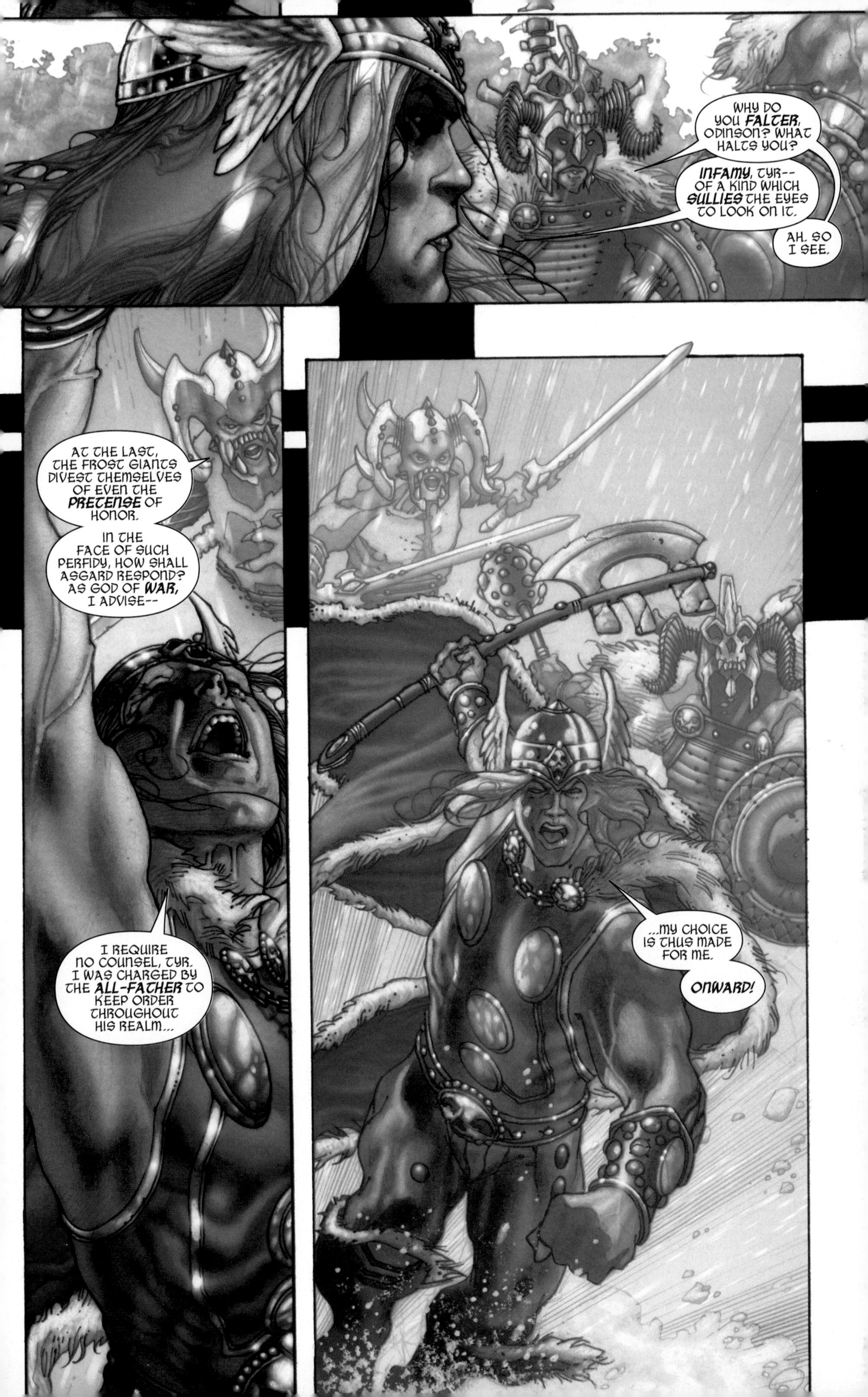
WHY DO YOU FALTER, ODINSON? WHAT HALTS YOU?
INFAMY, TYR-- OF A KIND WHICH SULLIES THE EYES TO LOOK ON IT.
AH. SO I SEE.
AT THE LAST, THE FROST GIANTS DIVEST THEMSELVES OF EVEN THE PRETENSE OF HONOR.
IN THE FACE OF SUCH PERFIDY, HOW SHALL ASGARD RESPOND? AS GOD OF WAR, I ADVISE--
I REQUIRE NO COUNSEL, TYR. I WAS CHARGED BY THE ALL-FATHER TO KEEP ORDER THROUGHOUT HIS REALM...
...MY CHOICE IS THUS MADE FOR ME.
ONWARD!

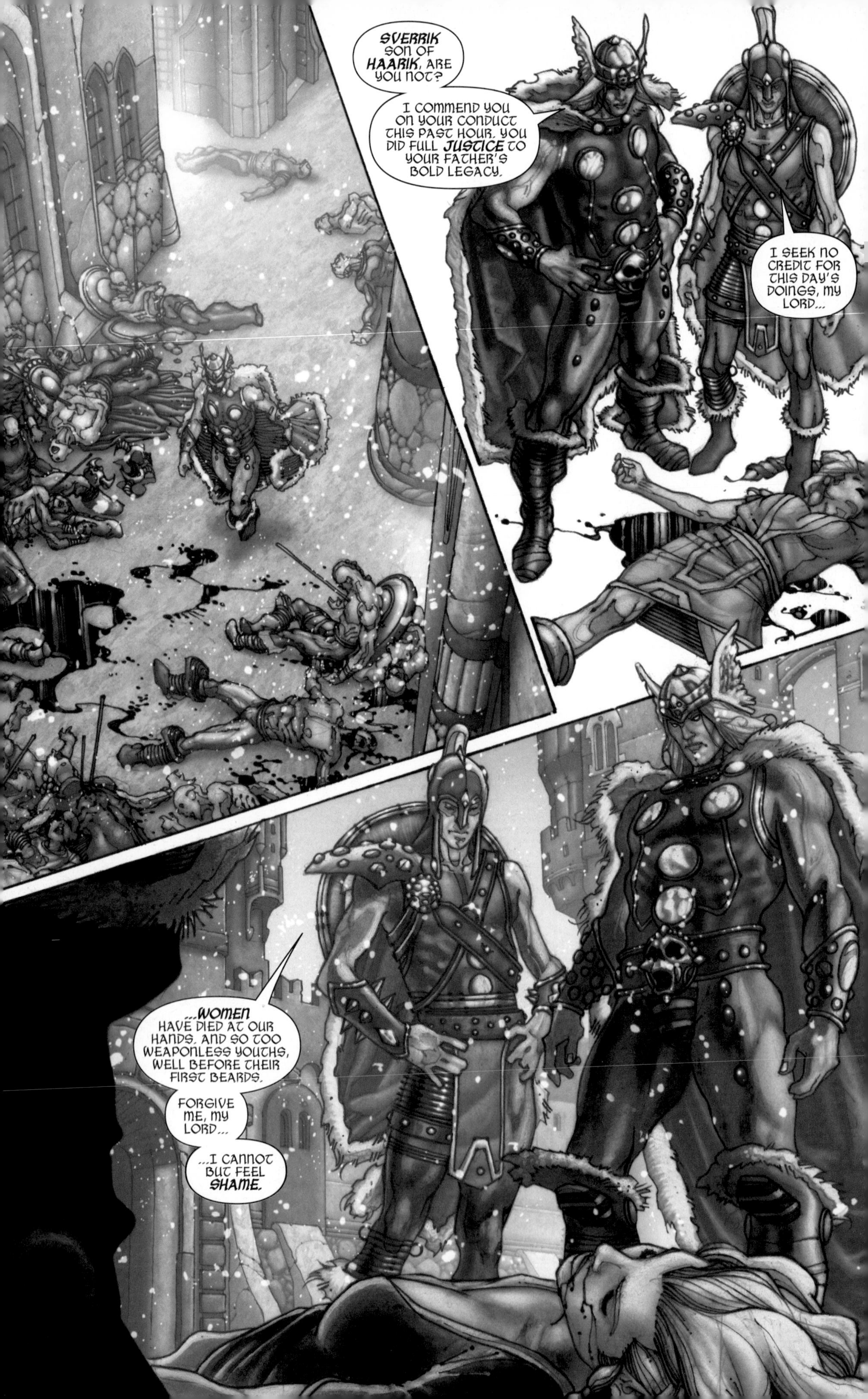
SVERRIK SON OF HAARIK, ARE YOU NOT?
I COMMEND YOU ON YOUR CONDUCT THIS PAST HOUR. YOU DID FULL JUSTICE TO YOUR FATHER'S BOLD LEGACY.
I SEEK NO CREDIT FOR THIS DAY'S DOINGS, MY LORD...
...WOMEN HAVE DIED AT OUR HANDS. AND SO TOO WEAPONLESS YOUTHS, WELL BEFORE THEIR FIRST BEARDS.
FORGIVE ME, MY LORD...
...I CANNOT BUT FEEL SHAME.

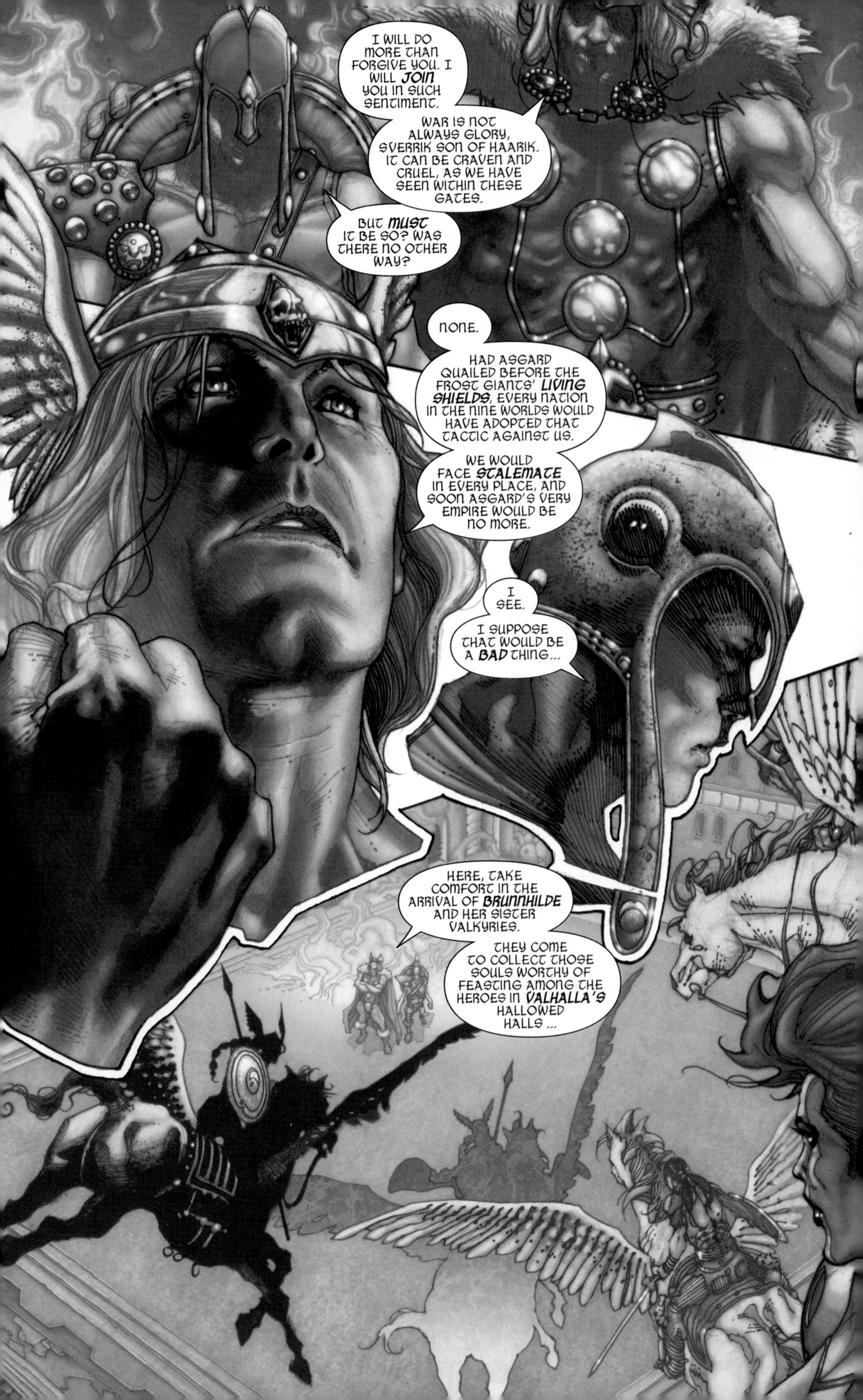
I WILL DO MORE THAN FORGIVE YOU. I WILL JOIN YOU IN SUCH SENTIMENT.
WAR IS NOT ALWAYS GLORY, SVERRIK SON OF HAARIK. IT CAN BE CRAVEN AND CRUEL, AS WE HAVE SEEN WITHIN THESE GATES.
BUT MUST IT BE SO? WAS THERE NO OTHER WAY?
NONE.
HAD ASGARD QUAILED BEFORE THE FROST GIANTS' LIVING SHIELDS, EVERY NATION IN THE NINE WORLDS WOULD HAVE ADOPTED THAT TACTIC AGAINST US.
WE WOULD FACE STALEMATE IN EVERY PLACE, AND SOON ASGARD'S VERY EMPIRE WOULD BE NO MORE.
I SEE.
I SUPPOSE THAT WOULD BE A BAD THING...
HERE, TAKE COMFORT IN THE ARRIVAL OF BRUNNHILDE AND HER SISTER VALKYRIES.
THEY COME TO COLLECT THOSE SOULS WORTHY OF FEASTING AMONG THE HEROES IN VALHALLA'S HALLOWED HALLS ...

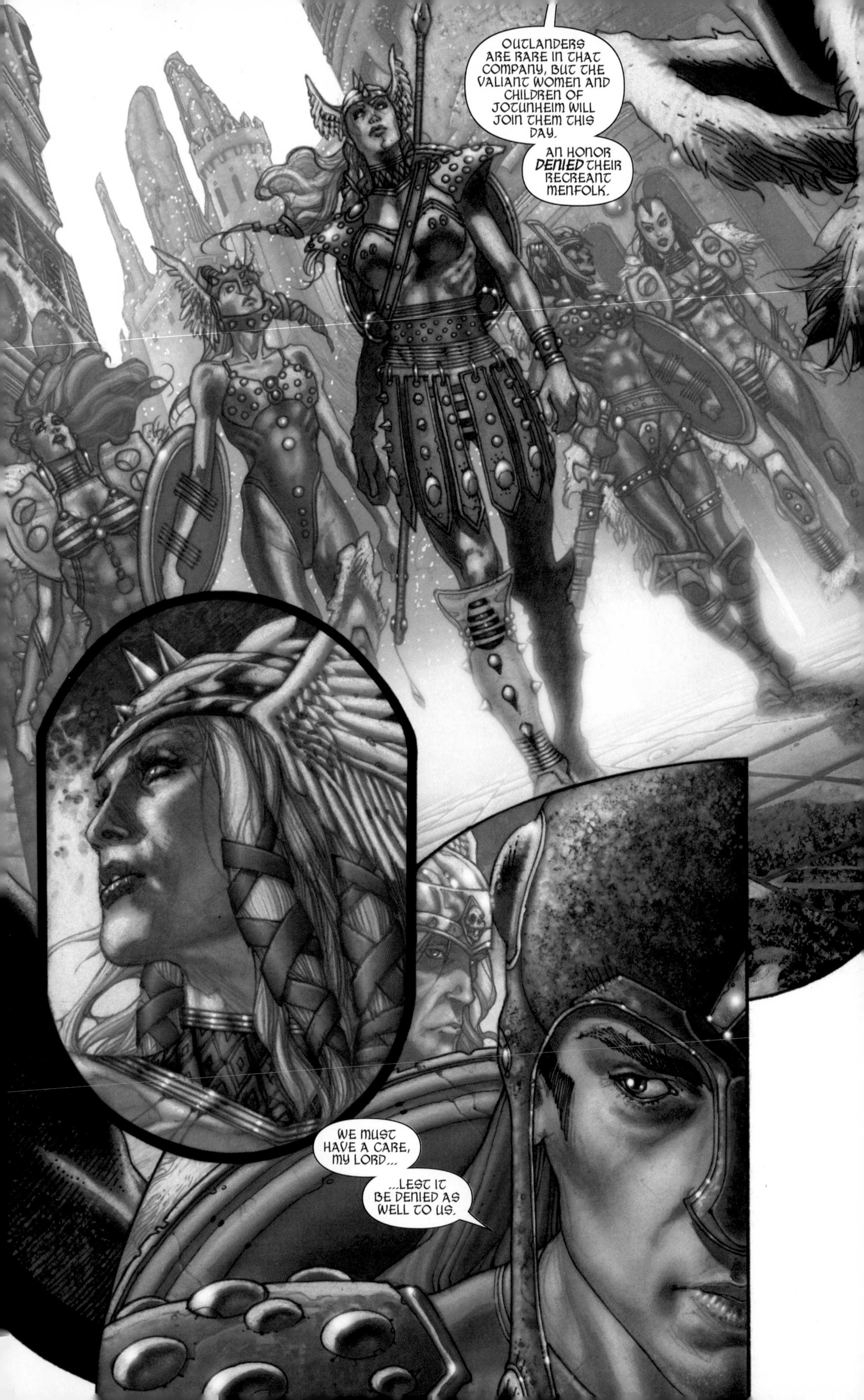
OUTLANDERS ARE RARE IN THAT COMPANY, BUT THE VALIANT WOMEN AND CHILDREN OF JOTUNHEIM WILL JOIN THEM THIS DAY.
AN HONOR DENIED THEIR RECREANT MENFOLK.
WE MUST HAVE A CARE, MY LORD...
...LEST IT BE DENIED AS WELL TO US.

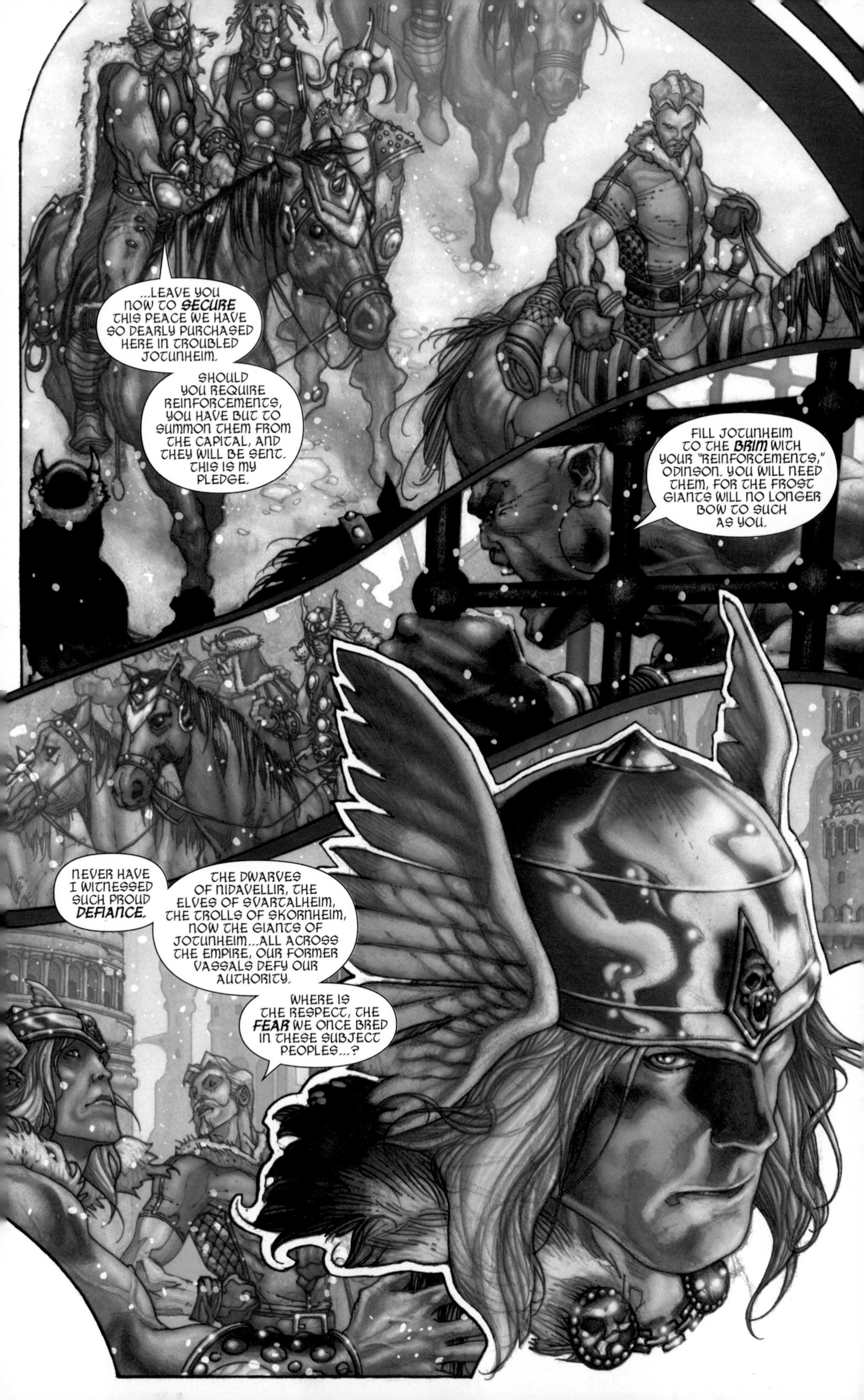
...LEAVE YOU NOW TO SECURE THIS PEACE WE HAVE SO DEARLY PURCHASED HERE IN TROUBLED JOTUNHEIM.
SHOULD YOU REQUIRE REINFORCEMENTS, YOU HAVE BUT TO SUMMON THEM FROM THE CAPITAL, AND THEY WILL BE SENT. THIS IS MY PLEDGE.
FILL JOTUNHEIM TO THE BRIM WITH YOUR "REINFORCEMENTS," ODINSON. YOU WILL NEED THEM, FOR THE FROST GIANTS WILL NO LONGER BOW TO SUCH AS YOU.
NEVER HAVE I WITNESSED SUCH PROUD DEFIANCE.
THE DWARVES OF NIDAVELLIR, THE ELVES OF SVARTALHEIM, THE TROLLS OF SKORNHEIM, NOW THE GIANTS OF JOTUNHEIM...ALL ACROSS THE EMPIRE, OUR FORMER VASSALS DEFY OUR AUTHORITY.
WHERE IS THE RESPECT, THE FEAR WE ONCE BRED IN THESE SUBJECT PEOPLES...?

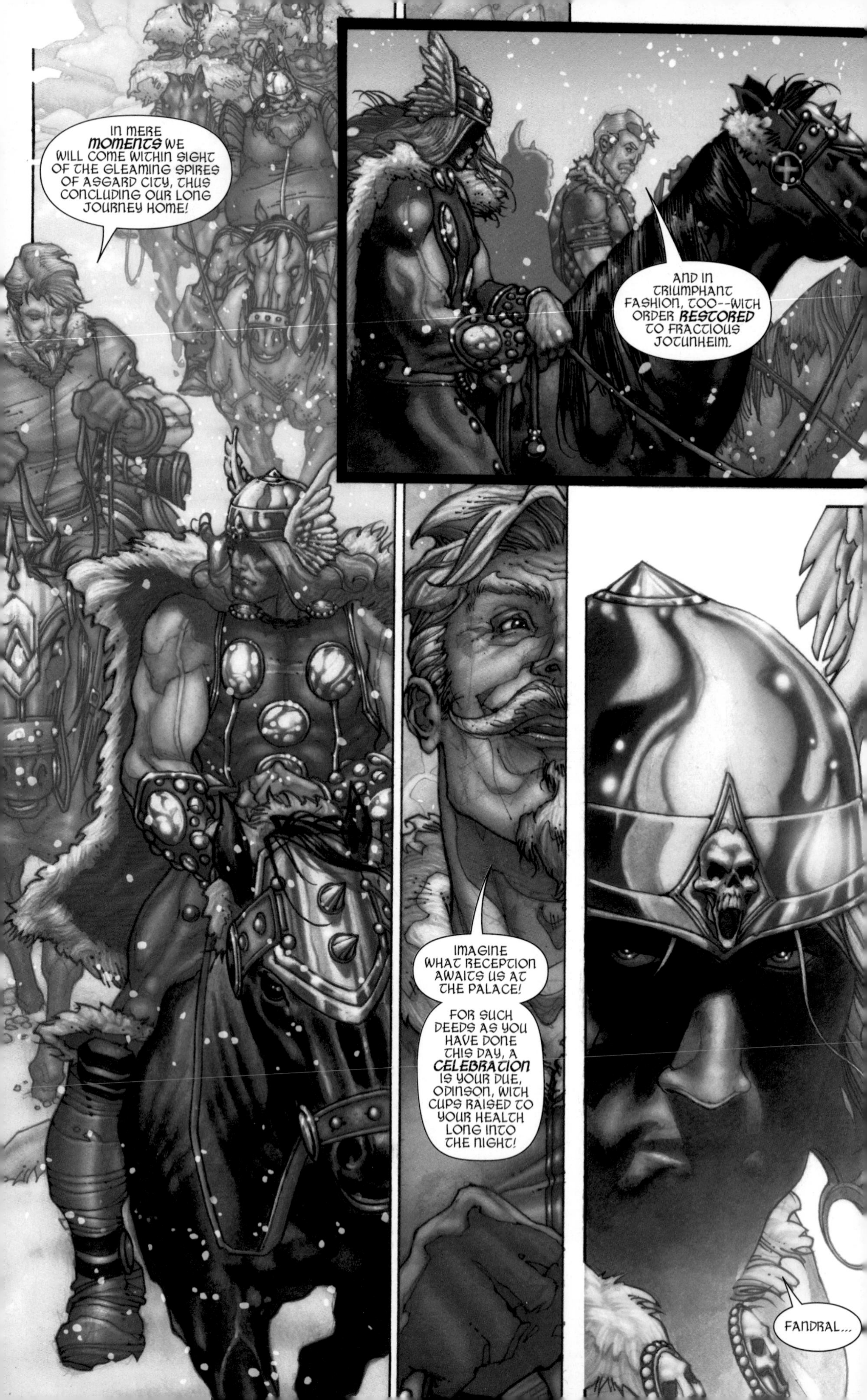
IN MERE MOMENTS WE WILL COME WITHIN SIGHT OF THE GLEAMING SPIRES OF ASGARD CITY, THUS CONCLUDING OUR LONG JOURNEY HOME!
AND IN TRIUMPHANT FASHION, TOO--WITH ORDER RESTORED TO FRACTIOUS JOTUNHEIM.
IMAGINE WHAT RECEPTION AWAITS US AT THE PALACE!
FOR SUCH DEEDS AS YOU HAVE DONE THIS DAY, A CELEBRATION IS YOUR DUE, ODINSON, WITH CUPS RAISED TO YOUR HEALTH LONG INTO THE NIGHT!
FANDRAL...

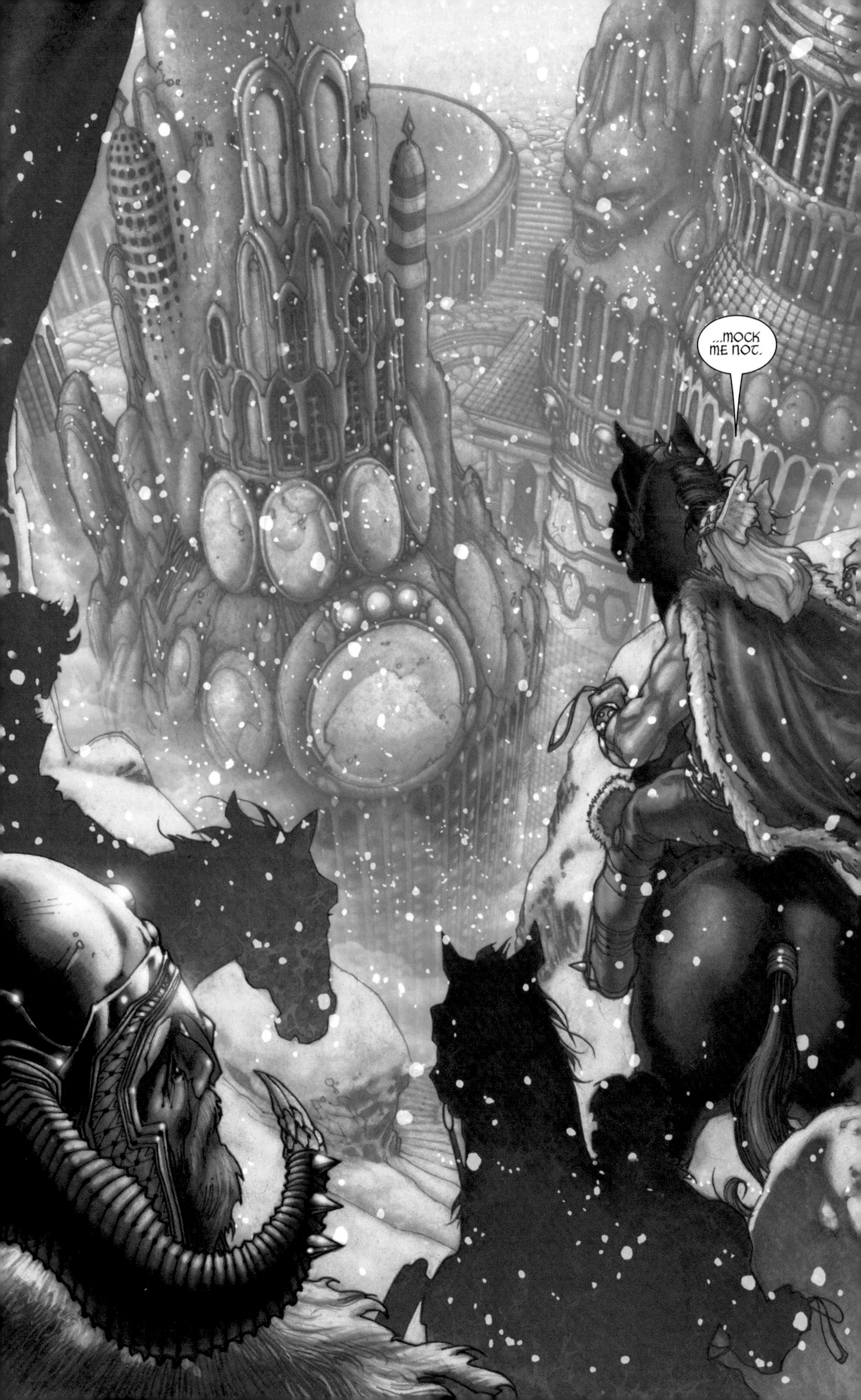
...MOCK ME NOT.

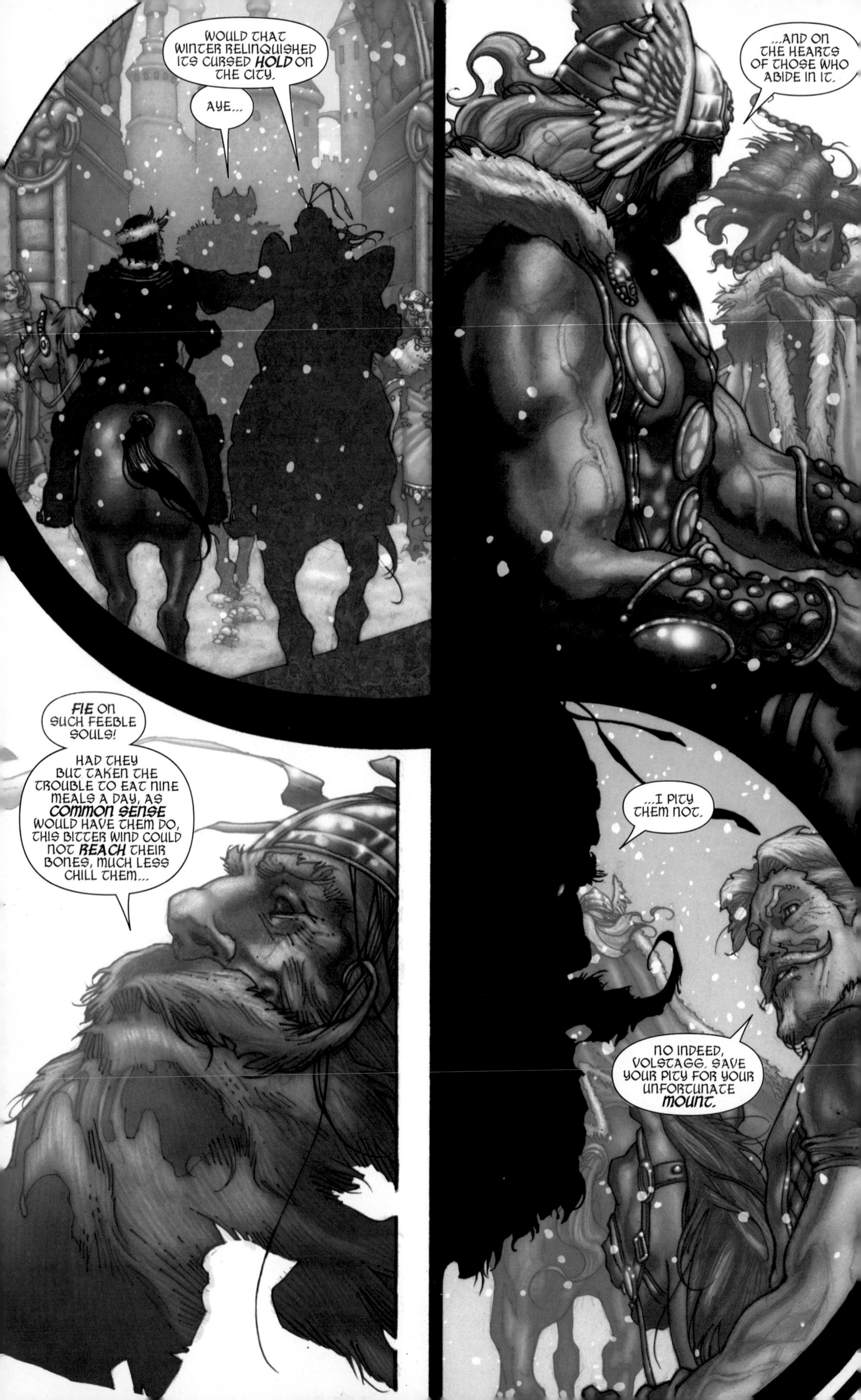
WOULD THAT WINTER RELINQUISHED ITS CURSED HOLD ON THE CITY.
AYE...
...AND ON THE HEARTS OF THOSE WHO ABIDE IN IT.
FIE ON SUCH FEEBLE SOULS!
HAD THEY BUT TAKEN THE TROUBLE TO EAT NINE MEALS A DAY, AS COMMON SENSE WOULD HAVE THEM DO, THIS BITTER WIND COULD NOT REACH THEIR BONES, MUCH LESS CHILL THEM...
...I PITY THEM NOT.
NO INDEED, VOLSTAGG. SAVE YOUR PITY FOR YOUR UNFORTUNATE MOUNT.

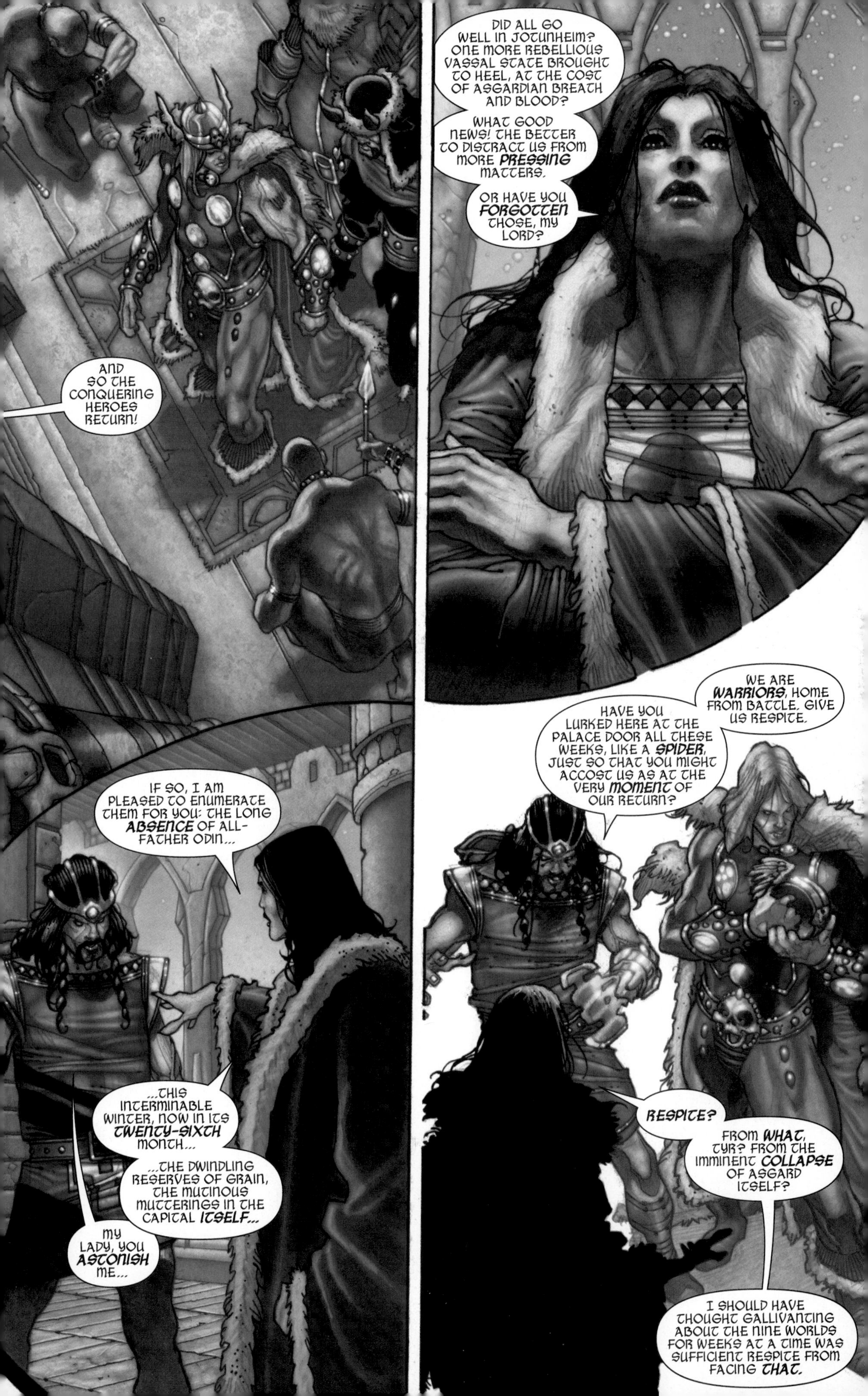
AND SO THE CONQUERING HEROES RETURN!
DID ALL GO WELL IN JOTUNHEIM? ONE MORE REBELLIOUS VASSAL STATE BROUGHT TO HEEL, AT THE COST OF ASGARDIAN BREATH AND BLOOD?
WHAT GOOD NEWS! THE BETTER TO DISTRACT US FROM MORE PRESSING MATTERS.
OR HAVE YOU FORGOTTEN THOSE, MY LORD?
IF SO, I AM PLEASED TO ENUMERATE THEM FOR YOU: THE LONG ABSENCE OF ALL-FATHER ODIN...
...THIS INTERMINABLE WINTER, NOW IN ITS TWENTY-SIXTH MONTH...
...THE DWINDLING RESERVES OF GRAIN, THE MUTINOUS MUTTERINGS IN THE CAPITAL ITSELF...
MY LADY, YOU ASTONISH ME...
HAVE YOU LURKED HERE AT THE PALACE DOOR ALL THESE WEEKS, LIKE A SPIDER, JUST SO THAT YOU MIGHT ACCOST US AS AT THE VERY MOMENT OF OUR RETURN?
WE ARE WARRIORS, HOME FROM BATTLE. GIVE US RESPITE.
RESPITE?
FROM WHAT, TYR? FROM THE IMMINENT COLLAPSE OF ASGARD ITSELF?
I SHOULD HAVE THOUGHT GALLIVANTING ABOUT THE NINE WORLDS FOR WEEKS AT A TIME WAS SUFFICIENT RESPITE FROM FACING THAT.

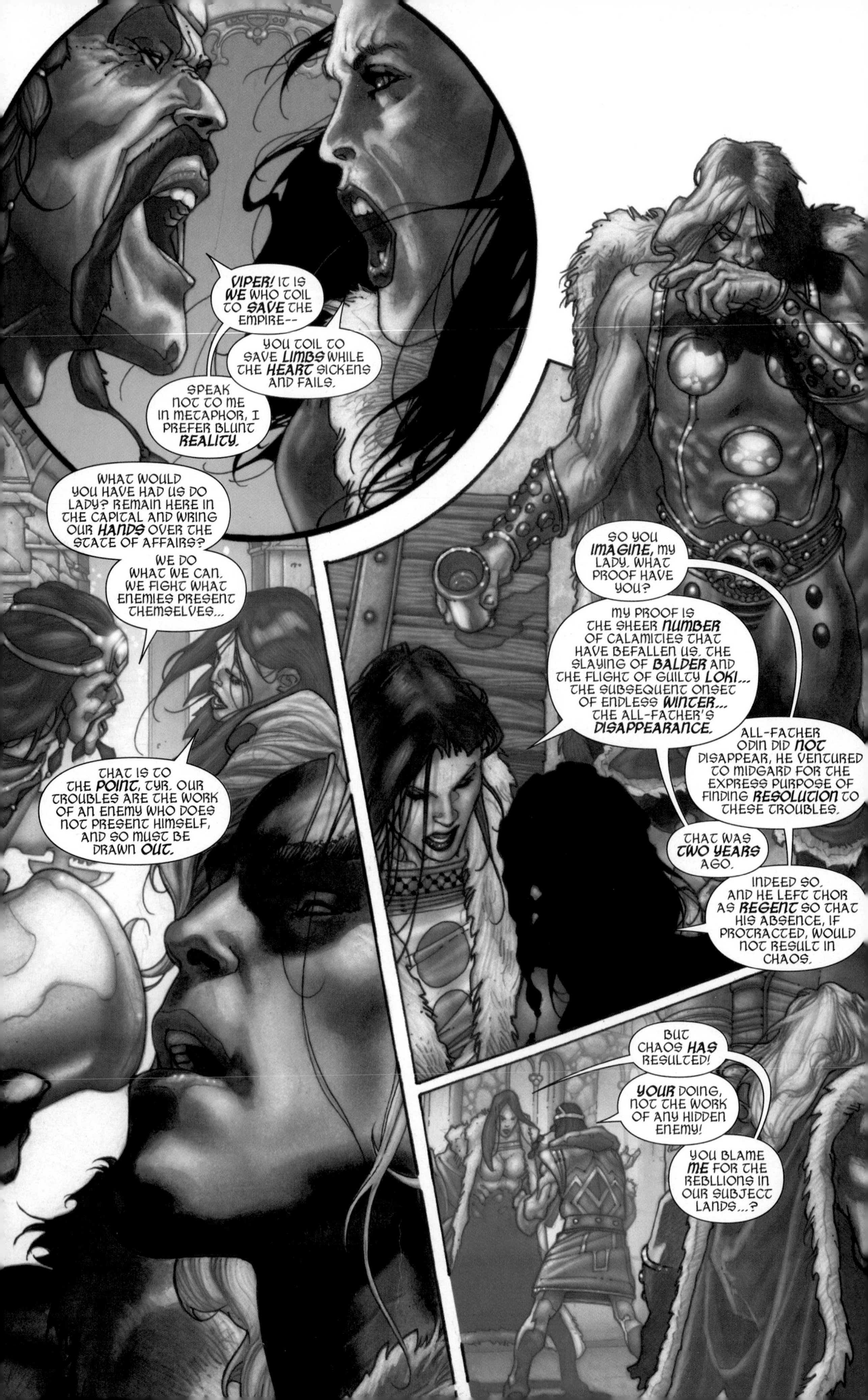
VIPER! IT IS WE WHO TOIL TO SAVE THE EMPIRE--
YOU TOIL TO SAVE LIMBS WHILE THE HEART SICKENS AND FAILS.
SPEAK NOT TO ME IN METAPHOR, I PREFER BLUNT REALITY.
WHAT WOULD YOU HAVE HAD US DO LADY? REMAIN HERE IN THE CAPITAL AND WRING OUR HANDS OVER THE STATE OF AFFAIRS?
WE DO WHAT WE CAN. WE FIGHT WHAT ENEMIES PRESENT THEMSELVES...
THAT IS TO THE POINT, TYR. OUR TROUBLES ARE THE WORK OF AN ENEMY WHO DOES NOT PRESENT HIMSELF, AND SO MUST BE DRAWN OUT.
SO YOU IMAGINE, MY LADY. WHAT PROOF HAVE YOU?
MY PROOF IS THE SHEER NUMBER OF CALAMITIES THAT HAVE BEFALLEN US. THE SLAYING OF BALDER AND THE FLIGHT OF GUILTY LOKI... THE SUBSEQUENT ONSET OF ENDLESS WINTER... THE ALL-FATHER'S DISAPPEARANCE.
ALL-FATHER ODIN DID NOT DISAPPEAR, HE VENTURED TO MIDGARD FOR THE EXPRESS PURPOSE OF FINDING RESOLUTION TO THESE TROUBLES.
THAT WAS TWO YEARS AGO.
INDEED SO. AND HE LEFT THOR AS REGENT SO THAT HIS ABSENCE, IF PROTRACTED, WOULD NOT RESULT IN CHAOS.
BUT CHAOS HAS RESULTED!
YOUR DOING, NOT THE WORK OF ANY HIDDEN ENEMY!
YOU BLAME ME FOR THE REBLLIONS IN OUR SUBJECT LANDS...?

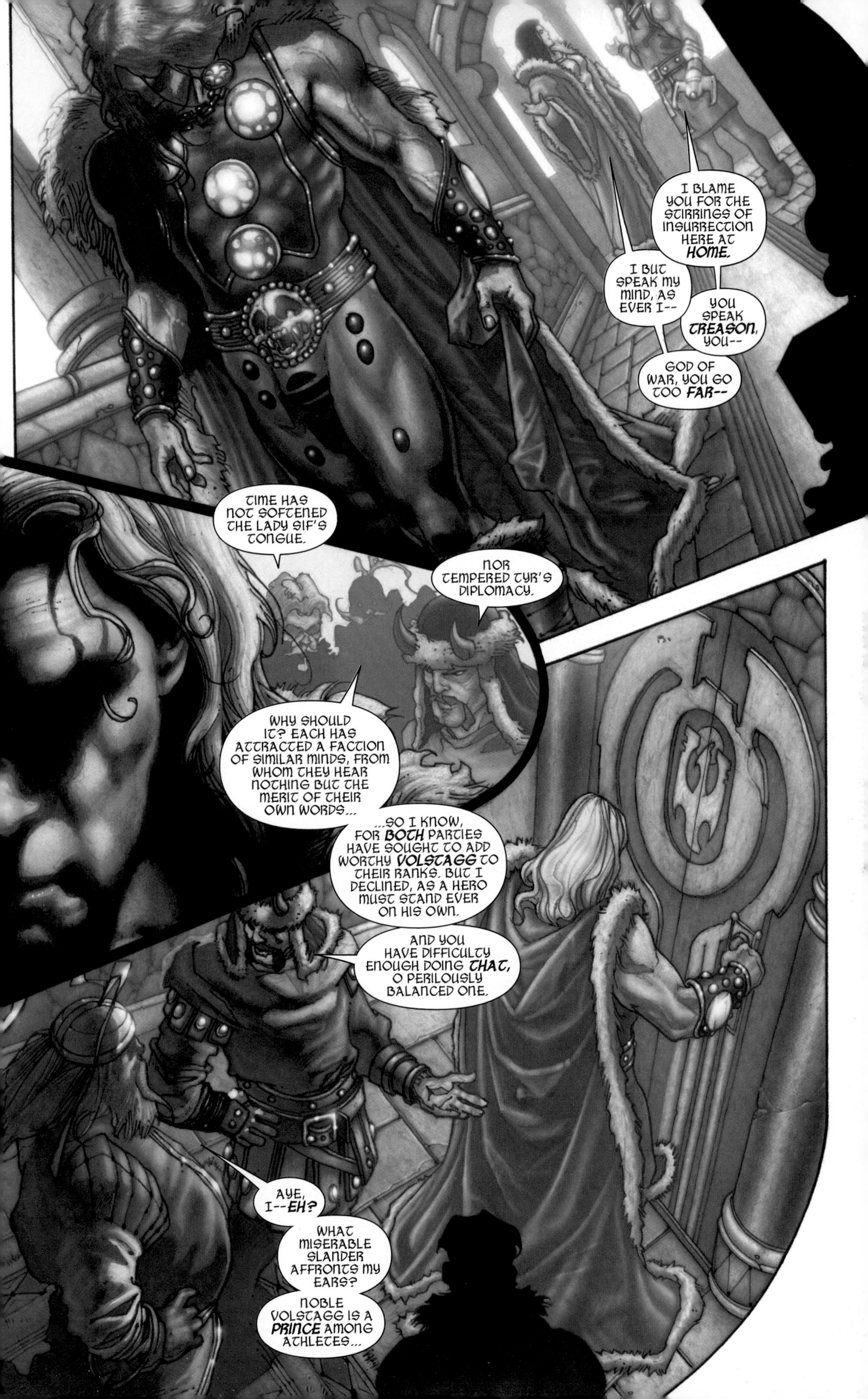
I BLAME YOU FOR THE STIRRINGS OF INSURRECTION HERE AT HOME.
I BUT SPEAK MY MIND, AS EVER I--
YOU SPEAK TREASON, YOU--
GOD OF WAR, YOU GO TOO FAR--
TIME HAS NOT SOFTENED THE LADY SIF'S TONGUE.
NOR TEMPERED TYR'S DIPLOMACY.
WHY SHOULD IT? EACH HAS ATTRACTED A FACTION OF SIMILAR MINDS, FROM WHOM THEY HEAR NOTHING BUT THE MERIT OF THEIR OWN WORDS...
...SO I KNOW, FOR BOTH PARTIES HAVE SOUGHT TO ADD WORTHY VOLSTAGG TO THEIR RANKS. BUT I DECLINED, AS A HERO MUST STAND EVER ON HIS OWN.
AND YOU HAVE DIFFICULTY ENOUGH DOING THAT, O PERILOUSLY BALANCED ONE.
AYE, I--EH?
WHAT MISERABLE SLANDER AFFRONTS MY EARS?
NOBLE VOLSTAGG IS A PRINCE AMONG ATHLETES...

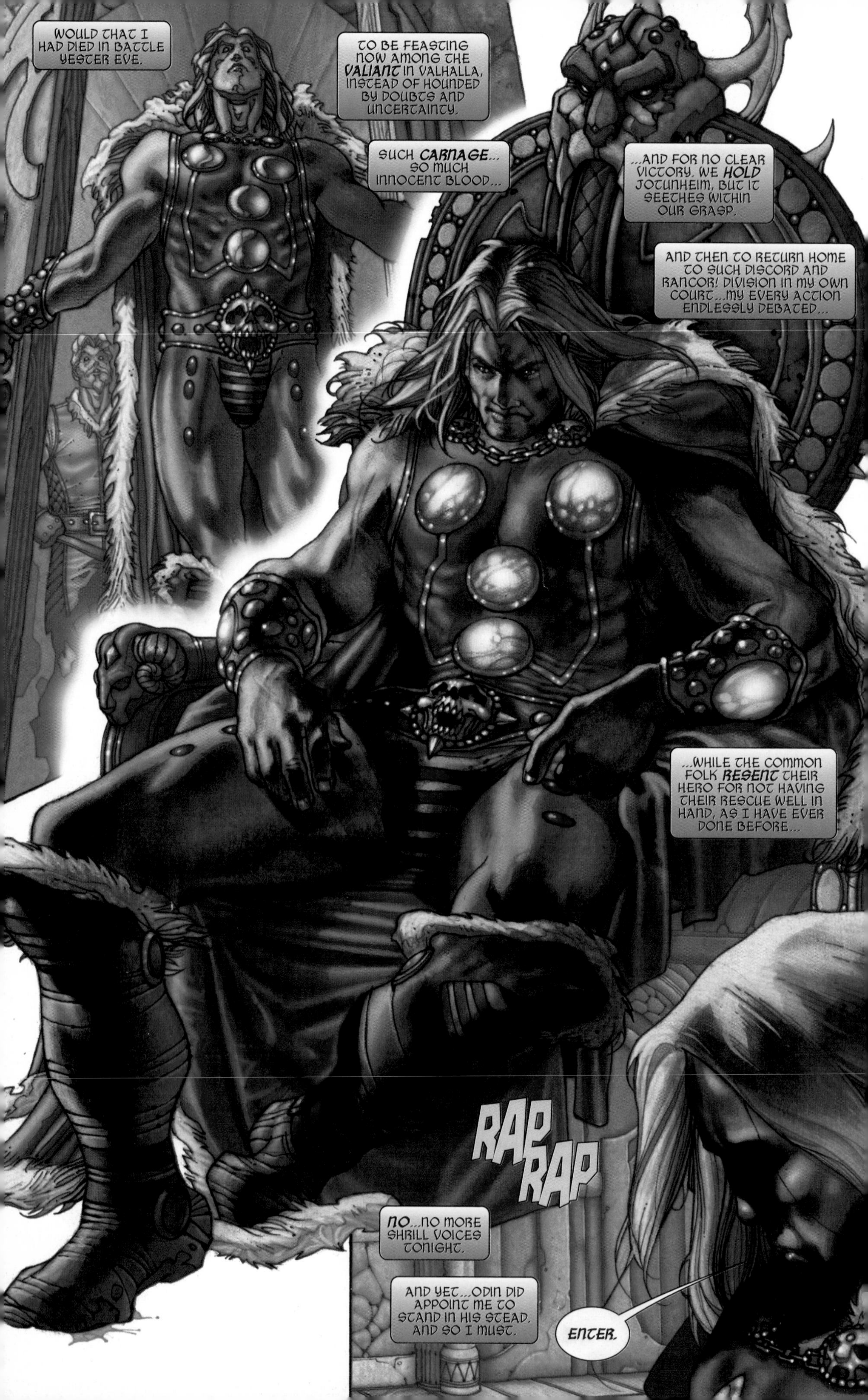
WOULD THAT I HAD DIED IN BATTLE YESTER EVE.
TO BE FEASTING NOW AMONG THE VALIANT IN VALHALLA, INSTEAD OF HOUNDED BY DOUBTS AND UNCERTAINTY.
SUCH CARNAGE... SO MUCH INNOCENT BLOOD...
...AND FOR NO CLEAR VICTORY. WE HOLD JOTUNHEIM, BUT IT SEETHES WITHIN OUR GRASP.
AND THEN TO RETURN HOME TO SUCH DISCORD AND RANCOR! DIVISION IN MY OWN COURT...MY EVERY ACTION ENDLESSLY DEBATED...
...WHILE THE COMMON FOLK RESENT THEIR HERO FOR NOT HAVING THEIR RESCUE WELL IN HAND, AS I HAVE EVER DONE BEFORE...
RAP RAP
NO...NO MORE SHRILL VOICES TONIGHT.
AND YET...ODIN DID APPOINT ME TO STAND IN HIS STEAD. AND SO I MUST.
ENTER.

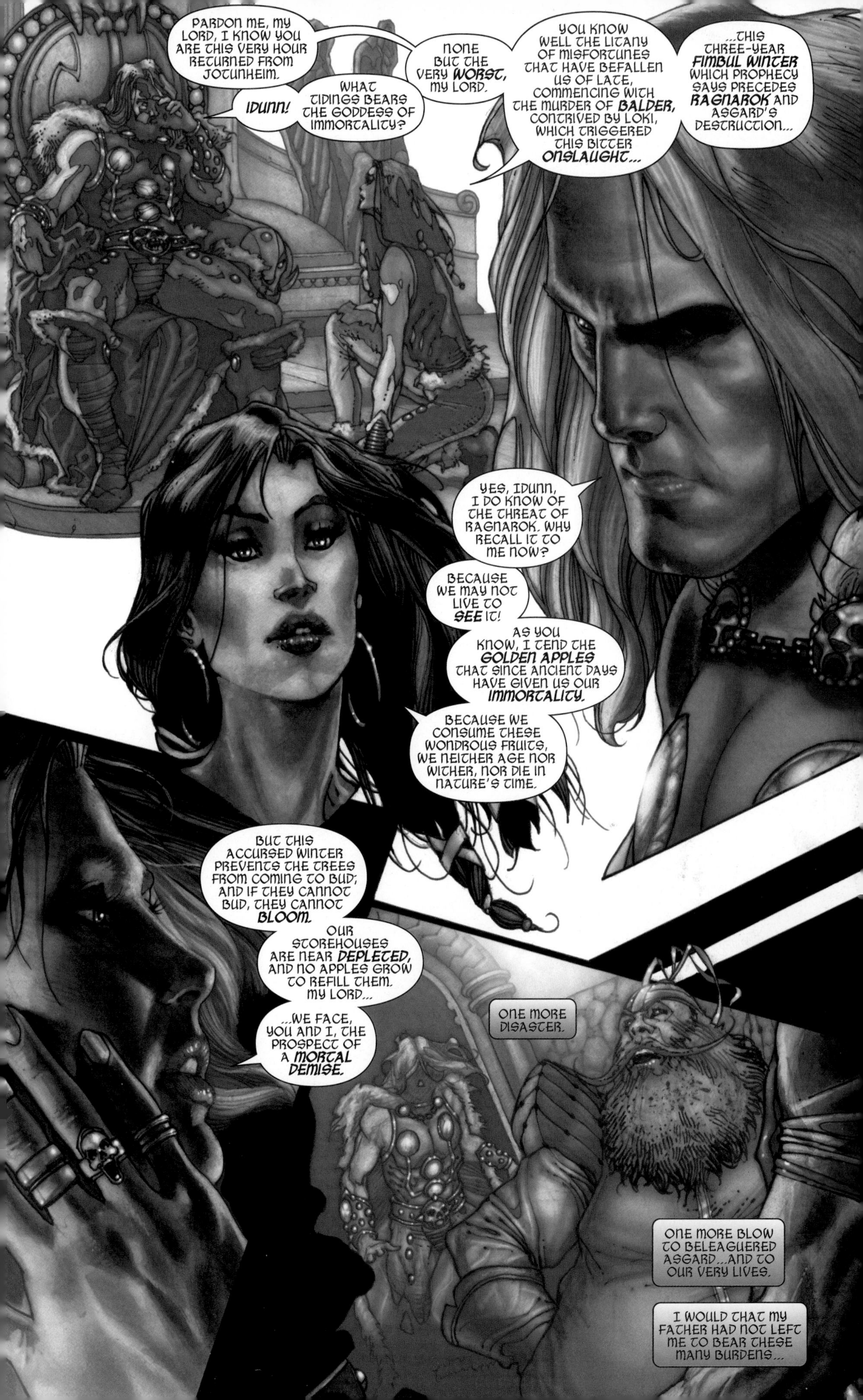
PARDON ME, MY LORD, I KNOW YOU ARE THIS VERY HOUR RETURNED FROM JOTUNHEIM.
IDUNN!
WHAT TIDINGS BEARS THE GODDESS OF IMMORTALITY?
NONE BUT THE VERY WORST, MY LORD.
YOU KNOW WELL THE LITANY OF MISFORTUNES THAT HAVE BEFALLEN US OF LATE, COMMENCING WITH THE MURDER OF BALDER, CONTRIVED BY LOKI, WHICH TRIGGERED THIS BITTER ONSLAUGHT...
...THIS THREE-YEAR FIMBUL WINTER WHICH PROPHECY SAYS PRECEDES RAGNAROK AND ASGARD'S DESTRUCTION...
YES, IDUNN, I DO KNOW OF THE THREAT OF RAGNAROK. WHY RECALL IT TO ME NOW?
BECAUSE WE MAY NOT LIVE TO SEE IT!
AS YOU KNOW, I TEND THE GOLDEN APPLES THAT SINCE ANCIENT DAYS HAVE GIVEN US OUR IMMORTALITY.
BECAUSE WE CONSUME THESE WONDROUS FRUITS, WE NEITHER AGE NOR WITHER, NOR DIE IN NATURE'S TIME.
BUT THIS ACCURSED WINTER PREVENTS THE TREES FROM COMING TO BUD; AND IF THEY CANNOT BUD, THEY CANNOT BLOOM.
OUR STOREHOUSES ARE NEAR DEPLETED, AND NO APPLES GROW TO REFILL THEM. MY LORD...
...WE FACE, YOU AND I, THE PROSPECT OF A MORTAL DEMISE.
ONE MORE DISASTER.
ONE MORE BLOW TO BELEAGUERED ASGARD...AND TO OUR VERY LIVES.
I WOULD THAT MY FATHER HAD NOT LEFT ME TO BEAR THESE MANY BURDENS...

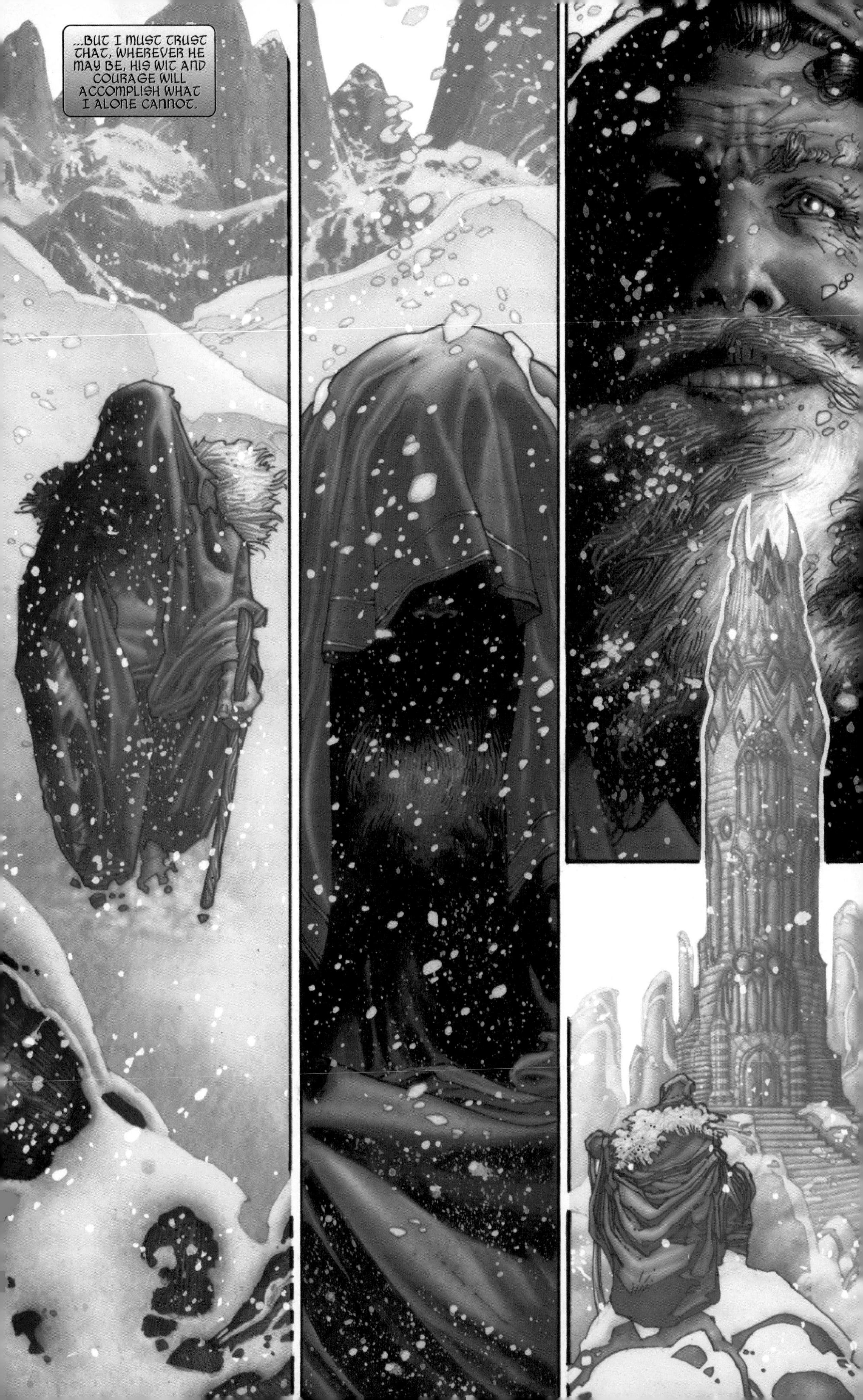
...BUT I MUST TRUST THAT, WHEREVER HE MAY BE, HIS WIT AND COURAGE WILL ACCOMPLISH WHAT I ALONE CANNOT.

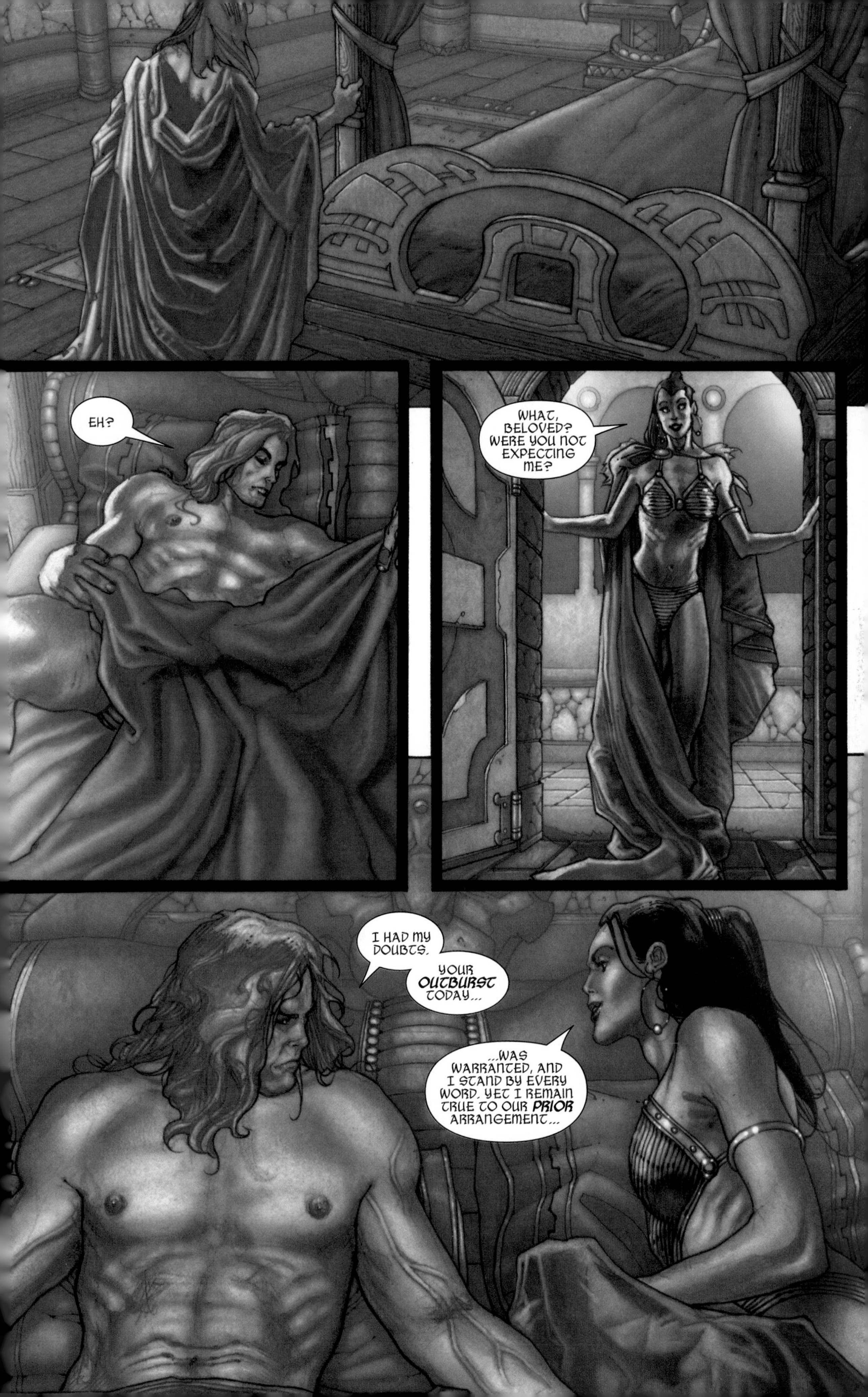
EH?
WHAT, BELOVED? WERE YOU NOT EXPECTING ME?
I HAD MY DOUBTS.
YOUR OUTBURST TODAY...
...WAS WARRANTED, AND I STAND BY EVERY WORD. YET I REMAIN TRUE TO OUR PRIOR ARRANGEMENT...

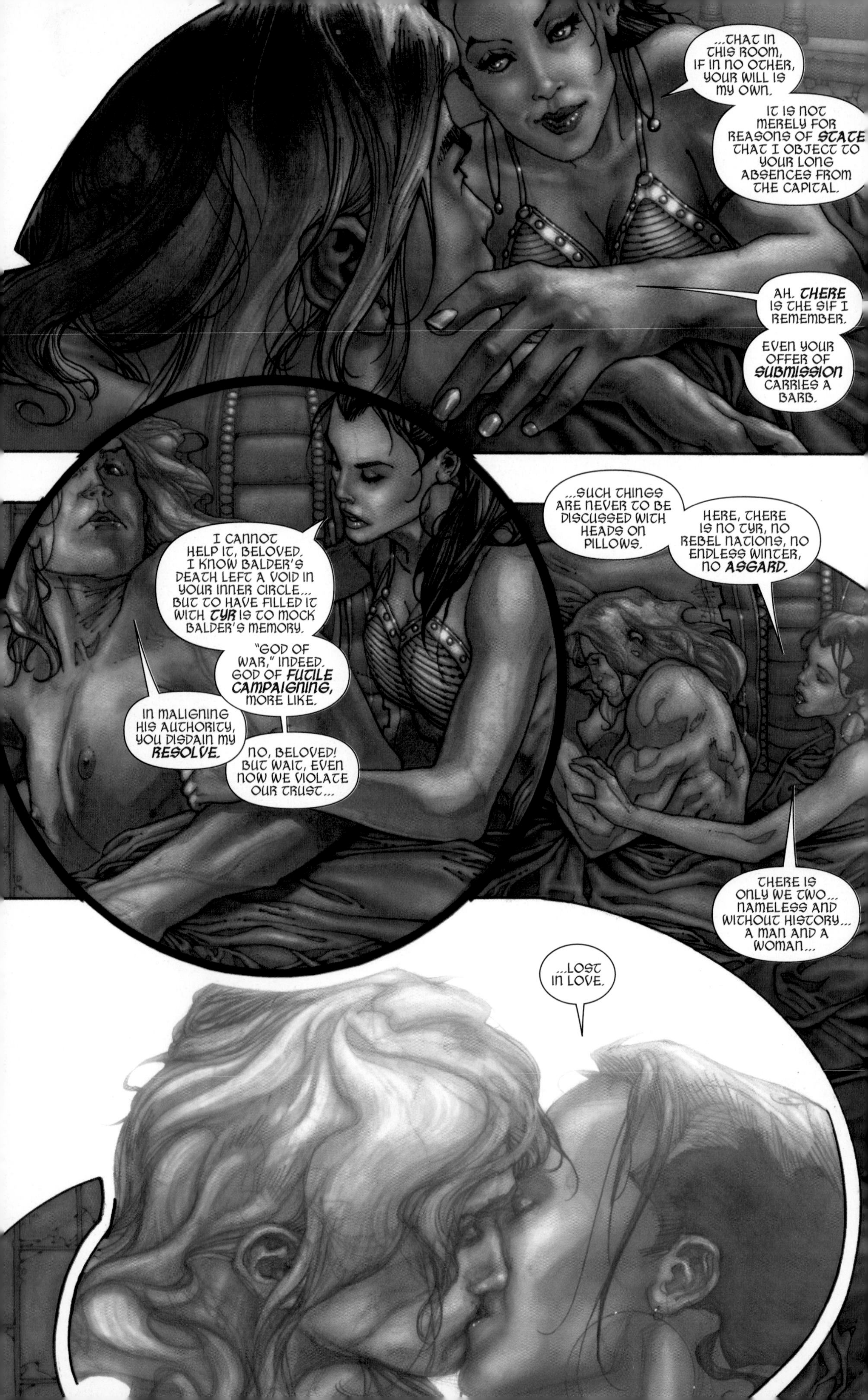
...THAT IN THIS ROOM, IF IN NO OTHER, YOUR WILL IS MY OWN.
IT IS NOT MERELY FOR REASONS OF STATE THAT I OBJECT TO YOUR LONG ABSENCES FROM THE CAPITAL.
AH. THERE IS THE SIF I REMEMBER.
EVEN YOUR OFFER OF SUBMISSION CARRIES A BARB.
I CANNOT HELP IT, BELOVED. I KNOW BALDER'S DEATH LEFT A VOID IN YOUR INNER CIRCLE... BUT TO HAVE FILLED IT WITH TYR IS TO MOCK BALDER'S MEMORY.
"GOD OF WAR," INDEED. GOD OF FUTILE CAMPAIGNING, MORE LIKE.
IN MALIGNING HIS AUTHORITY, YOU DISDAIN MY RESOLVE.
NO, BELOVED! BUT WAIT, EVEN NOW WE VIOLATE OUR TRUST...
...SUCH THINGS ARE NEVER TO BE DISCUSSED WITH HEADS ON PILLOWS.
HERE, THERE IS NO TYR, NO REBEL NATIONS, NO ENDLESS WINTER, NO ASGARD.
THERE IS ONLY WE TWO... NAMELESS AND WITHOUT HISTORY... A MAN AND A WOMAN...
...LOST IN LOVE.

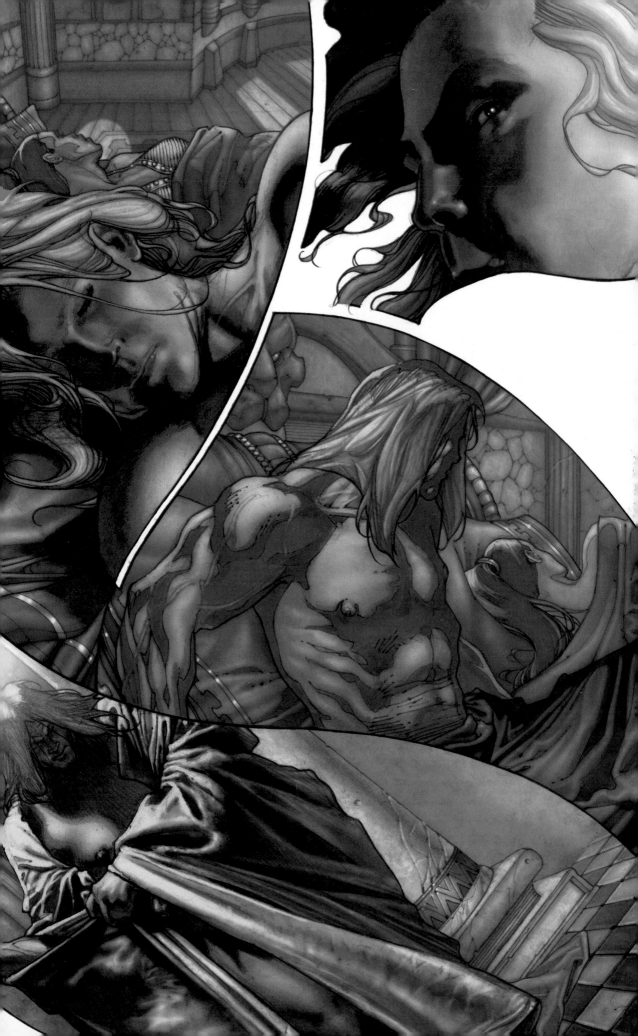

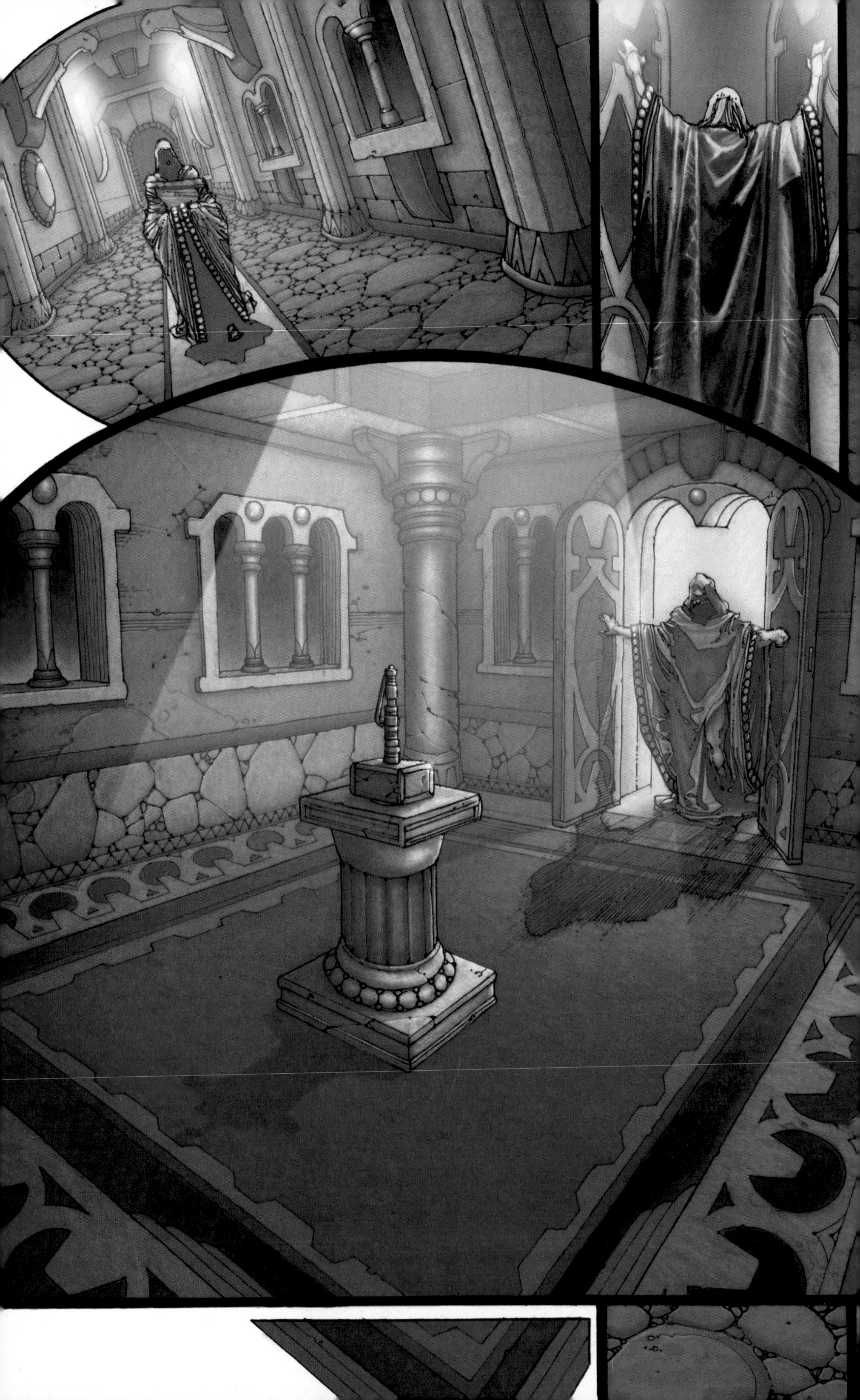

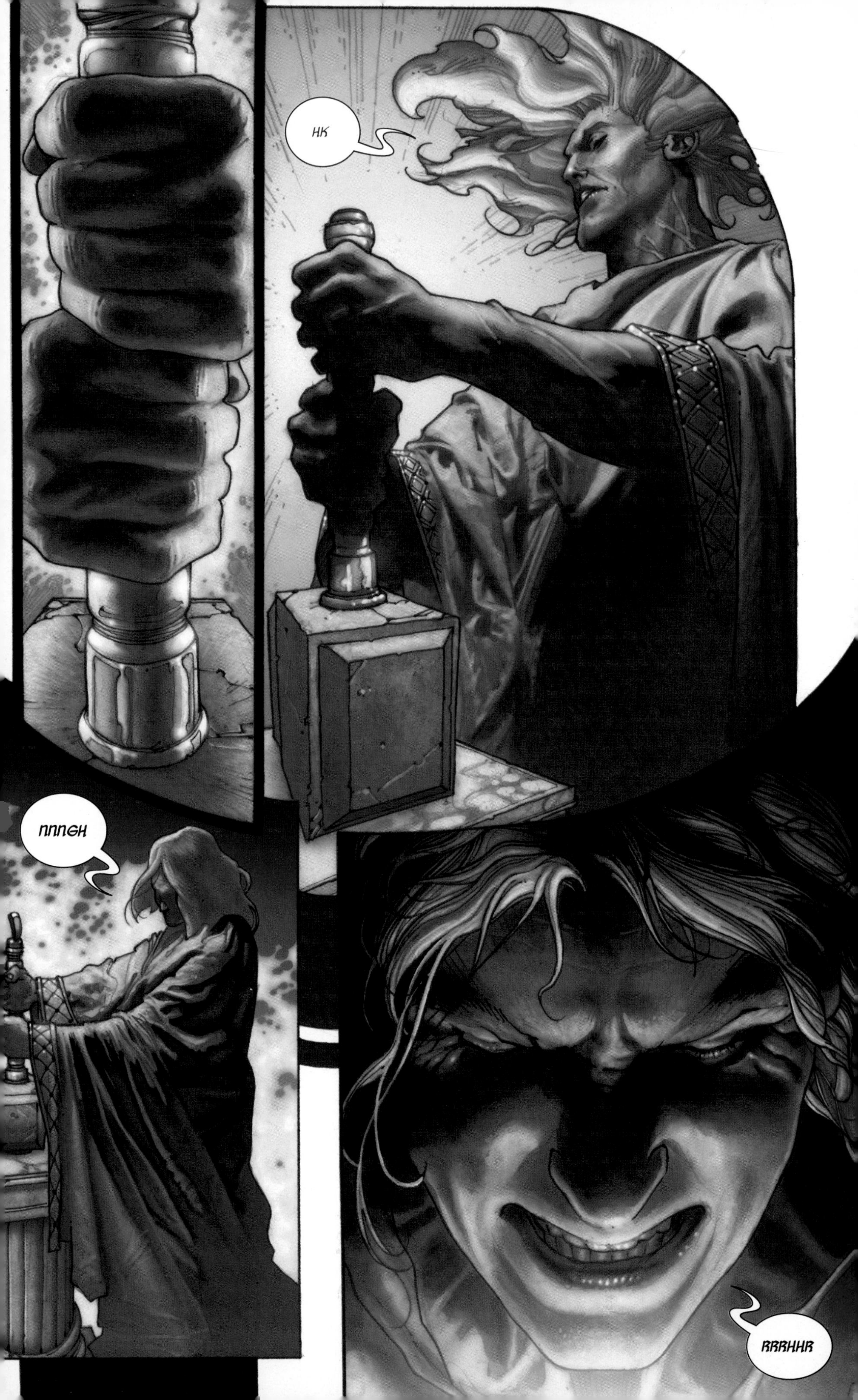
HK
NNNGH
RRRHHR

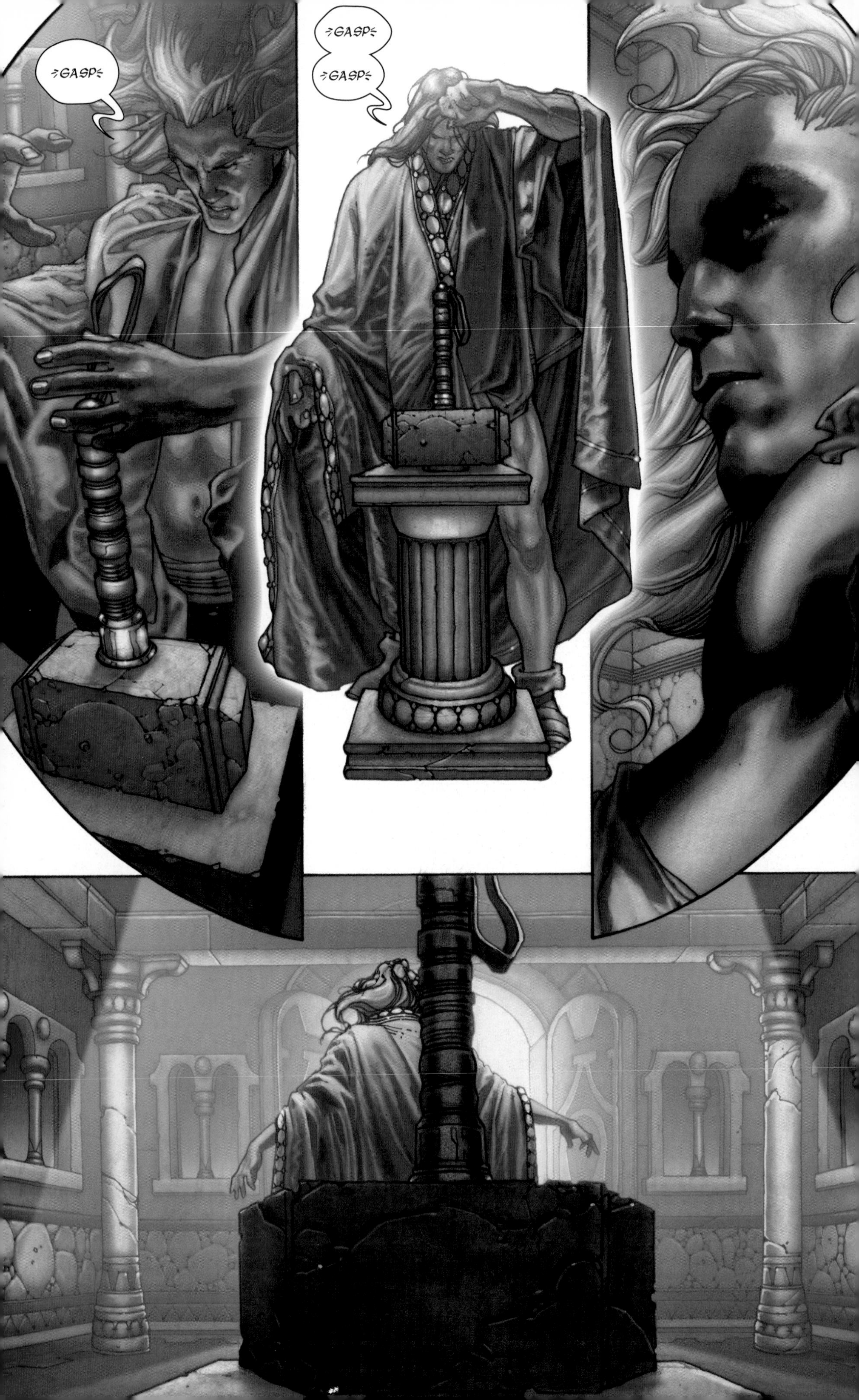
GASP
GASP
GASP

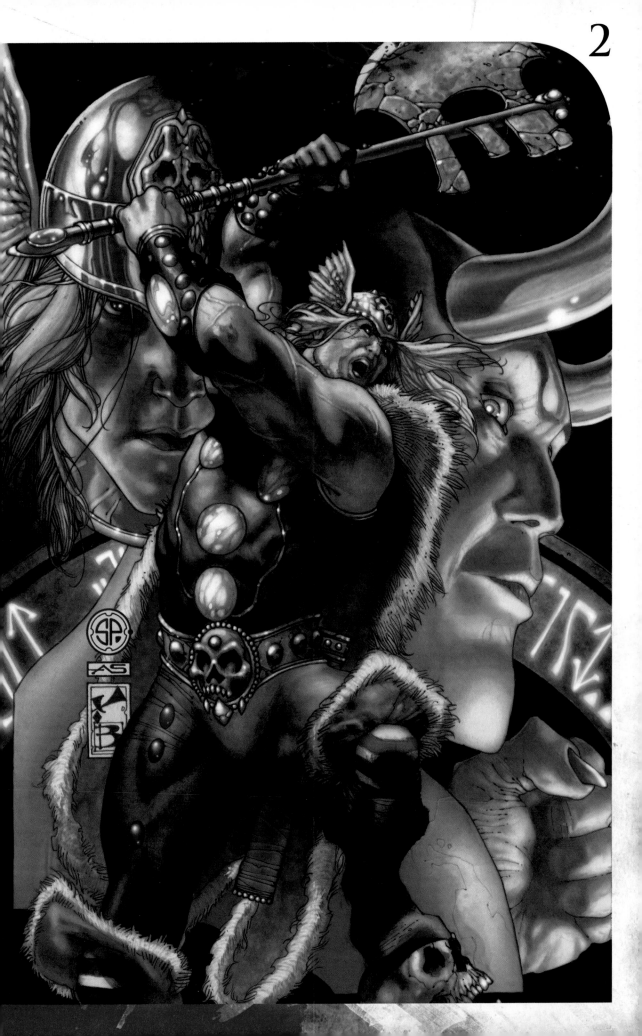

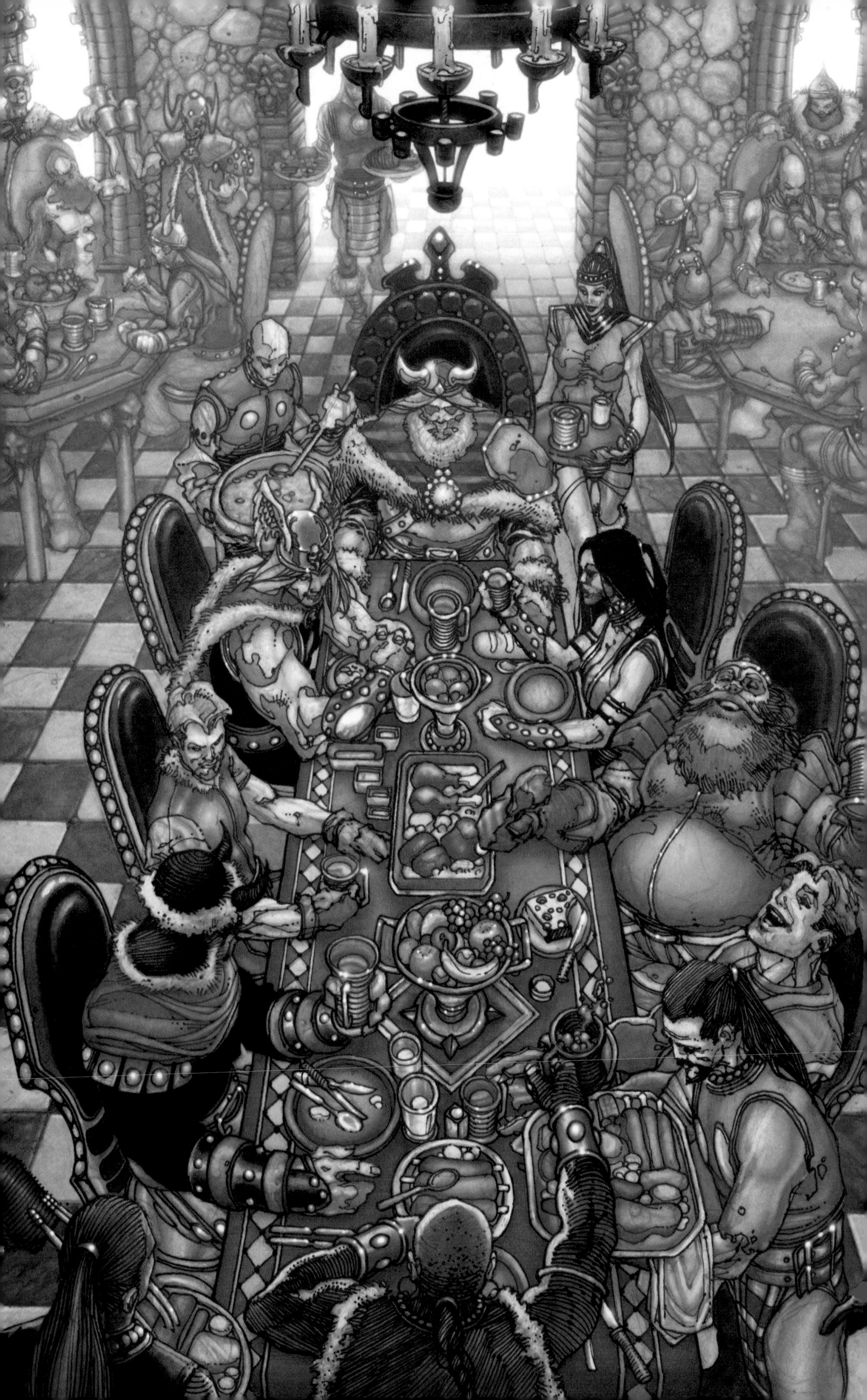

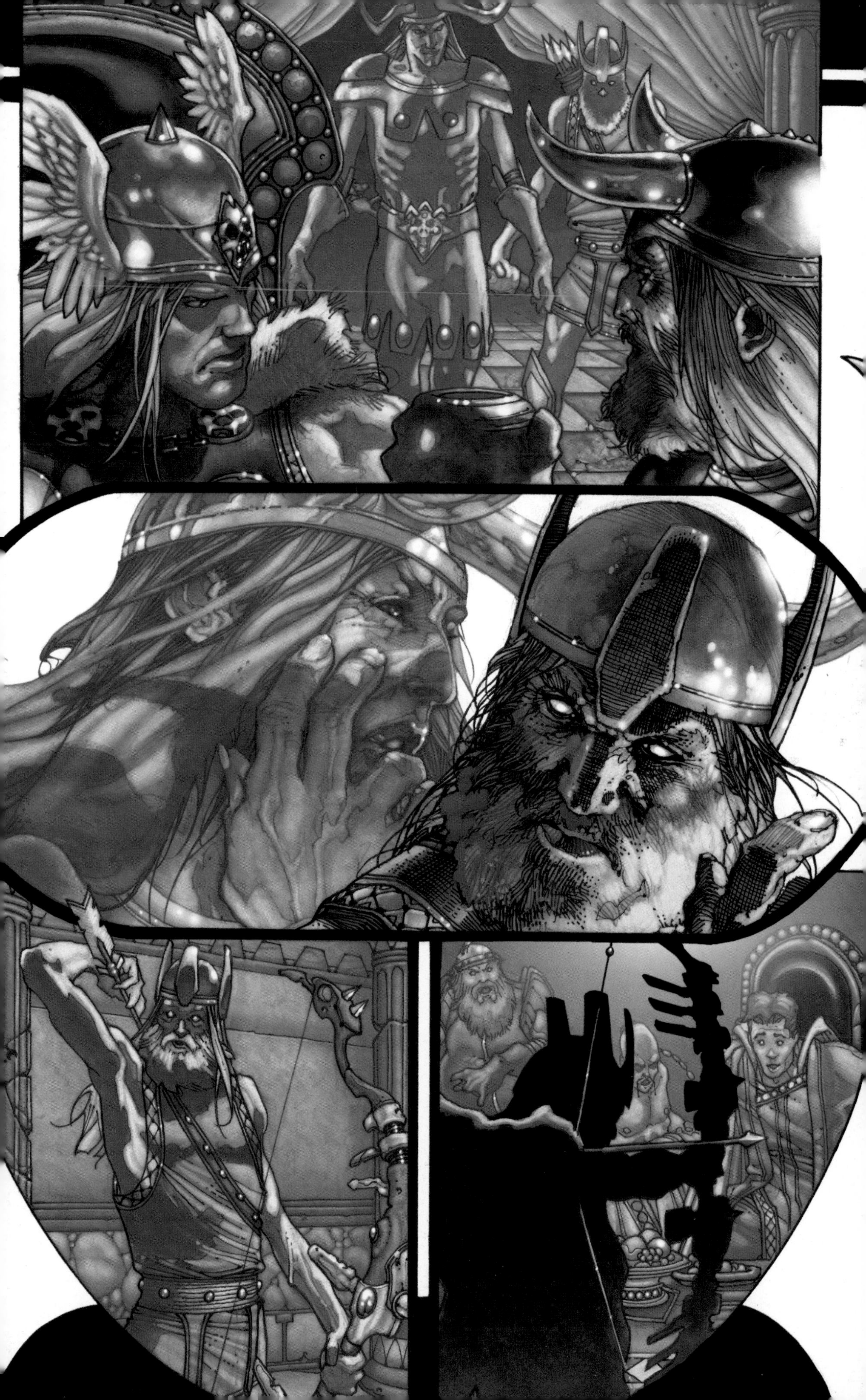

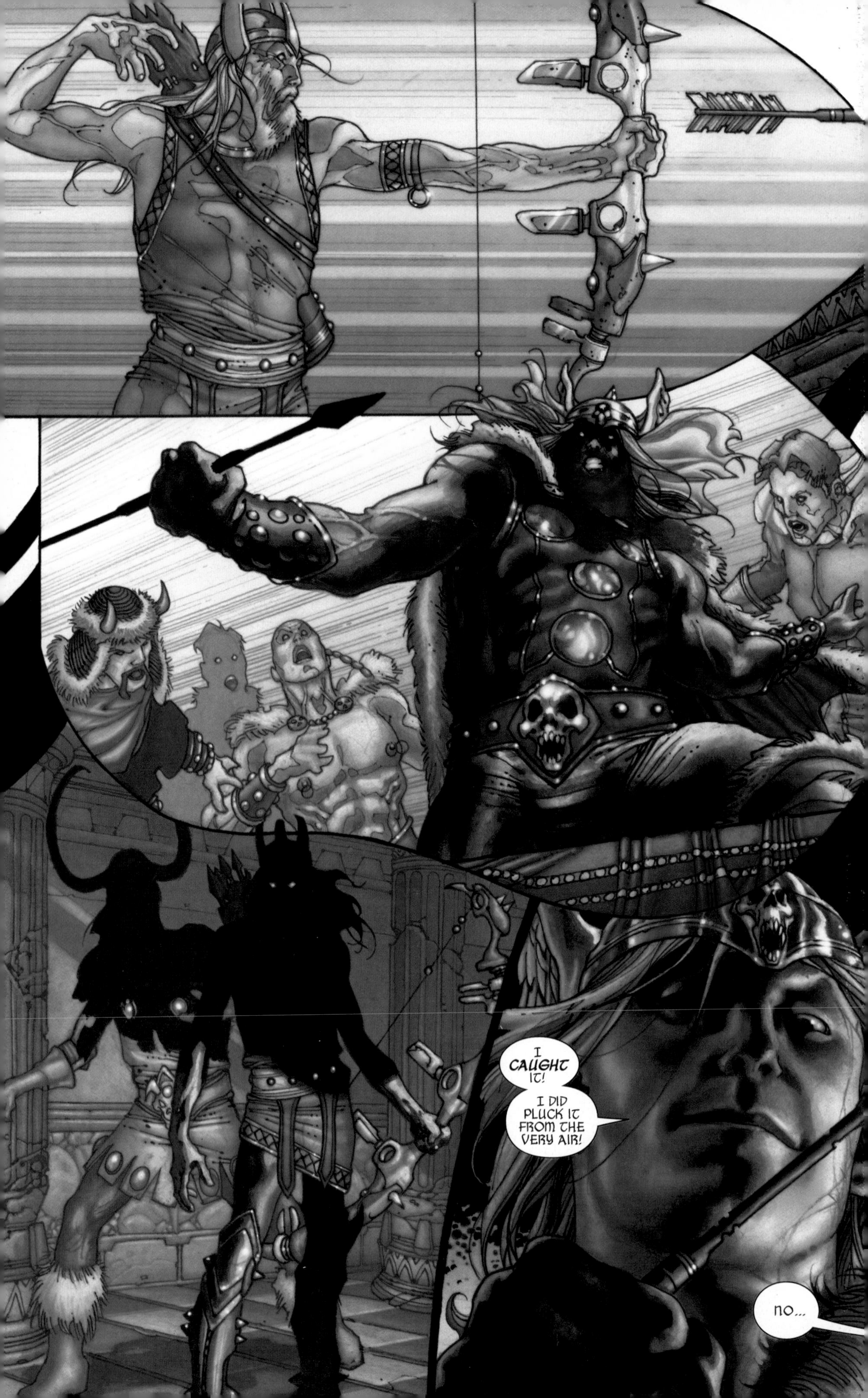

I CAUGHT IT!
I DID PLUCK IT FROM THE VERY AIR!
no...

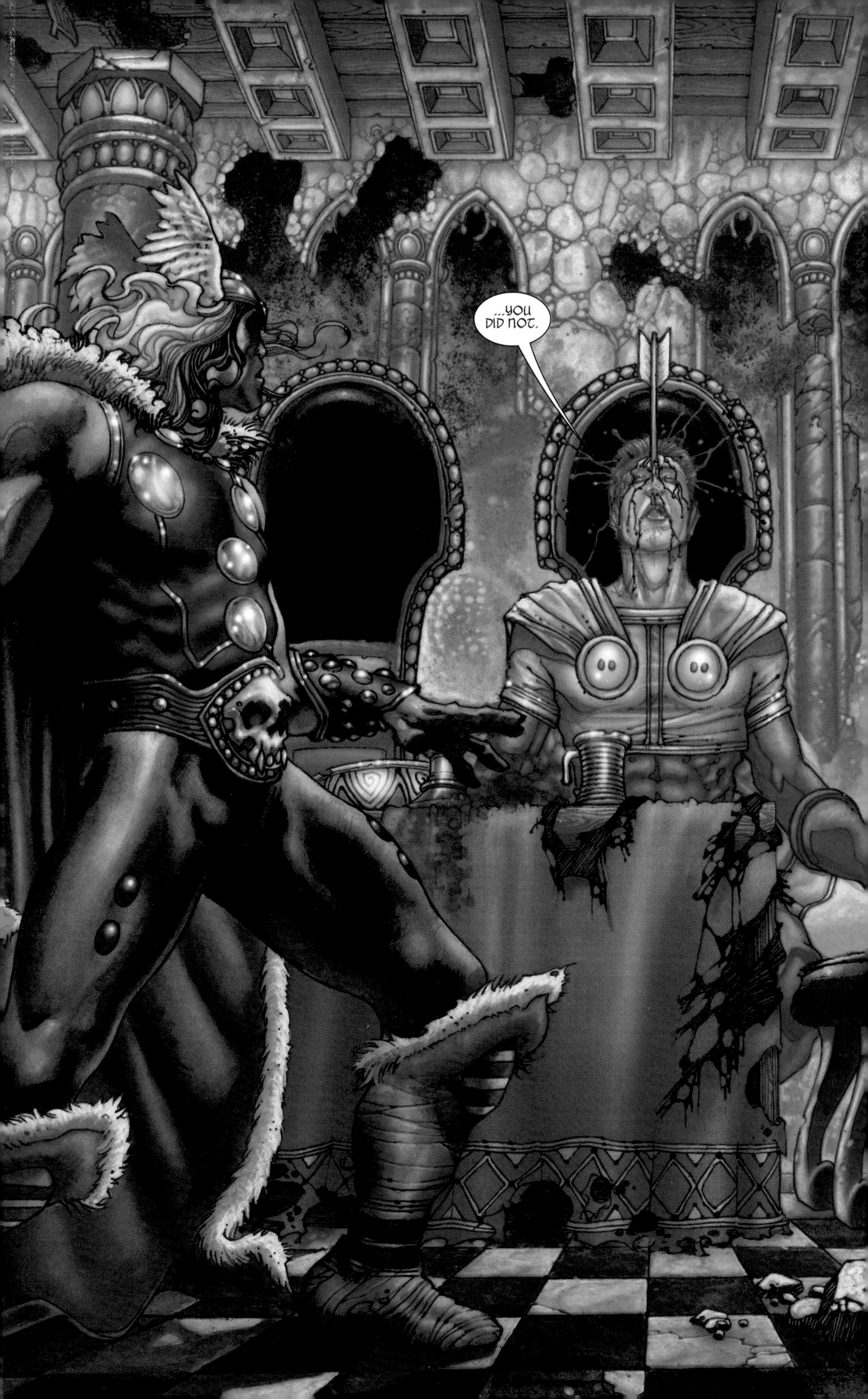
...YOU DID NOT.

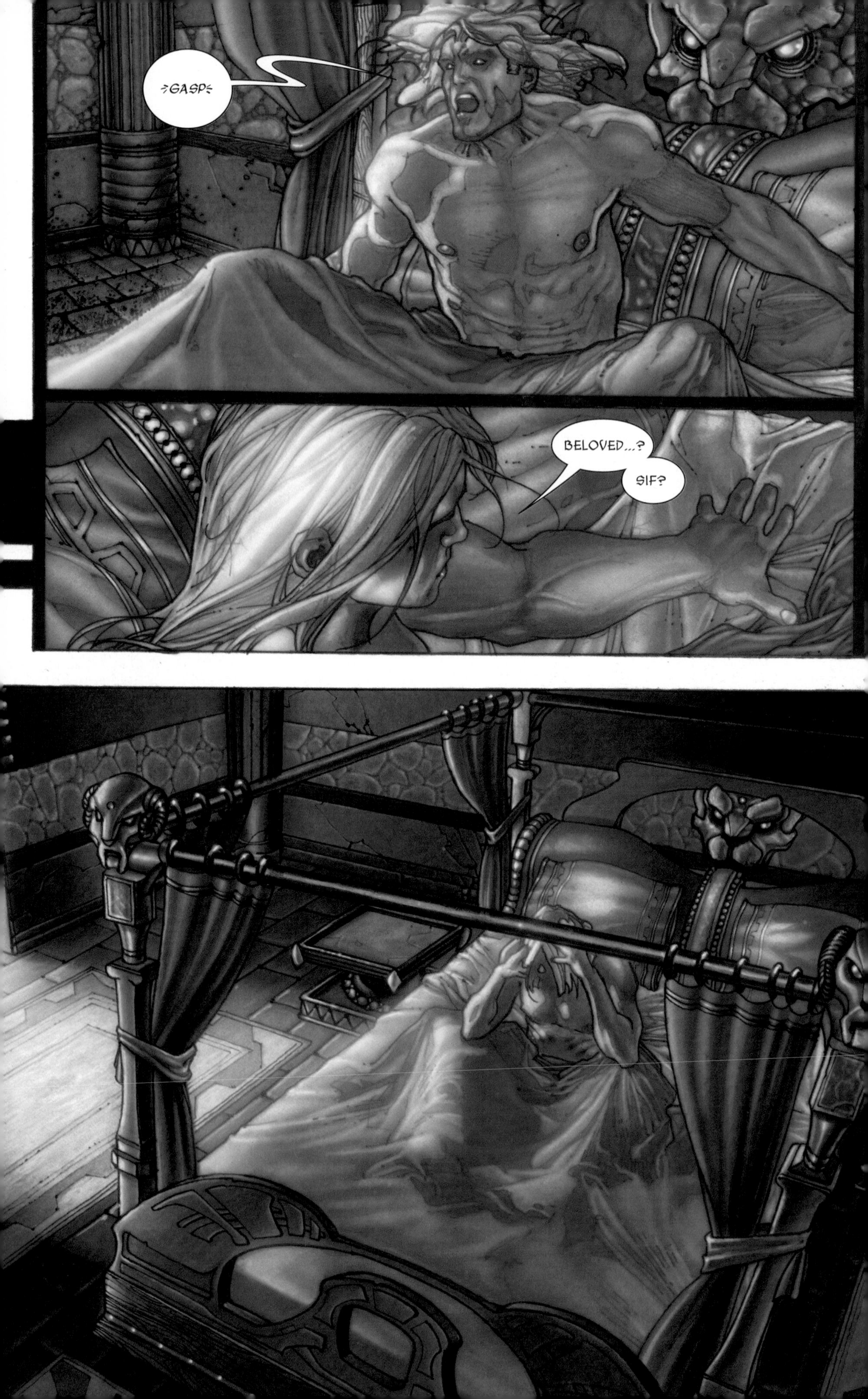
GASP
BELOVED...?
SIF?

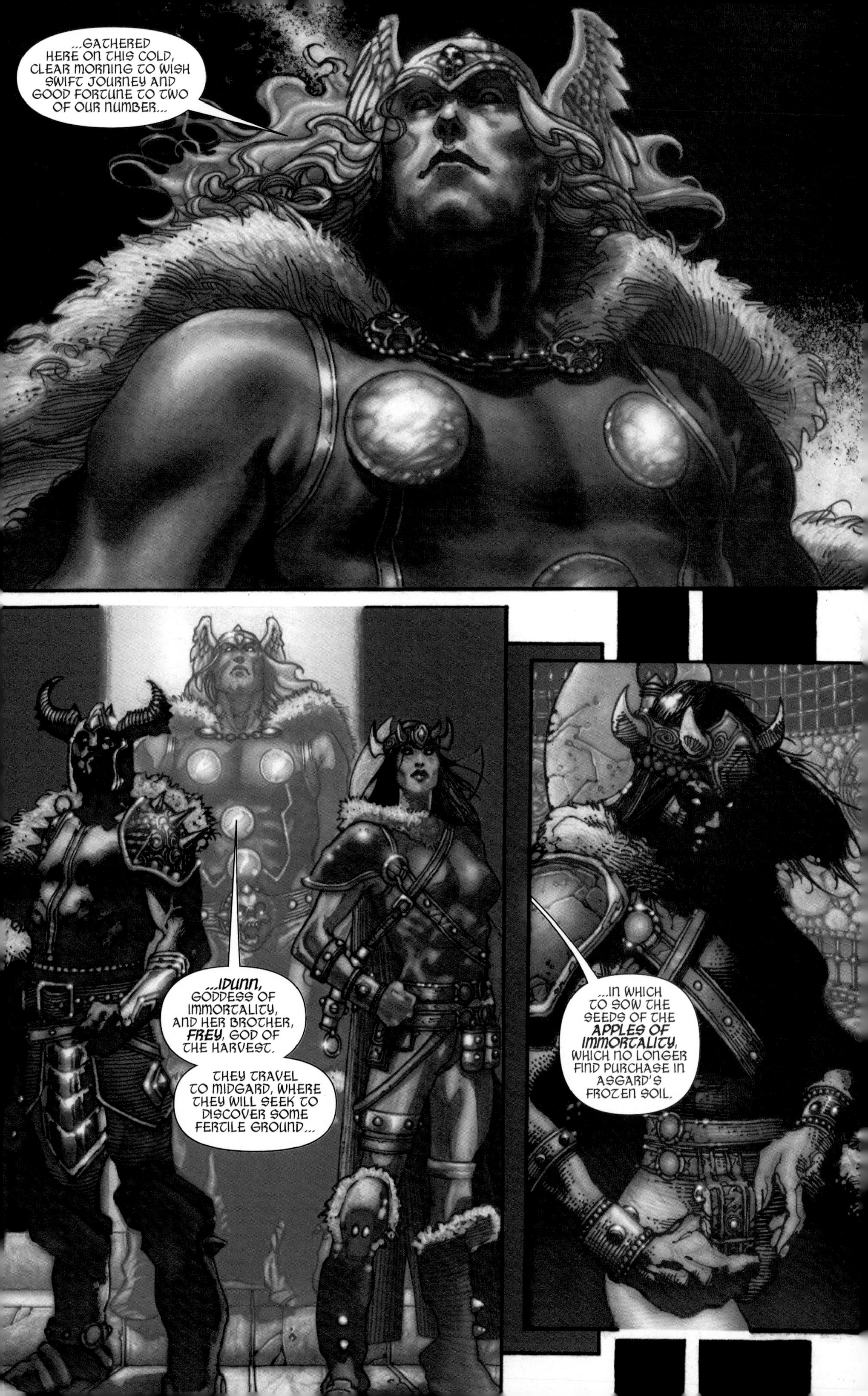
...GATHERED HERE ON THIS COLD, CLEAR MORNING TO WISH SWIFT JOURNEY AND GOOD FORTUNE TO TWO OF OUR NUMBER...
...IDUNN, GODDESS OF IMMORTALITY, AND HER BROTHER, FREY, GOD OF THE HARVEST.
THEY TRAVEL TO MIDGARD, WHERE THEY WILL SEEK TO DISCOVER SOME FERTILE GROUND...
...IN WHICH TO SOW THE SEEDS OF THE APPLES OF IMMORTALITY, WHICH NO LONGER FIND PURCHASE IN ASGARD'S FROZEN SOIL.

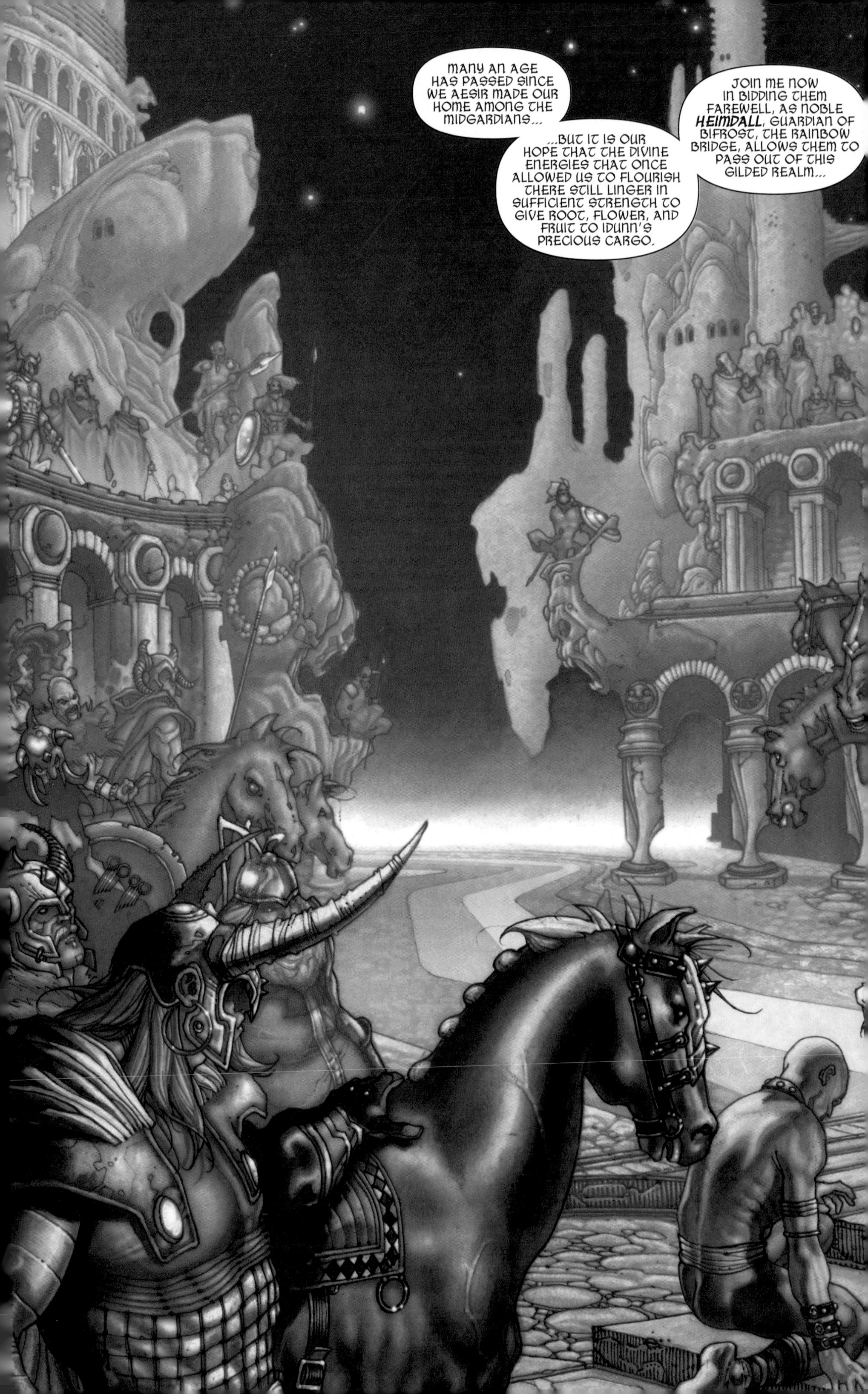
MANY AN AGE HAS PASSED SINCE WE AESIR MADE OUR HOME AMONG THE MIDGARDIANS...
...BUT IT IS OUR HOPE THAT THE DIVINE ENERGIES THAT ONCE ALLOWED US TO FLOURISH THERE STILL LINGER IN SUFFICIENT STRENGTH TO GIVE ROOT, FLOWER, AND FRUIT TO IDUNN'S PRECIOUS CARGO.
JOIN ME NOW IN BIDDING THEM FAREWELL, AS NOBLE HEIMDALL, GUARDIAN OF BIFROST, THE RAINBOW BRIDGE, ALLOWS THEM TO PASS OUT OF THIS GILDED REALM...

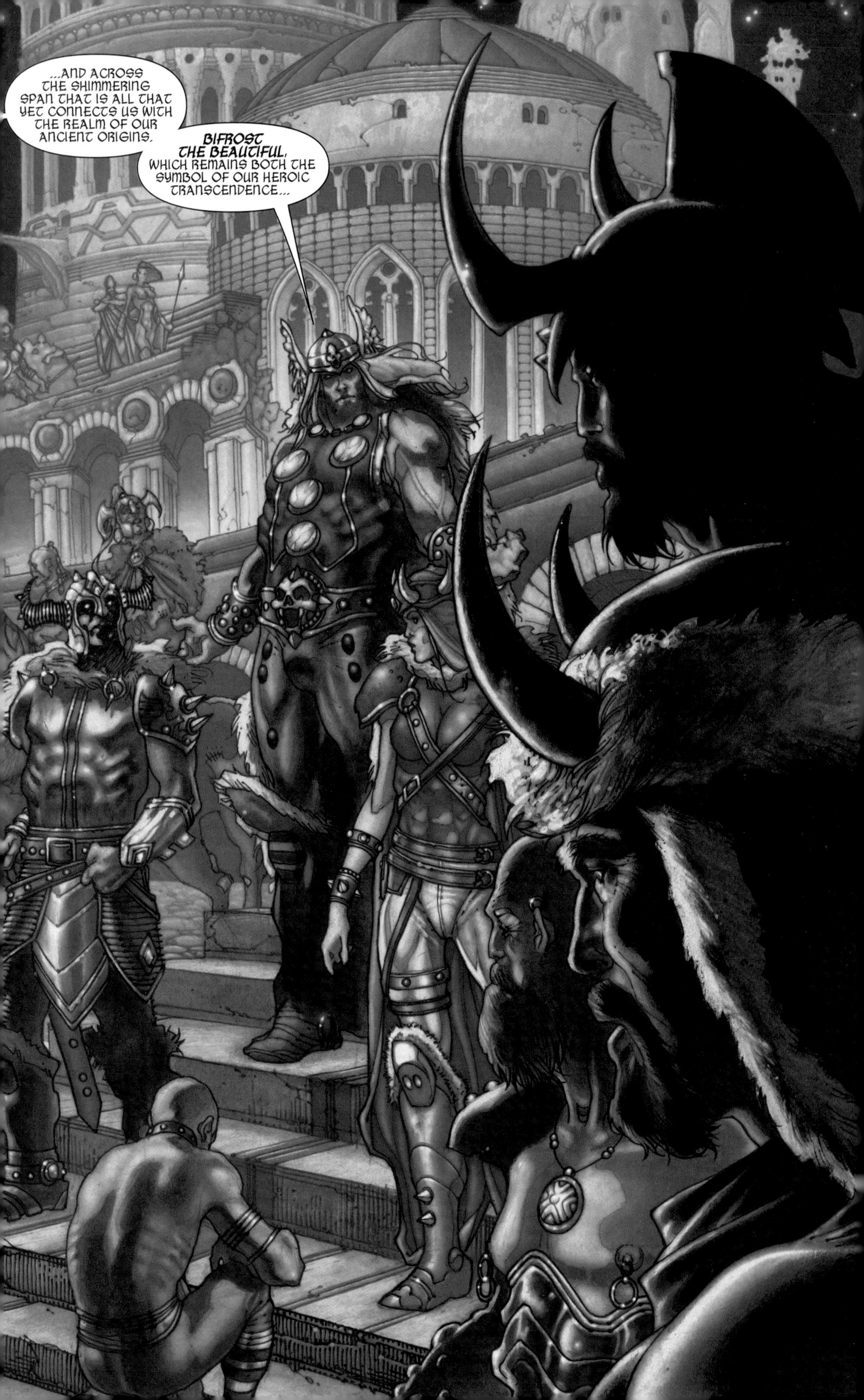
...AND ACROSS THE SHIMMERING SPAN THAT IS ALL THAT YET CONNECTS US WITH THE REALM OF OUR ANCIENT ORIGINS.
BIFROST THE BEAUTIFUL, WHICH REMAINS BOTH THE SYMBOL OF OUR HEROIC TRANSCENDENCE...

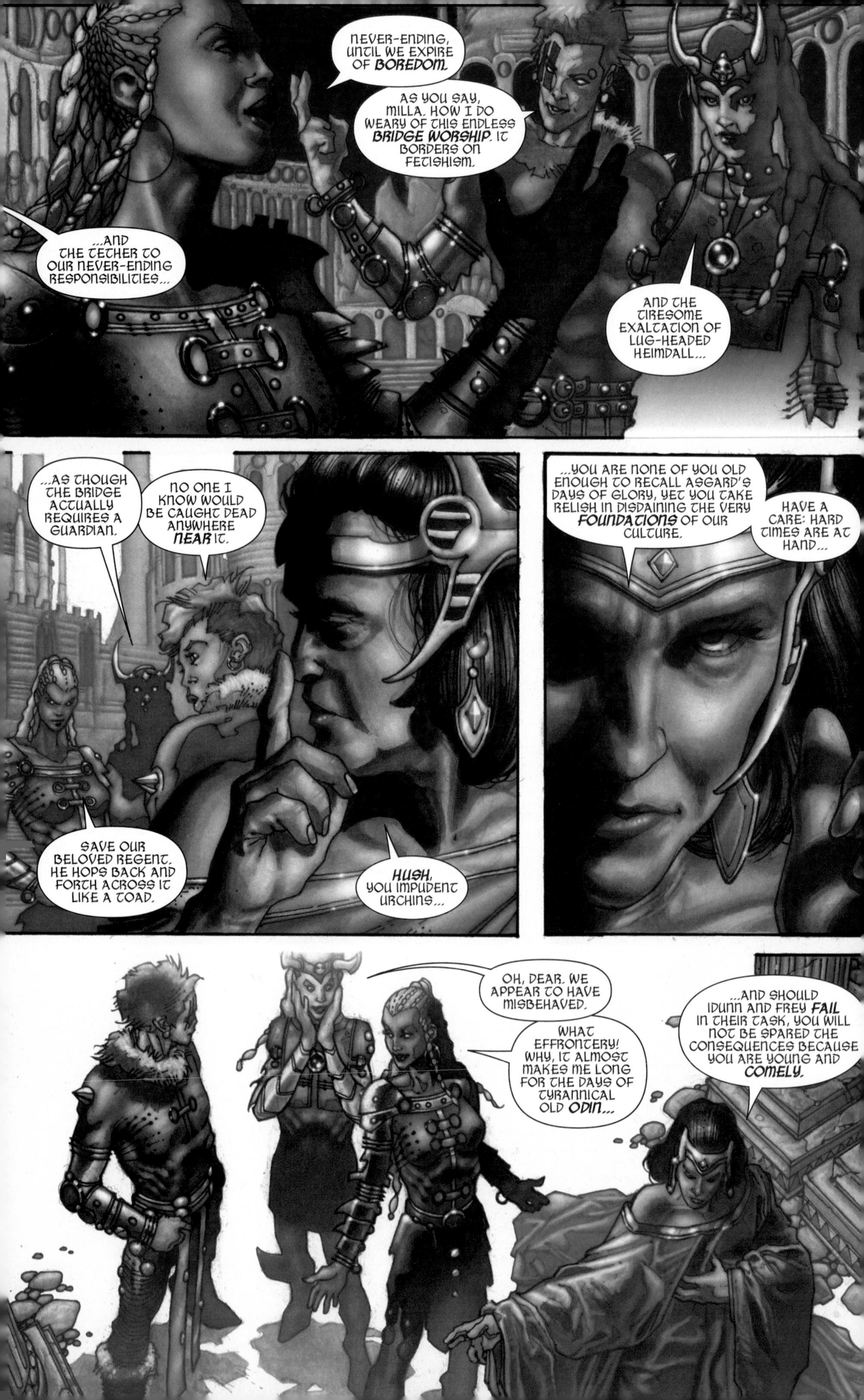
NEVER-ENDING, UNTIL WE EXPIRE OF BOREDOM.
AS YOU SAY, MILLA. HOW I DO WEARY OF THIS ENDLESS BRIDGE WORSHIP. IT BORDERS ON FETISHISM.
...AND THE TETHER TO OUR NEVER-ENDING RESPONSIBILITIES...
AND THE TIRESOME EXALTATION OF LUG-HEADED HEIMDALL...
...AS THOUGH THE BRIDGE ACTUALLY REQUIRES A GUARDIAN.
NO ONE I KNOW WOULD BE CAUGHT DEAD ANYWHERE NEAR IT.
SAVE OUR BELOVED REGENT. HE HOPS BACK AND FORTH ACROSS IT LIKE A TOAD.
HUSH, YOU IMPUDENT URCHINS...
...YOU ARE NONE OF YOU OLD ENOUGH TO RECALL ASGARD'S DAYS OF GLORY, YET YOU TAKE RELISH IN DISDAINING THE VERY FOUNDATIONS OF OUR CULTURE.
HAVE A CARE: HARD TIMES ARE AT HAND...
OH, DEAR. WE APPEAR TO HAVE MISBEHAVED.
WHAT EFFRONTERY! WHY, IT ALMOST MAKES ME LONG FOR THE DAYS OF TYRANNICAL OLD ODIN...
...AND SHOULD IDUNN AND FREY FAIL IN THEIR TASK, YOU WILL NOT BE SPARED THE CONSEQUENCES BECAUSE YOU ARE YOUNG AND COMELY.

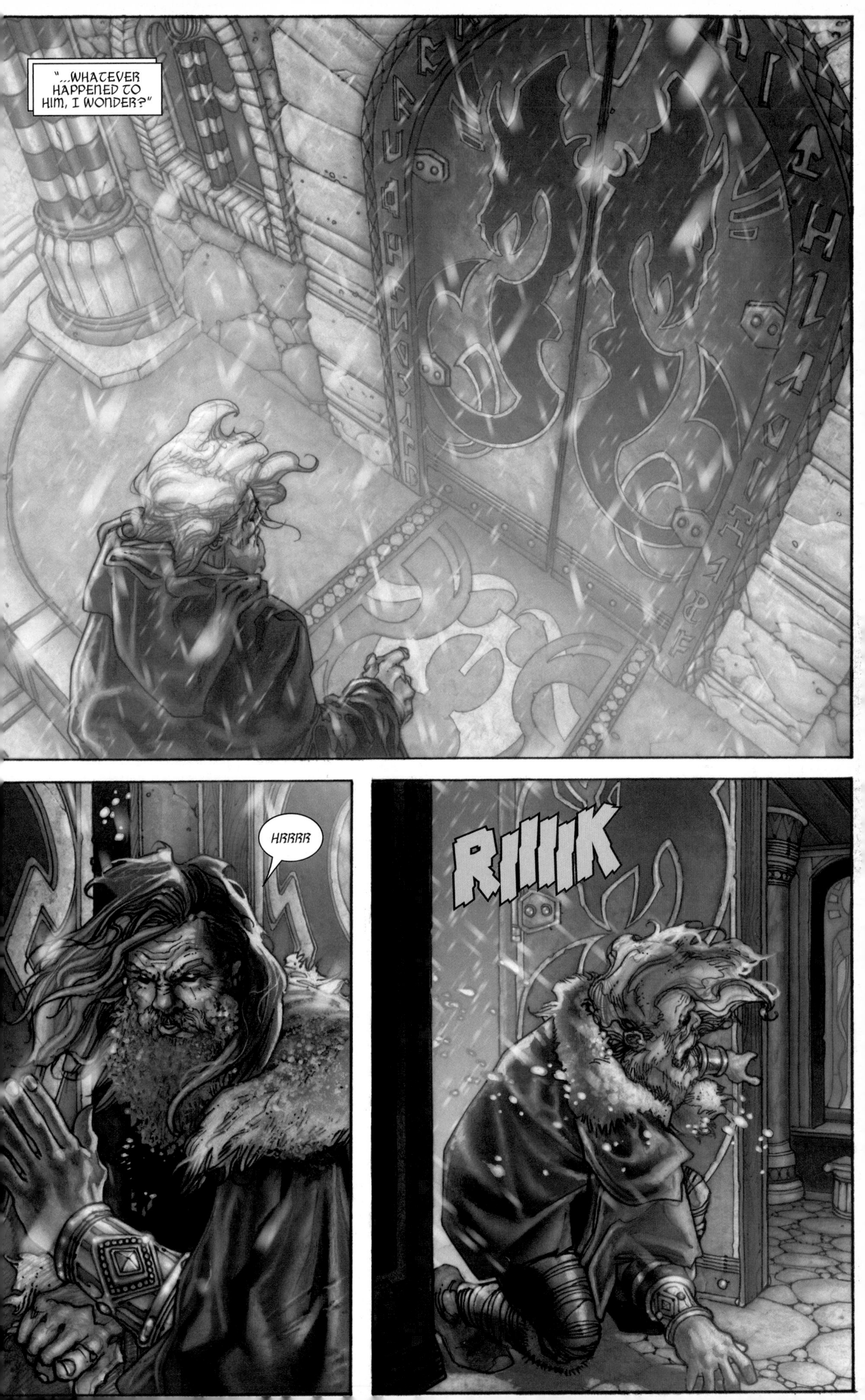
"...WHATEVER HAPPENED TO HIM, I WONDER?"
HRRRR
RIIIIK

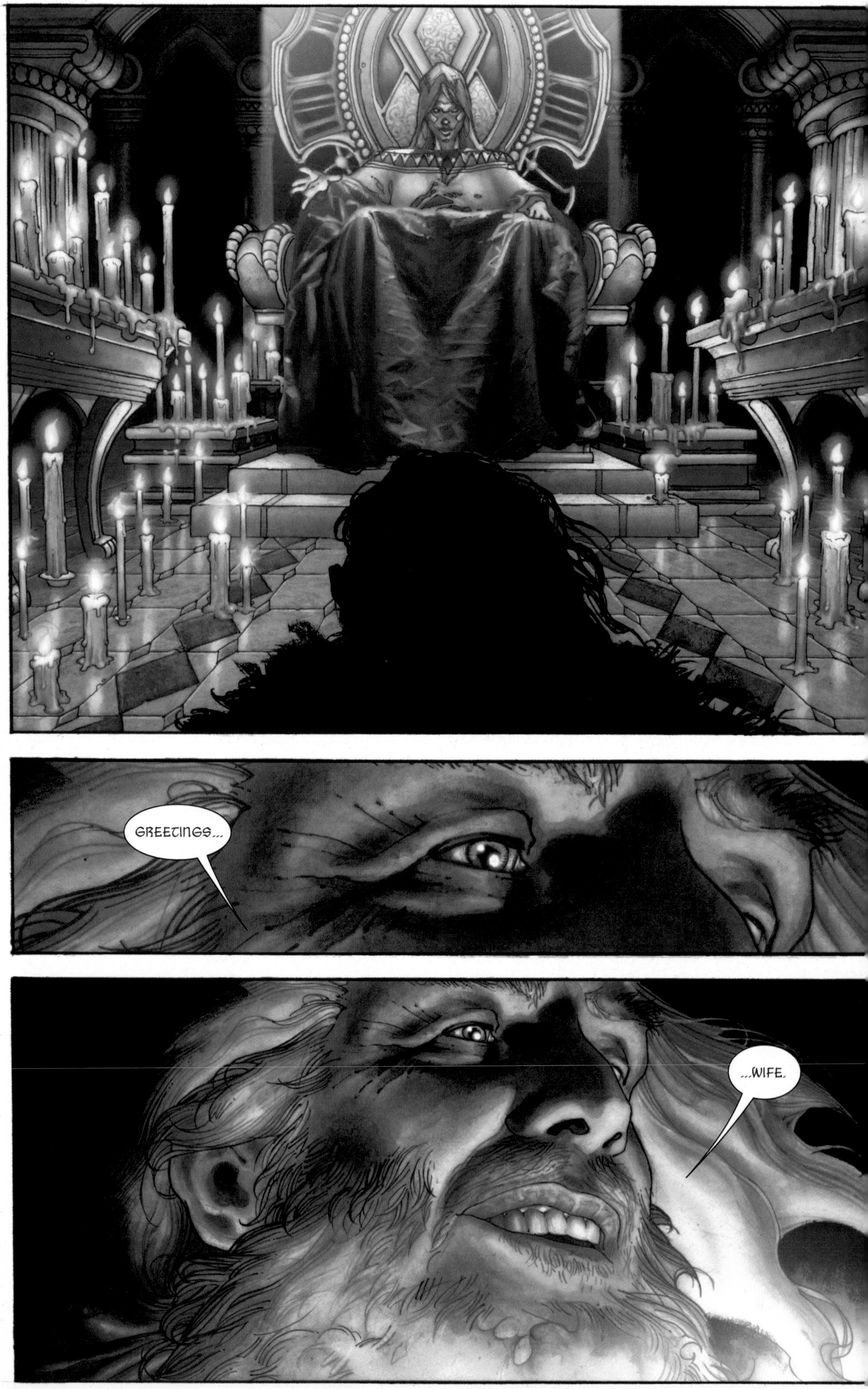
GREETINGS...
...WIFE.

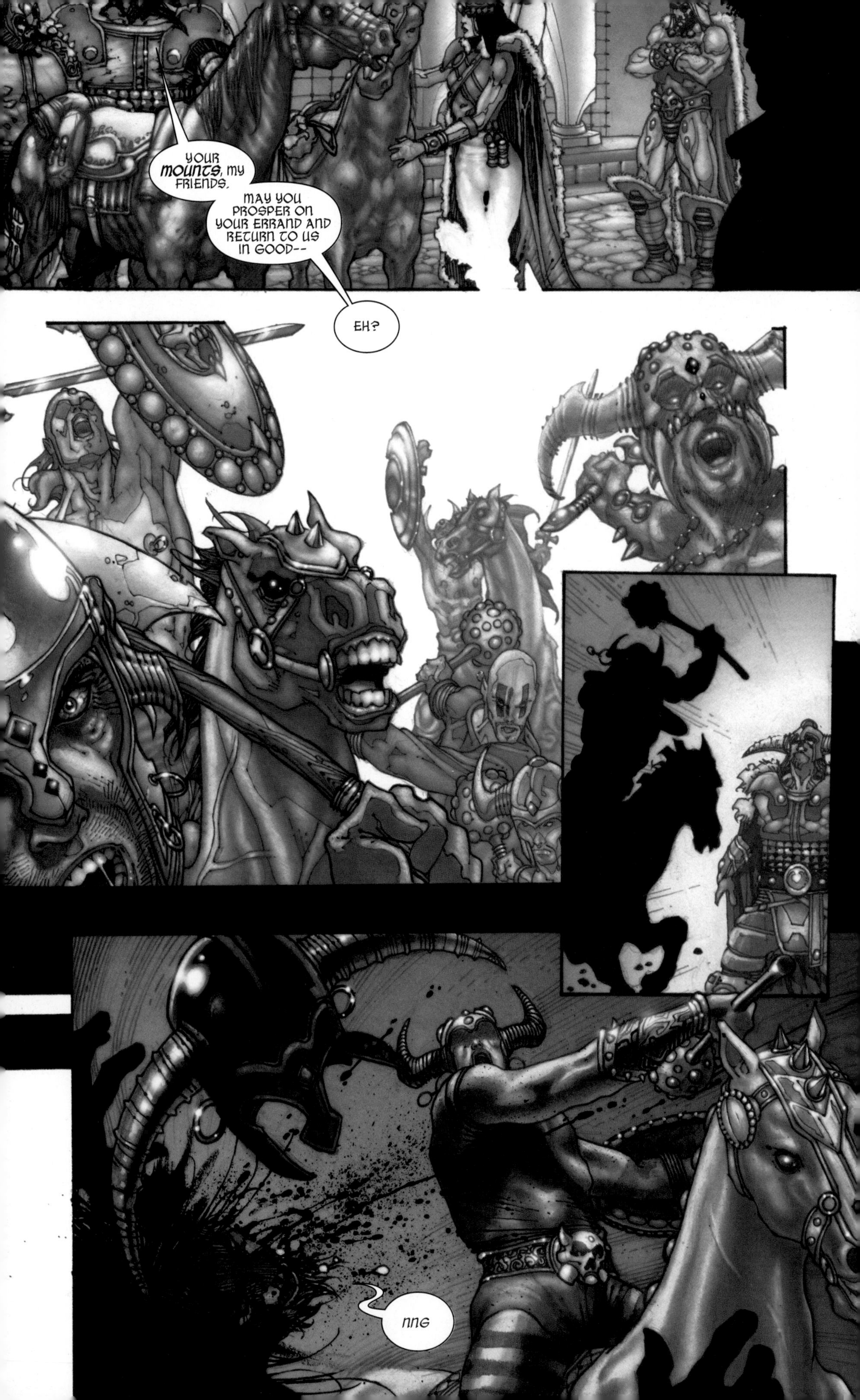
YOUR MOUNTS, MY FRIENDS.
MAY YOU PROSPER ON YOUR ERRAND AND RETURN TO US IN GOOD--
EH?
NNG

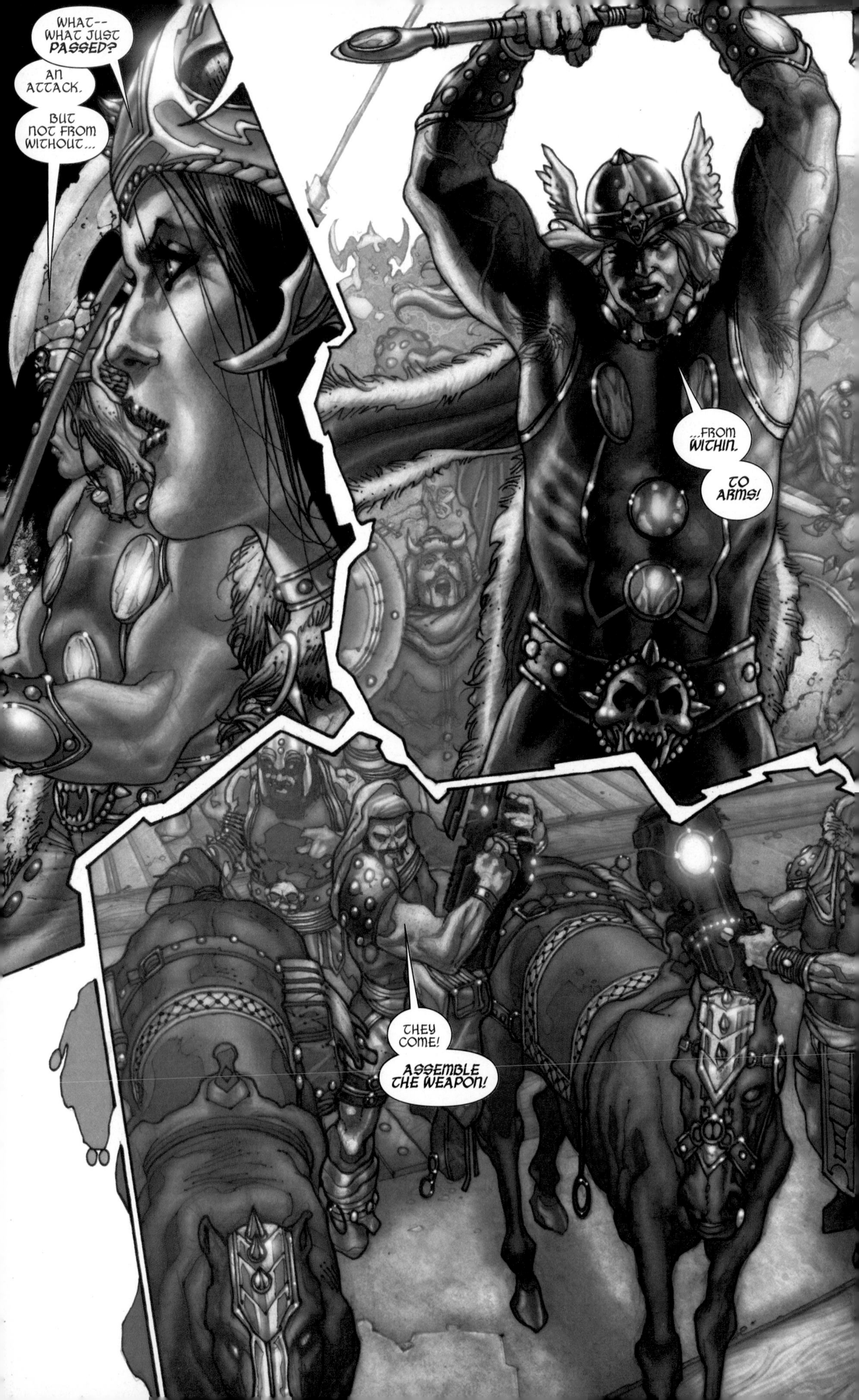
WHAT-- WHAT JUST PASSED?
AN ATTACK.
BUT NOT FROM WITHOUT...
...FROM WITHIN.
TO ARMS!
THEY COME!
ASSEMBLE THE WEAPON!

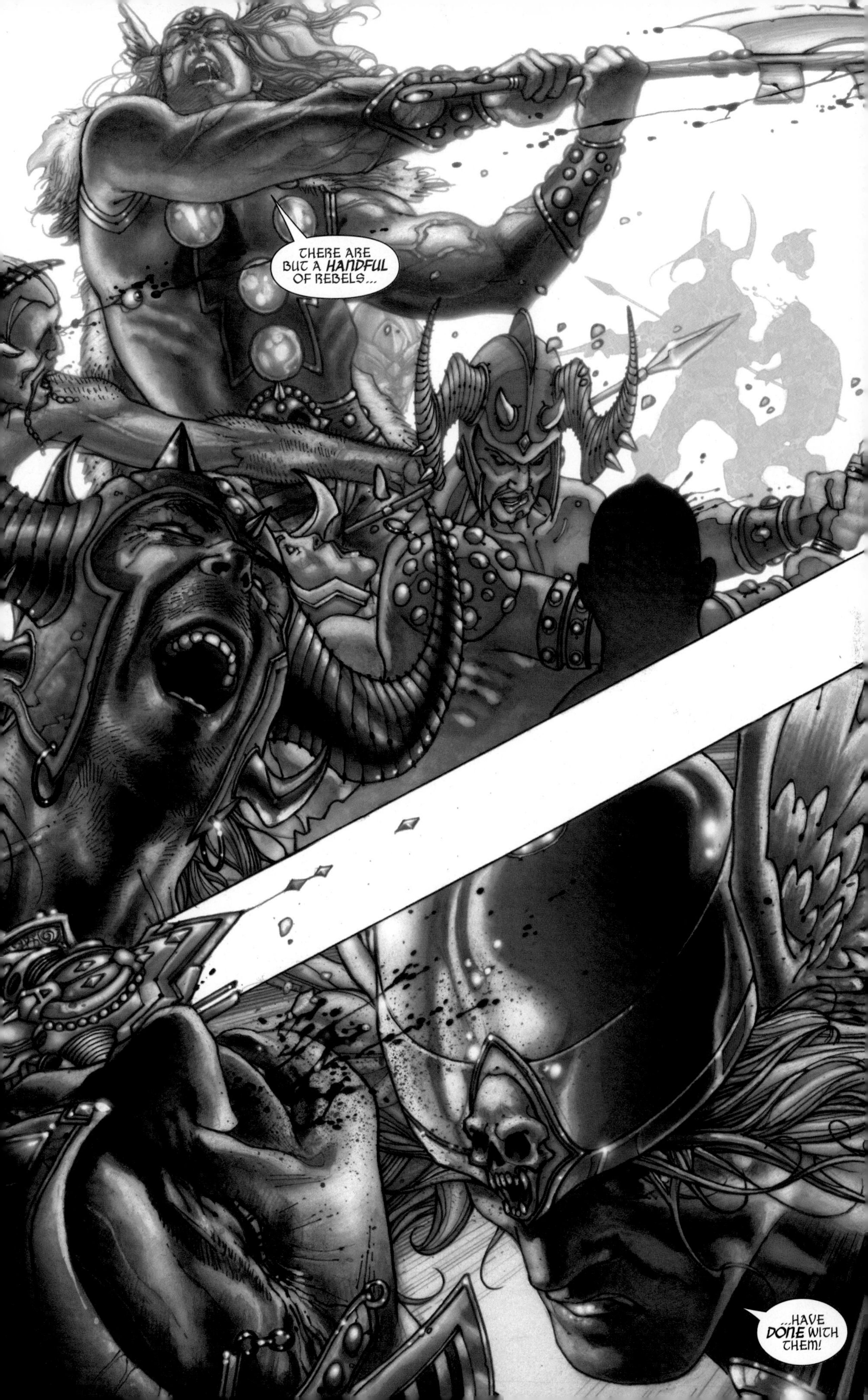
THERE ARE BUT A HANDFUL OF REBELS...
...HAVE DONE WITH THEM!

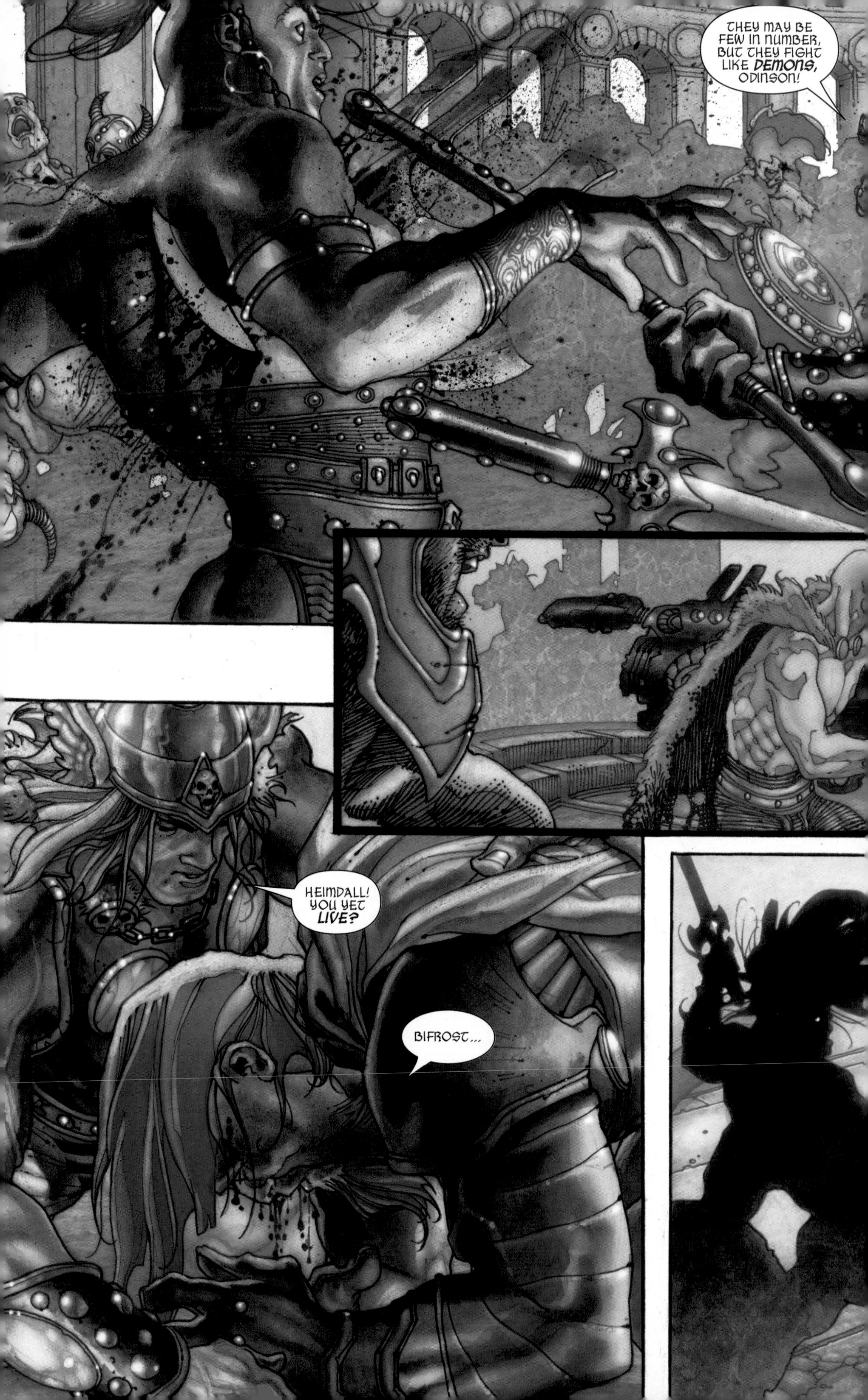
THEY MAY BE FEW IN NUMBER, BUT THEY FIGHT LIKE DEMONS, ODINSON!
HEIMDALL! YOU YET LIVE?
BIFROST...

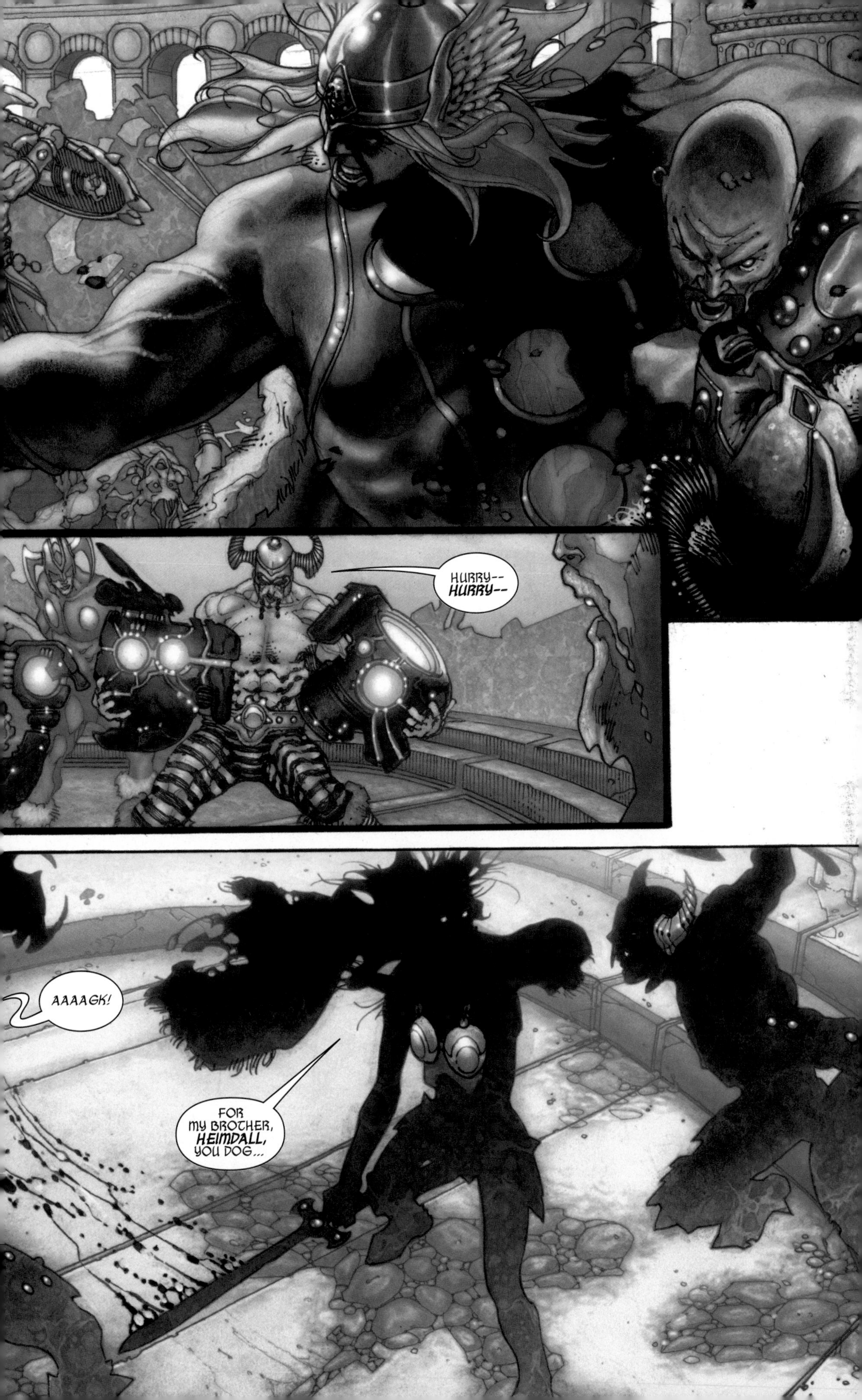
HURRY--
HURRY--
AAAAGK!
FOR MY BROTHER, HEIMDALL, YOU DOG...

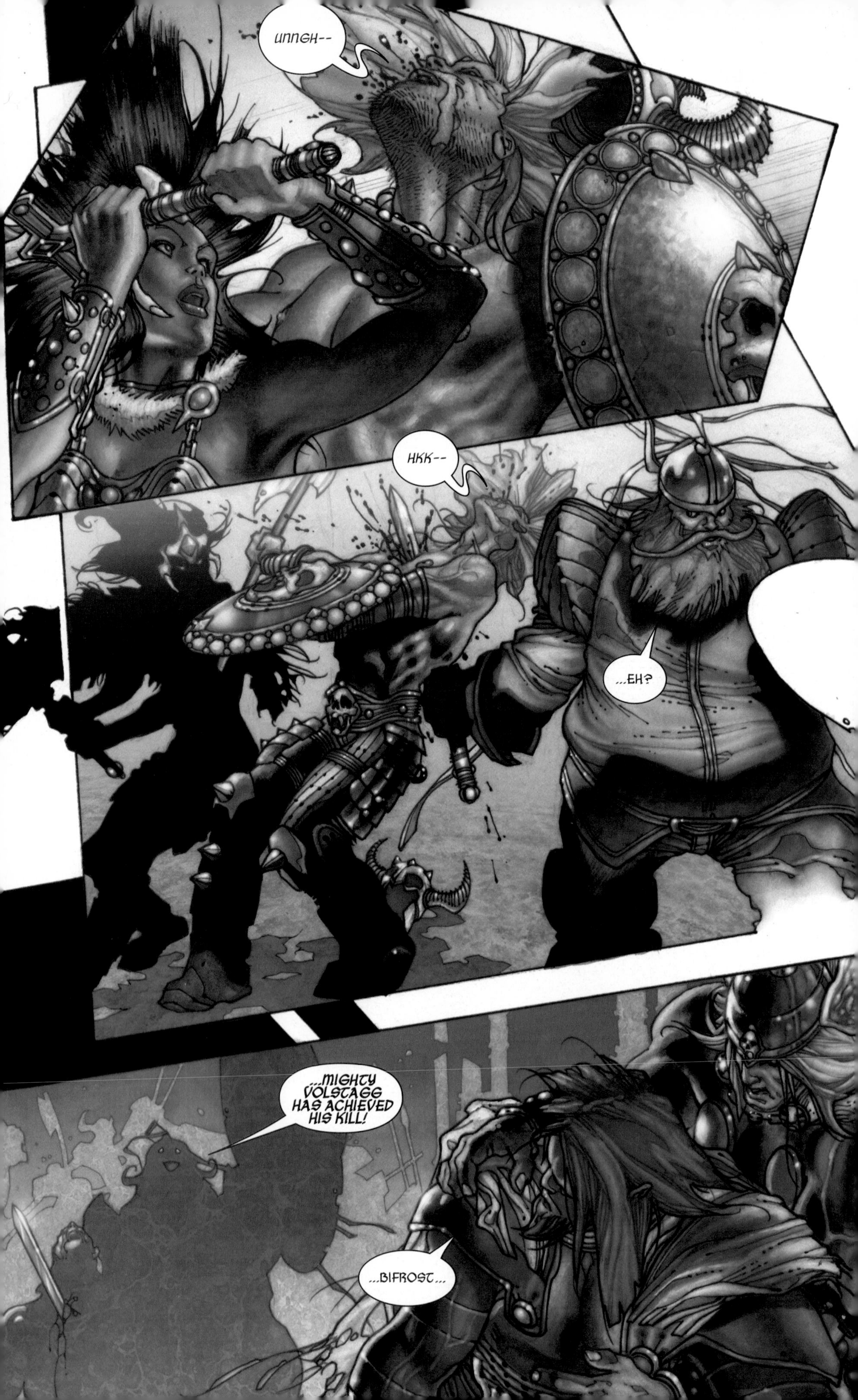
UNNGH--
HKK--
...EH?
...MIGHTY VOLSTAGG HAS ACHIEVED HIS KILL!
...BIFROST...

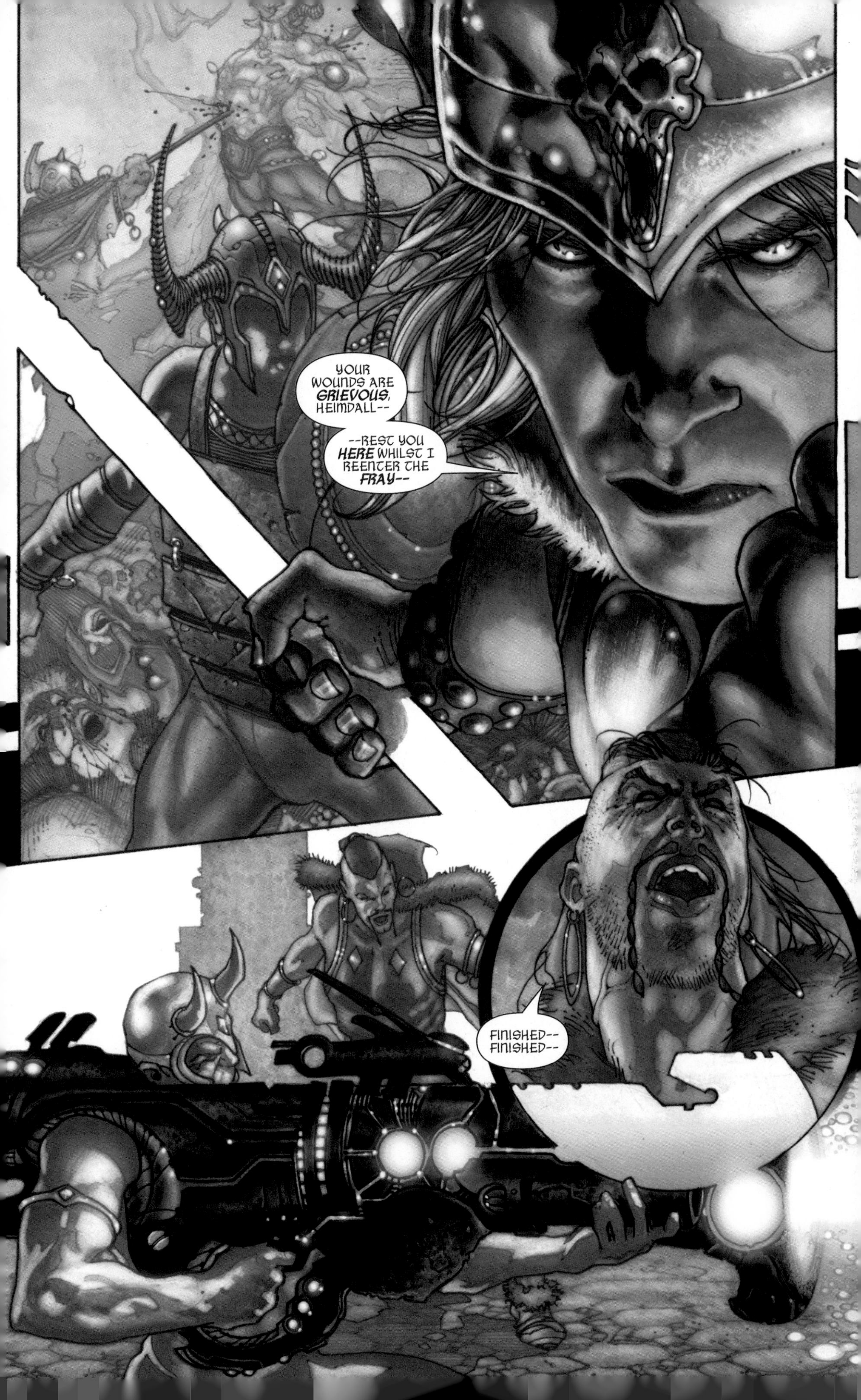
YOUR WOUNDS ARE GRIEVOUS, HEIMDALL--
--REST YOU HERE WHILST I REENTER THE FRAY--
FINISHED-- FINISHED--

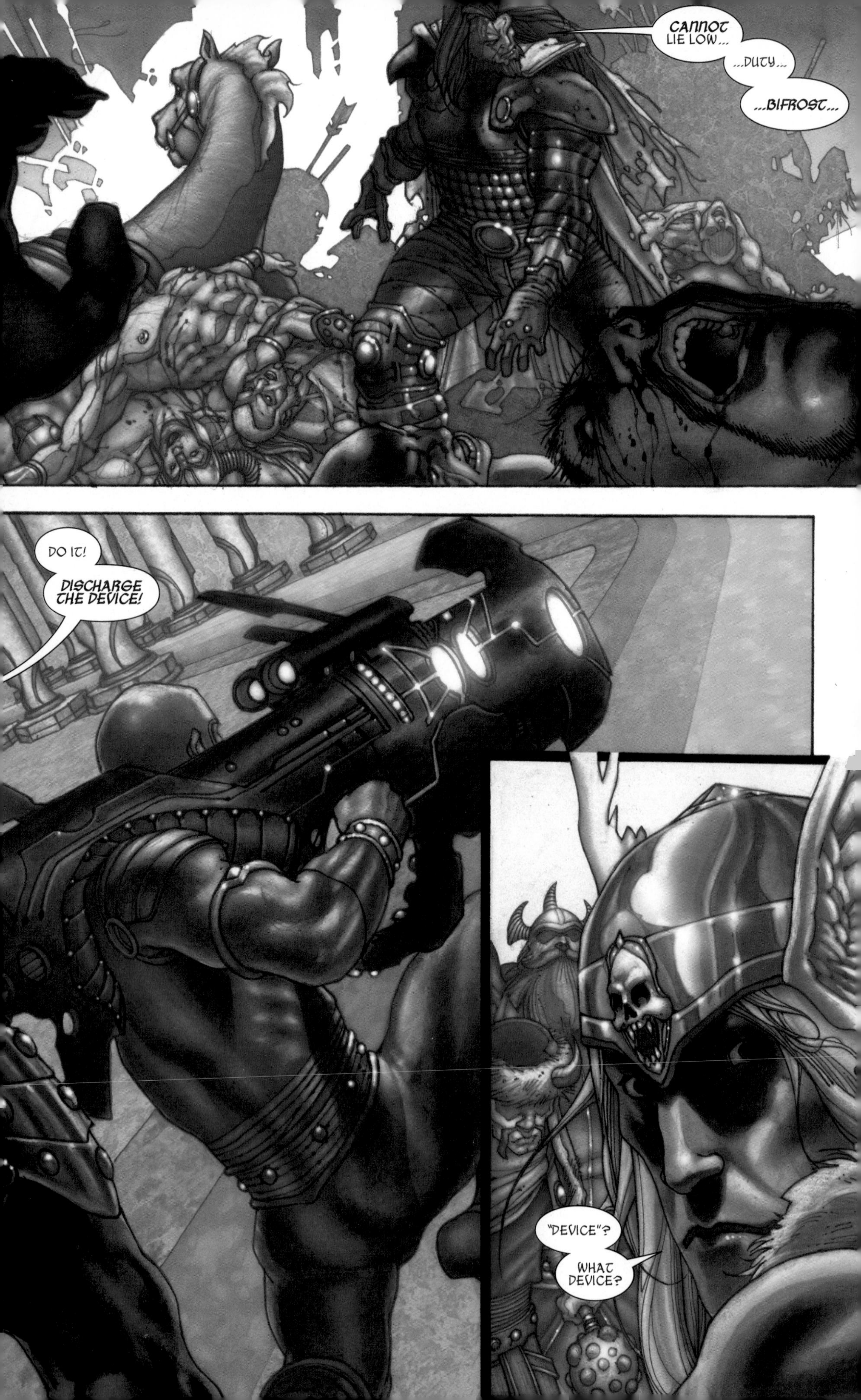
CANNOT LIE LOW...
...DUTY...
...BIFROST...
DO IT!
DISCHARGE THE DEVICE!
"DEVICE"?
WHAT DEVICE?

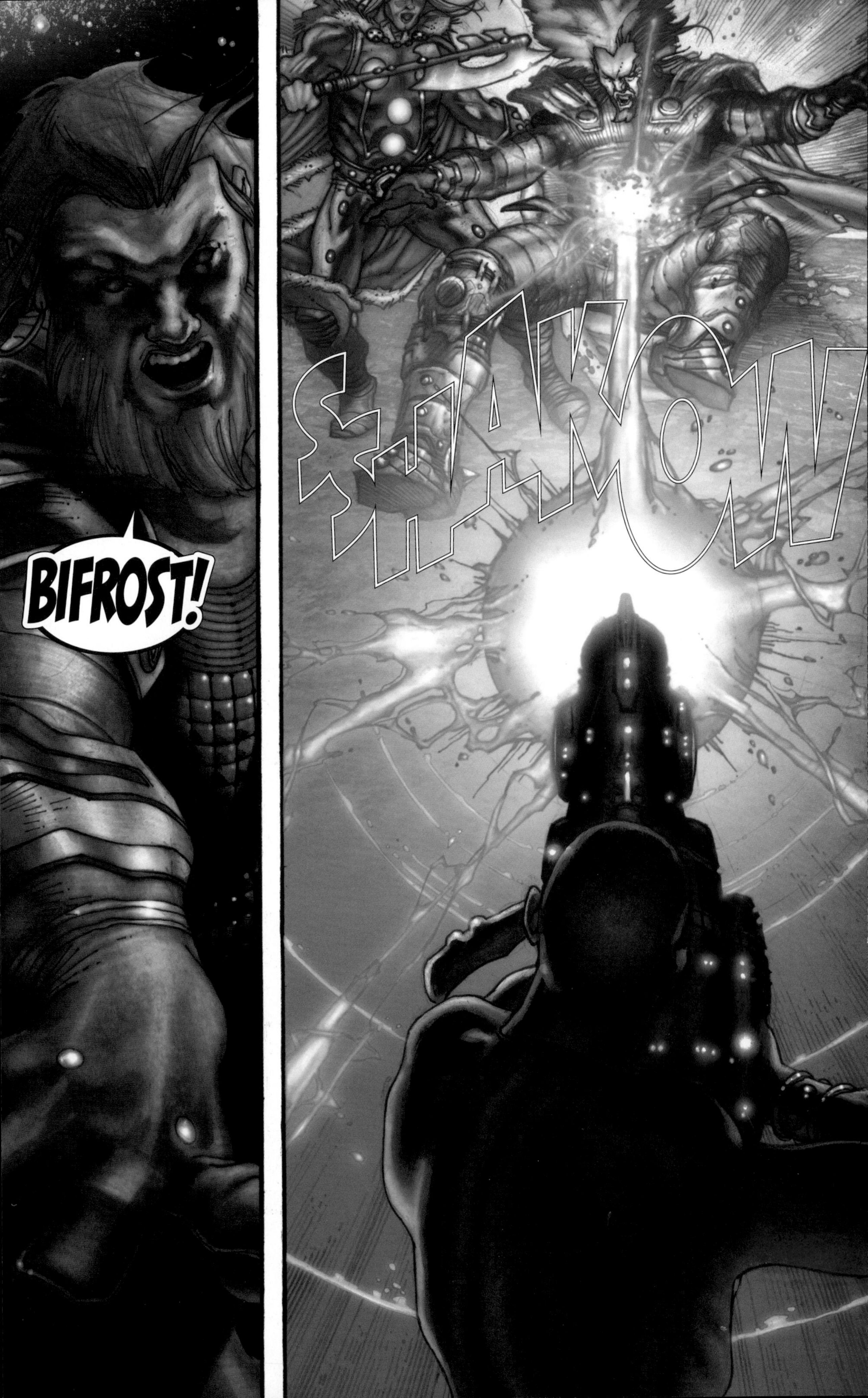
BIFROST!
SHAKOW

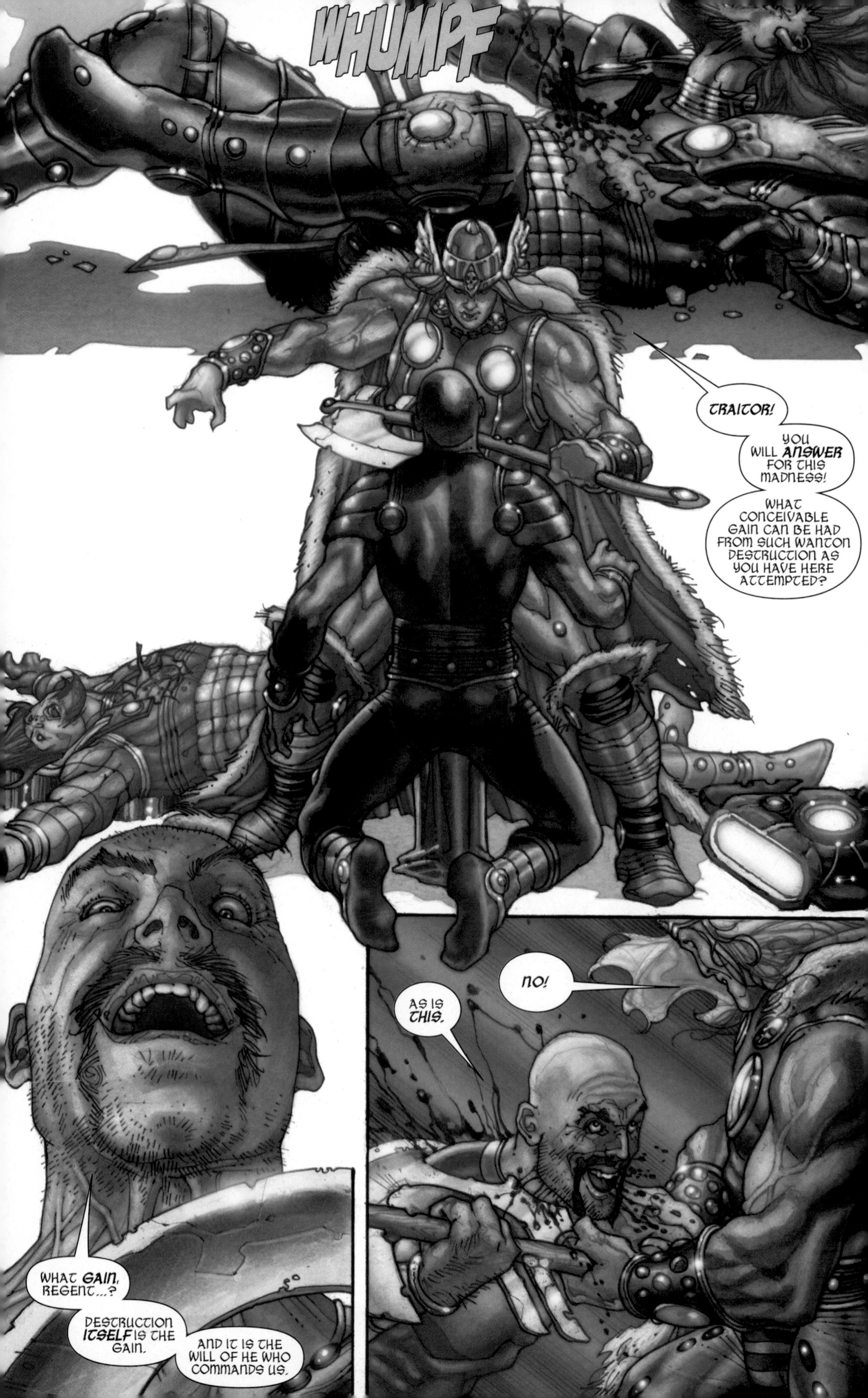
WHUMPF
TRAITOR!
YOU WILL ANSWER FOR THIS MADNESS!
WHAT CONCEIVABLE GAIN CAN BE HAD FROM SUCH WANTON DESTRUCTION AS YOU HAVE HERE ATTEMPTED?
WHAT GAIN, REGENT...?
DESTRUCTION ITSELF IS THE GAIN.
AND IT IS THE WILL OF HE WHO COMMANDS US.
NO!
AS IS THIS.

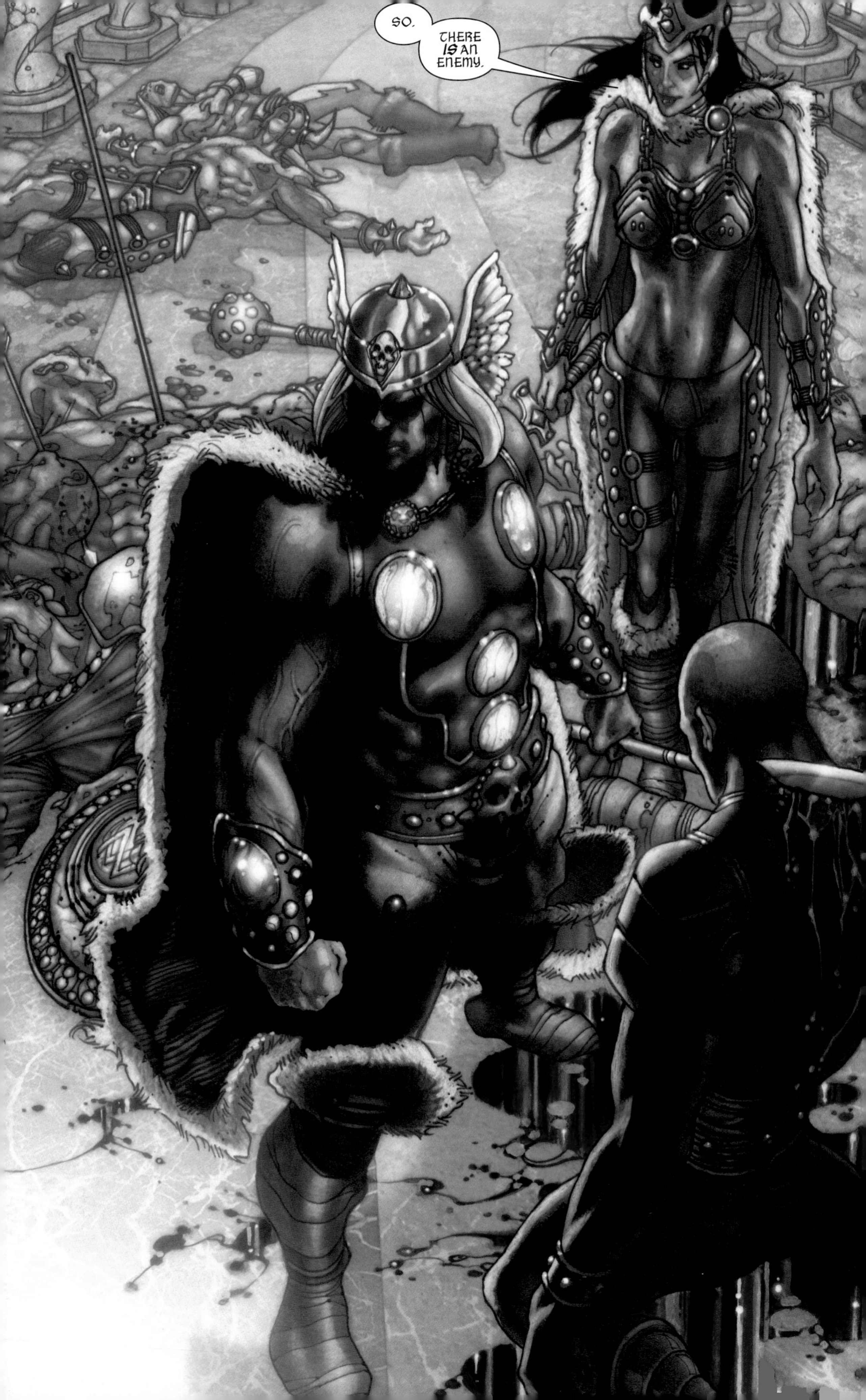
SO.
THERE IS AN ENEMY.

3

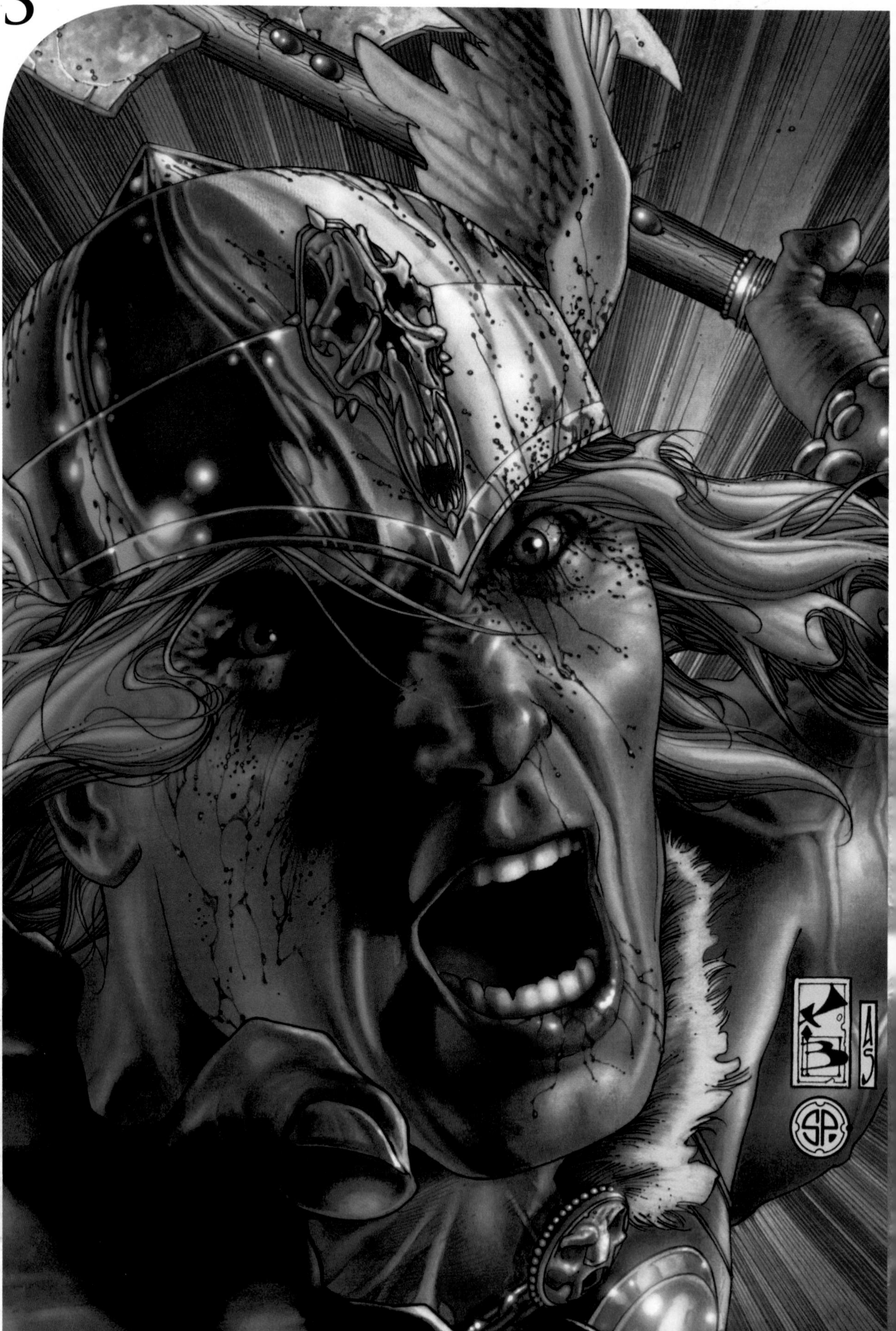

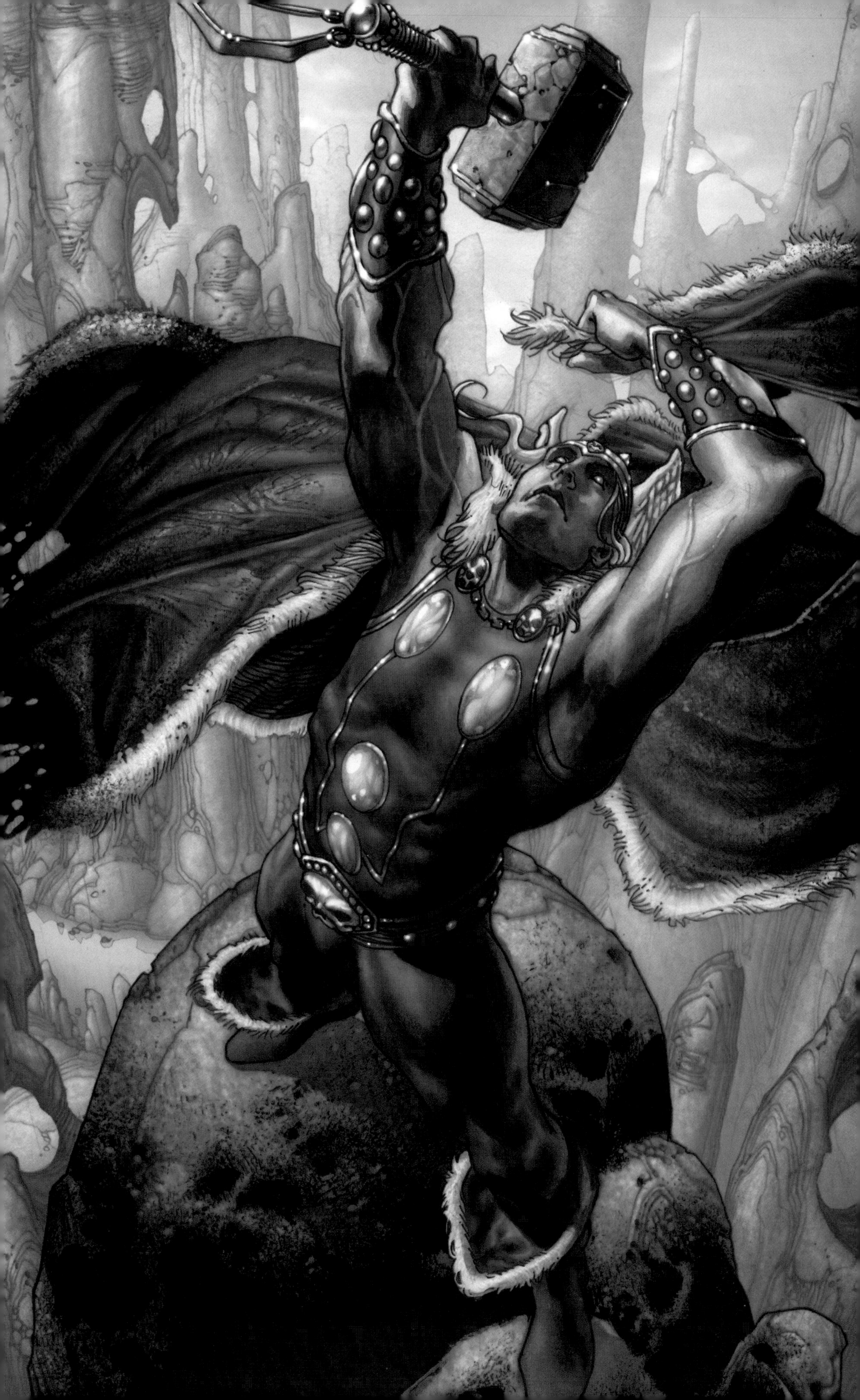

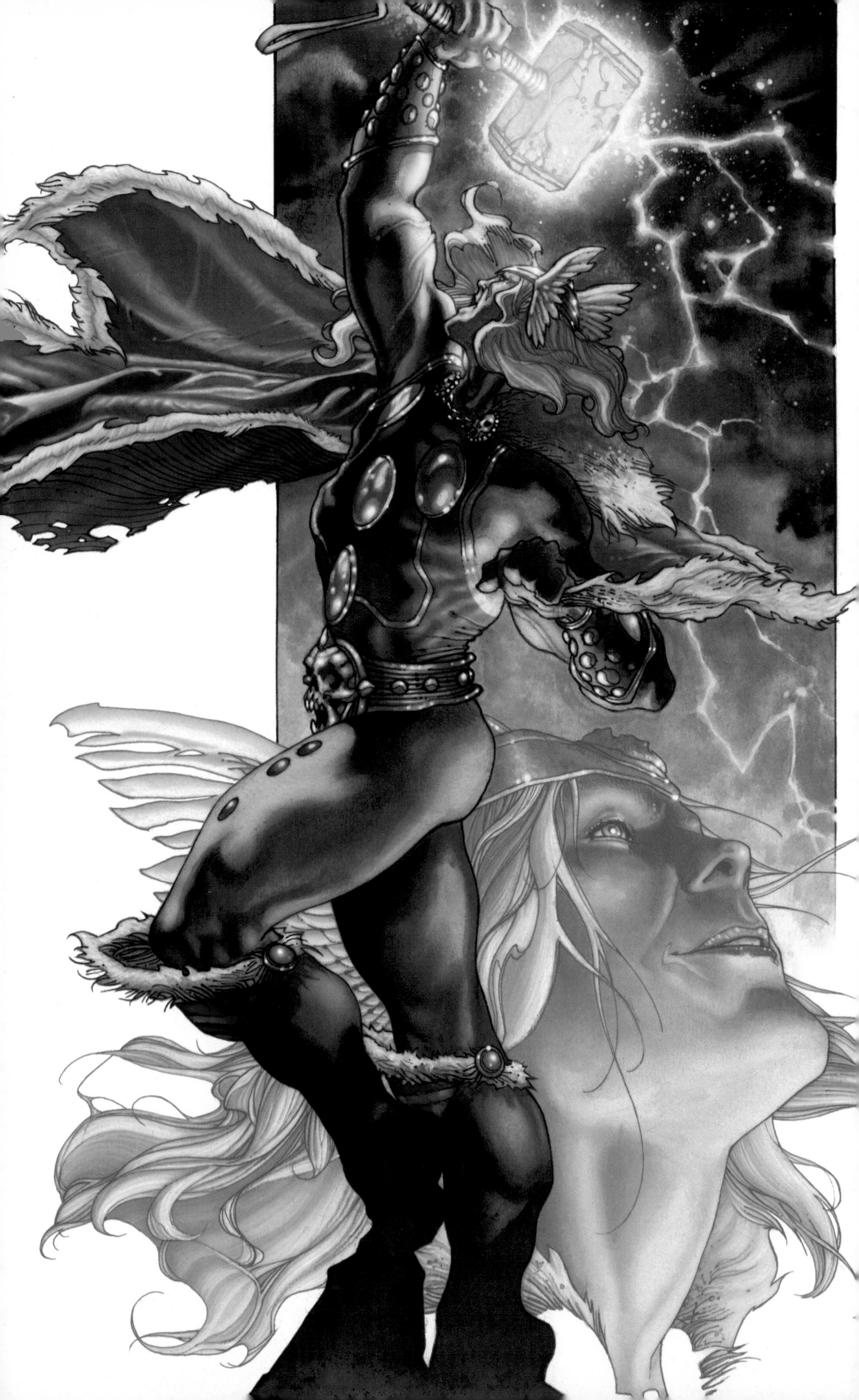

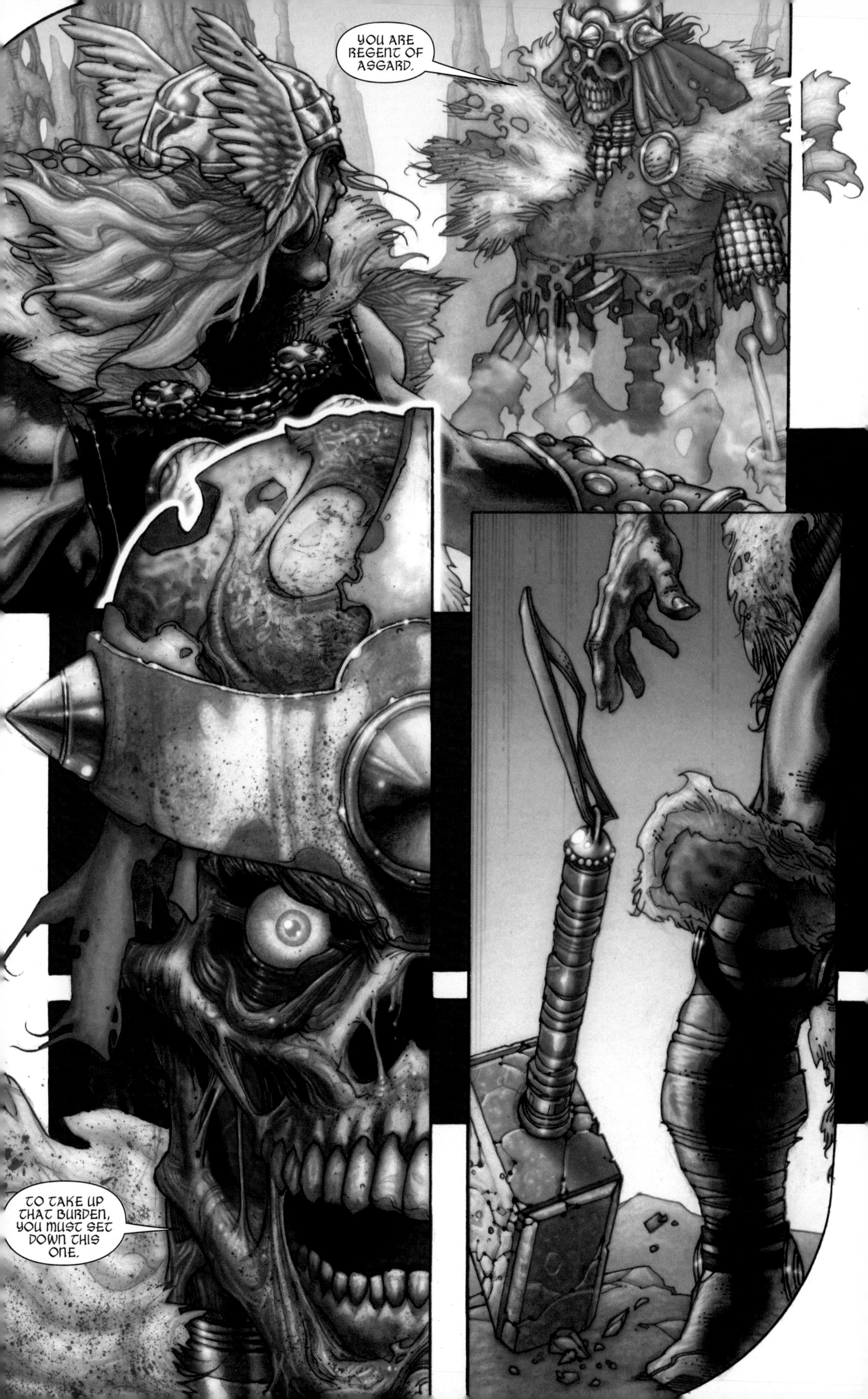
YOU ARE REGENT OF ASGARD.
TO TAKE UP THAT BURDEN, YOU MUST SET DOWN THIS ONE.

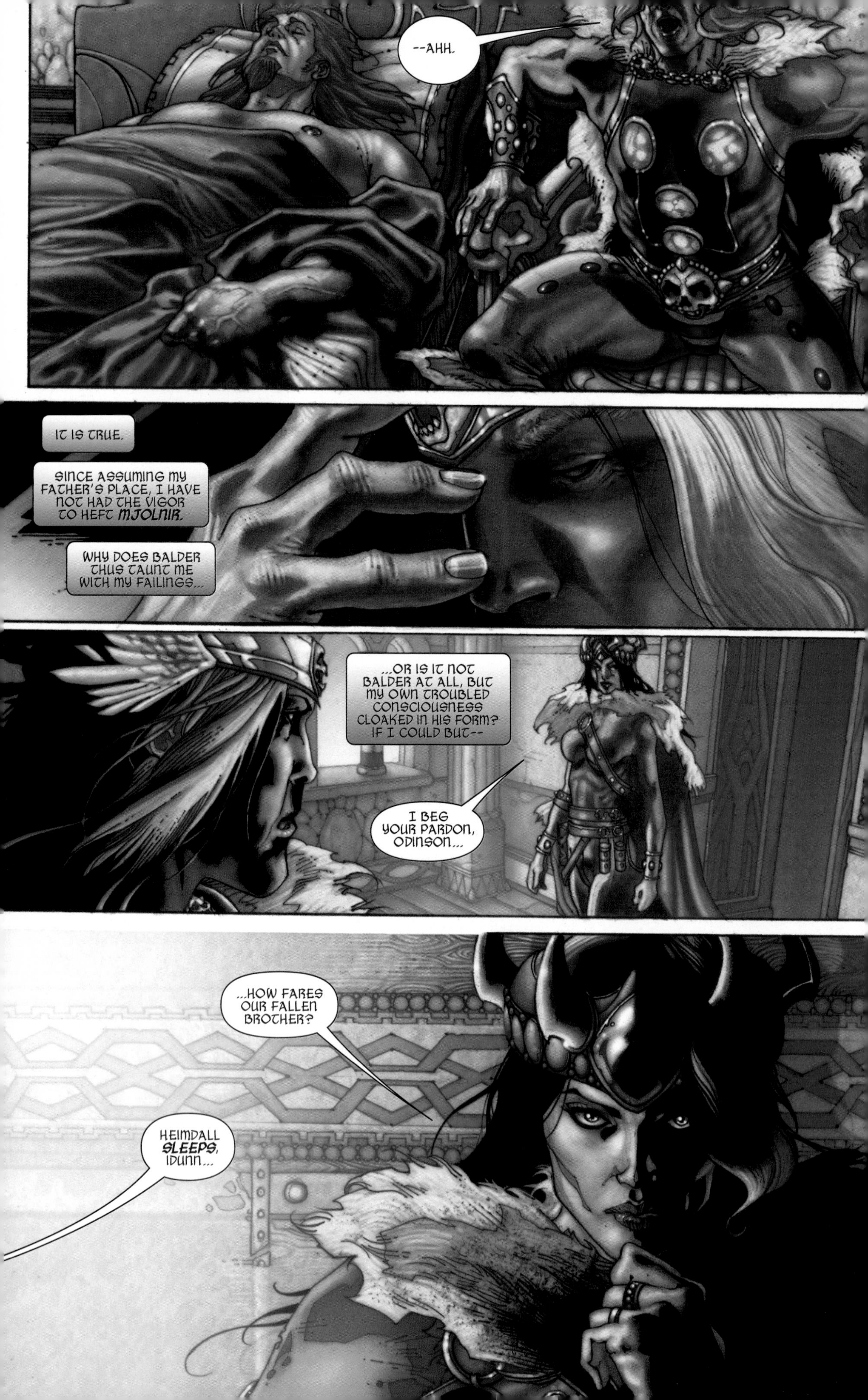
--AHH.
IT IS TRUE.
SINCE ASSUMING MY FATHER'S PLACE, I HAVE NOT HAD THE VIGOR TO HEFT MJOLNIR.
WHY DOES BALDER THUS TAUNT ME WITH MY FAILINGS...
...OR IS IT NOT BALDER AT ALL, BUT MY OWN TROUBLED CONSCIOUSNESS CLOAKED IN HIS FORM? IF I COULD BUT--
I BEG YOUR PARDON, ODINSON...
...HOW FARES OUR FALLEN BROTHER?
HEIMDALL SLEEPS, IDUNN...

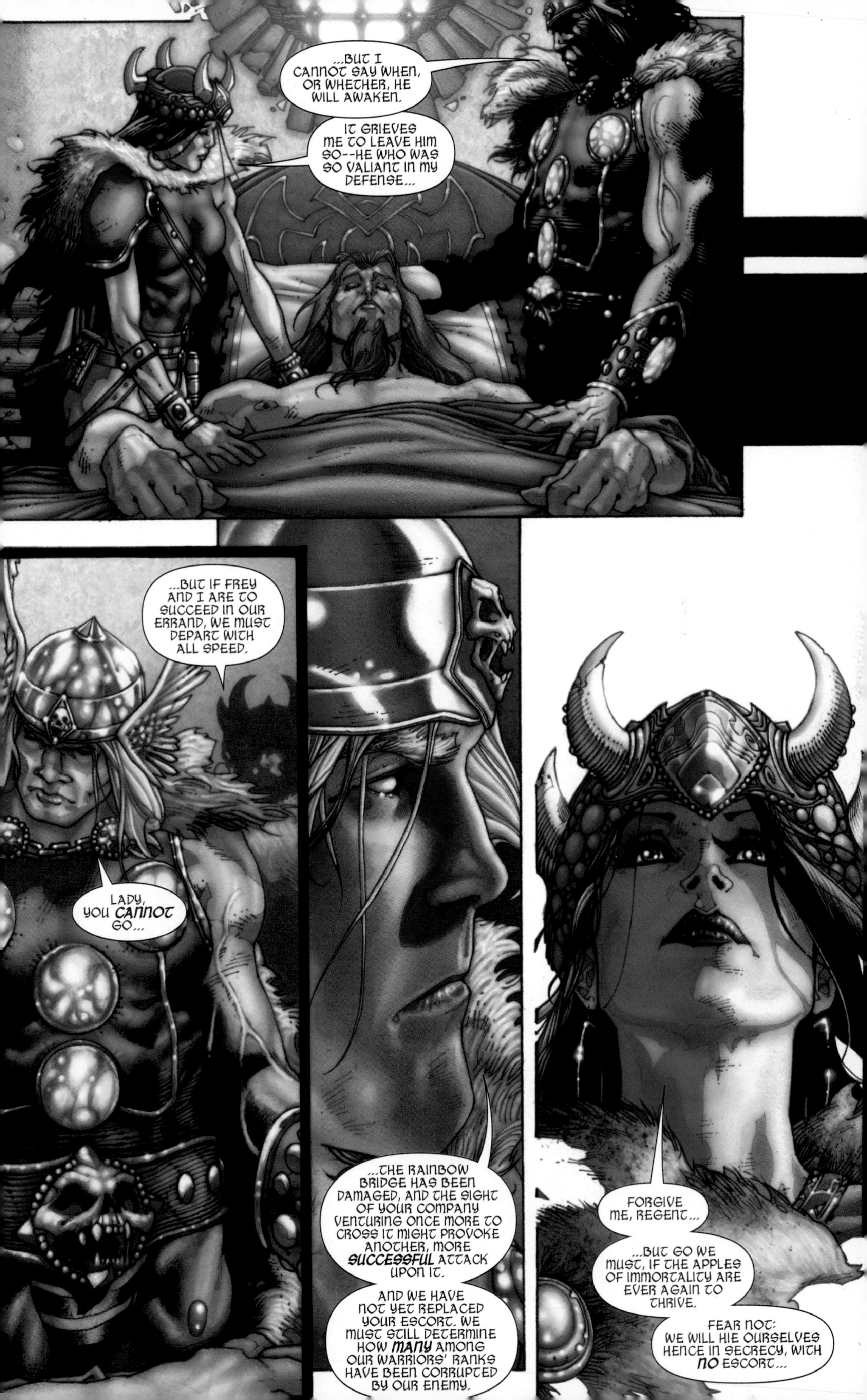
...BUT I CANNOT SAY WHEN, OR WHETHER, HE WILL AWAKEN.
IT GRIEVES ME TO LEAVE HIM SO--HE WHO WAS SO VALIANT IN MY DEFENSE...
...BUT IF FREY AND I ARE TO SUCCEED IN OUR ERRAND, WE MUST DEPART WITH ALL SPEED.
LADY, YOU CANNOT GO...
...THE RAINBOW BRIDGE HAS BEEN DAMAGED, AND THE SIGHT OF YOUR COMPANY VENTURING ONCE MORE TO CROSS IT MIGHT PROVOKE ANOTHER, MORE SUCCESSFUL ATTACK UPON IT.
AND WE HAVE NOT YET REPLACED YOUR ESCORT. WE MUST STILL DETERMINE HOW MANY AMONG OUR WARRIORS' RANKS HAVE BEEN CORRUPTED BY OUR ENEMY.
FORGIVE ME, REGENT...
...BUT GO WE MUST, IF THE APPLES OF IMMORTALITY ARE EVER AGAIN TO THRIVE.
FEAR NOT: WE WILL HIE OURSELVES HENCE IN SECRECY, WITH NO ESCORT...

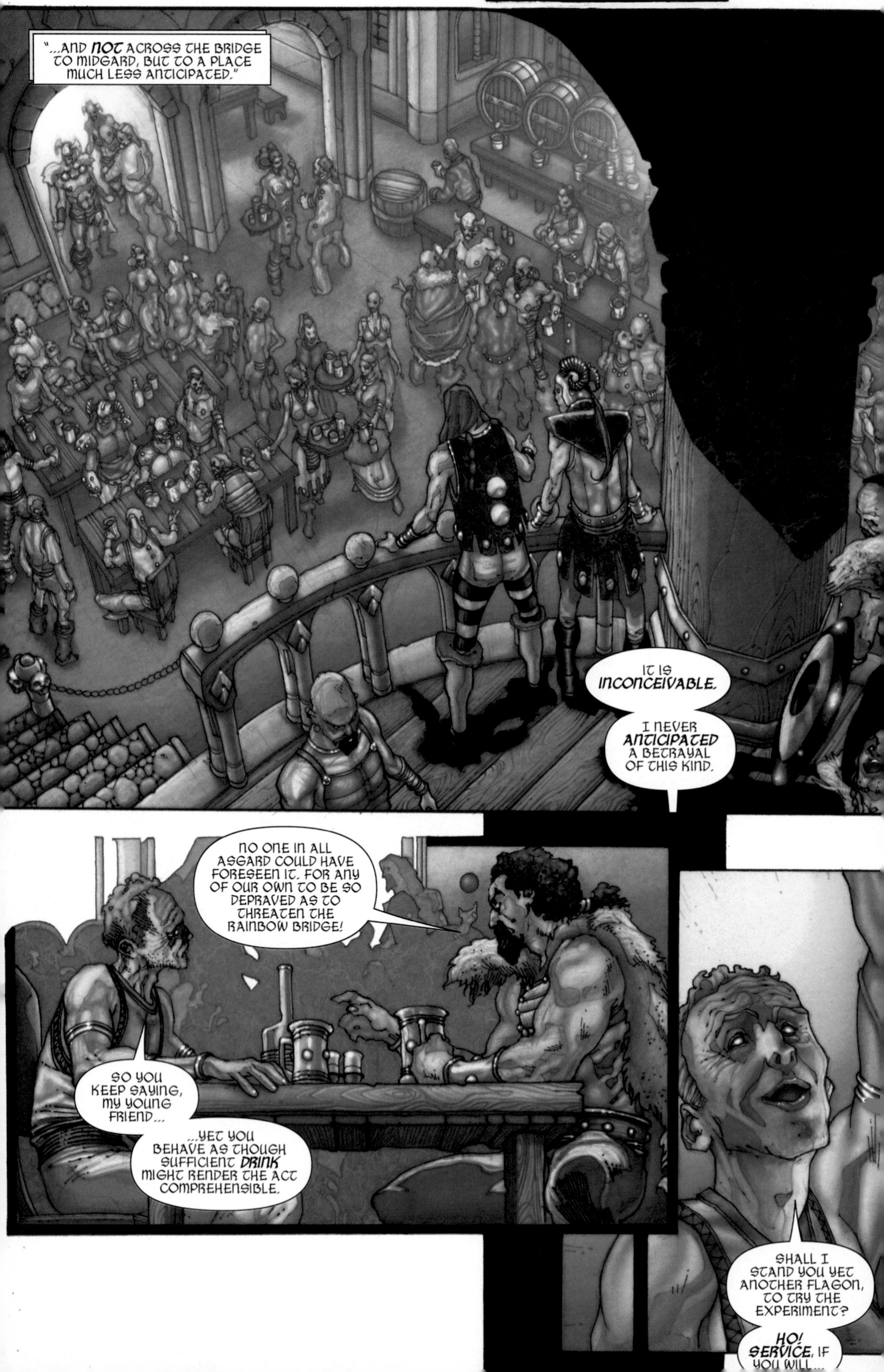
"...AND NOT ACROSS THE BRIDGE TO MIDGARD, BUT TO A PLACE MUCH LESS ANTICIPATED."
IT IS INCONCEIVABLE.
I NEVER ANTICIPATED A BETRAYAL OF THIS KIND.
NO ONE IN ALL ASGARD COULD HAVE FORESEEN IT. FOR ANY OF OUR OWN TO BE SO DEPRAVED AS TO THREATEN THE RAINBOW BRIDGE!
SO YOU KEEP SAYING, MY YOUNG FRIEND...
...YET YOU BEHAVE AS THOUGH SUFFICIENT DRINK MIGHT RENDER THE ACT COMPREHENSIBLE.
SHALL I STAND YOU YET ANOTHER FLAGON, TO TRY THE EXPERIMENT?
HO! SERVICE, IF YOU WILL...

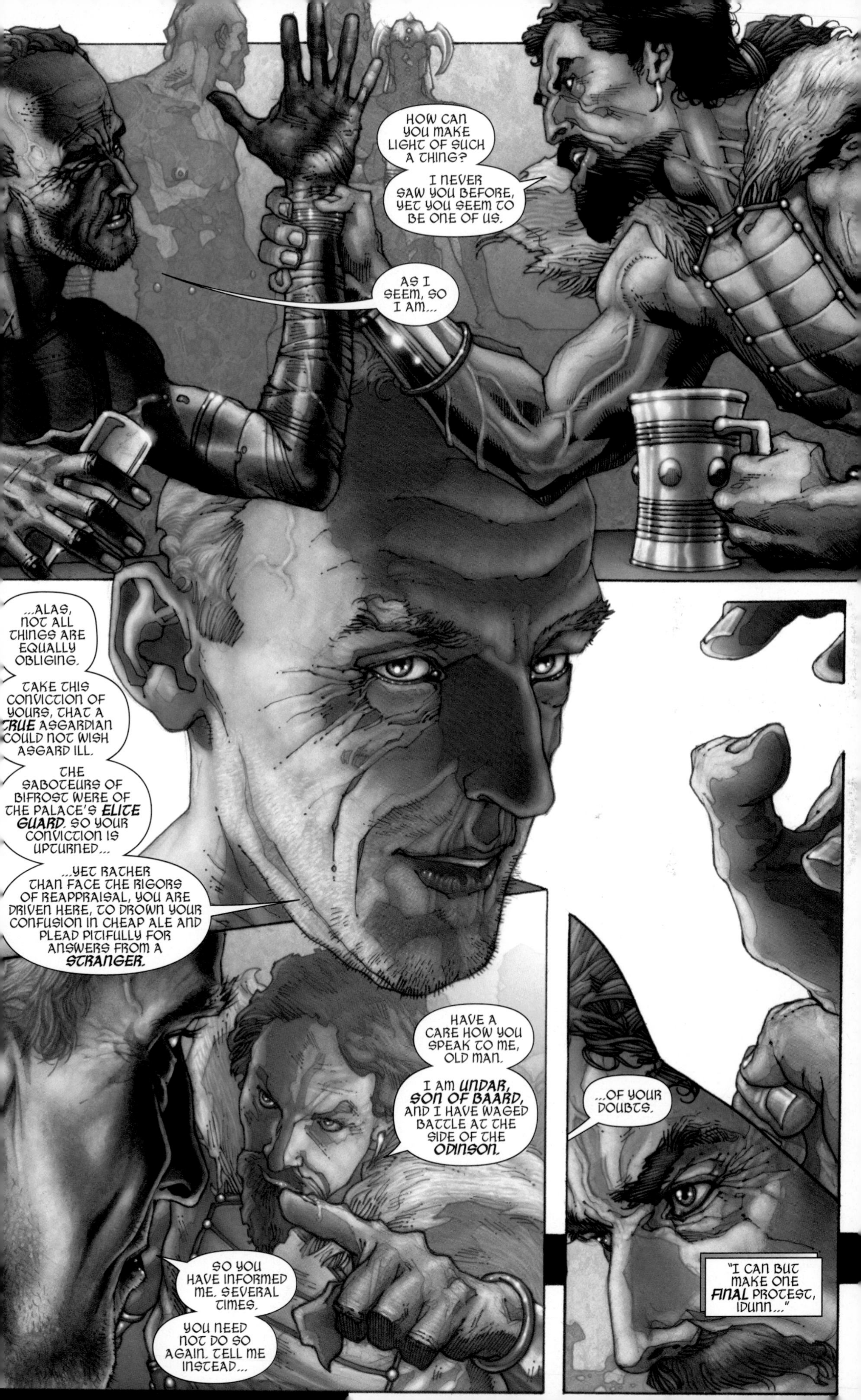
HOW CAN YOU MAKE LIGHT OF SUCH A THING?
I NEVER SAW YOU BEFORE, YET YOU SEEM TO BE ONE OF US.
AS I SEEM, SO I AM...
...ALAS, NOT ALL THINGS ARE EQUALLY OBLIGING.
TAKE THIS CONVICTION OF YOURS, THAT A TRUE ASGARDIAN COULD NOT WISH ASGARD ILL.
THE SABOTEURS OF BIFROST WERE OF THE PALACE'S ELITE GUARD. SO YOUR CONVICTION IS UPTURNED...
...YET RATHER THAN FACE THE RIGORS OF REAPPRAISAL, YOU ARE DRIVEN HERE, TO DROWN YOUR CONFUSION IN CHEAP ALE AND PLEAD PITIFULLY FOR ANSWERS FROM A STRANGER.
HAVE A CARE HOW YOU SPEAK TO ME, OLD MAN.
I AM UNDAR, SON OF BAARD, AND I HAVE WAGED BATTLE AT THE SIDE OF THE ODINSON.
SO YOU HAVE INFORMED ME. SEVERAL TIMES.
YOU NEED NOT DO SO AGAIN. TELL ME INSTEAD...
...OF YOUR DOUBTS.
"I CAN BUT MAKE ONE FINAL PROTEST, IDUNN..."

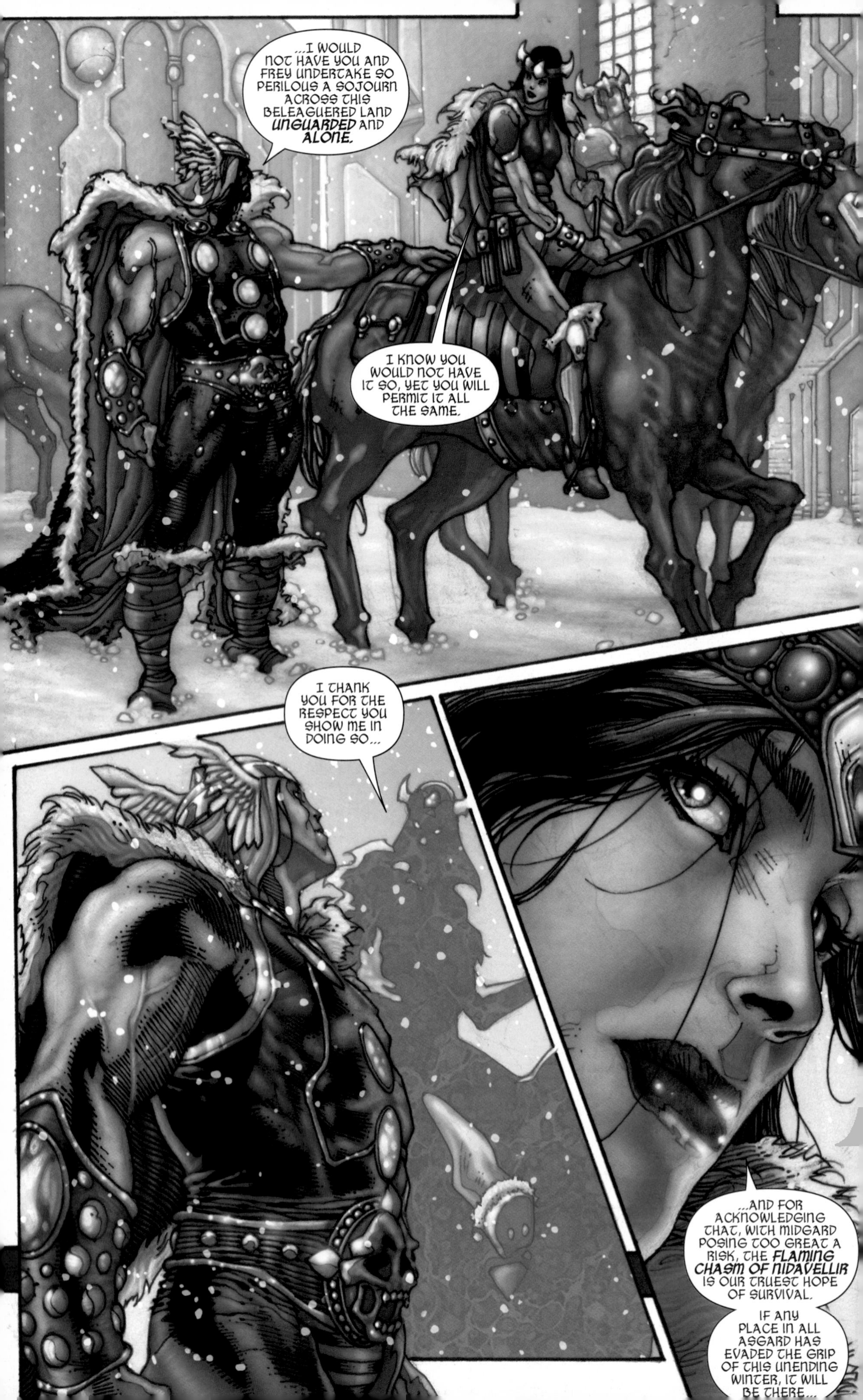
...I WOULD NOT HAVE YOU AND FREY UNDERTAKE SO PERILOUS A SOJOURN ACROSS THIS BELEAGUERED LAND UNGUARDED AND ALONE.
I KNOW YOU WOULD NOT HAVE IT SO, YET YOU WILL PERMIT IT ALL THE SAME.
I THANK YOU FOR THE RESPECT YOU SHOW ME IN DOING SO...
...AND FOR ACKNOWLEDGING THAT, WITH MIDGARD POSING TOO GREAT A RISK, THE FLAMING CHASM OF NIDAVELLIR IS OUR TRUEST HOPE OF SURVIVAL.
IF ANY PLACE IN ALL ASGARD HAS EVADED THE GRIP OF THIS UNENDING WINTER, IT WILL BE THERE...

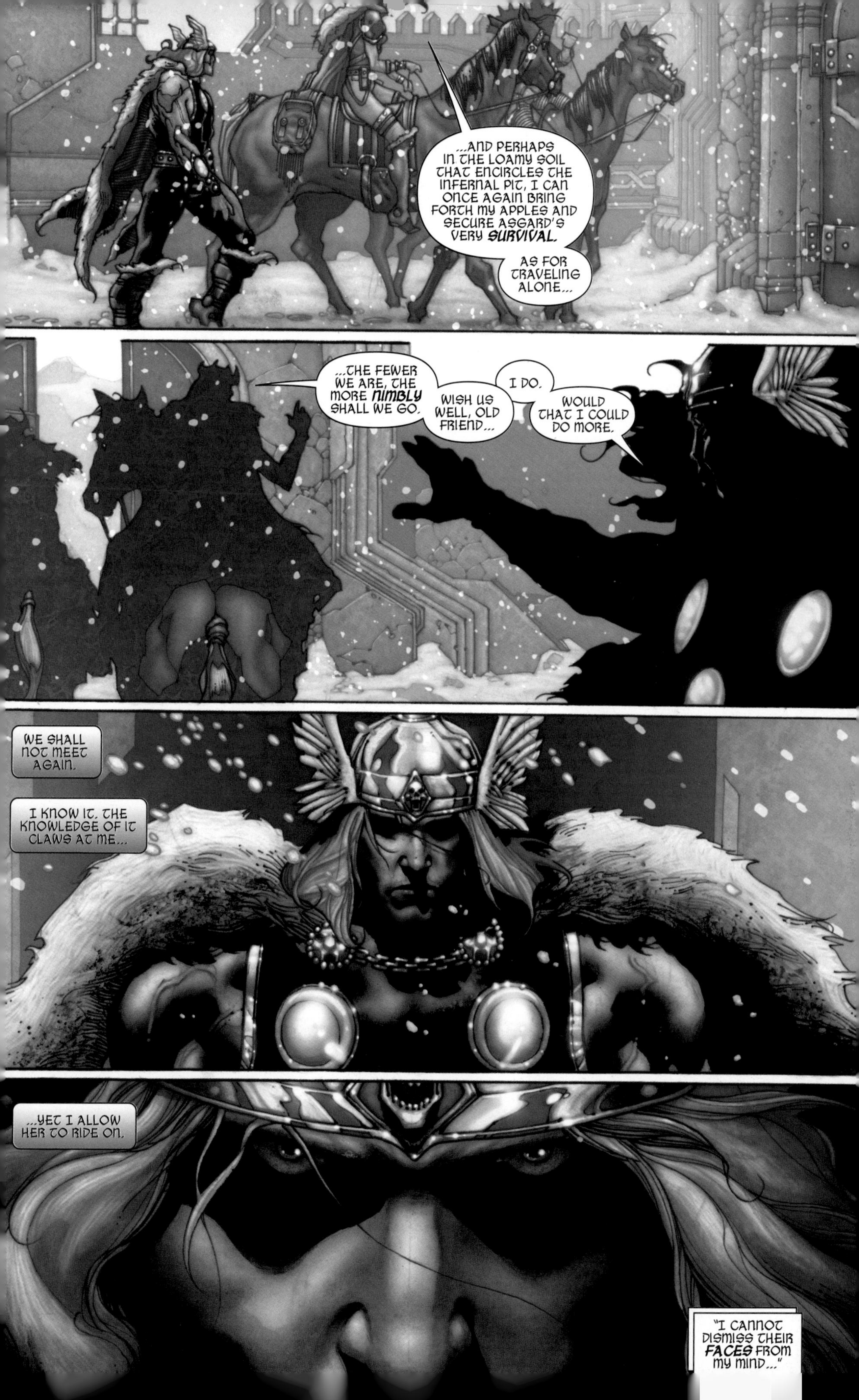

...AND PERHAPS IN THE LOAMY SOIL THAT ENCIRCLES THE INFERNAL PIT, I CAN ONCE AGAIN BRING FORTH MY APPLES AND SECURE ASGARD'S VERY SURVIVAL.
AS FOR TRAVELING ALONE...
...THE FEWER WE ARE, THE MORE NIMBLY SHALL WE GO.
WISH US WELL, OLD FRIEND...
I DO.
WOULD THAT I COULD DO MORE.
WE SHALL NOT MEET AGAIN.
I KNOW IT. THE KNOWLEDGE OF IT CLAWS AT ME...
...YET I ALLOW HER TO RIDE ON.
"I CANNOT DISMISS THEIR FACES FROM MY MIND..."

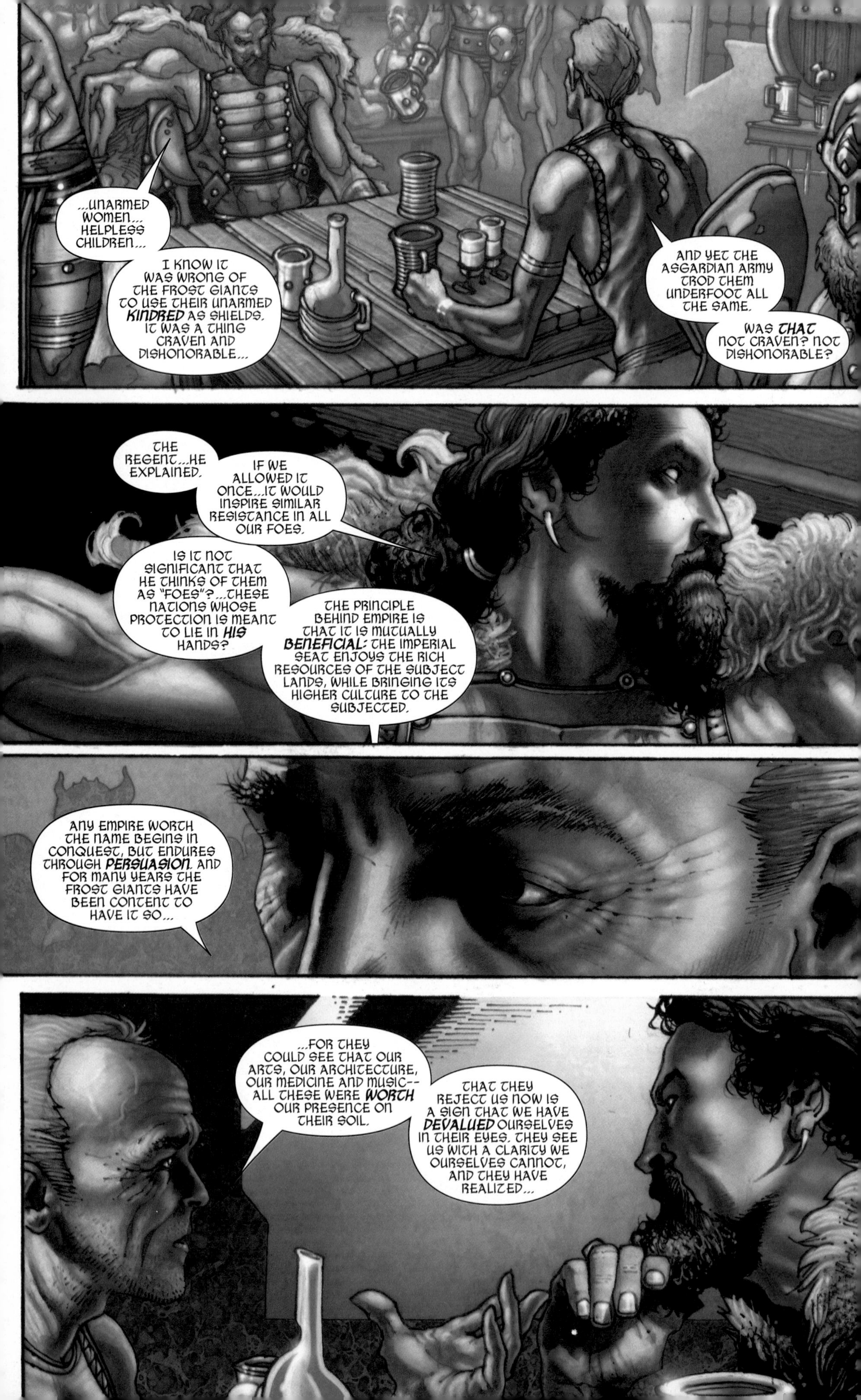
...UNARMED WOMEN... HELPLESS CHILDREN...
I KNOW IT WAS WRONG OF THE FROST GIANTS TO USE THEIR UNARMED KINDRED AS SHIELDS. IT WAS A THING CRAVEN AND DISHONORABLE...
AND YET THE ASGARDIAN ARMY TROD THEM UNDERFOOT ALL THE SAME.
WAS THAT NOT CRAVEN? NOT DISHONORABLE?
THE REGENT...HE EXPLAINED.
IF WE ALLOWED IT ONCE...IT WOULD INSPIRE SIMILAR RESISTANCE IN ALL OUR FOES.
IS IT NOT SIGNIFICANT THAT HE THINKS OF THEM AS "FOES"?...THESE NATIONS WHOSE PROTECTION IS MEANT TO LIE IN HIS HANDS?
THE PRINCIPLE BEHIND EMPIRE IS THAT IT IS MUTUALLY BENEFICIAL: THE IMPERIAL SEAT ENJOYS THE RICH RESOURCES OF THE SUBJECT LANDS, WHILE BRINGING ITS HIGHER CULTURE TO THE SUBJECTED.
ANY EMPIRE WORTH THE NAME BEGINS IN CONQUEST, BUT ENDURES THROUGH PERSUASION. AND FOR MANY YEARS THE FROST GIANTS HAVE BEEN CONTENT TO HAVE IT SO...
...FOR THEY COULD SEE THAT OUR ARTS, OUR ARCHITECTURE, OUR MEDICINE AND MUSIC--ALL THESE WERE WORTH OUR PRESENCE ON THEIR SOIL.
THAT THEY REJECT US NOW IS A SIGN THAT WE HAVE DEVALUED OURSELVES IN THEIR EYES. THEY SEE US WITH A CLARITY WE OURSELVES CANNOT, AND THEY HAVE REALIZED...

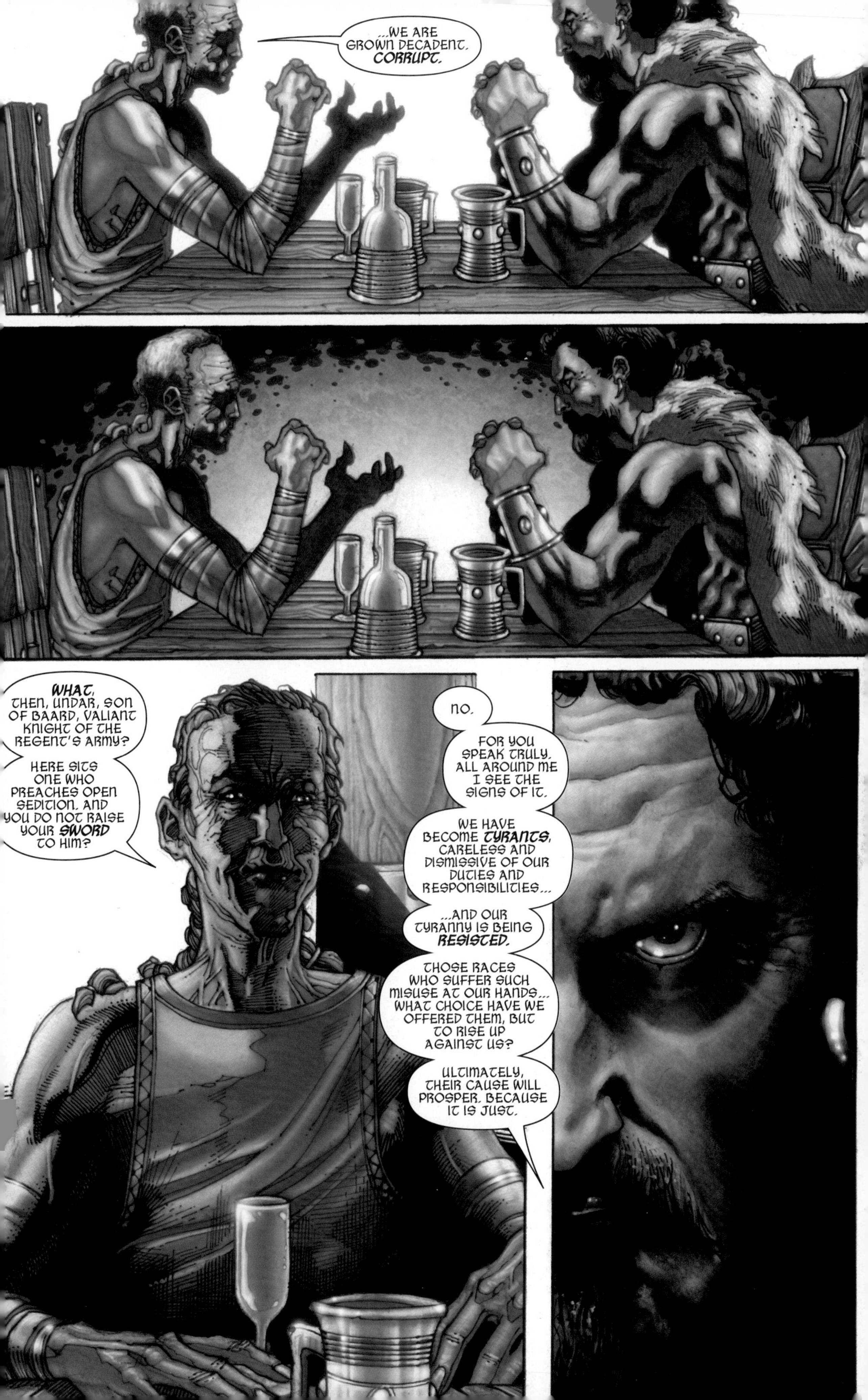
...WE ARE GROWN DECADENT. CORRUPT.
WHAT, THEN, UNDAR, SON OF BAARD, VALIANT KNIGHT OF THE REGENT'S ARMY?
HERE SITS ONE WHO PREACHES OPEN SEDITION, AND YOU DO NOT RAISE YOUR SWORD TO HIM?
NO.
FOR YOU SPEAK TRULY. ALL AROUND ME I SEE THE SIGNS OF IT.
WE HAVE BECOME TYRANTS, CARELESS AND DISMISSIVE OF OUR DUTIES AND RESPONSIBILITIES...
...AND OUR TYRANNY IS BEING RESISTED.
THOSE RACES WHO SUFFER SUCH MISUSE AT OUR HANDS... WHAT CHOICE HAVE WE OFFERED THEM, BUT TO RISE UP AGAINST US?
ULTIMATELY, THEIR CAUSE WILL PROSPER, BECAUSE IT IS JUST.

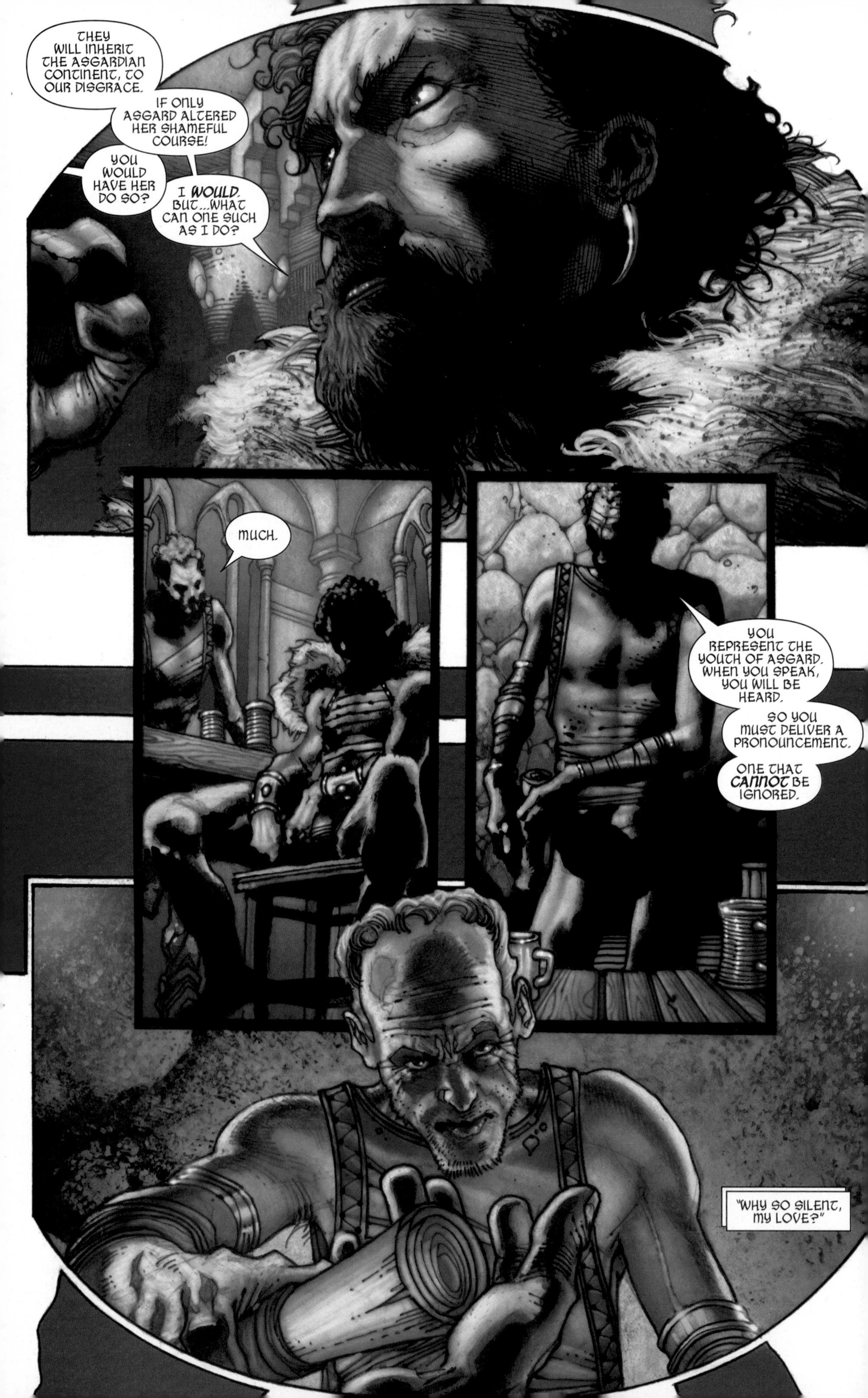
THEY WILL INHERIT THE ASGARDIAN CONTINENT, TO OUR DISGRACE.
IF ONLY ASGARD ALTERED HER SHAMEFUL COURSE!
YOU WOULD HAVE HER DO SO?
I WOULD. BUT...WHAT CAN ONE SUCH AS I DO?
MUCH.
YOU REPRESENT THE YOUTH OF ASGARD. WHEN YOU SPEAK, YOU WILL BE HEARD.
SO YOU MUST DELIVER A PRONOUNCEMENT.
ONE THAT CANNOT BE IGNORED.
"WHY SO SILENT, MY LOVE?"

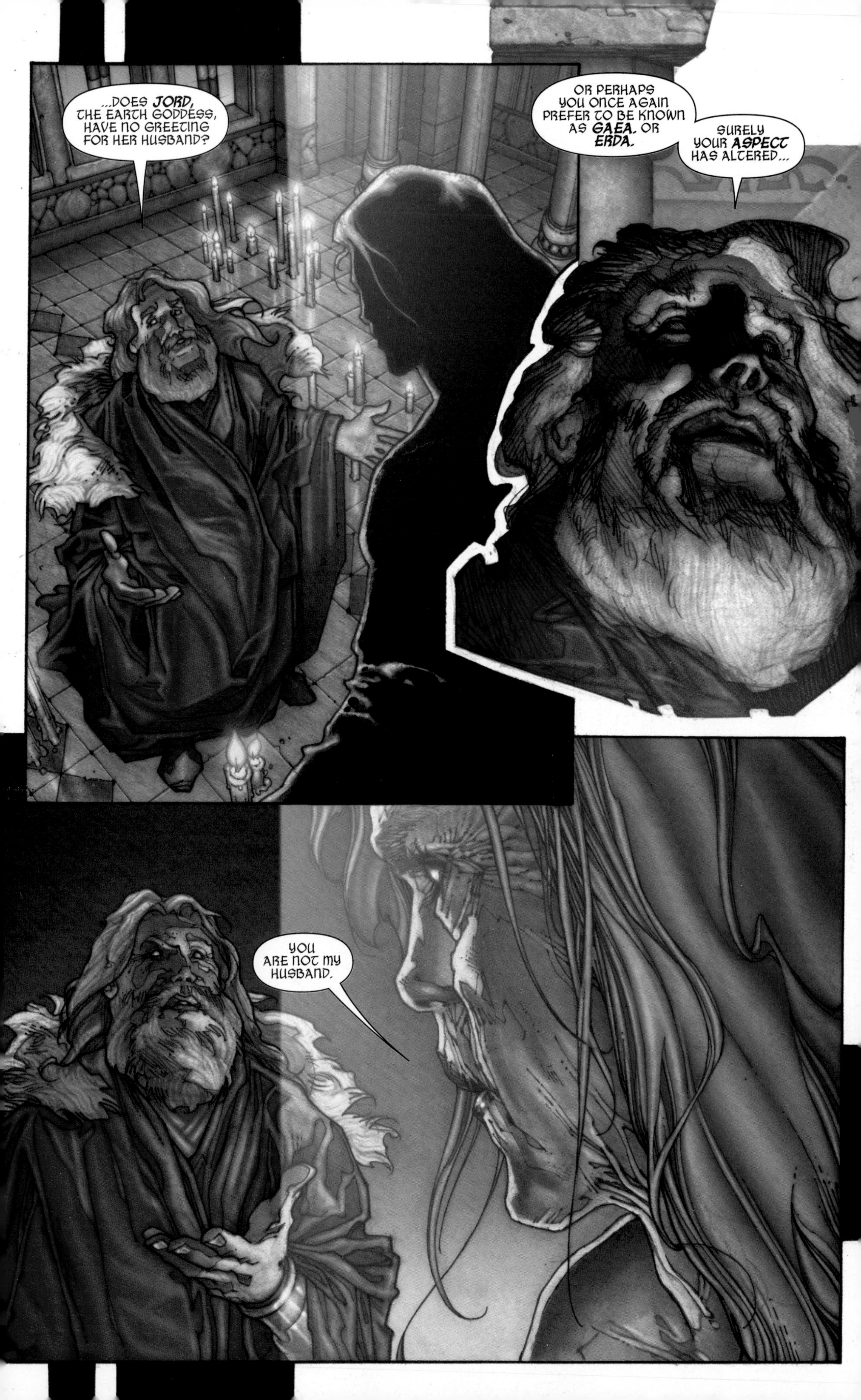
...DOES JORD, THE EARTH GODDESS, HAVE NO GREETING FOR HER HUSBAND?
OR PERHAPS YOU ONCE AGAIN PREFER TO BE KNOWN AS GAEA, OR ERDA.
SURELY YOUR ASPECT HAS ALTERED...
YOU ARE NOT MY HUSBAND.

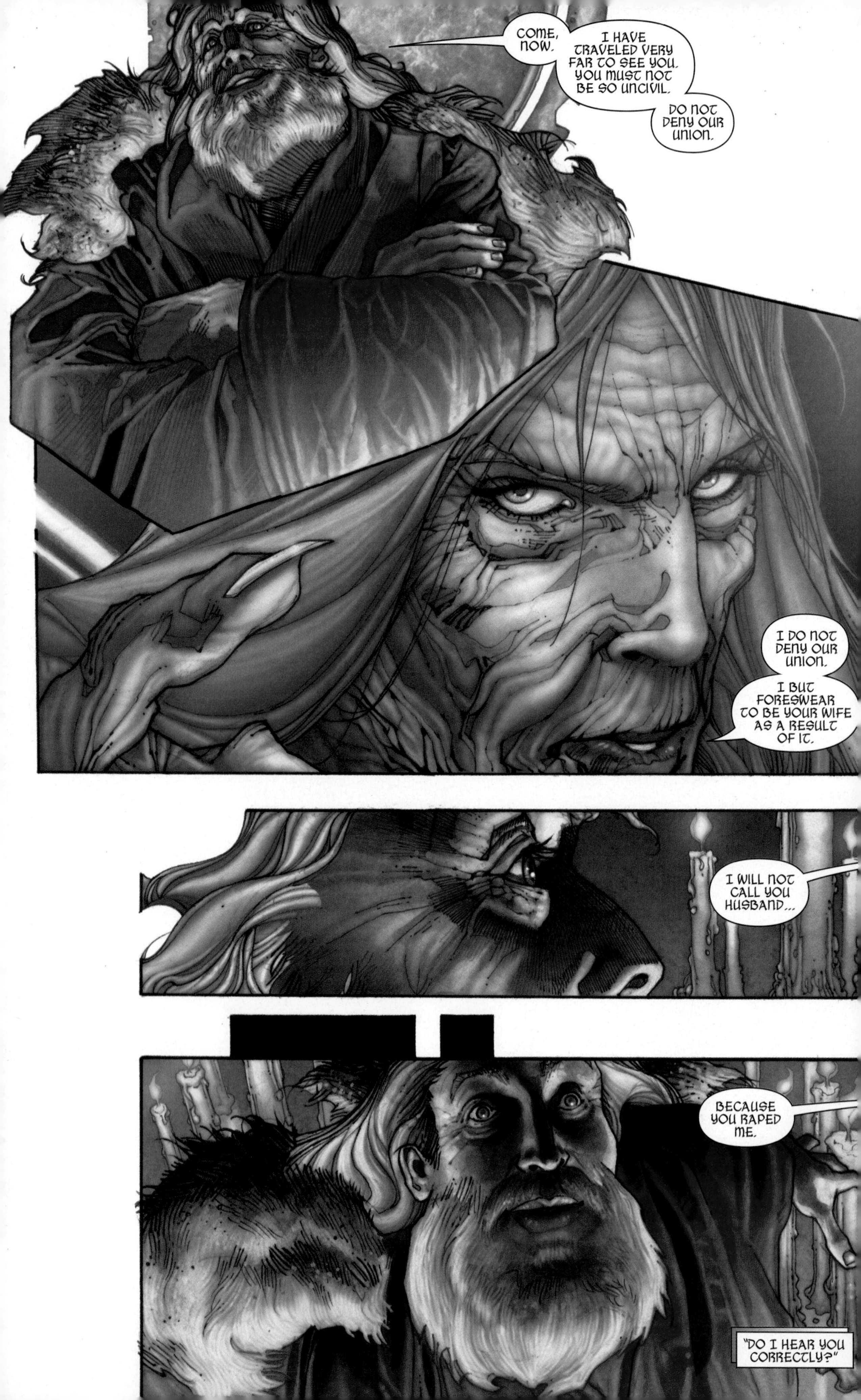
COME, NOW.
I HAVE TRAVELED VERY FAR TO SEE YOU. YOU MUST NOT BE SO UNCIVIL.
DO NOT DENY OUR UNION.
I DO NOT DENY OUR UNION.
I BUT FORESWEAR TO BE YOUR WIFE AS A RESULT OF IT.
I WILL NOT CALL YOU HUSBAND...
BECAUSE YOU RAPED ME.
"DO I HEAR YOU CORRECTLY?"

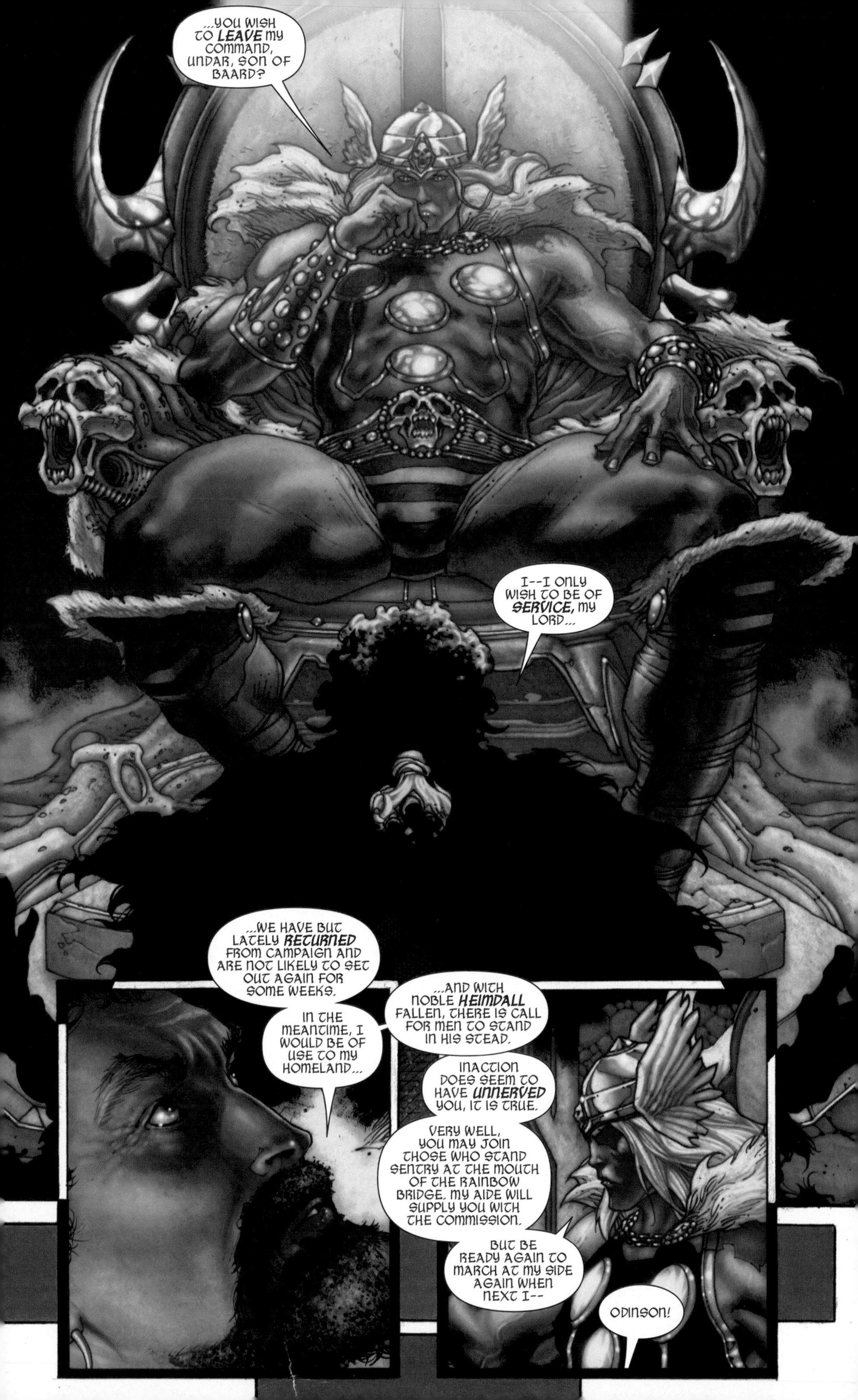
...YOU WISH TO LEAVE MY COMMAND, UNDAR, SON OF BAARD?
I--I ONLY WISH TO BE OF SERVICE, MY LORD...
...WE HAVE BUT LATELY RETURNED FROM CAMPAIGN AND ARE NOT LIKELY TO SET OUT AGAIN FOR SOME WEEKS.
IN THE MEANTIME, I WOULD BE OF USE TO MY HOMELAND...
...AND WITH NOBLE HEIMDALL FALLEN, THERE IS CALL FOR MEN TO STAND IN HIS STEAD.
INACTION DOES SEEM TO HAVE UNNERVED YOU, IT IS TRUE.
VERY WELL, YOU MAY JOIN THOSE WHO STAND SENTRY AT THE MOUTH OF THE RAINBOW BRIDGE. MY AIDE WILL SUPPLY YOU WITH THE COMMISSION.
BUT BE READY AGAIN TO MARCH AT MY SIDE AGAIN WHEN NEXT I--
ODINSON!

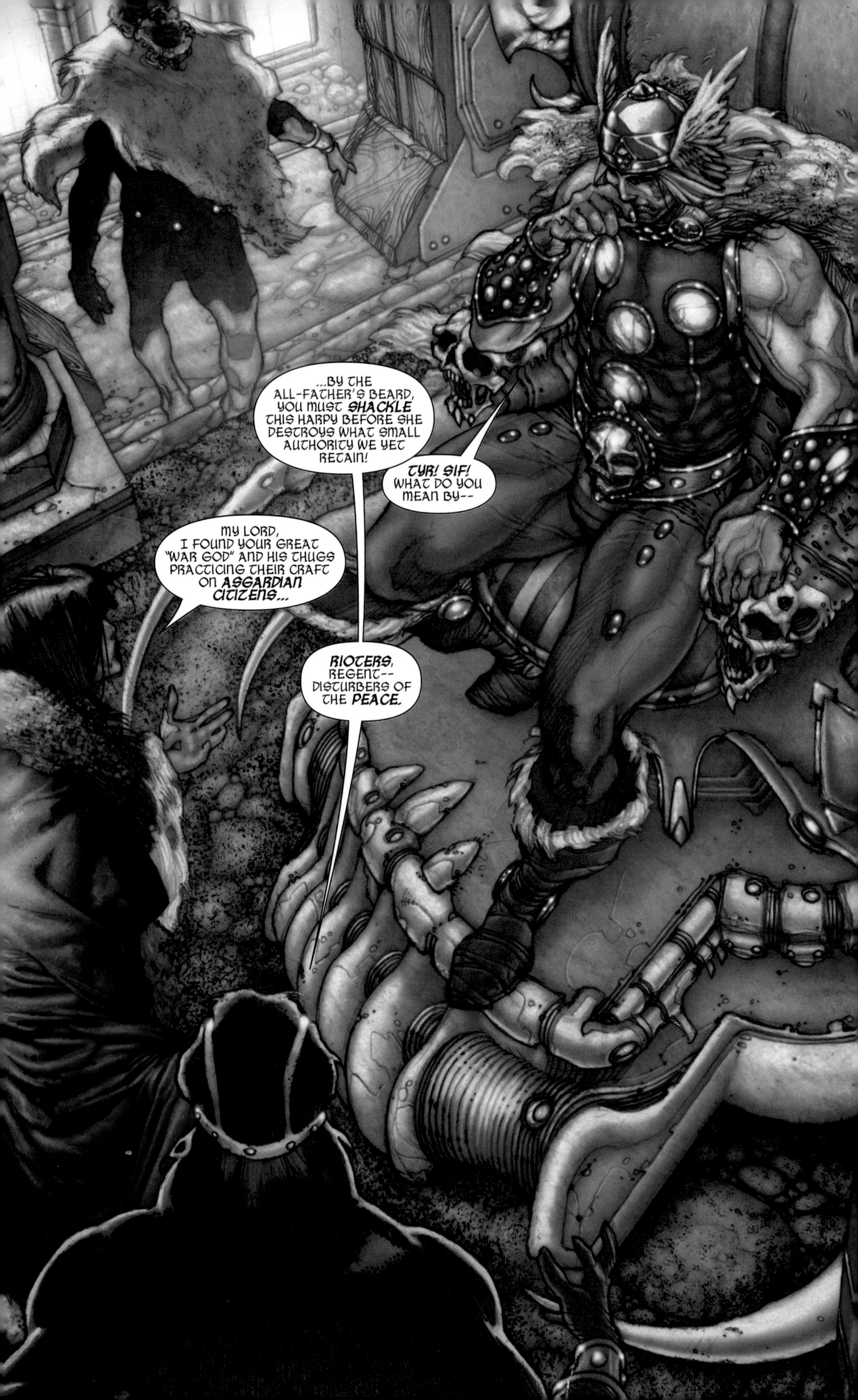

...BY THE ALL-FATHER'S BEARD, YOU MUST **SHACKLE** THIS HARPY BEFORE SHE DESTROYS WHAT SMALL AUTHORITY WE YET RETAIN!
TYR! SIF! WHAT DO YOU MEAN BY--
MY LORD, I FOUND YOUR GREAT "WAR GOD" AND HIS THUGS PRACTICING THEIR CRAFT ON **ASGARDIAN CITIZENS...**
RIOTERS, REGENT-- DISTURBERS OF THE **PEACE.**

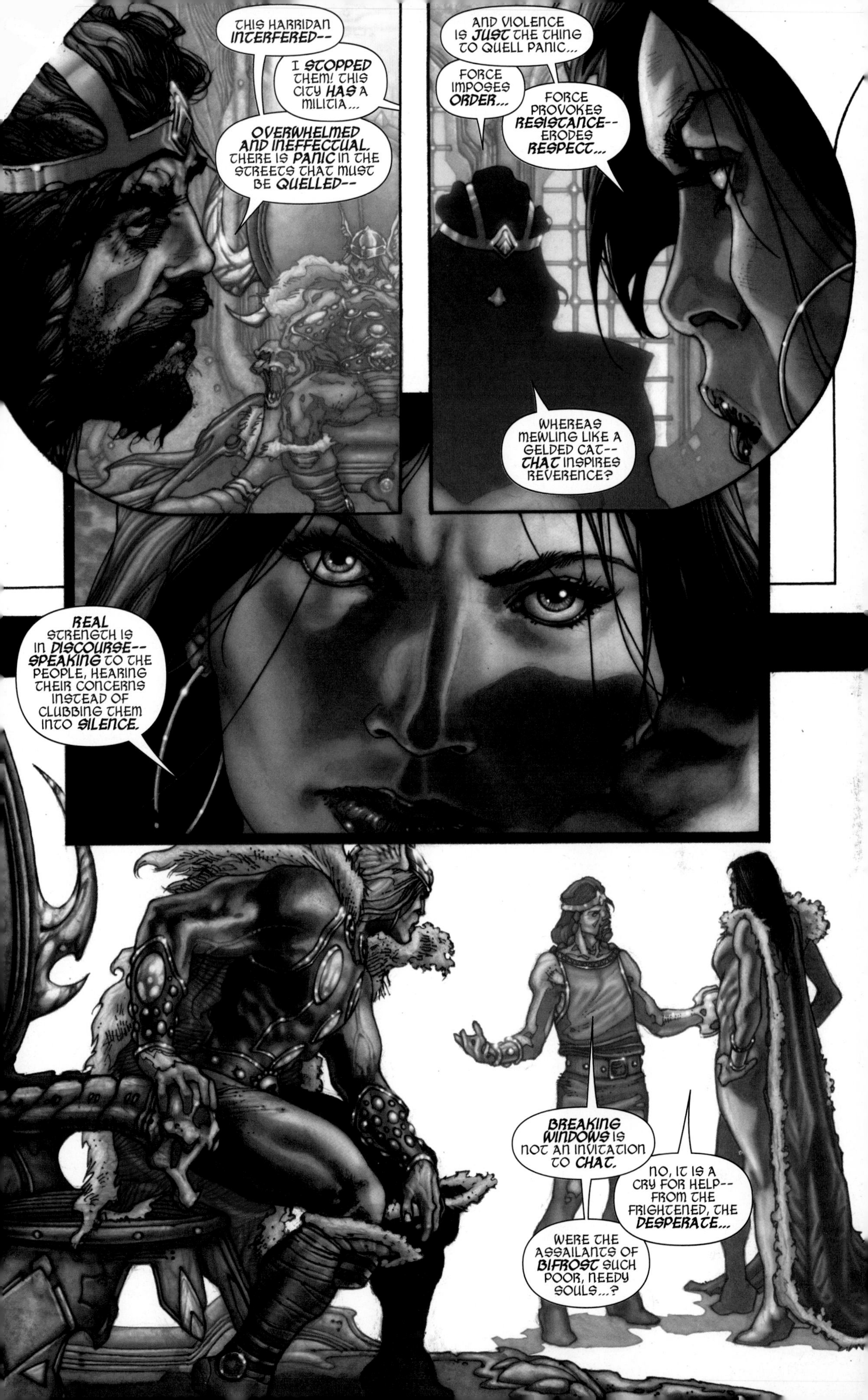

THIS HARRIDAN INTERFERED--
I STOPPED THEM! THIS CITY HAS A MILITIA...
OVERWHELMED AND INEFFECTUAL. THERE IS PANIC IN THE STREETS THAT MUST BE QUELLED--
AND VIOLENCE IS JUST THE THING TO QUELL PANIC...
FORCE IMPOSES ORDER...
FORCE PROVOKES RESISTANCE-- ERODES RESPECT...
WHEREAS MEWLING LIKE A GELDED CAT-- THAT INSPIRES REVERENCE?
REAL STRENGTH IS IN DISCOURSE-- SPEAKING TO THE PEOPLE, HEARING THEIR CONCERNS INSTEAD OF CLUBBING THEM INTO SILENCE.
BREAKING WINDOWS IS NOT AN INVITATION TO CHAT.
NO, IT IS A CRY FOR HELP-- FROM THE FRIGHTENED, THE DESPERATE...
WERE THE ASSAILANTS OF BIFROST SUCH POOR, NEEDY SOULS...?

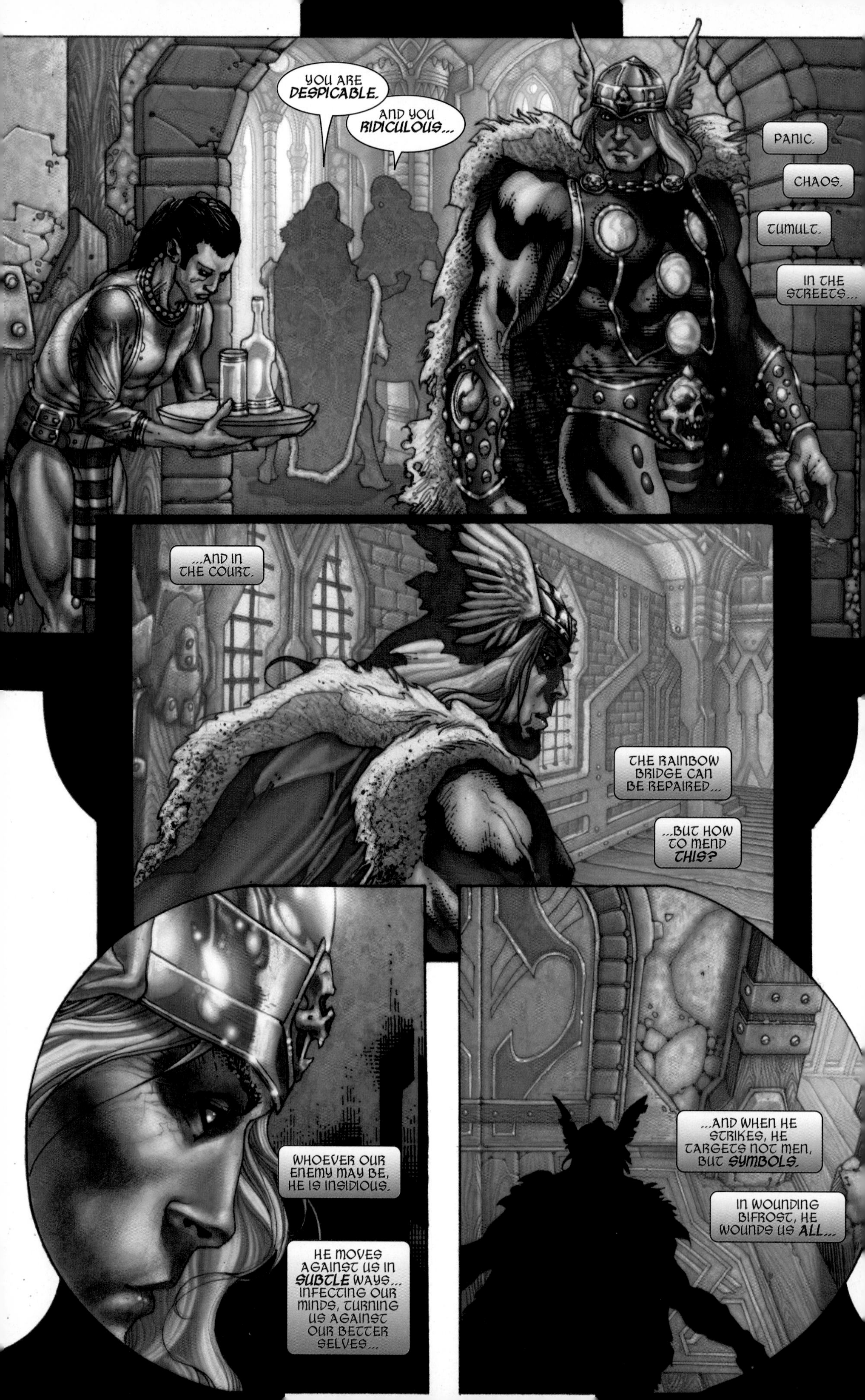

YOU ARE DESPICABLE.
AND YOU RIDICULOUS...
PANIC.
CHAOS.
TUMULT.
IN THE STREETS...
...AND IN THE COURT.
THE RAINBOW BRIDGE CAN BE REPAIRED...
...BUT HOW TO MEND THIS?
WHOEVER OUR ENEMY MAY BE, HE IS INSIDIOUS.
HE MOVES AGAINST US IN SUBTLE WAYS... INFECTING OUR MINDS, TURNING US AGAINST OUR BETTER SELVES...
...AND WHEN HE STRIKES, HE TARGETS NOT MEN, BUT SYMBOLS.
IN WOUNDING BIFROST, HE WOUNDS US ALL...

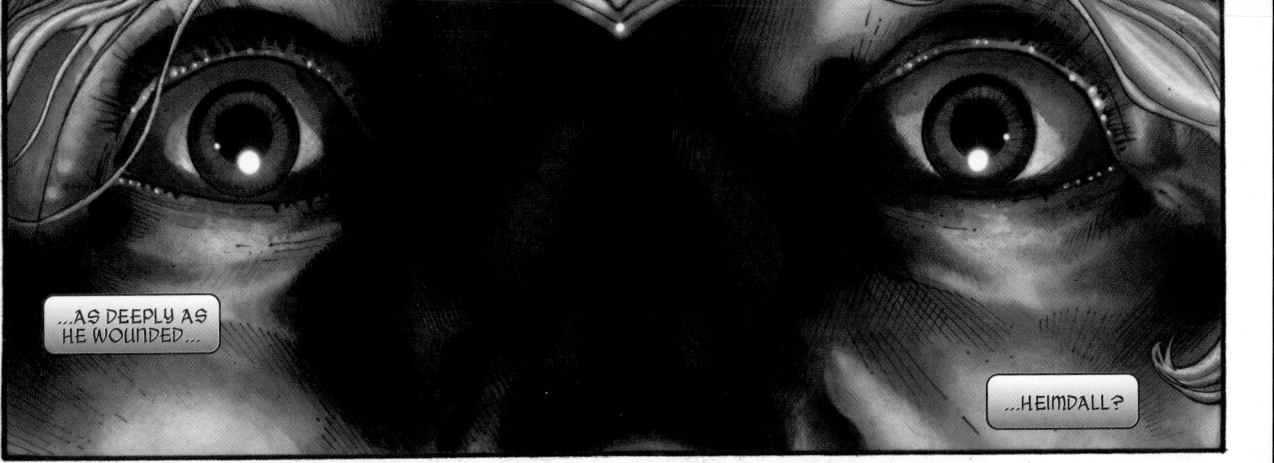
...AS DEEPLY AS HE WOUNDED...
...HEIMDALL?
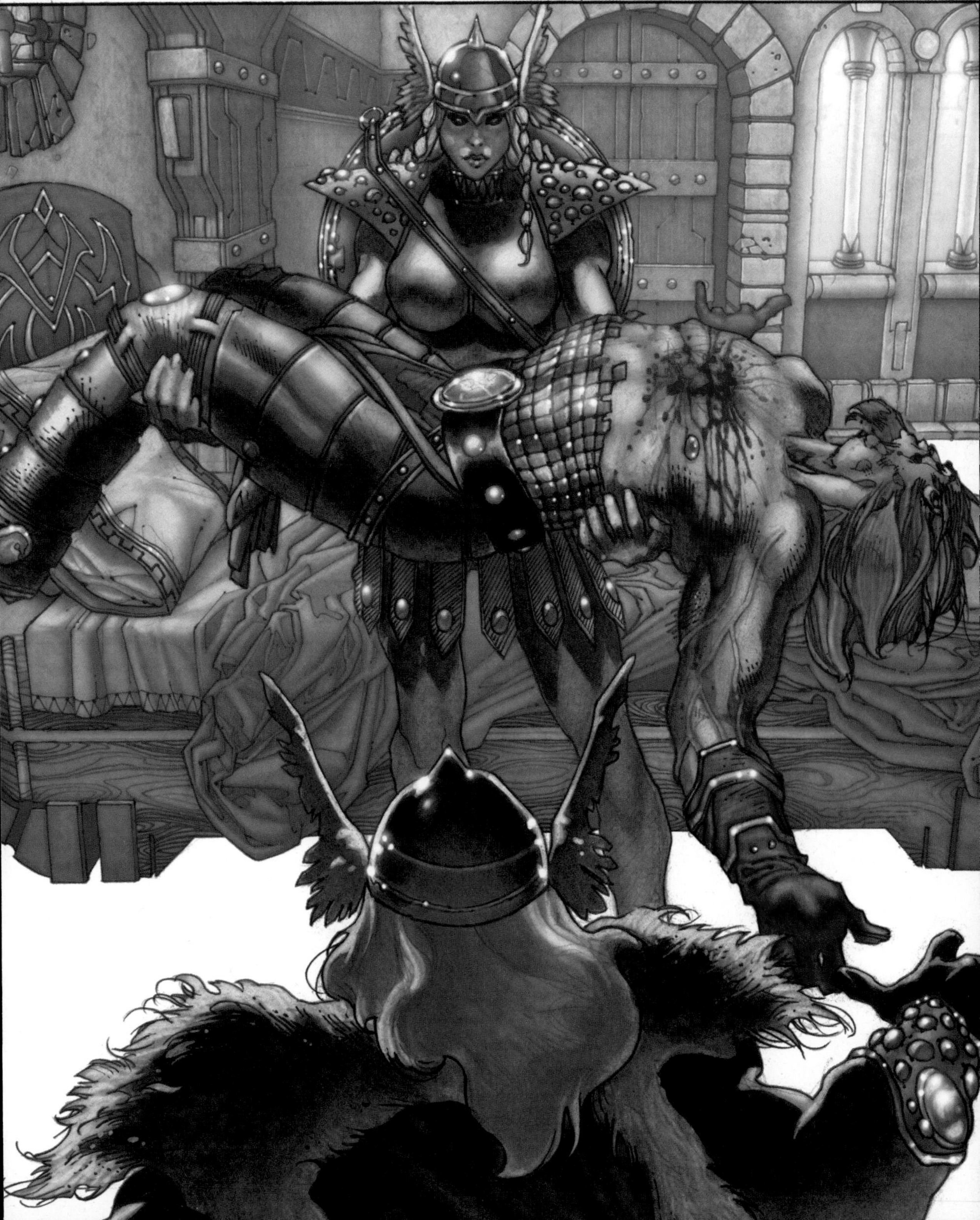

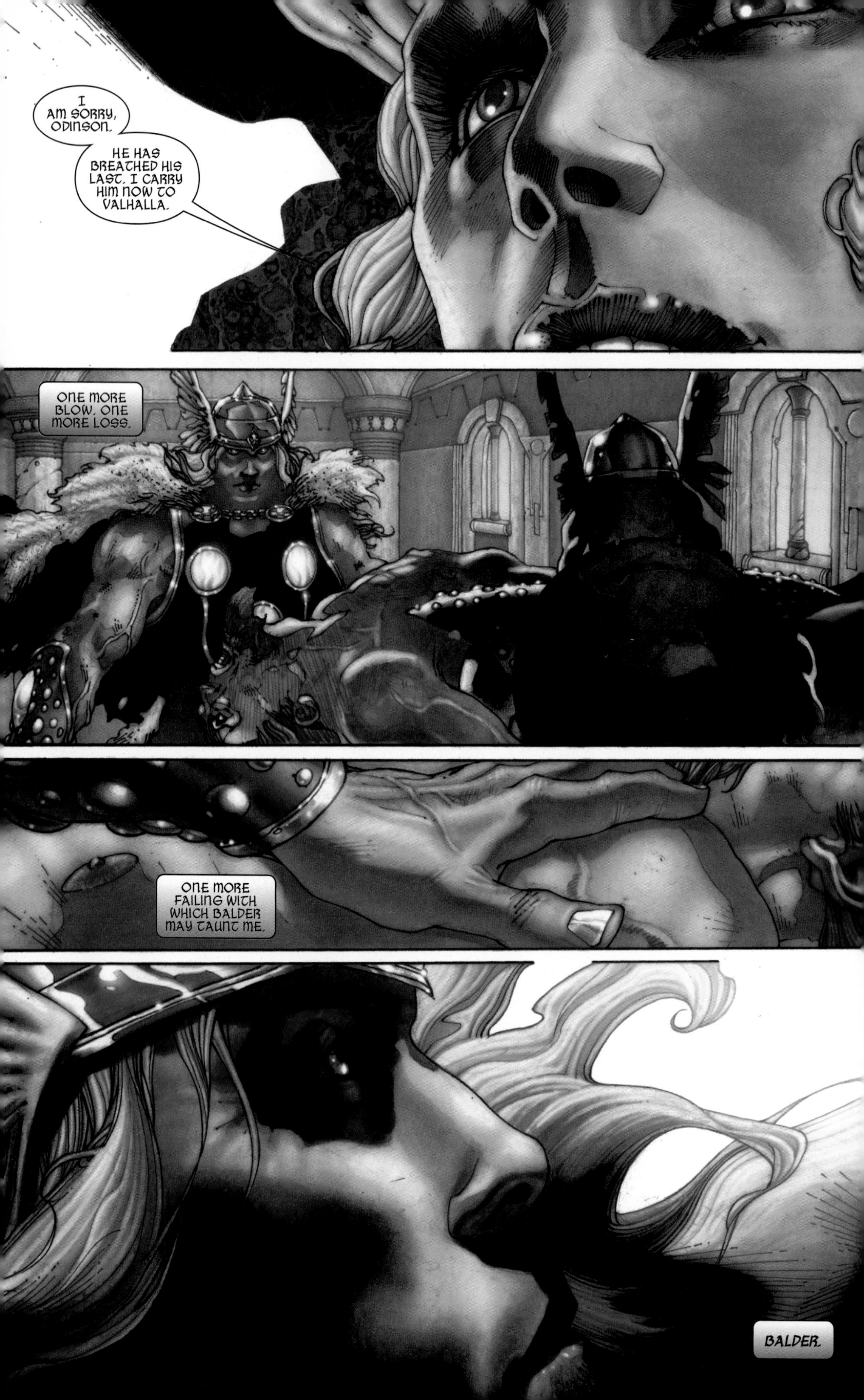
I AM SORRY, ODINSON.
HE HAS BREATHED HIS LAST. I CARRY HIM NOW TO VALHALLA.
ONE MORE BLOW. ONE MORE LOSS.
ONE MORE FAILING WITH WHICH BALDER MAY TAUNT ME.
BALDER.

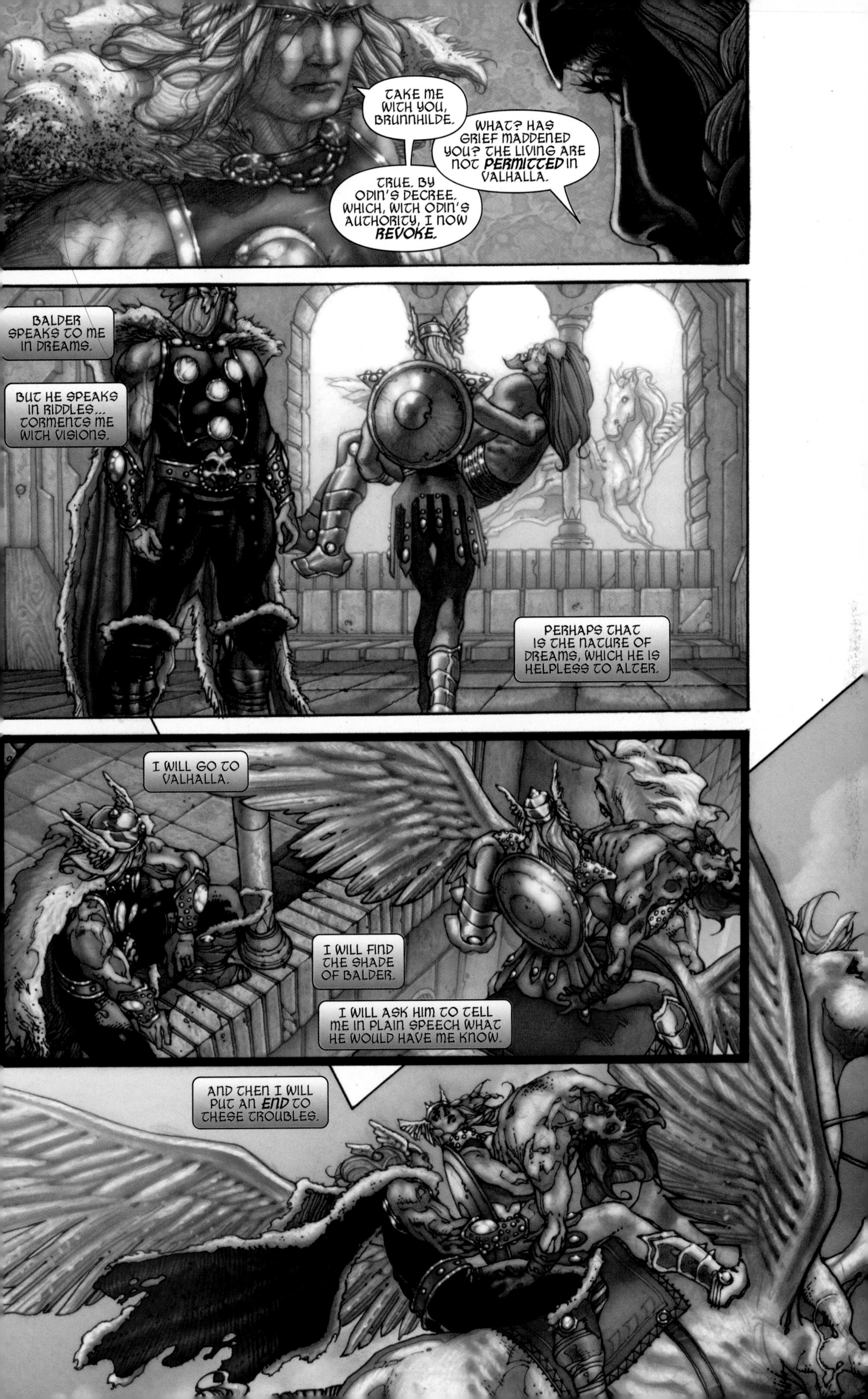
TAKE ME WITH YOU, BRUNNHILDE.
WHAT? HAS GRIEF MADDENED YOU? THE LIVING ARE NOT PERMITTED IN VALHALLA.
TRUE. BY ODIN'S DECREE. WHICH, WITH ODIN'S AUTHORITY, I NOW REVOKE.
BALDER SPEAKS TO ME IN DREAMS.
BUT HE SPEAKS IN RIDDLES... TORMENTS ME WITH VISIONS.
PERHAPS THAT IS THE NATURE OF DREAMS, WHICH HE IS HELPLESS TO ALTER.
I WILL GO TO VALHALLA.
I WILL FIND THE SHADE OF BALDER.
I WILL ASK HIM TO TELL ME IN PLAIN SPEECH WHAT HE WOULD HAVE ME KNOW.
AND THEN I WILL PUT AN END TO THESE TROUBLES.

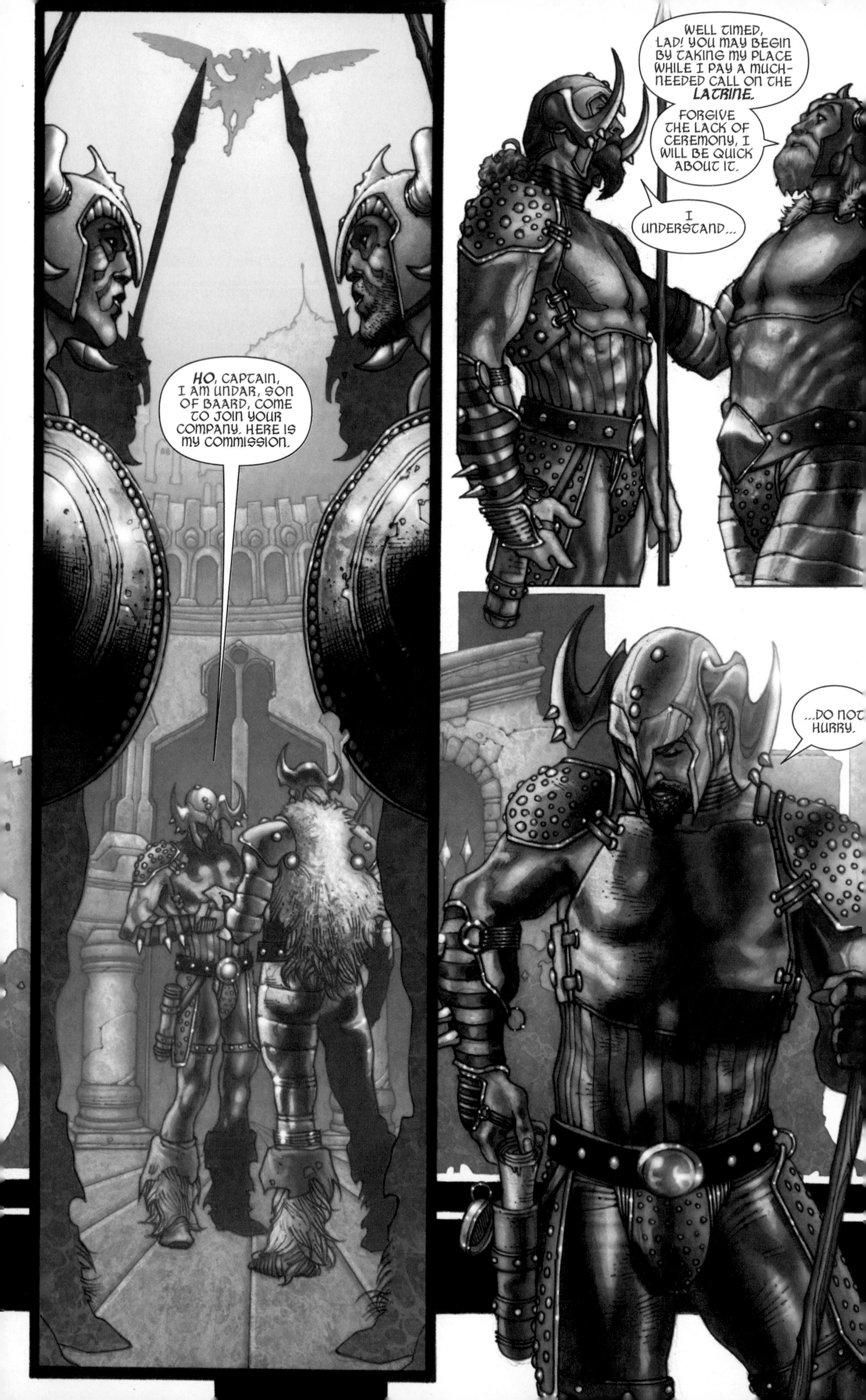
HO, CAPTAIN, I AM UNDAR, SON OF BAARD, COME TO JOIN YOUR COMPANY. HERE IS MY COMMISSION.
WELL TIMED, LAD! YOU MAY BEGIN BY TAKING MY PLACE WHILE I PAY A MUCH-NEEDED CALL ON THE LATRINE.
FORGIVE THE LACK OF CEREMONY, I WILL BE QUICK ABOUT IT.
I UNDERSTAND...
...DO NOT HURRY.

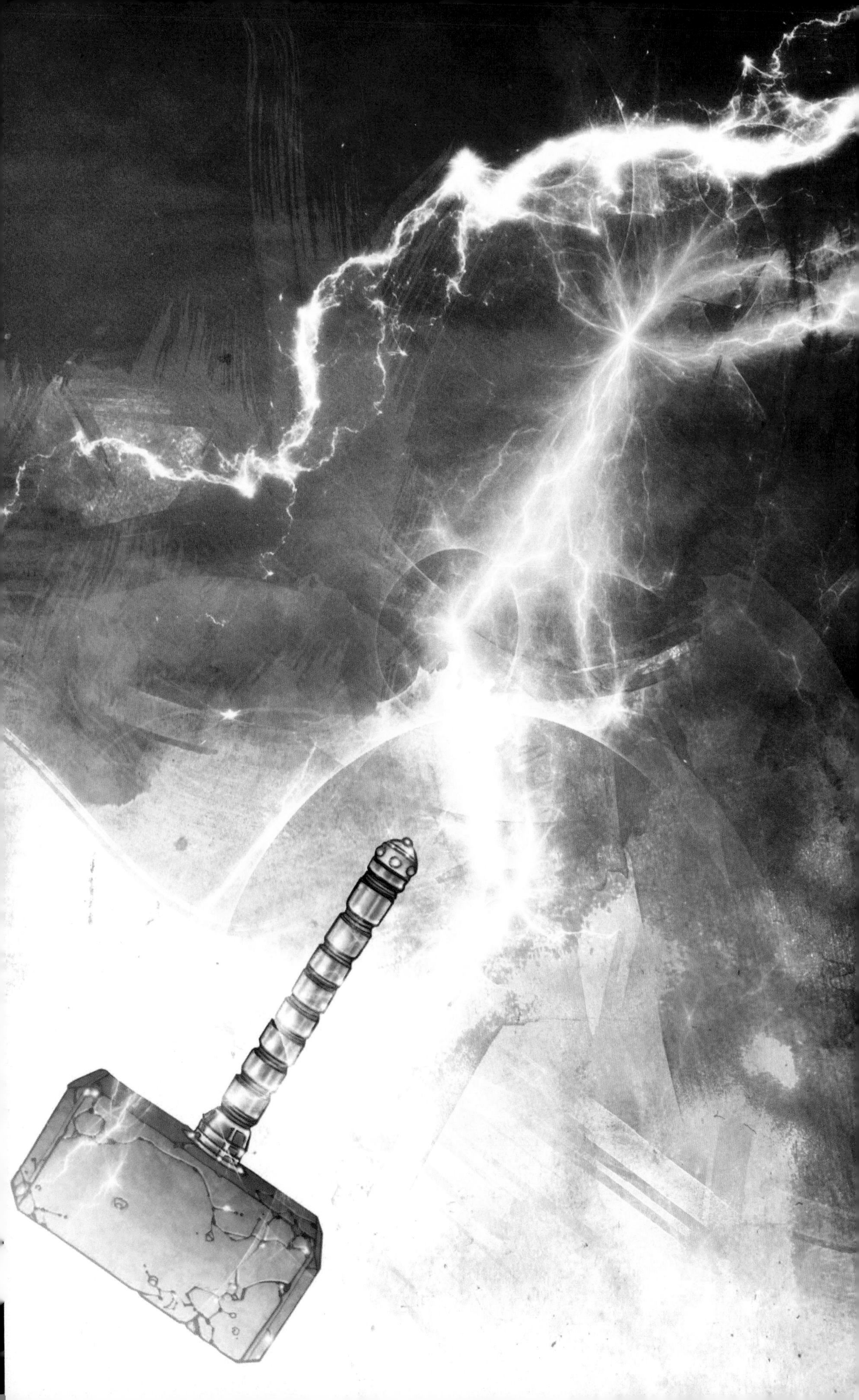

4

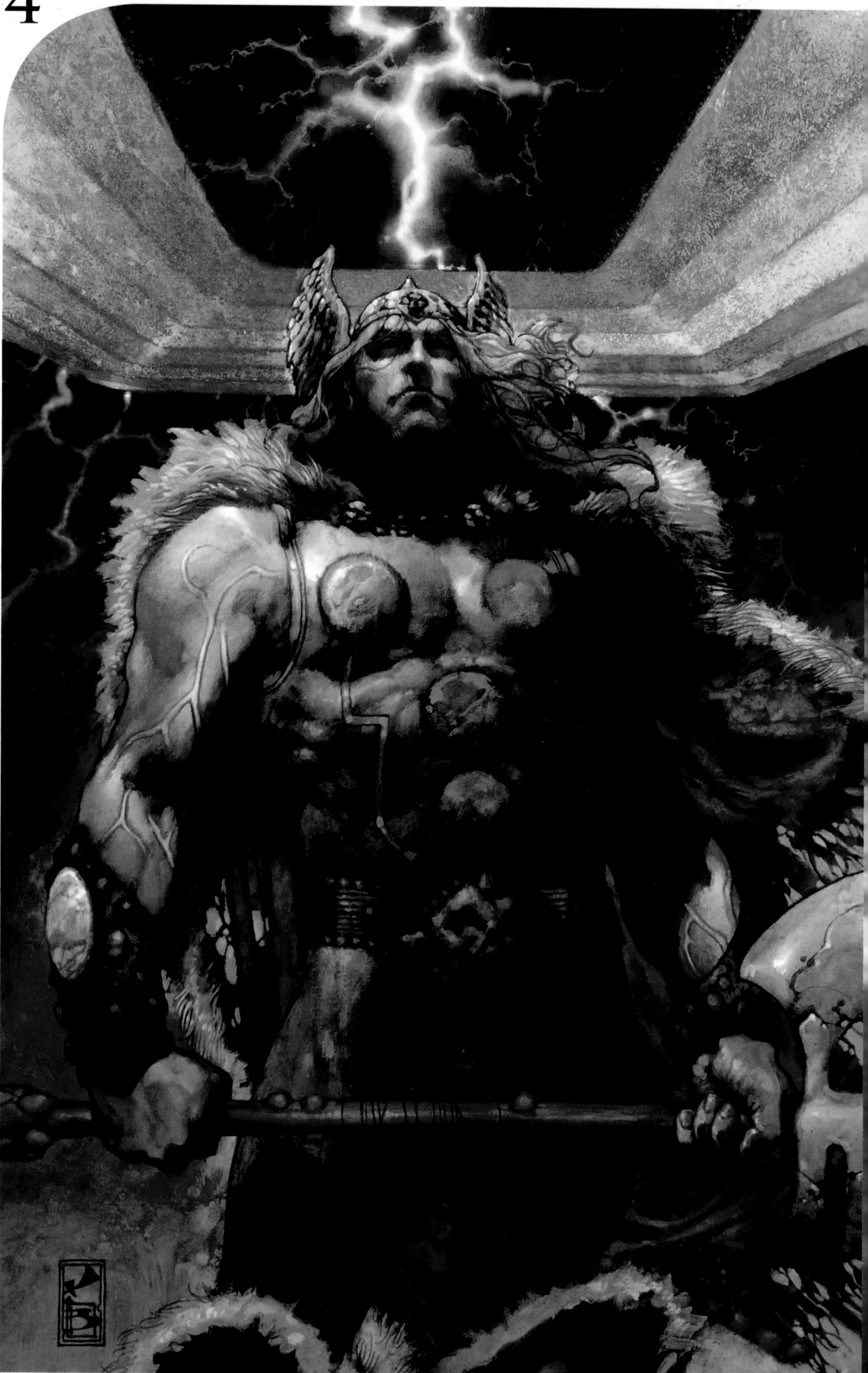

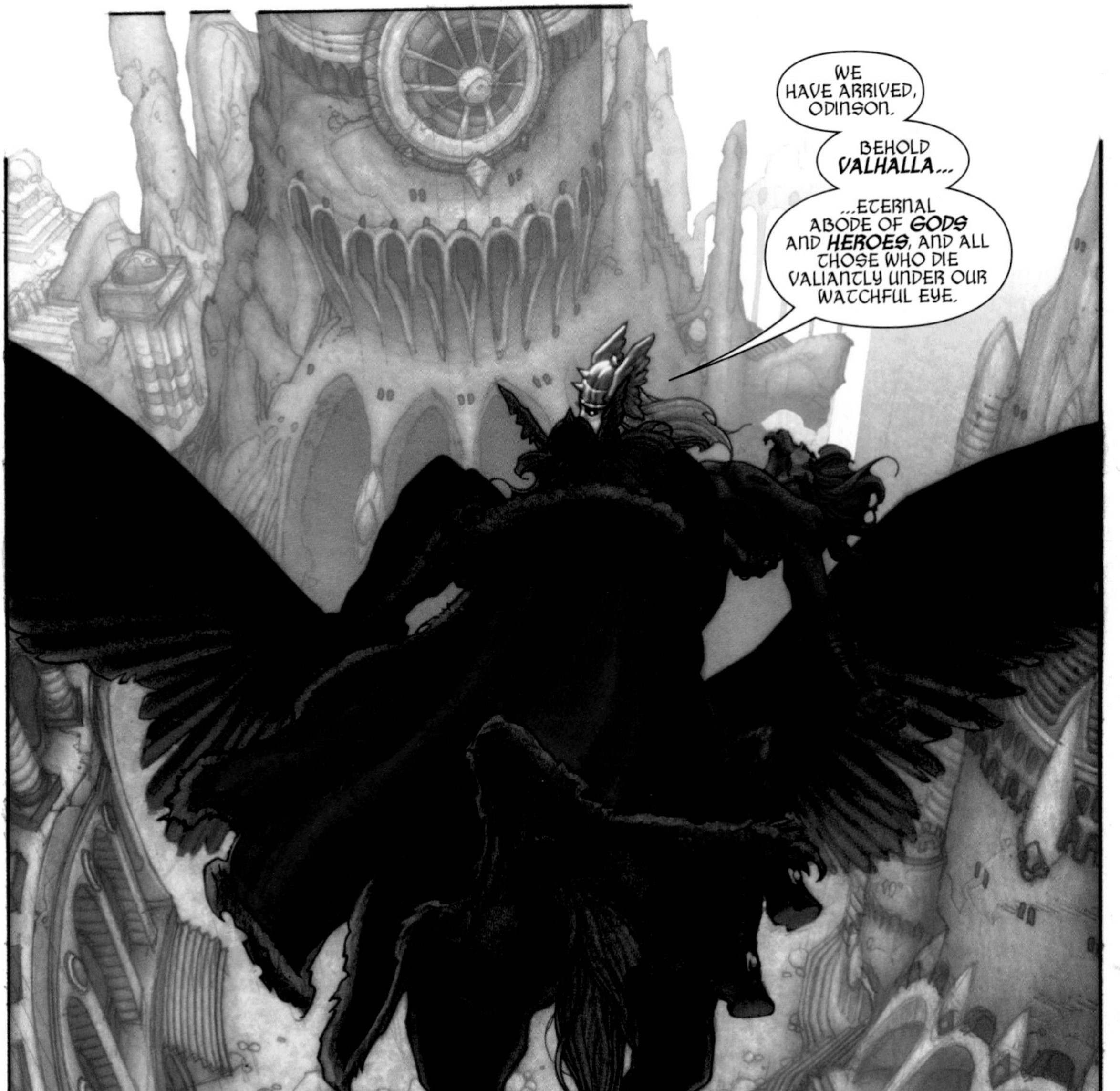
WE HAVE ARRIVED, ODINSON.
BEHOLD VALHALLA...
...ETERNAL ABODE OF GODS AND HEROES, AND ALL THOSE WHO DIE VALIANTLY UNDER OUR WATCHFUL EYE.

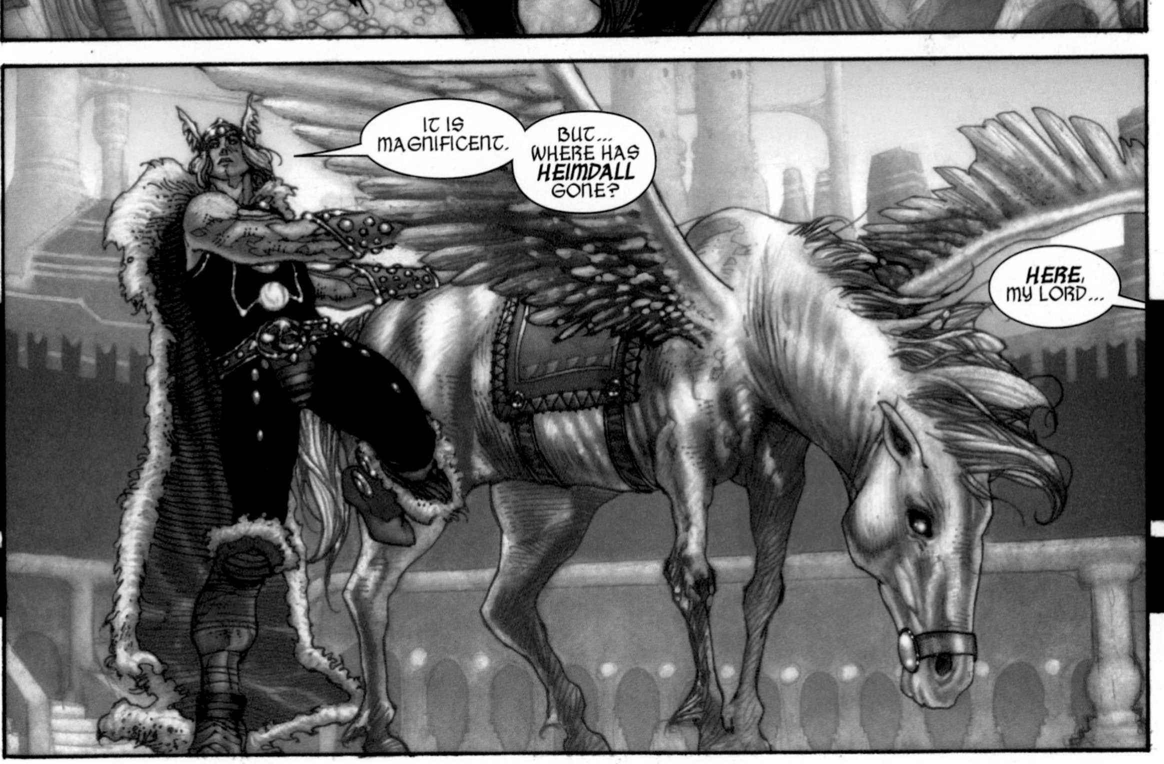
IT IS MAGNIFICENT.
BUT... WHERE HAS HEIMDALL GONE?
HERE, MY LORD...

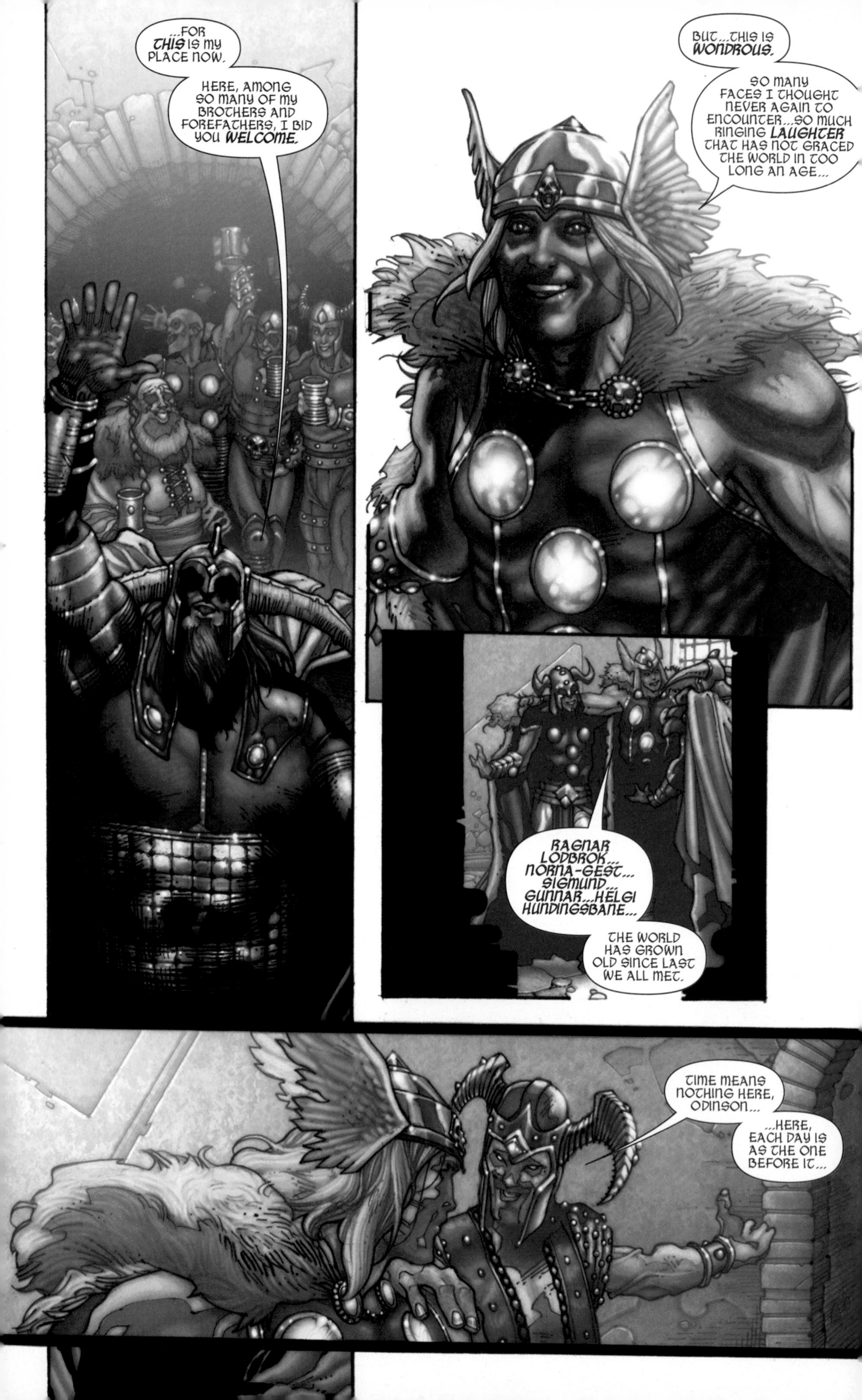
...FOR THIS IS MY PLACE NOW.
HERE, AMONG SO MANY OF MY BROTHERS AND FOREFATHERS, I BID YOU WELCOME.
BUT...THIS IS WONDROUS.
SO MANY FACES I THOUGHT NEVER AGAIN TO ENCOUNTER...SO MUCH RINGING LAUGHTER THAT HAS NOT GRACED THE WORLD IN TOO LONG AN AGE...
RAGNAR LODBROK... NORNA-GEST... SIGMUND... GUNNAR...HELGI HUNDINGSBANE...
THE WORLD HAS GROWN OLD SINCE LAST WE ALL MET.
TIME MEANS NOTHING HERE, ODINSON...
...HERE, EACH DAY IS AS THE ONE BEFORE IT...

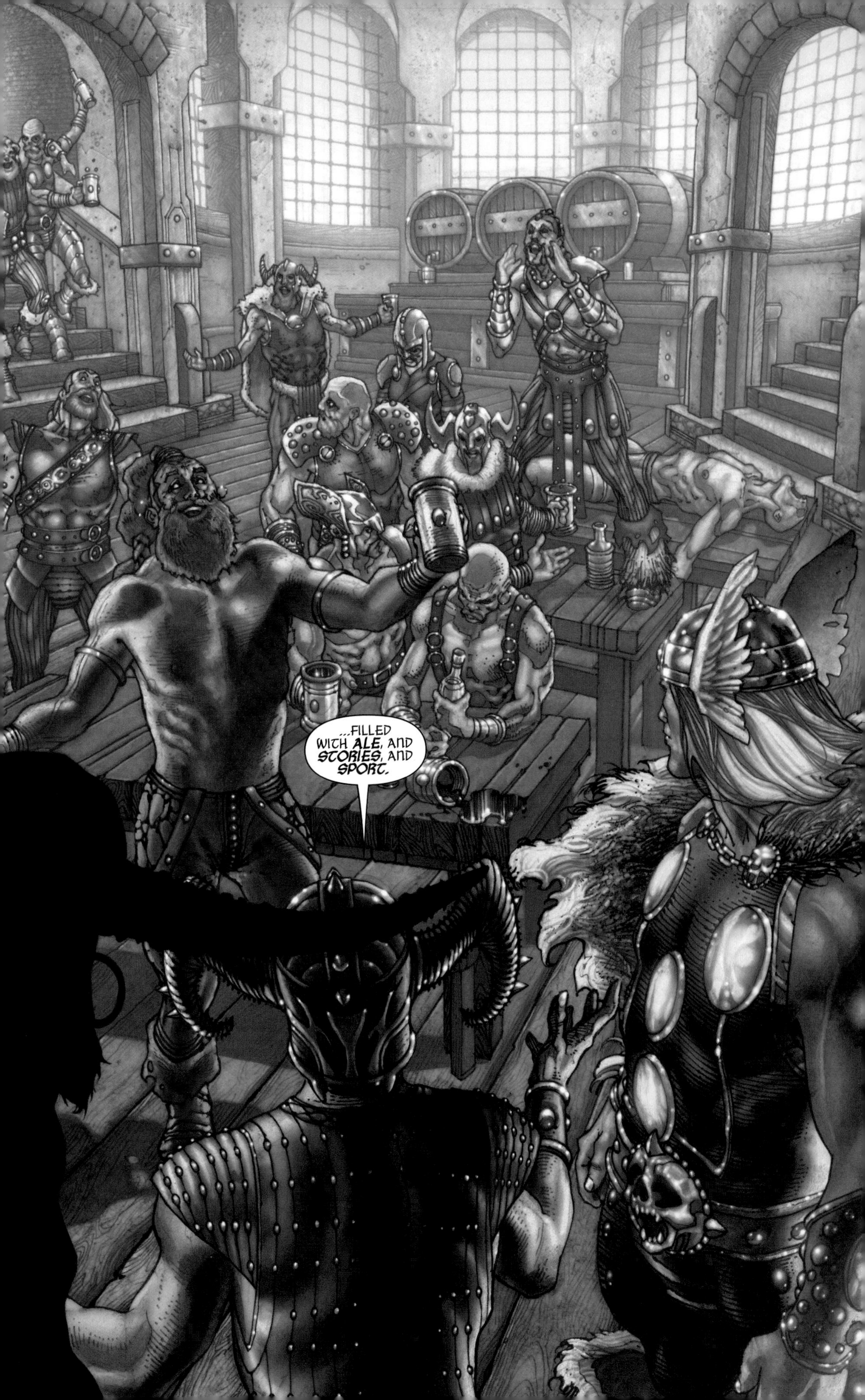
...FILLED WITH ALE, AND STORIES, AND SPORT.

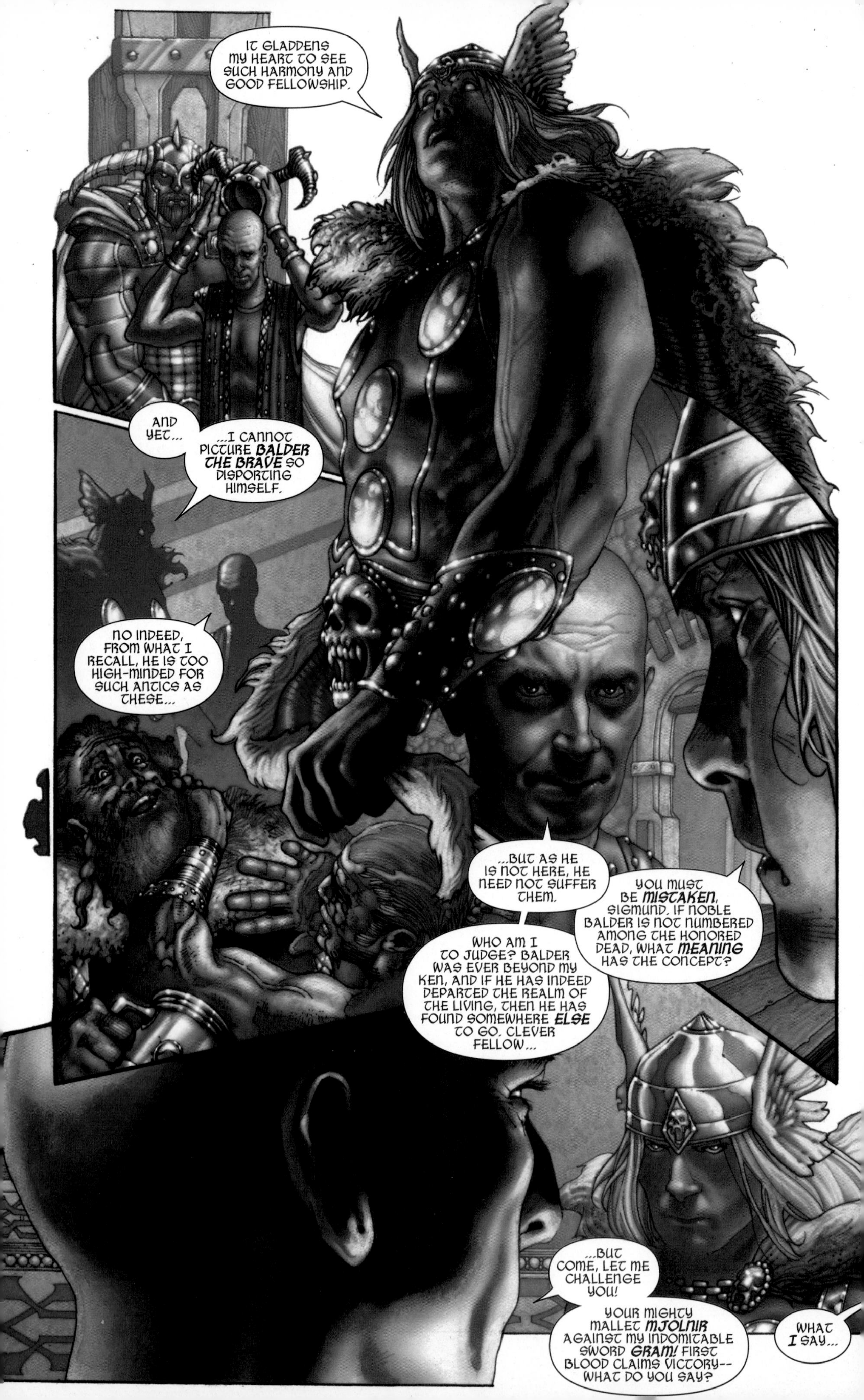
IT GLADDENS MY HEART TO SEE SUCH HARMONY AND GOOD FELLOWSHIP.
AND YET...
...I CANNOT PICTURE BALDER THE BRAVE SO DISPORTING HIMSELF.
NO INDEED, FROM WHAT I RECALL, HE IS TOO HIGH-MINDED FOR SUCH ANTICS AS THESE...
...BUT AS HE IS NOT HERE, HE NEED NOT SUFFER THEM.
YOU MUST BE MISTAKEN, SIGMUND. IF NOBLE BALDER IS NOT NUMBERED AMONG THE HONORED DEAD, WHAT MEANING HAS THE CONCEPT?
WHO AM I TO JUDGE? BALDER WAS EVER BEYOND MY KEN, AND IF HE HAS INDEED DEPARTED THE REALM OF THE LIVING, THEN HE HAS FOUND SOMEWHERE ELSE TO GO. CLEVER FELLOW...
...BUT COME, LET ME CHALLENGE YOU!
YOUR MIGHTY MALLET MJOLNIR AGAINST MY INDOMITABLE SWORD GRAM! FIRST BLOOD CLAIMS VICTORY--WHAT DO YOU SAY?
WHAT I SAY...

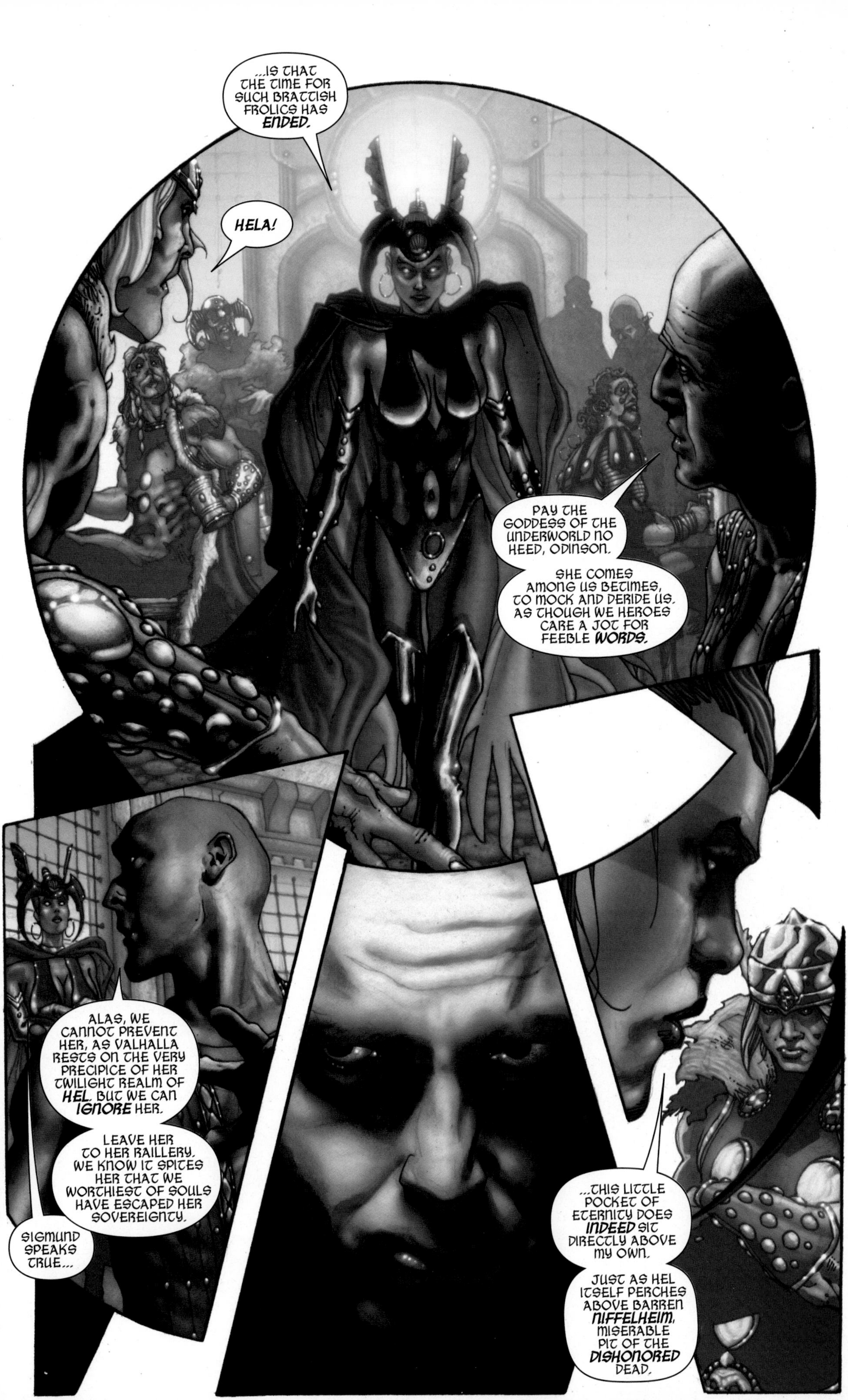

...IS THAT THE TIME FOR SUCH BRATTISH FROLICS HAS ENDED.
HELA!
PAY THE GODDESS OF THE UNDERWORLD NO HEED, ODINSON.
SHE COMES AMONG US BETIMES, TO MOCK AND DERIDE US. AS THOUGH WE HEROES CARE A JOT FOR FEEBLE WORDS.
ALAS, WE CANNOT PREVENT HER, AS VALHALLA RESTS ON THE VERY PRECIPICE OF HER TWILIGHT REALM OF HEL. BUT WE CAN IGNORE HER.
LEAVE HER TO HER RAILLERY. WE KNOW IT SPITES HER THAT WE WORTHIEST OF SOULS HAVE ESCAPED HER SOVEREIGNTY.
SIGMUND SPEAKS TRUE...
...THIS LITTLE POCKET OF ETERNITY DOES INDEED SIT DIRECTLY ABOVE MY OWN.
JUST AS HEL ITSELF PERCHES ABOVE BARREN NIFFELHEIM, MISERABLE PIT OF THE DISHONORED DEAD.

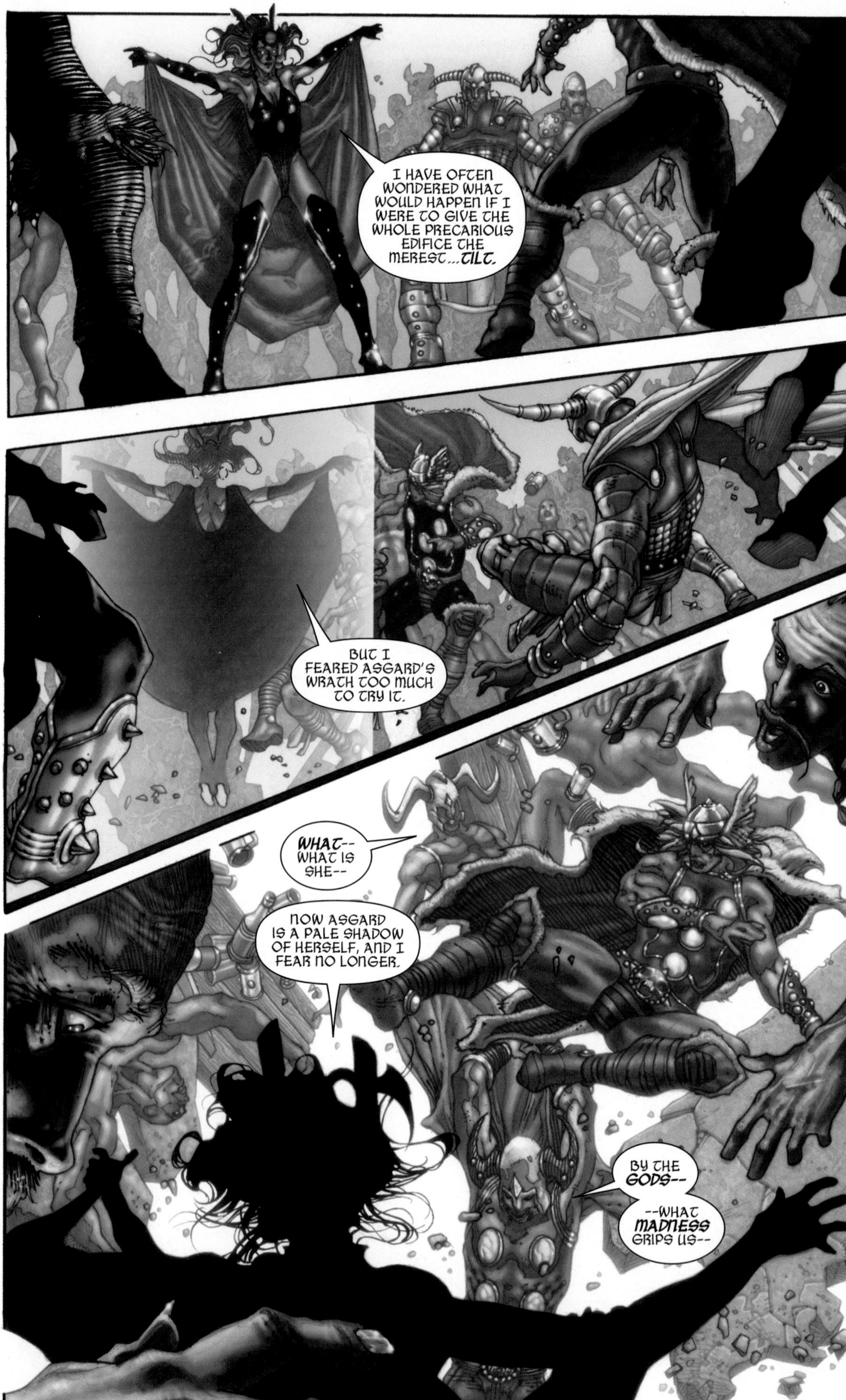
I HAVE OFTEN WONDERED WHAT WOULD HAPPEN IF I WERE TO GIVE THE WHOLE PRECARIOUS EDIFICE THE MEREST... TILT.
BUT I FEARED ASGARD'S WRATH TOO MUCH TO TRY IT.
WHAT-- WHAT IS SHE--
NOW ASGARD IS A PALE SHADOW OF HERSELF, AND I FEAR NO LONGER.
BY THE GODS--
--WHAT MADNESS GRIPS US--

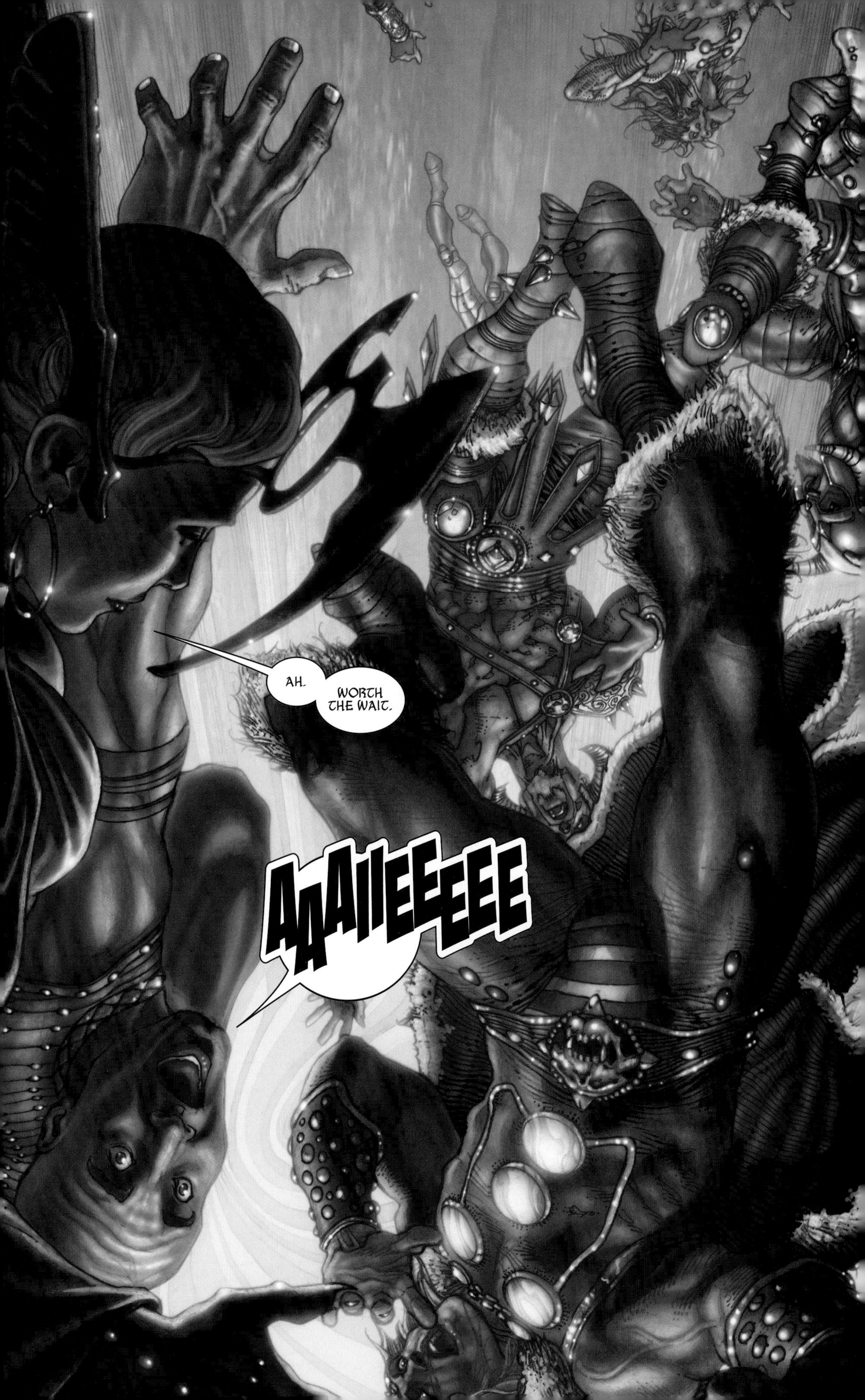
AH.
WORTH THE WAIT.
AAAIIEEEEE

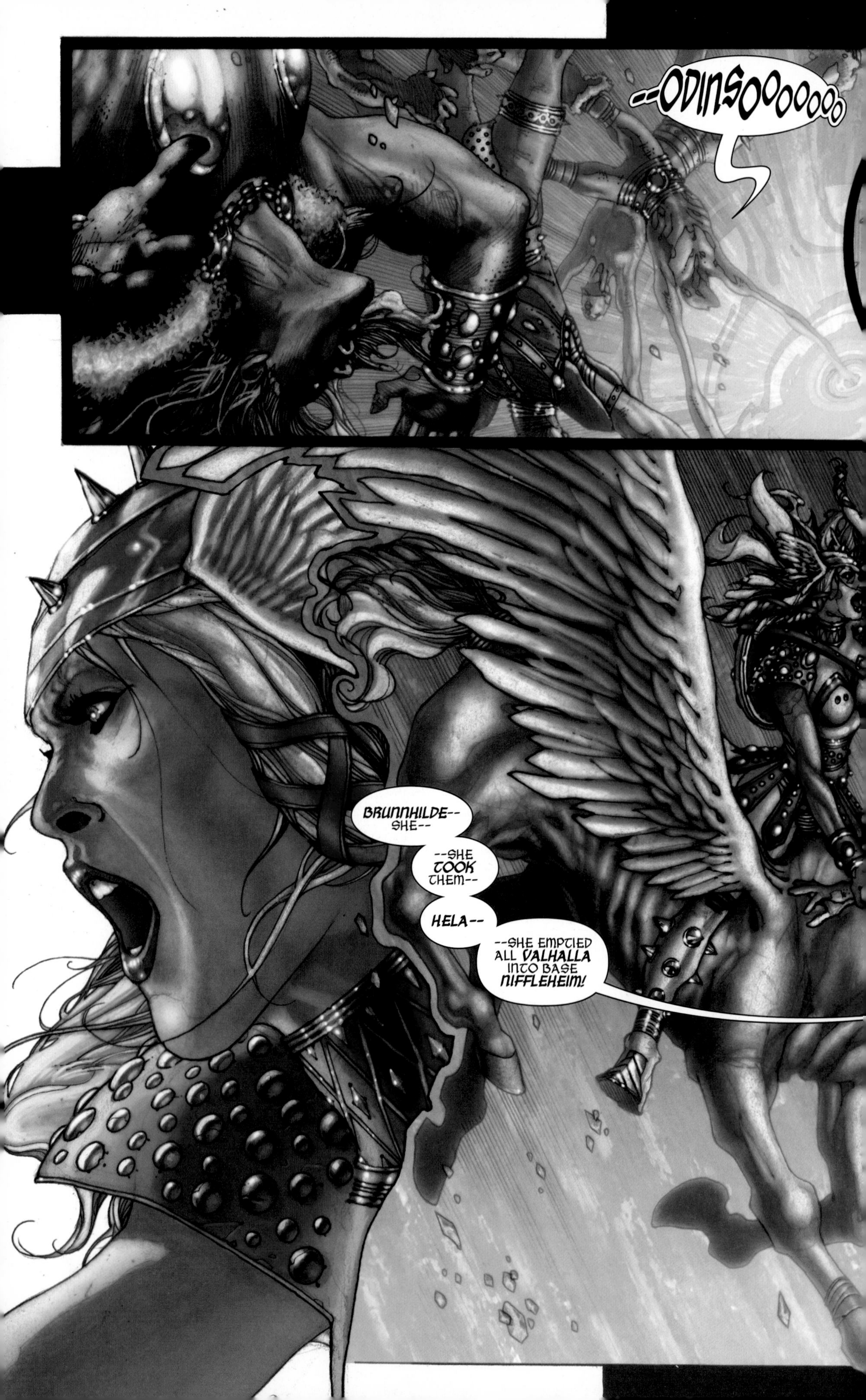
--ODINSOOOOOOO
BRUNNHILDE-- SHE--
--SHE TOOK THEM--
HELA--
--SHE EMPTIED ALL VALHALLA INTO BASE NIFFLEHEIM!

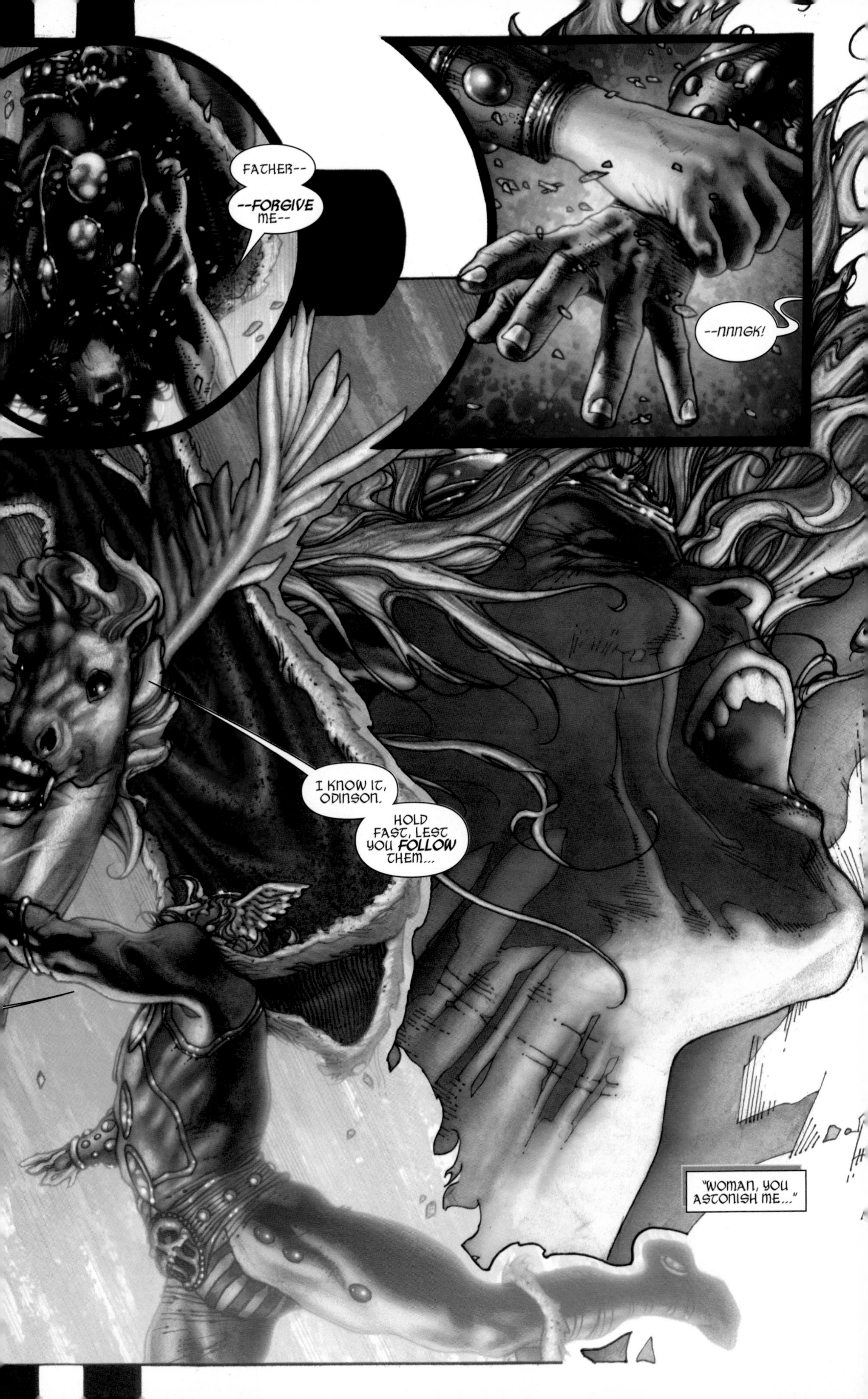
FATHER--
--FORGIVE ME--
--NNNGK!
I KNOW IT, ODINSON.
HOLD FAST, LEST YOU FOLLOW THEM...
"WOMAN, YOU ASTONISH ME..."

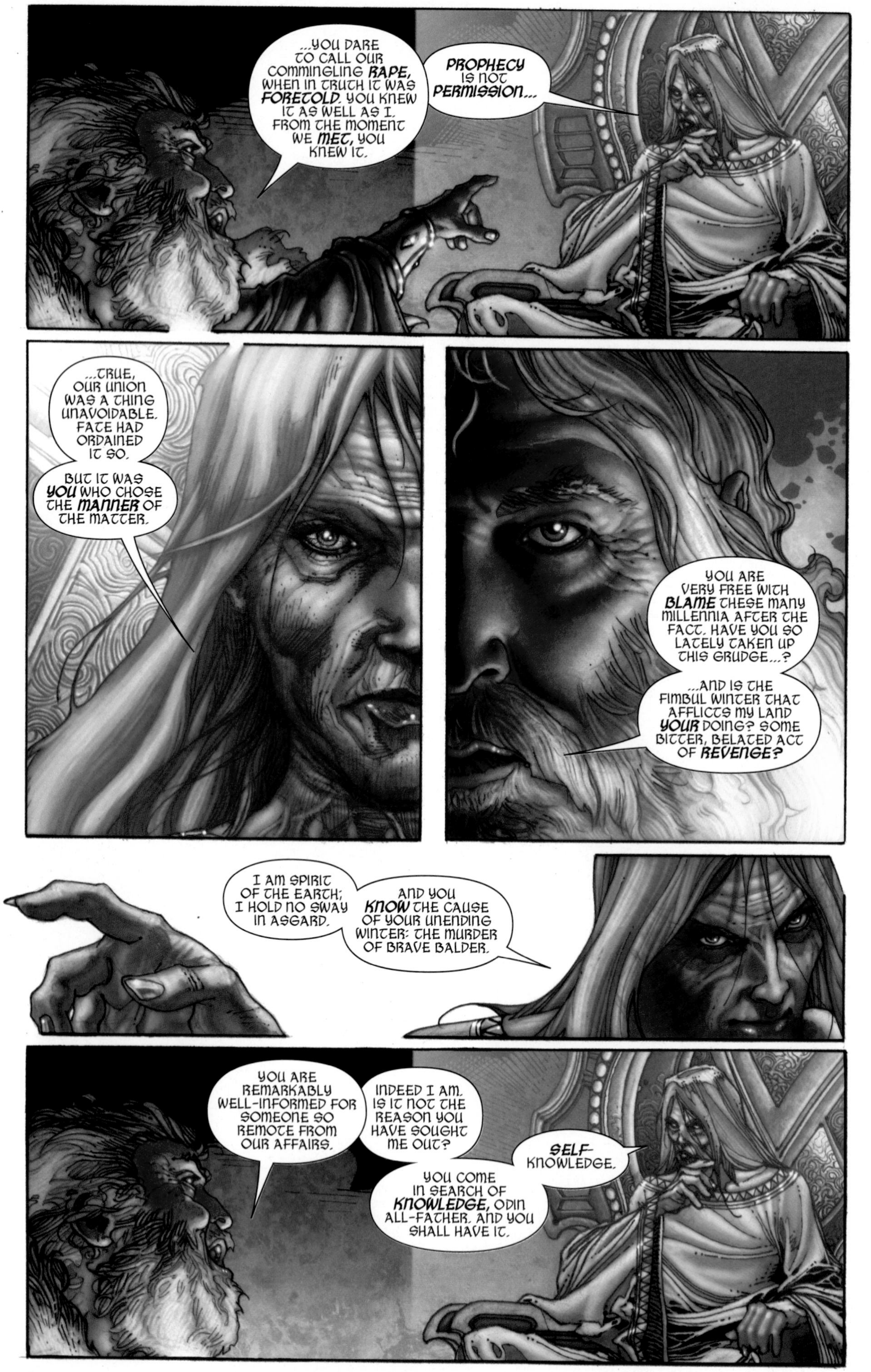
...YOU DARE TO CALL OUR COMMINGLING **RAPE,** WHEN IN TRUTH IT WAS **FORETOLD.** YOU KNEW IT AS WELL AS I. FROM THE MOMENT WE **MET,** YOU KNEW IT.
PROPHECY IS NOT **PERMISSION...**
...TRUE, OUR UNION WAS A THING UNAVOIDABLE. FATE HAD ORDAINED IT SO.
BUT IT WAS **YOU** WHO CHOSE THE **MANNER** OF THE MATTER.
YOU ARE VERY FREE WITH **BLAME** THESE MANY MILLENNIA AFTER THE FACT. HAVE YOU SO LATELY TAKEN UP THIS GRUDGE...?
...AND IS THE FIMBUL WINTER THAT AFFLICTS MY LAND **YOUR** DOING? SOME BITTER, BELATED ACT OF **REVENGE?**
I AM SPIRIT OF THE EARTH; I HOLD NO SWAY IN ASGARD.
AND YOU **KNOW** THE CAUSE OF YOUR UNENDING WINTER: THE MURDER OF BRAVE BALDER.
YOU ARE REMARKABLY WELL-INFORMED FOR SOMEONE SO REMOTE FROM OUR AFFAIRS.
INDEED I AM. IS IT NOT THE REASON YOU HAVE SOUGHT ME OUT?
SELF-KNOWLEDGE.
YOU COME IN SEARCH OF **KNOWLEDGE,** ODIN ALL-FATHER. AND YOU SHALL HAVE IT.

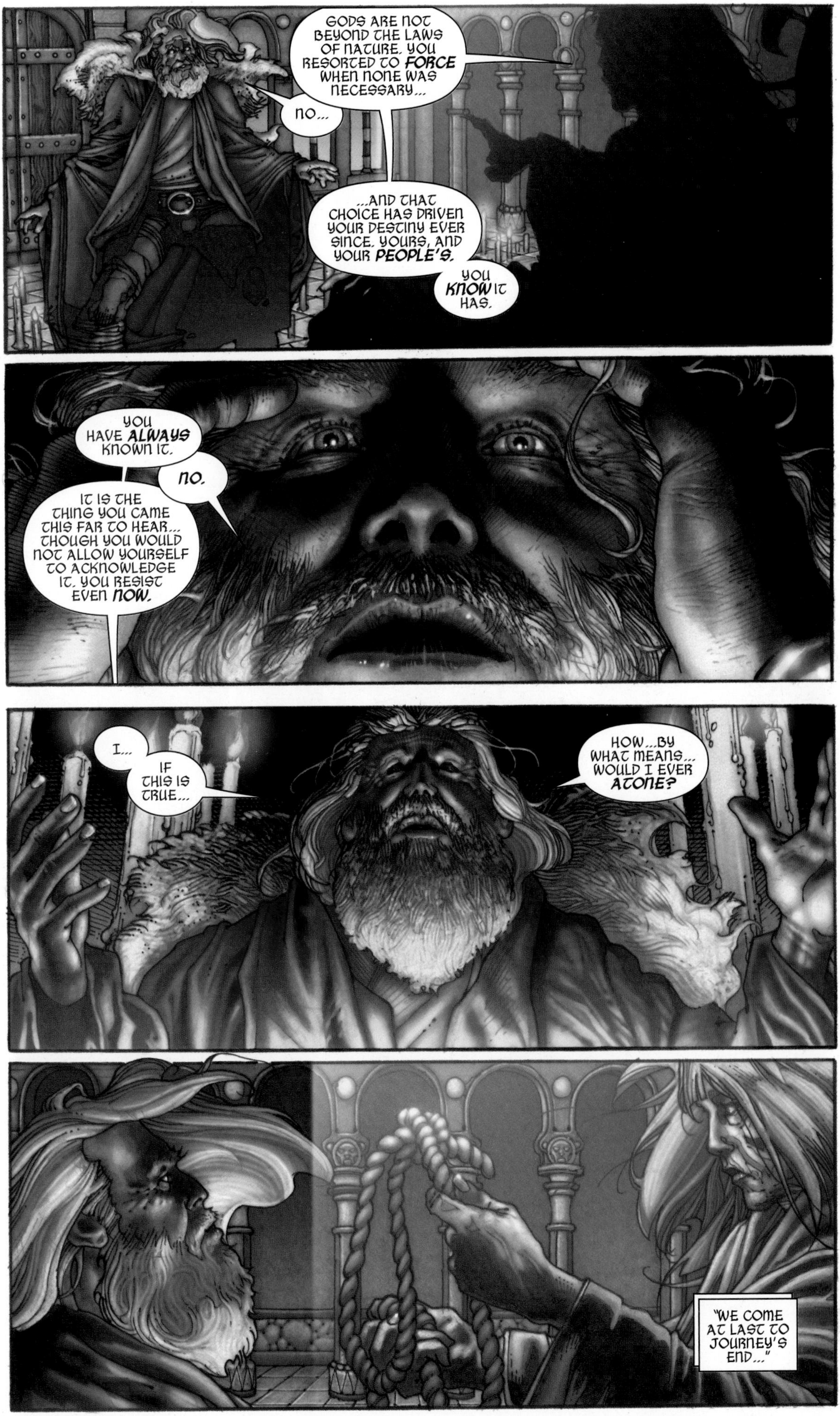
GODS ARE NOT BEYOND THE LAWS OF NATURE. YOU RESORTED TO FORCE WHEN NONE WAS NECESSARY...
NO...
...AND THAT CHOICE HAS DRIVEN YOUR DESTINY EVER SINCE. YOURS, AND YOUR PEOPLE'S.
YOU KNOW IT HAS.
YOU HAVE ALWAYS KNOWN IT.
NO.
IT IS THE THING YOU CAME THIS FAR TO HEAR... THOUGH YOU WOULD NOT ALLOW YOURSELF TO ACKNOWLEDGE IT. YOU RESIST EVEN NOW.
I...
IF THIS IS TRUE...
HOW...BY WHAT MEANS... WOULD I EVER ATONE?
"WE COME AT LAST TO JOURNEY'S END..."

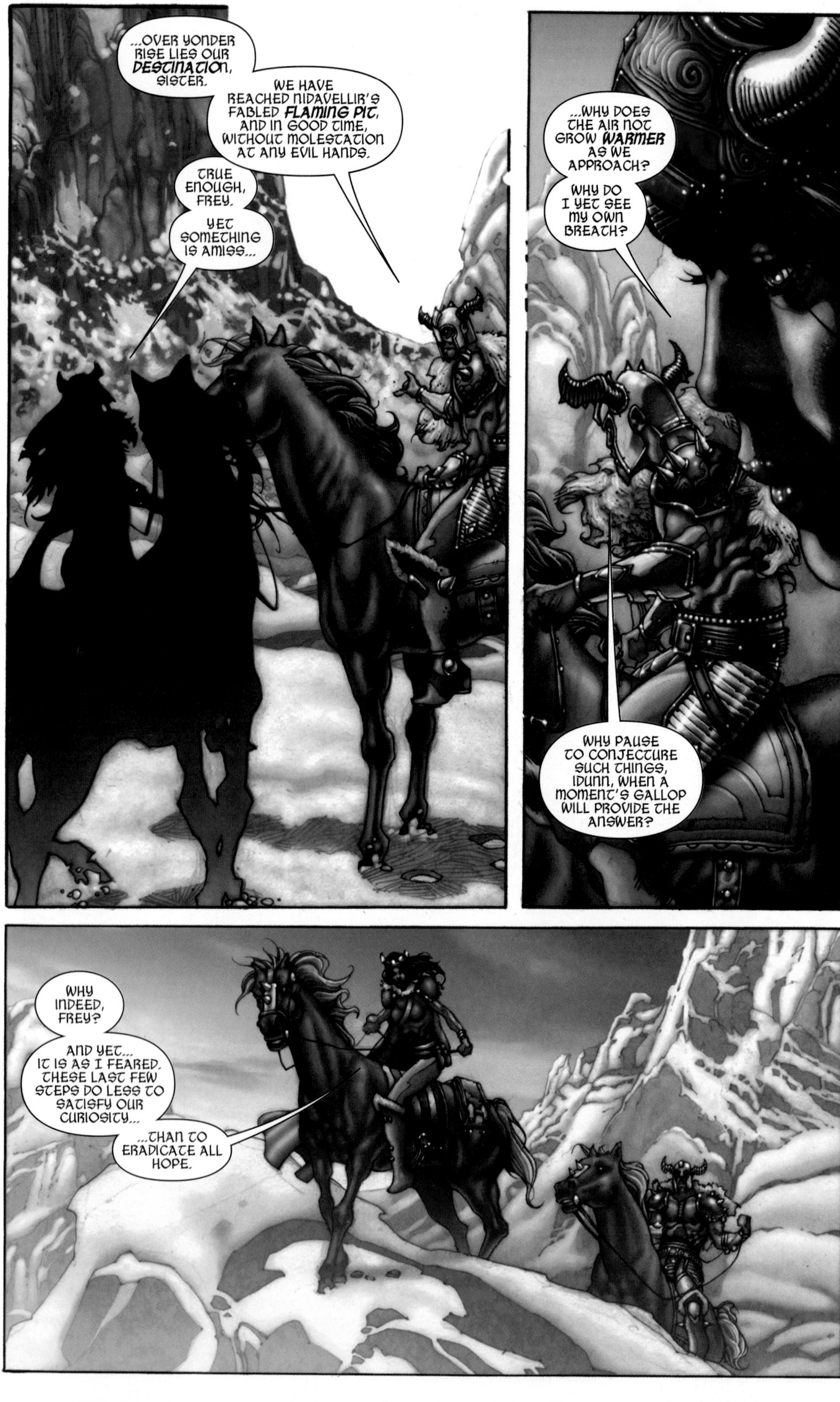
...OVER YONDER RISE LIES OUR DESTINATION, SISTER.
WE HAVE REACHED NIDAVELLIR'S FABLED FLAMING PIT, AND IN GOOD TIME, WITHOUT MOLESTATION AT ANY EVIL HANDS.
TRUE ENOUGH, FREY.
YET SOMETHING IS AMISS...
...WHY DOES THE AIR NOT GROW WARMER AS WE APPROACH?
WHY DO I YET SEE MY OWN BREATH?
WHY PAUSE TO CONJECTURE SUCH THINGS, IDUNN, WHEN A MOMENT'S GALLOP WILL PROVIDE THE ANSWER?
WHY INDEED, FREY?
AND YET... IT IS AS I FEARED. THESE LAST FEW STEPS DO LESS TO SATISFY OUR CURIOSITY...
...THAN TO ERADICATE ALL HOPE.

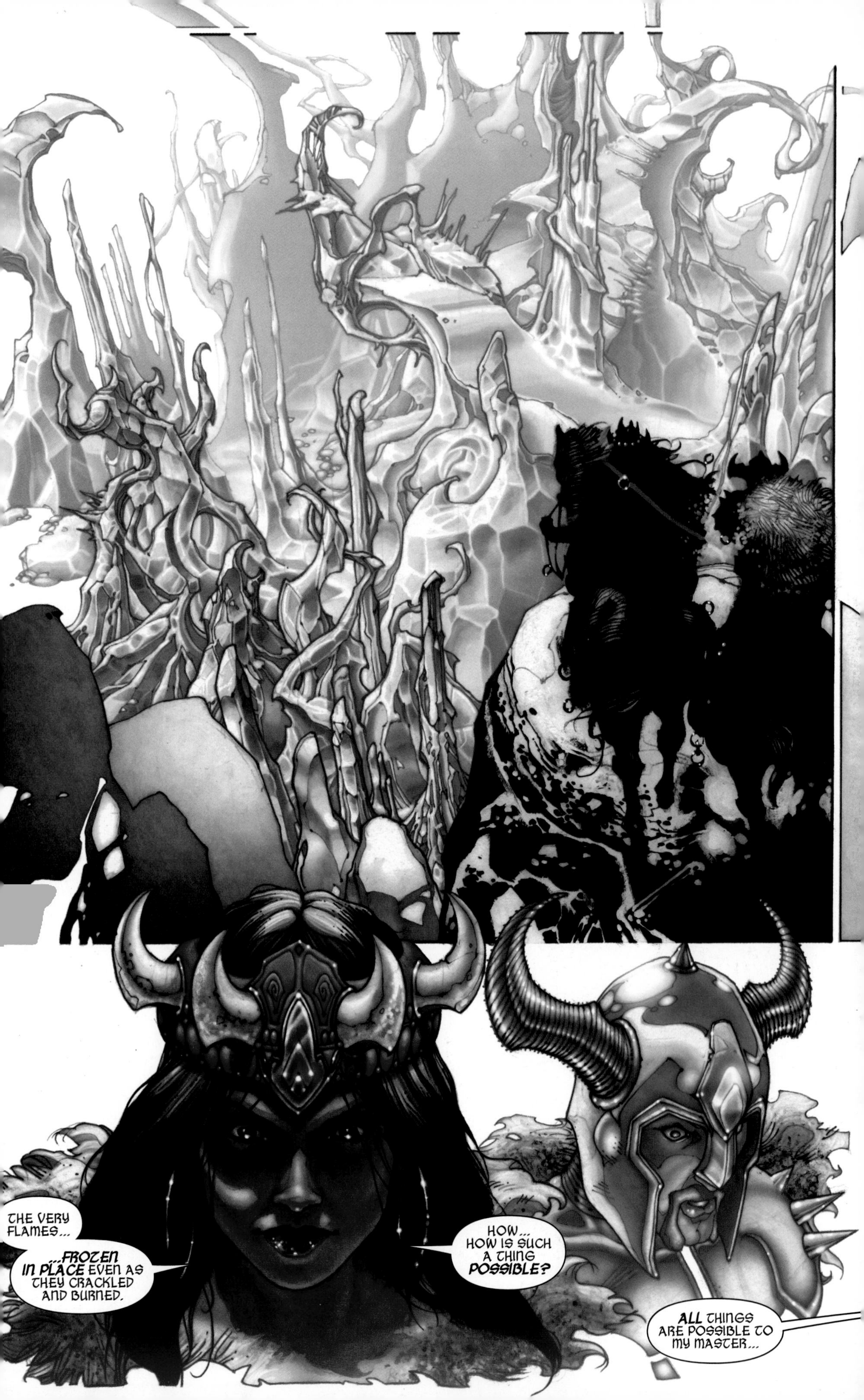

THE VERY FLAMES...
...FROZEN IN PLACE EVEN AS THEY CRACKLED AND BURNED.
HOW... HOW IS SUCH A THING POSSIBLE?
ALL THINGS ARE POSSIBLE TO MY MASTER...

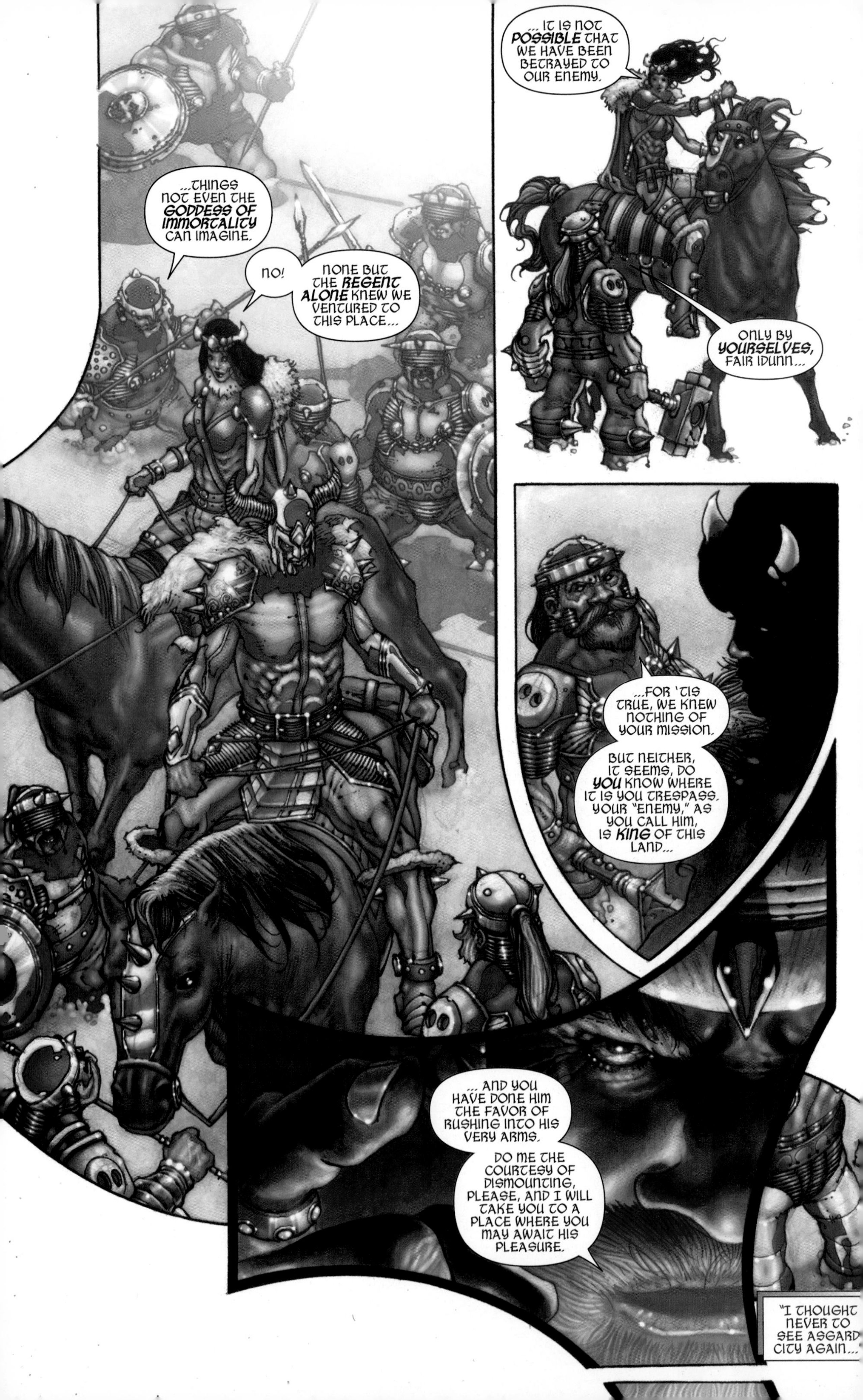
...THINGS NOT EVEN THE GODDESS OF IMMORTALITY CAN IMAGINE.
NO!
NONE BUT THE REGENT ALONE KNEW WE VENTURED TO THIS PLACE...
...IT IS NOT POSSIBLE THAT WE HAVE BEEN BETRAYED TO OUR ENEMY.
ONLY BY YOURSELVES, FAIR IDUNN...
...FOR 'TIS TRUE, WE KNEW NOTHING OF YOUR MISSION.
BUT NEITHER, IT SEEMS, DO YOU KNOW WHERE IT IS YOU TRESPASS. YOUR "ENEMY," AS YOU CALL HIM, IS KING OF THIS LAND...
...AND YOU HAVE DONE HIM THE FAVOR OF RUSHING INTO HIS VERY ARMS.
DO ME THE COURTESY OF DISMOUNTING, PLEASE, AND I WILL TAKE YOU TO A PLACE WHERE YOU MAY AWAIT HIS PLEASURE.
"I THOUGHT NEVER TO SEE ASGARD CITY AGAIN...

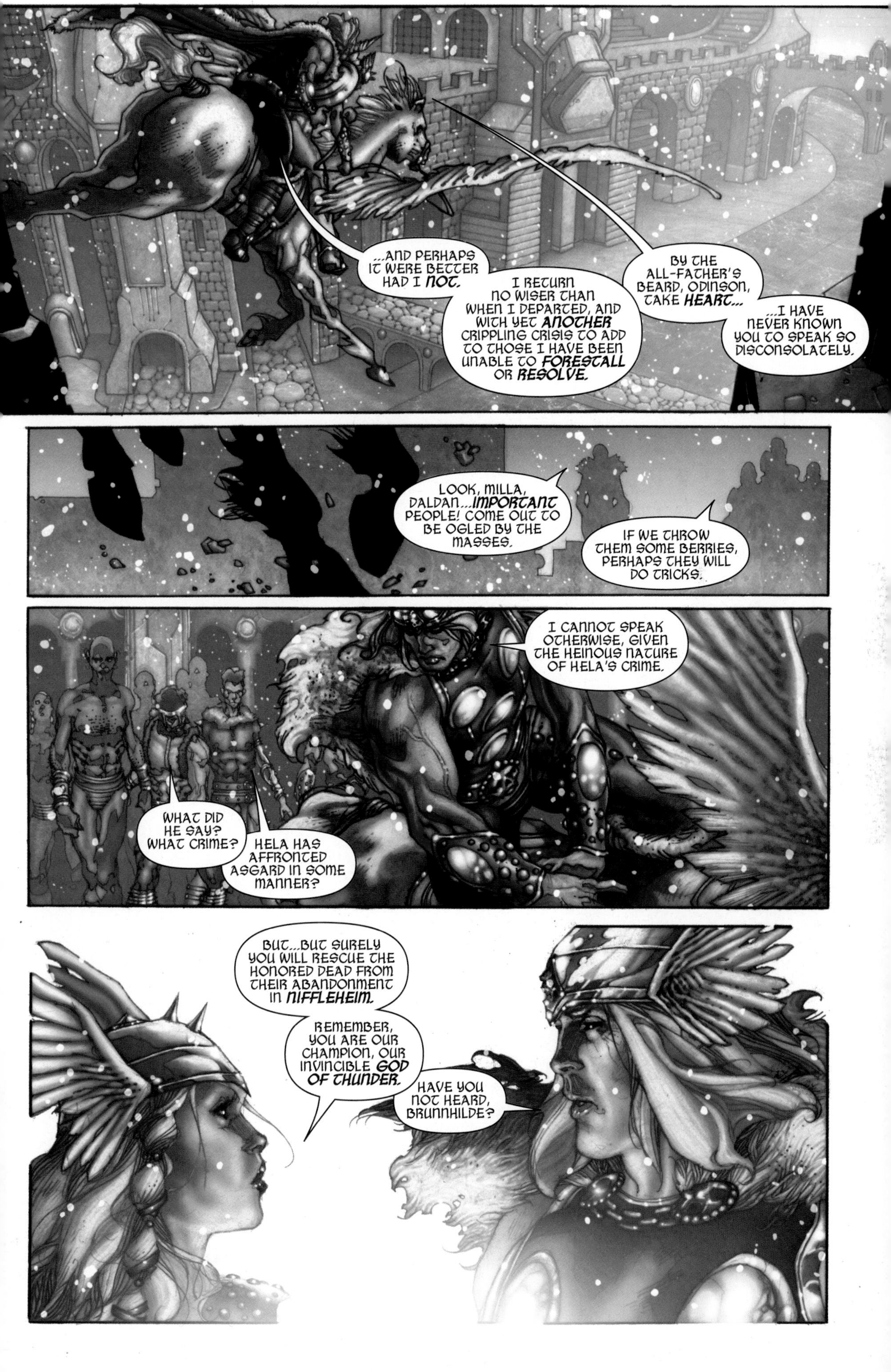

...AND PERHAPS IT WERE BETTER HAD I NOT.
I RETURN NO WISER THAN WHEN I DEPARTED, AND WITH YET ANOTHER CRIPPLING CRISIS TO ADD TO THOSE I HAVE BEEN UNABLE TO FORESTALL OR RESOLVE.
BY THE ALL-FATHER'S BEARD, ODINSON, TAKE HEART...
...I HAVE NEVER KNOWN YOU TO SPEAK SO DISCONSOLATELY.
LOOK, MILLA, DALDAN...IMPORTANT PEOPLE! COME OUT TO BE OGLED BY THE MASSES.
IF WE THROW THEM SOME BERRIES, PERHAPS THEY WILL DO TRICKS.
I CANNOT SPEAK OTHERWISE, GIVEN THE HEINOUS NATURE OF HELA'S CRIME.
WHAT DID HE SAY? WHAT CRIME?
HELA HAS AFFRONTED ASGARD IN SOME MANNER?
BUT...BUT SURELY YOU WILL RESCUE THE HONORED DEAD FROM THEIR ABANDONMENT IN NIFFLEHEIM.
REMEMBER, YOU ARE OUR CHAMPION, OUR INVINCIBLE GOD OF THUNDER.
HAVE YOU NOT HEARD, BRUNNHILDE?

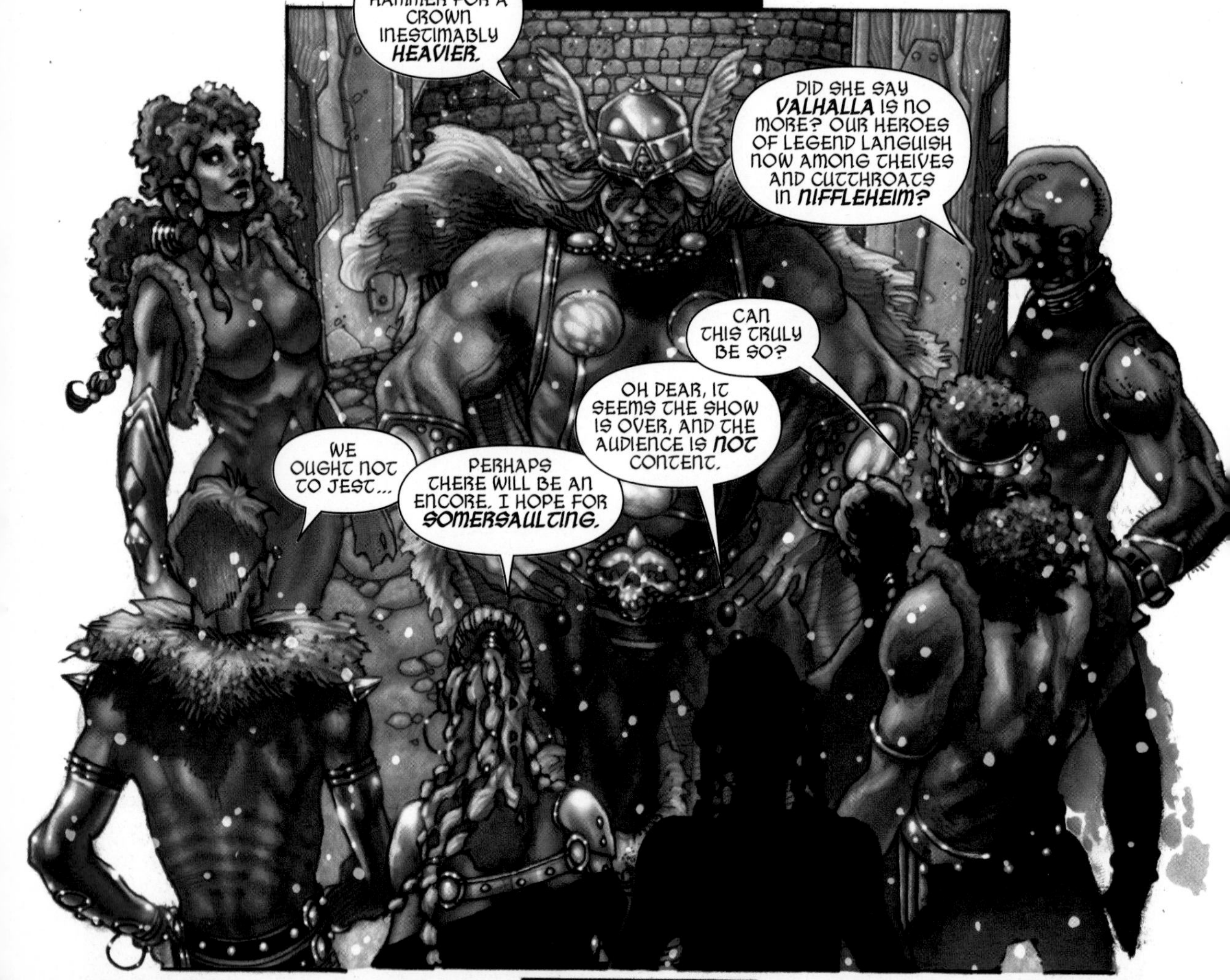
...I HAVE SET DOWN MY HAMMER FOR A CROWN INESTIMABLY **HEAVIER**.
DID SHE SAY **VALHALLA** IS NO MORE? OUR HEROES OF LEGEND LANGUISH NOW AMONG THEIVES AND CUTTHROATS IN **NIFFLEHEIM?**
CAN THIS TRULY BE SO?
OH DEAR, IT SEEMS THE SHOW IS OVER, AND THE AUDIENCE IS **NOT** CONTENT.
WE OUGHT NOT TO JEST...
PERHAPS THERE WILL BE AN ENCORE. I HOPE FOR **SOMERSAULTING**.

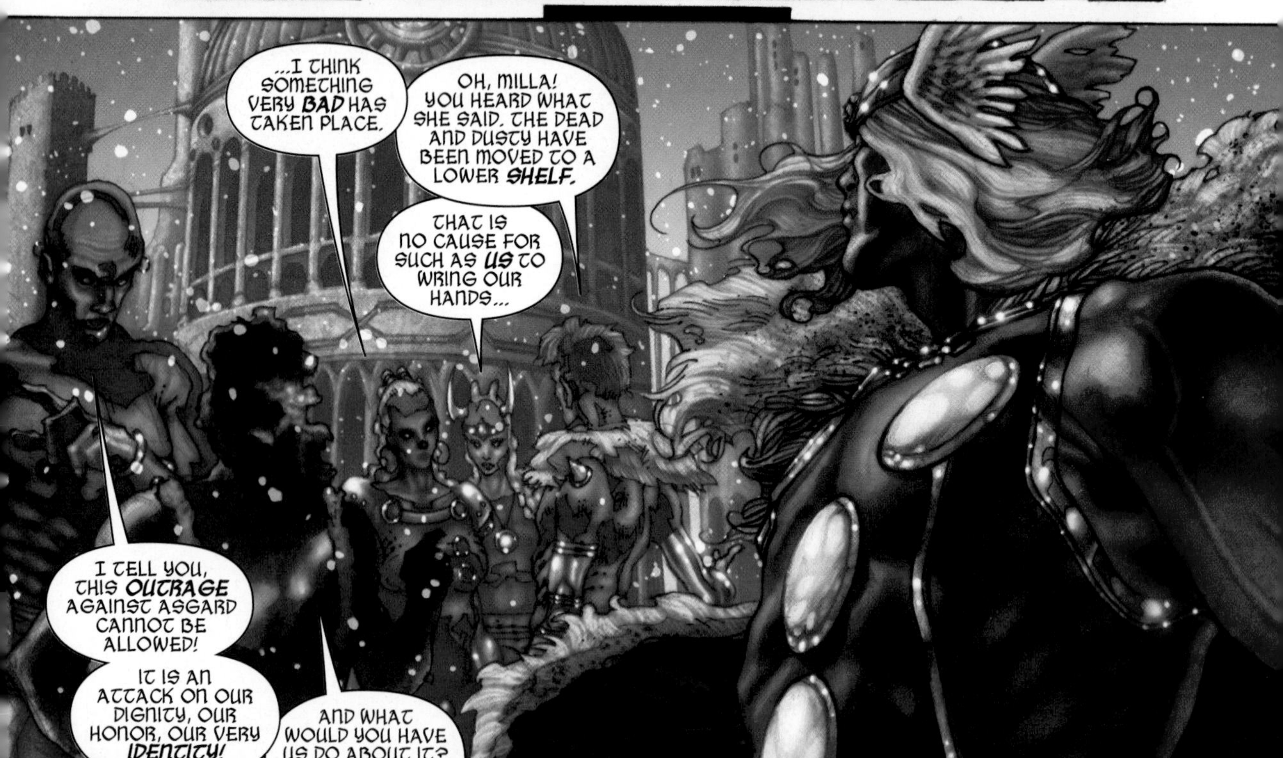
...I THINK SOMETHING VERY **BAD** HAS TAKEN PLACE.
OH, MILLA! YOU HEARD WHAT SHE SAID. THE DEAD AND DUSTY HAVE BEEN MOVED TO A LOWER **SHELF**.
THAT IS NO CAUSE FOR SUCH AS **US** TO WRING OUR HANDS...
I TELL YOU, THIS **OUTRAGE** AGAINST ASGARD CANNOT BE ALLOWED!
IT IS AN ATTACK ON OUR DIGNITY, OUR HONOR, OUR VERY **IDENTITY!**
AND WHAT WOULD YOU HAVE US DO ABOUT IT? MARCH ON THE QUEEN OF HEL?

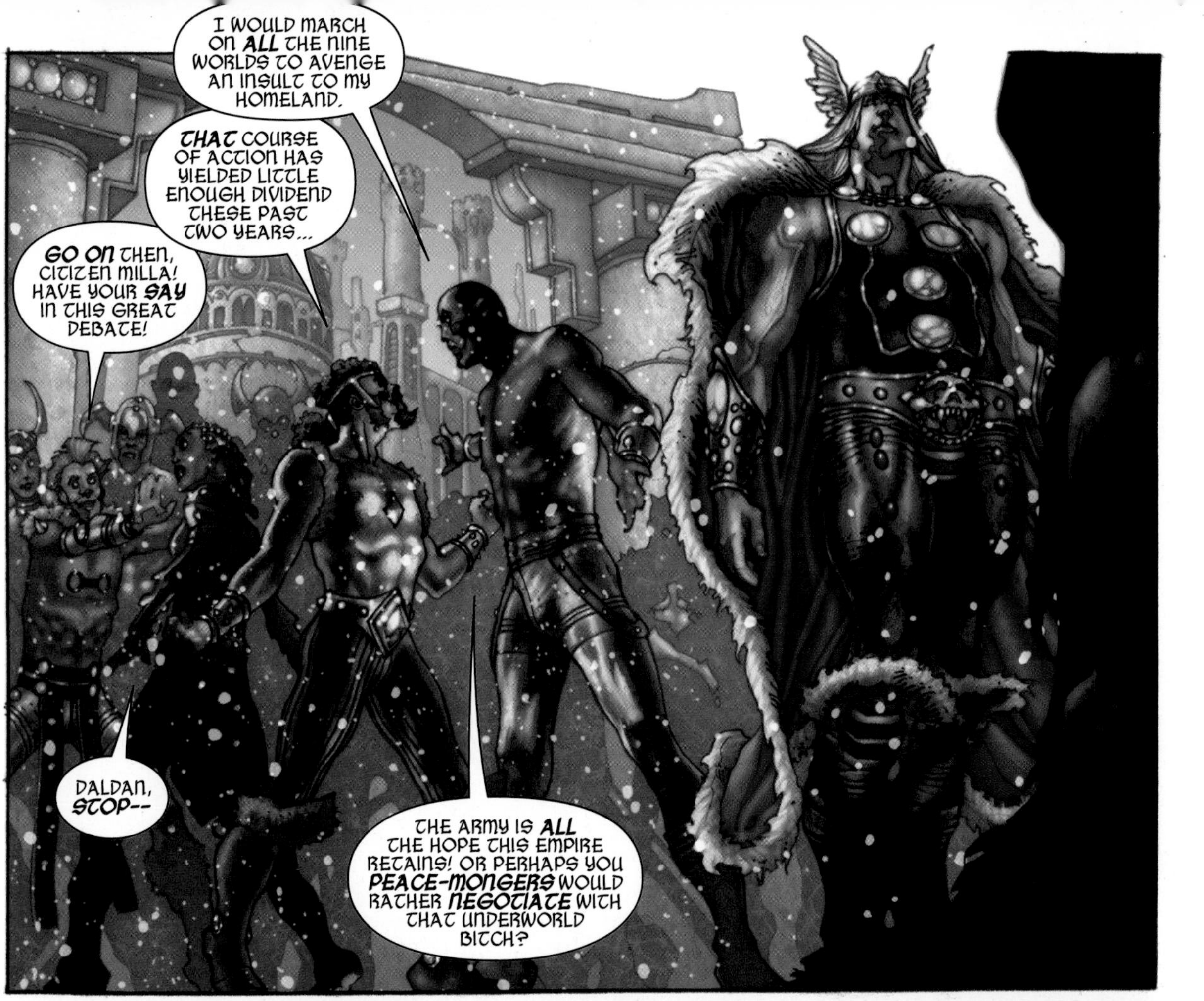
GO ON THEN, CITIZEN MILLA! HAVE YOUR SAY IN THIS GREAT DEBATE!
THAT COURSE OF ACTION HAS YIELDED LITTLE ENOUGH DIVIDEND THESE PAST TWO YEARS...
I WOULD MARCH ON ALL THE NINE WORLDS TO AVENGE AN INSULT TO MY HOMELAND.
DALDAN, STOP--
THE ARMY IS ALL THE HOPE THIS EMPIRE RETAINS! OR PERHAPS YOU PEACE-MONGERS WOULD RATHER NEGOTIATE WITH THAT UNDERWORLD BITCH?

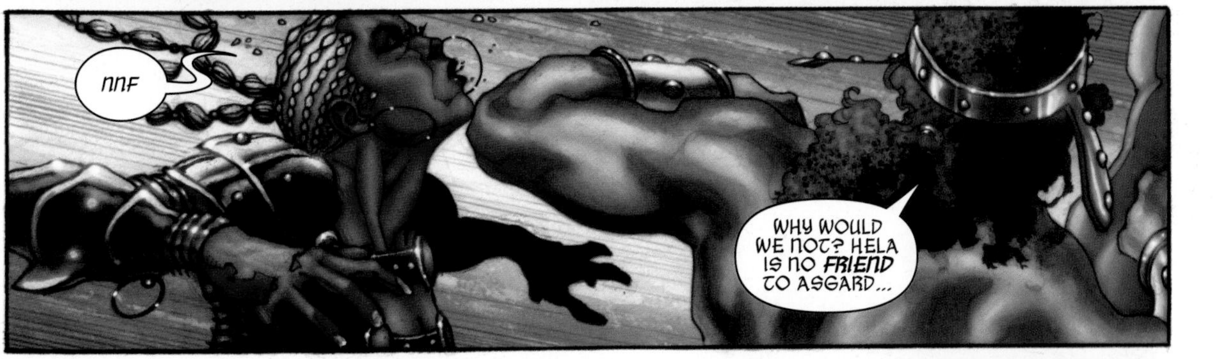
NNF
WHY WOULD WE NOT? HELA IS NO FRIEND TO ASGARD...

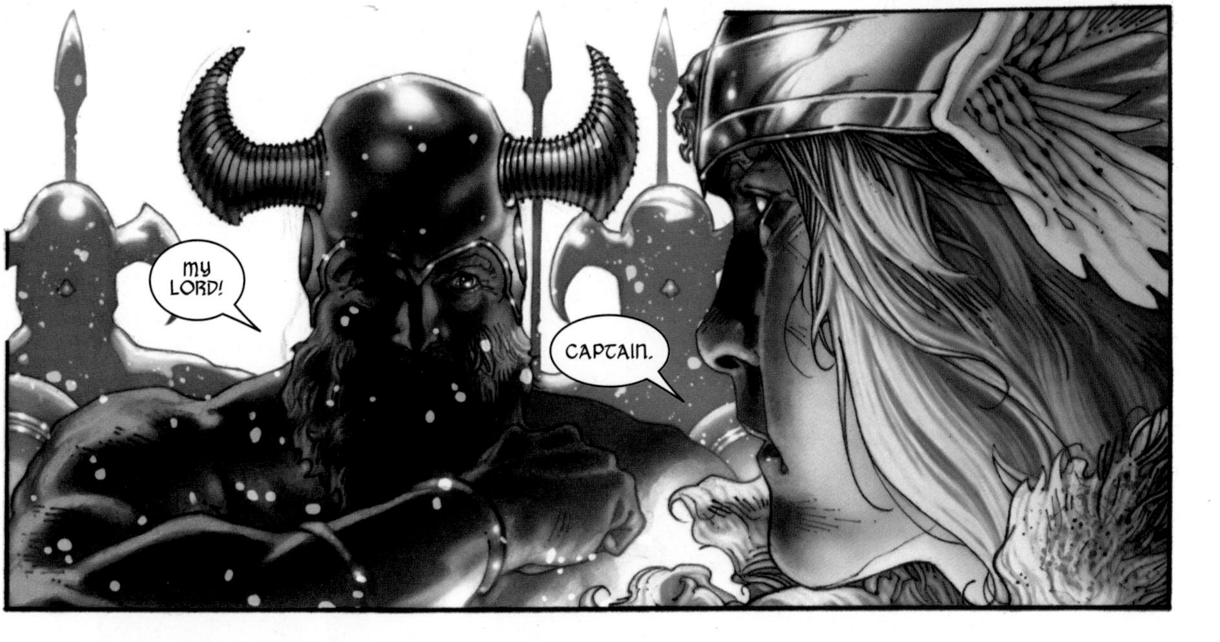
MY LORD!
CAPTAIN.

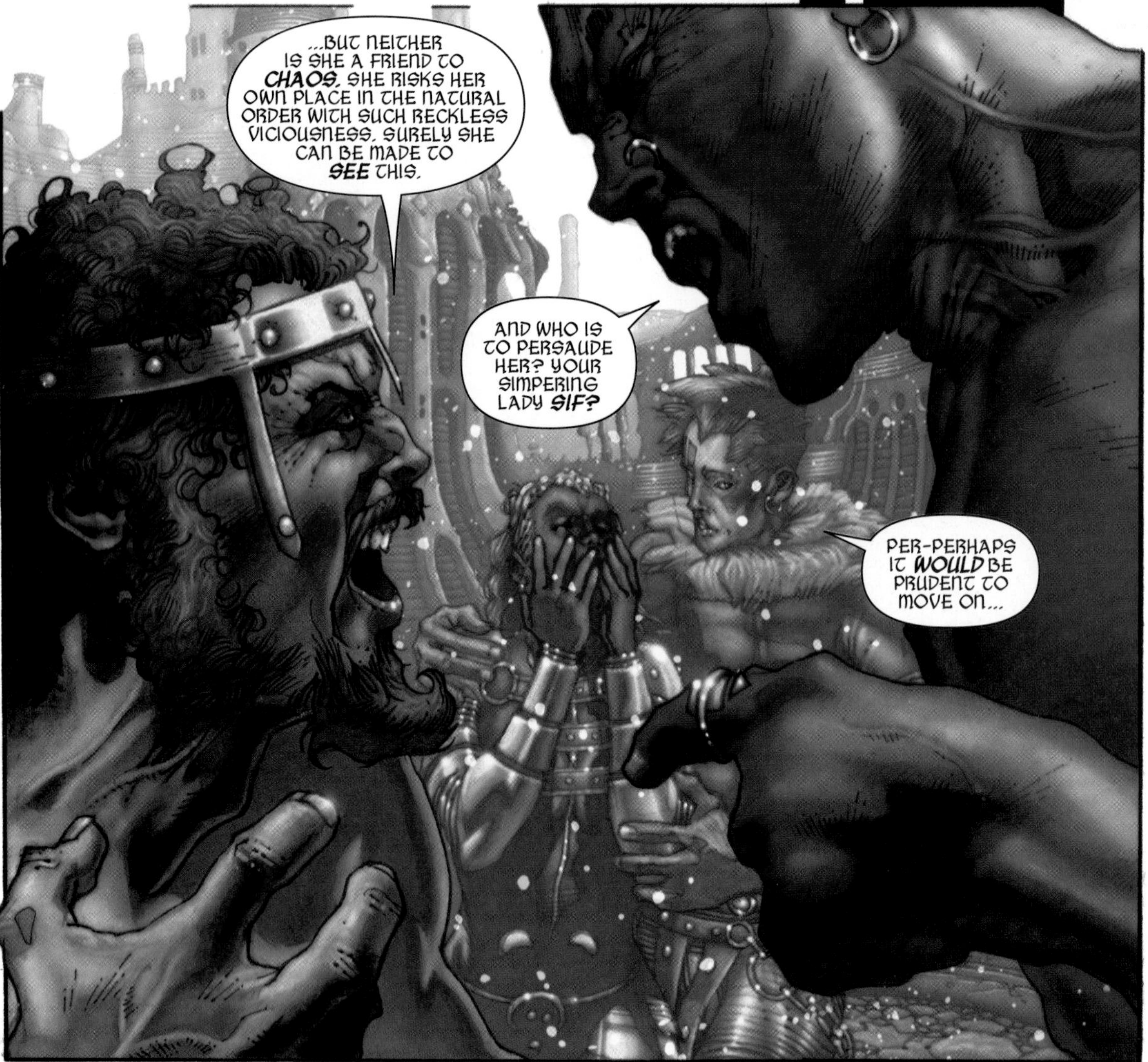
...BUT NEITHER IS SHE A FRIEND TO CHAOS. SHE RISKS HER OWN PLACE IN THE NATURAL ORDER WITH SUCH RECKLESS VICIOUSNESS. SURELY SHE CAN BE MADE TO SEE THIS.
AND WHO IS TO PERSAUDE HER? YOUR SIMPERING LADY SIF?
PER-PERHAPS IT WOULD BE PRUDENT TO MOVE ON...

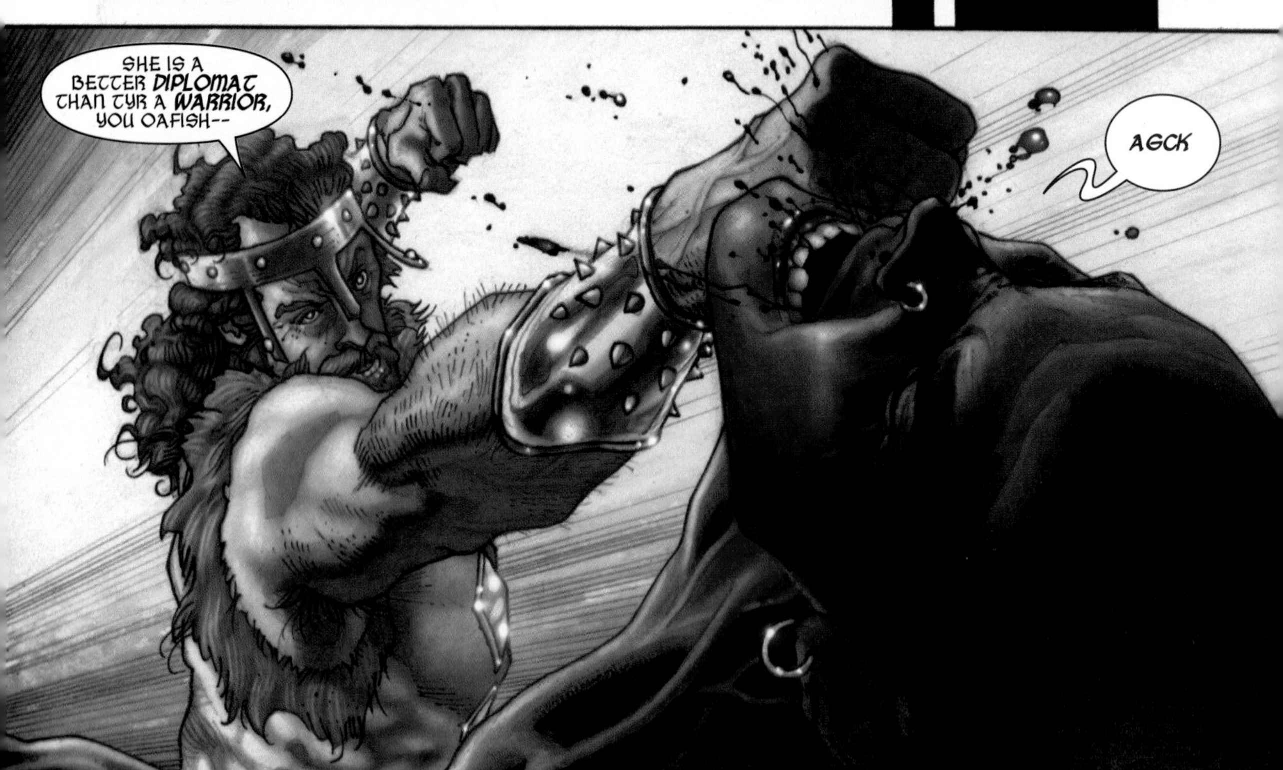
SHE IS A BETTER DIPLOMAT THAN TYR A WARRIOR, YOU OAFISH--
AGCK

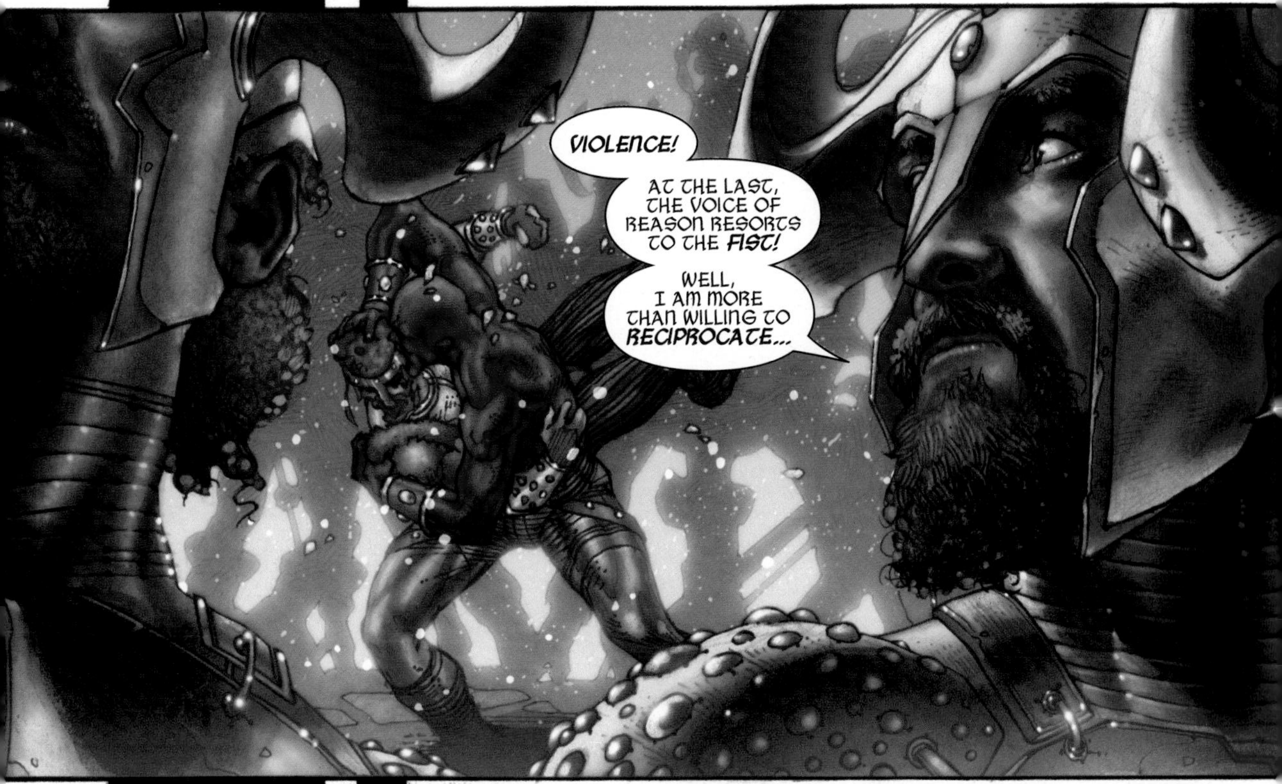
VIOLENCE!
AT THE LAST, THE VOICE OF REASON RESORTS TO THE FIST!
WELL, I AM MORE THAN WILLING TO RECIPROCATE...

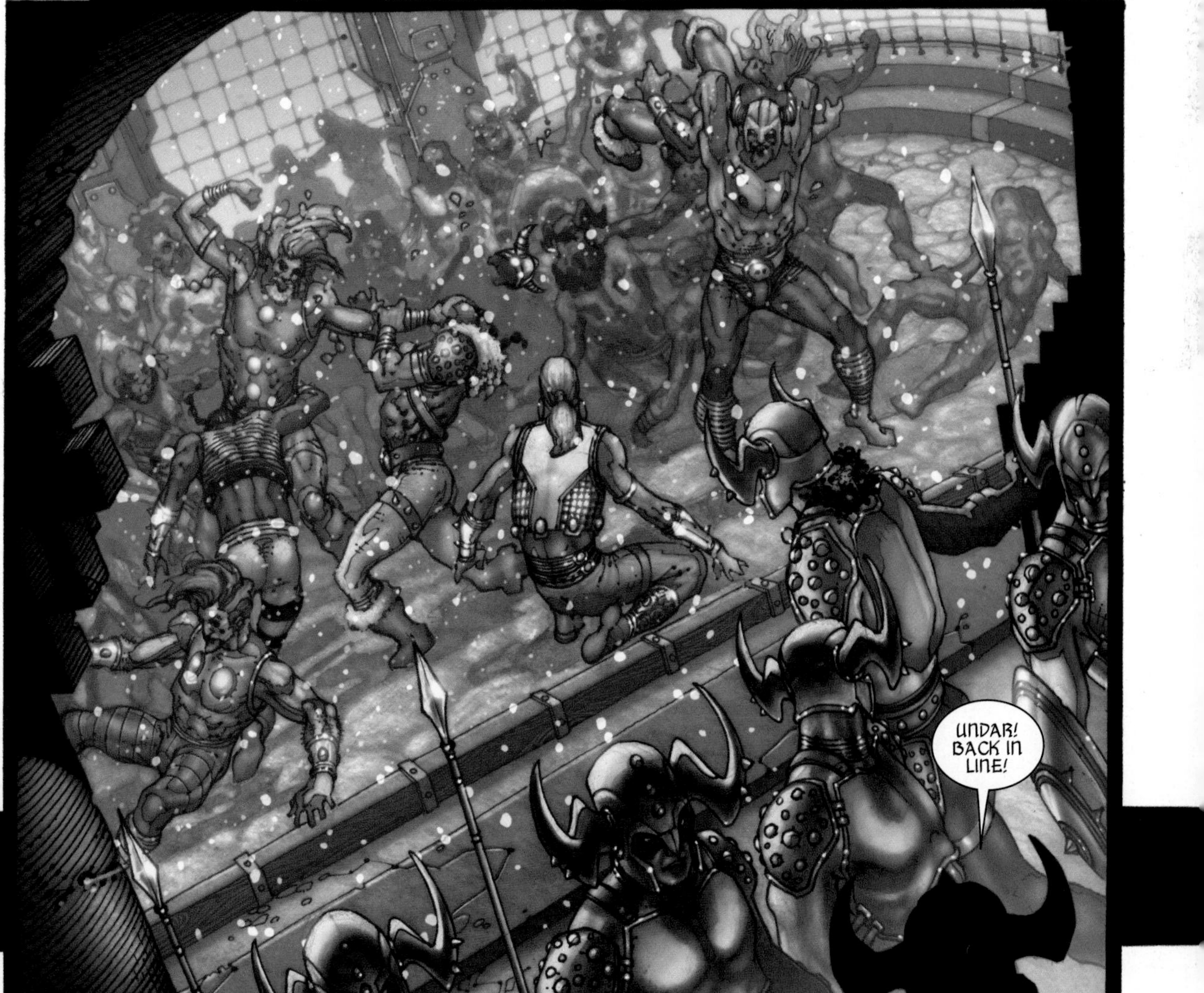
UNDAR! BACK IN LINE!

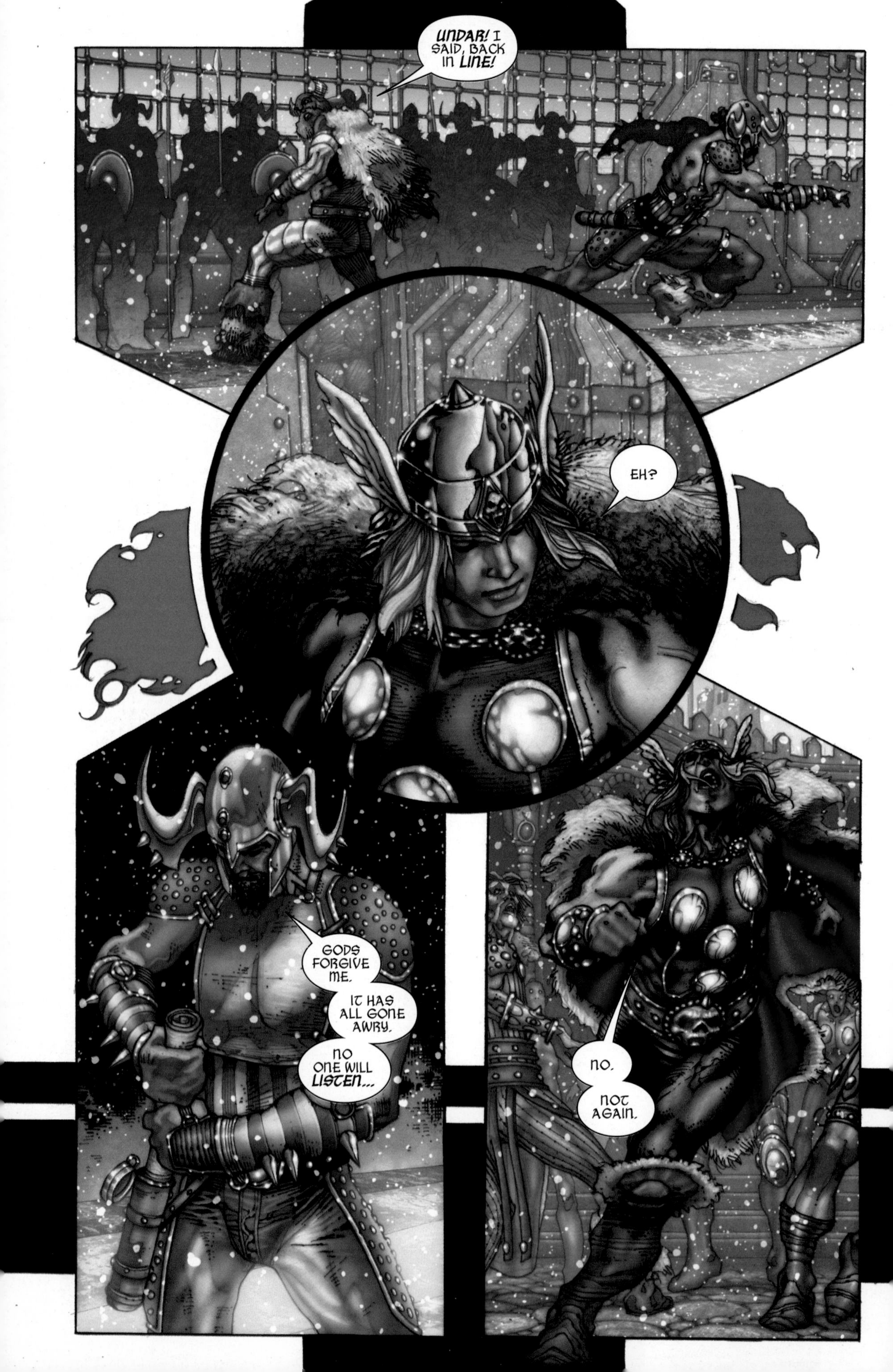
UNDAR! I SAID, BACK IN LINE!
EH?
GODS FORGIVE ME.
IT HAS ALL GONE AWRY.
NO ONE WILL LISTEN...
NO.
NOT AGAIN.

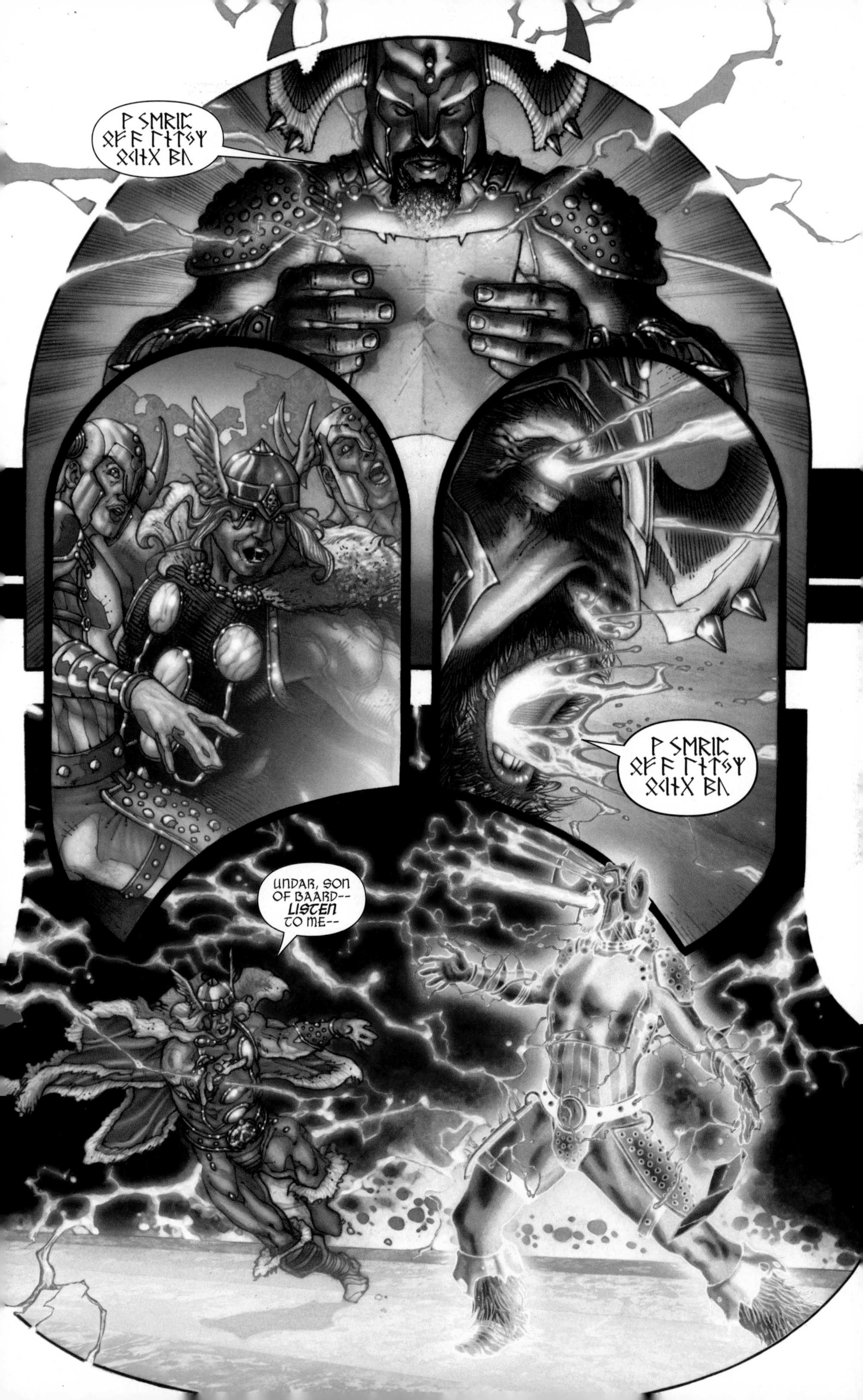
UNDAR, SON OF BAARD-- LISTEN TO ME--

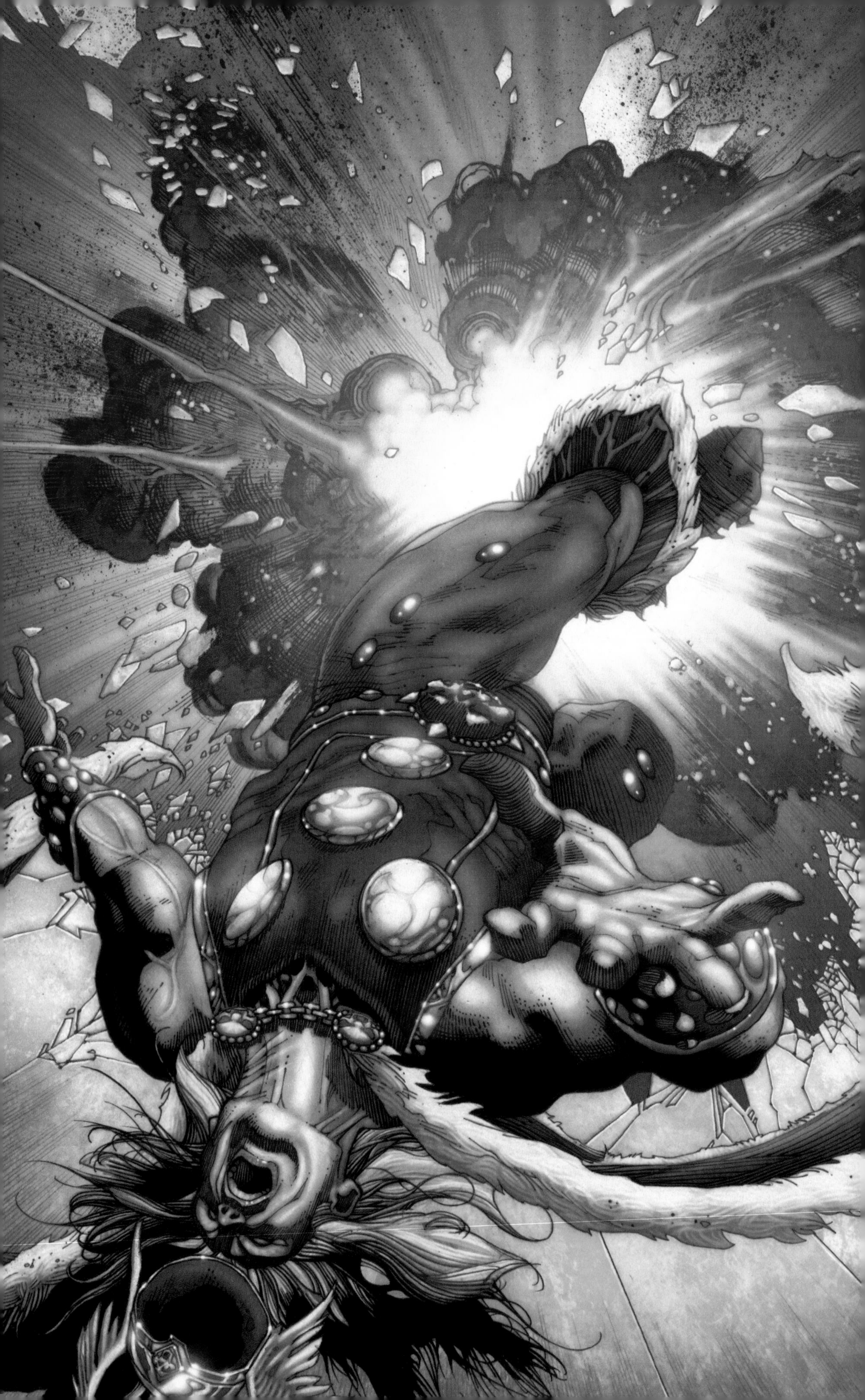

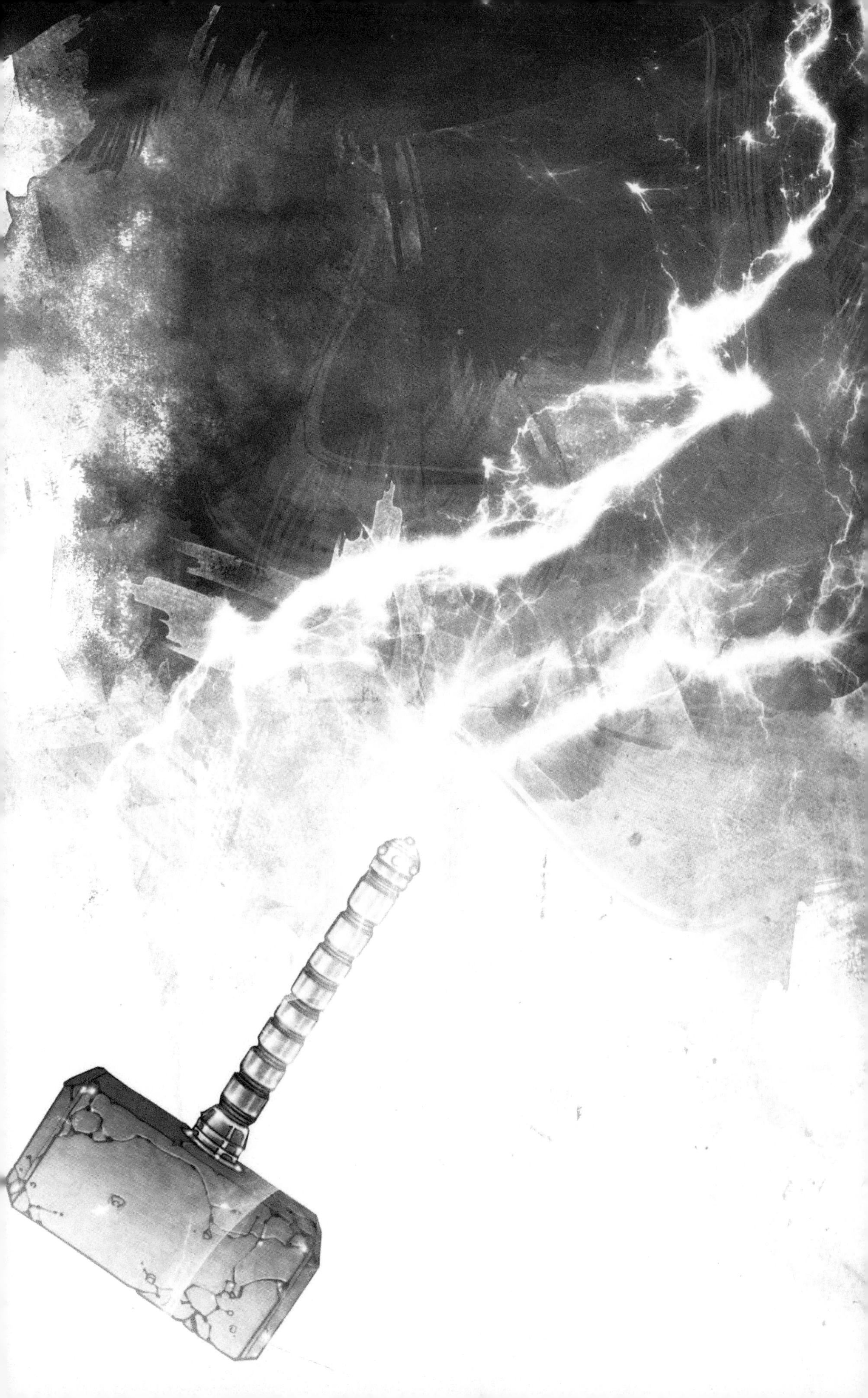

5

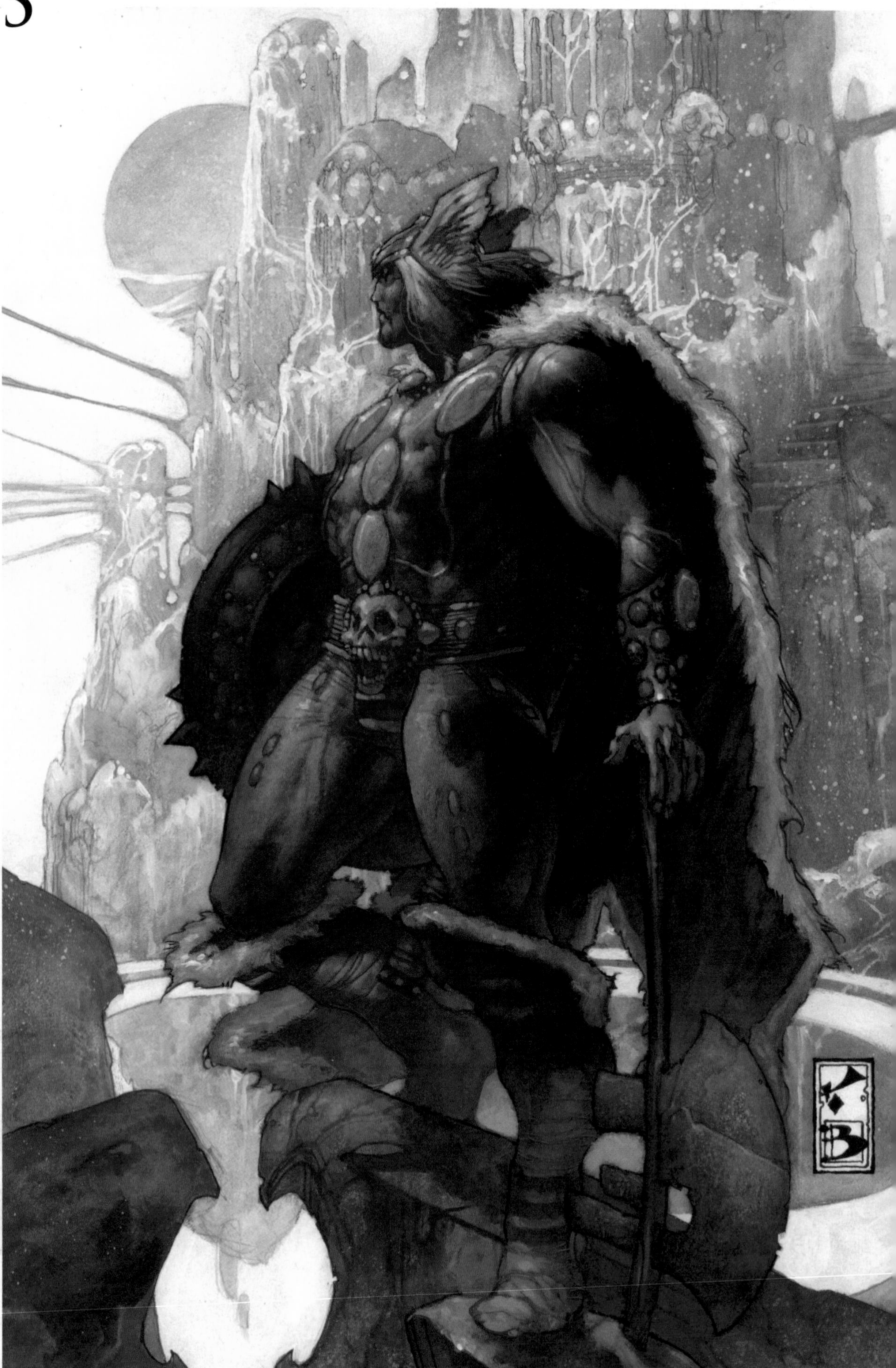

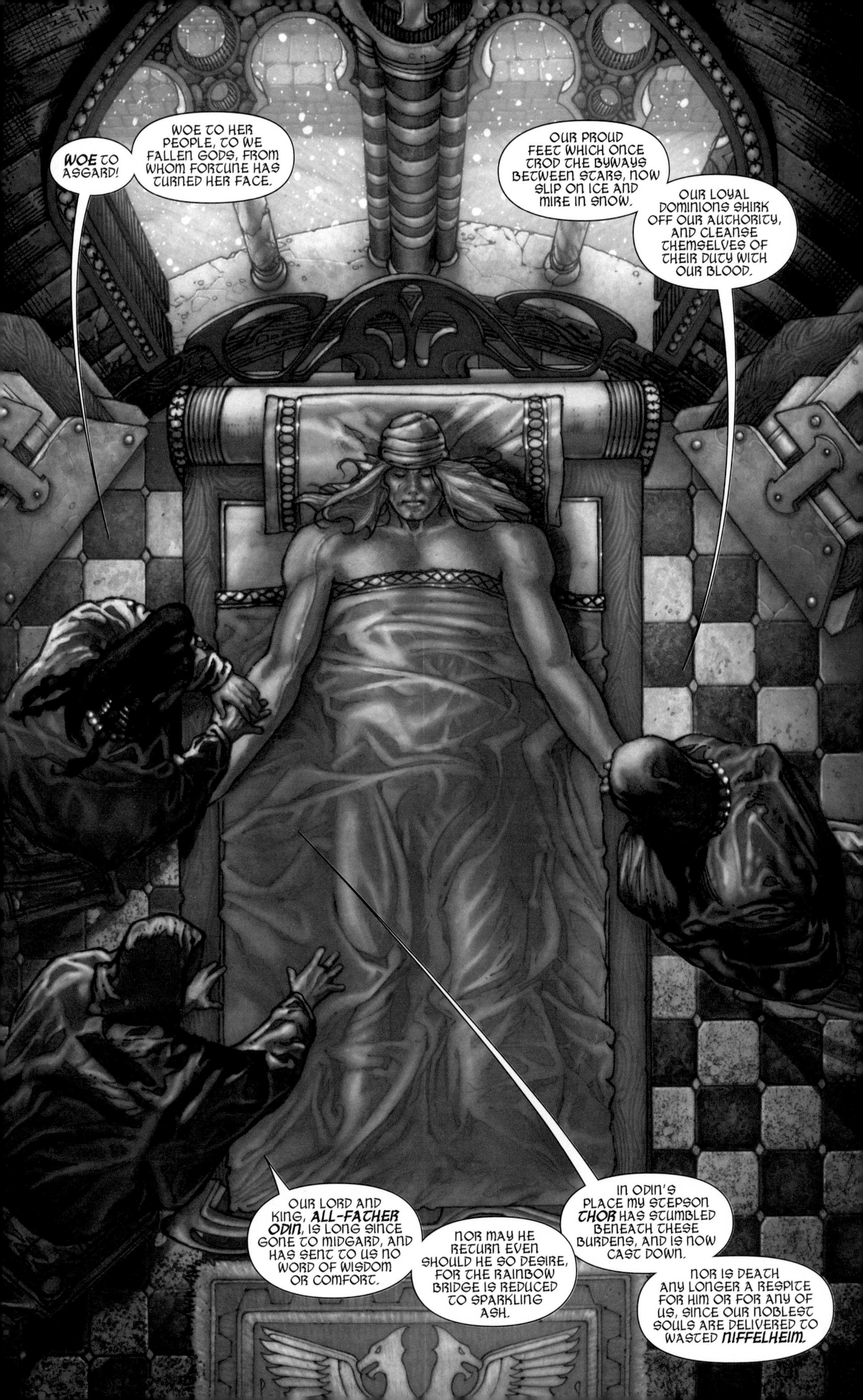
WOE TO ASGARD!
WOE TO HER PEOPLE, TO WE FALLEN GODS, FROM WHOM FORTUNE HAS TURNED HER FACE.
OUR PROUD FEET WHICH ONCE TROD THE BYWAYS BETWEEN STARS, NOW SLIP ON ICE AND MIRE IN SNOW.
OUR LOYAL DOMINIONS SHIRK OFF OUR AUTHORITY, AND CLEANSE THEMSELVES OF THEIR DUTY WITH OUR BLOOD.
OUR LORD AND KING, ALL-FATHER ODIN, IS LONG SINCE GONE TO MIDGARD, AND HAS SENT TO US NO WORD OF WISDOM OR COMFORT.
NOR MAY HE RETURN EVEN SHOULD HE SO DESIRE, FOR THE RAINBOW BRIDGE IS REDUCED TO SPARKLING ASH.
IN ODIN'S PLACE MY STEPSON THOR HAS STUMBLED BENEATH THESE BURDENS, AND IS NOW CAST DOWN.
NOR IS DEATH ANY LONGER A RESPITE FOR HIM OR FOR ANY OF US, SINCE OUR NOBLEST SOULS ARE DELIVERED TO WASTED NIFFELHEIM.

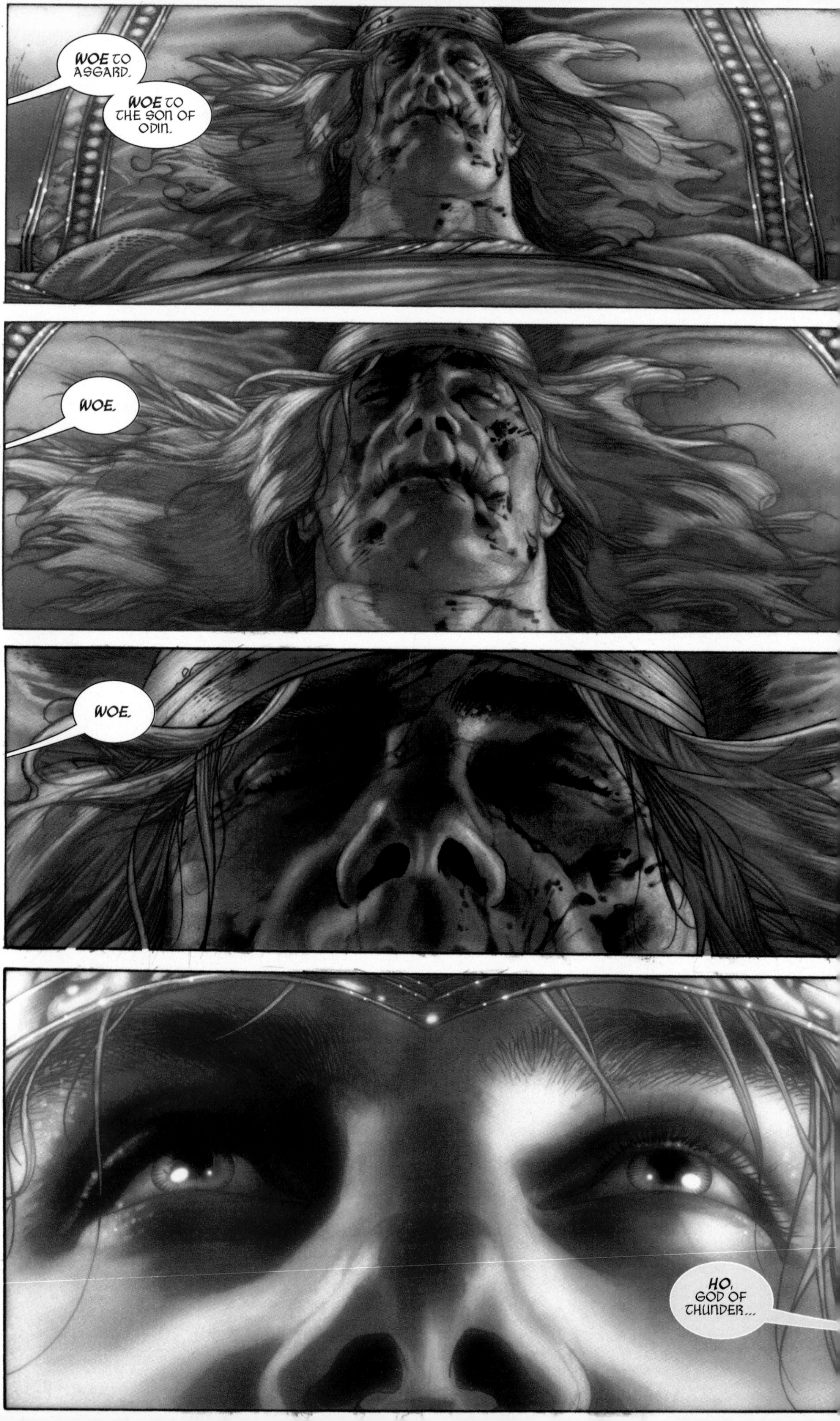
WOE TO ASGARD.
WOE TO THE SON OF ODIN.
WOE.
WOE.
HO, GOD OF THUNDER...

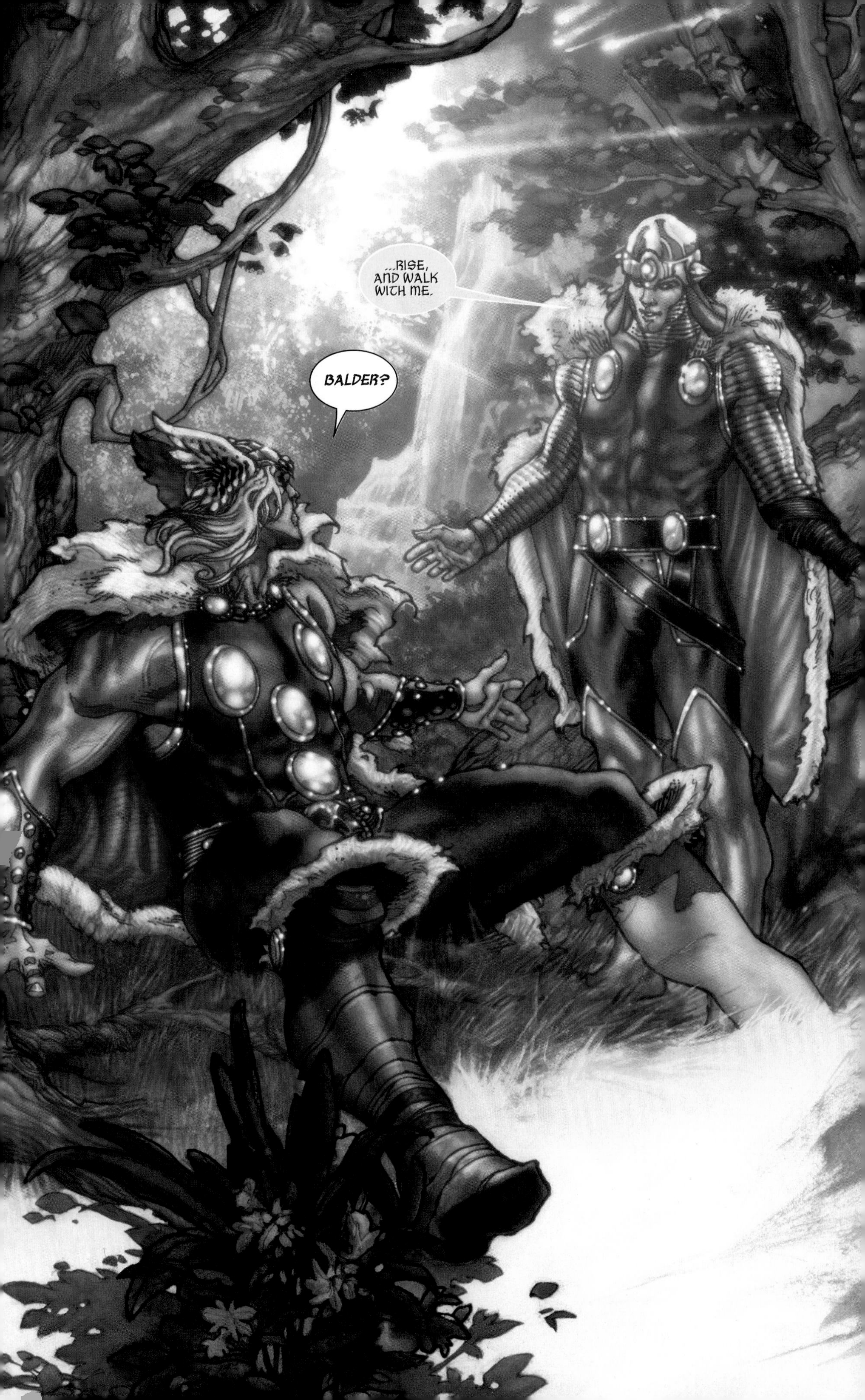
...RISE, AND WALK WITH ME.
BALDER?

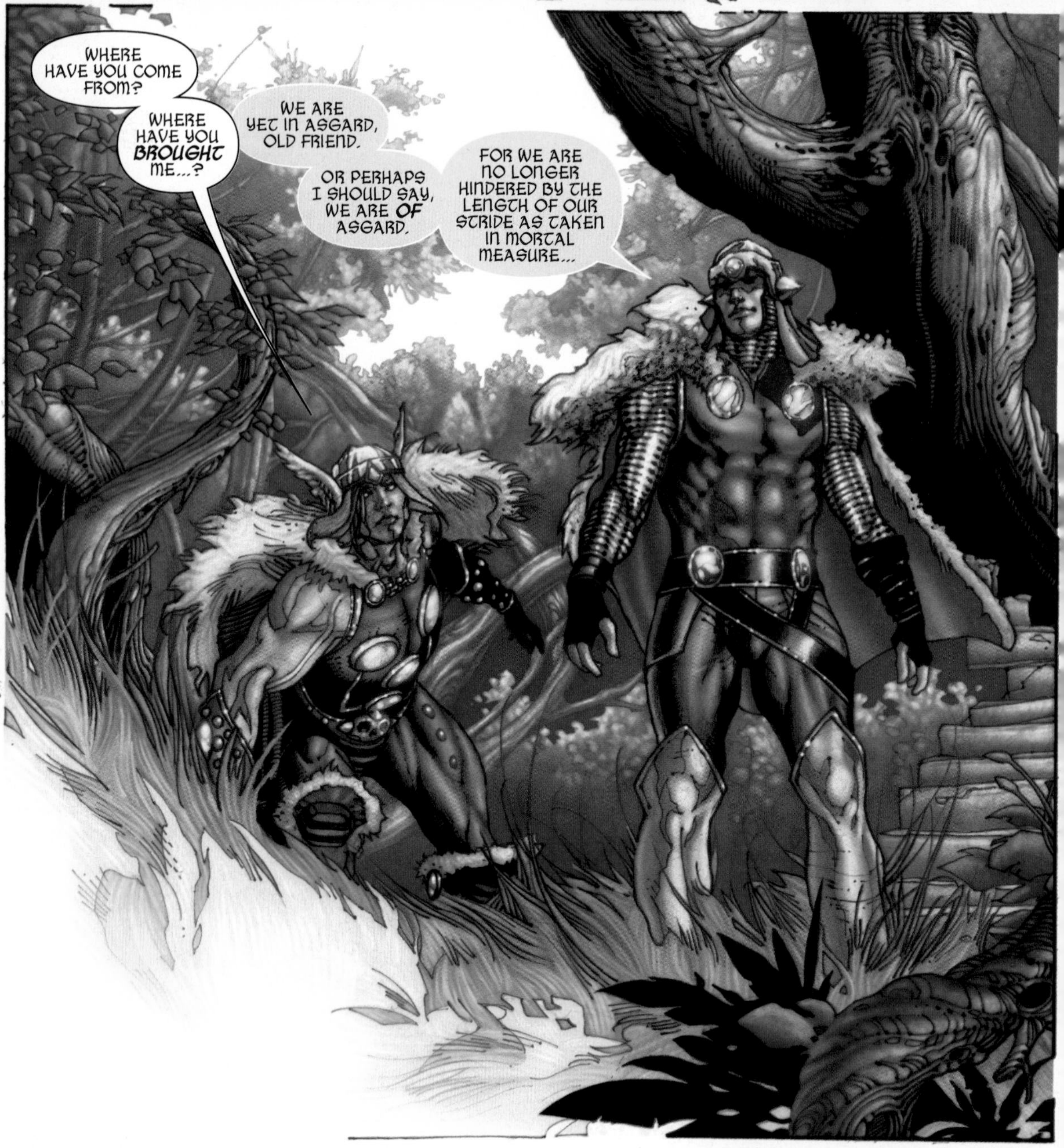
WHERE HAVE YOU COME FROM?
WHERE HAVE YOU BROUGHT ME...?
WE ARE YET IN ASGARD, OLD FRIEND.
OR PERHAPS I SHOULD SAY, WE ARE OF ASGARD.
FOR WE ARE NO LONGER HINDERED BY THE LENGTH OF OUR STRIDE AS TAKEN IN MORTAL MEASURE...

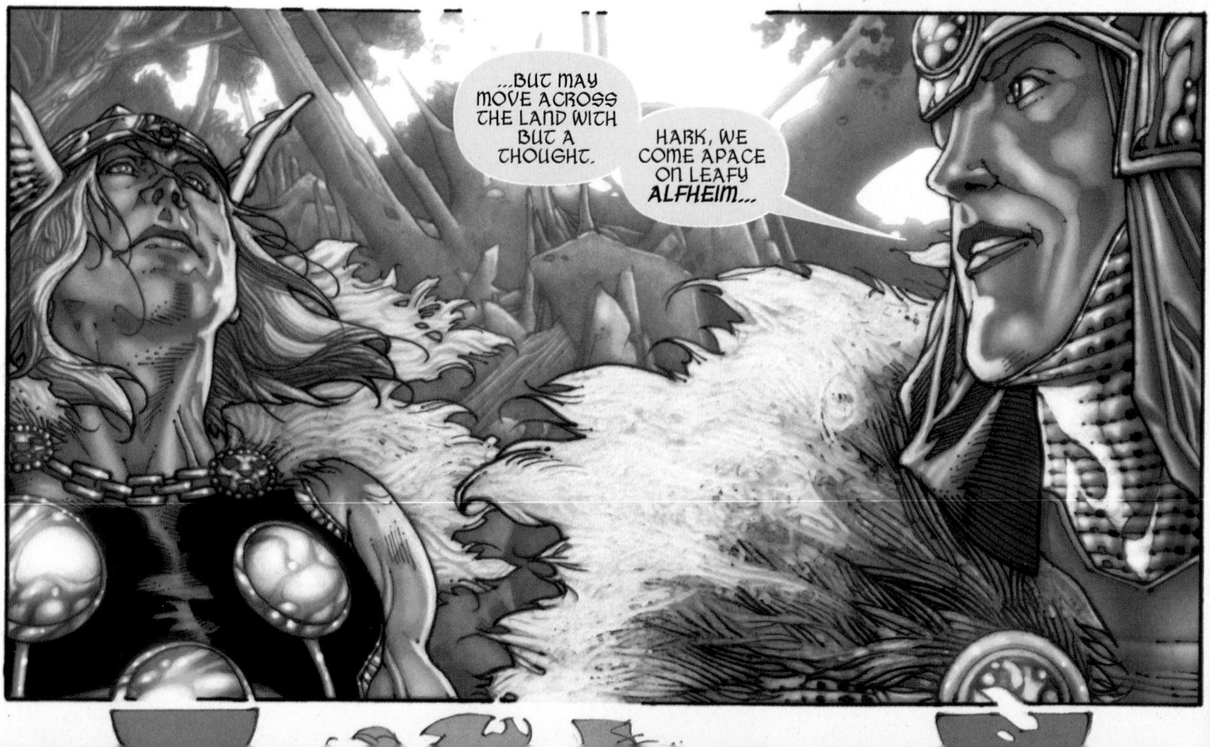
...BUT MAY MOVE ACROSS THE LAND WITH BUT A THOUGHT.
HARK, WE COME APACE ON LEAFY ALFHEIM...

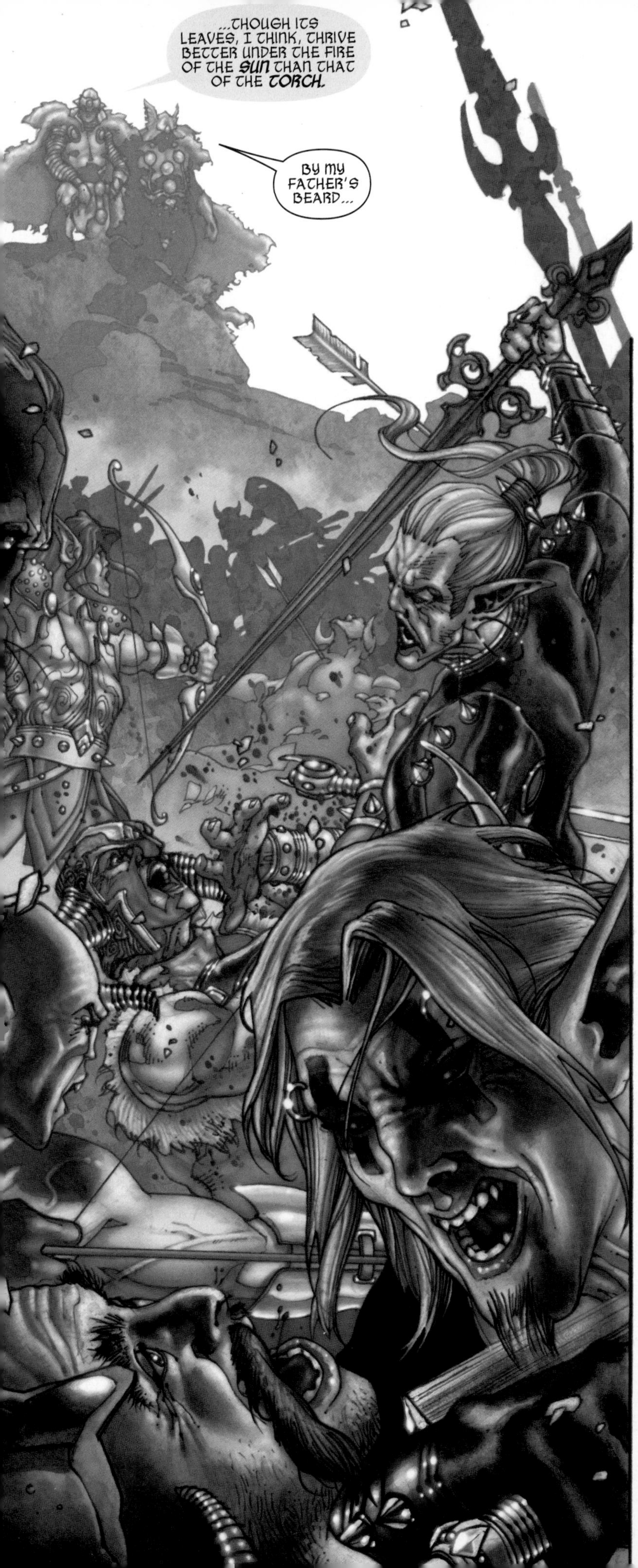
...THOUGH ITS LEAVES, I THINK, THRIVE BETTER UNDER THE FIRE OF THE SUN THAN THAT OF THE TORCH.
BY MY FATHER'S BEARD...

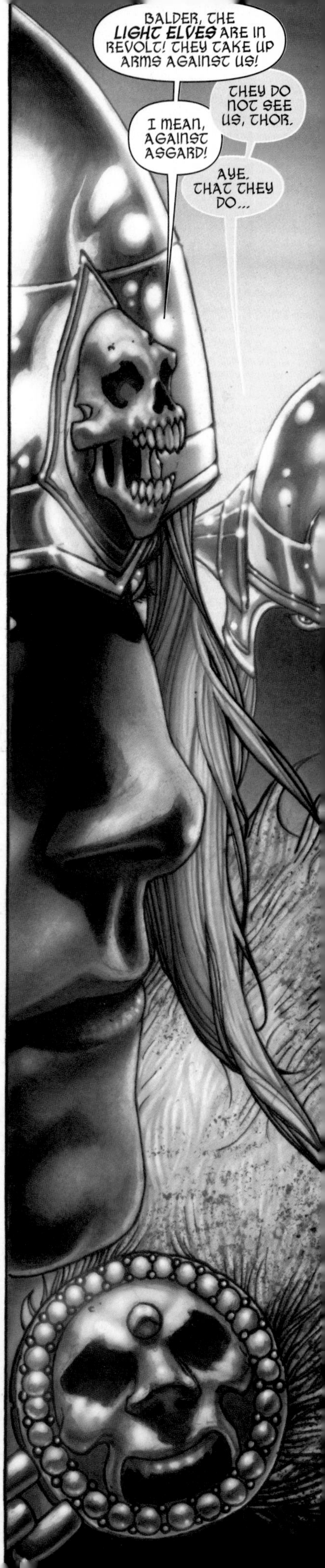
BALDER, THE LIGHT ELVES ARE IN REVOLT! THEY TAKE UP ARMS AGAINST US!
I MEAN, AGAINST ASGARD!
THEY DO NOT SEE US, THOR.
AYE. THAT THEY DO...

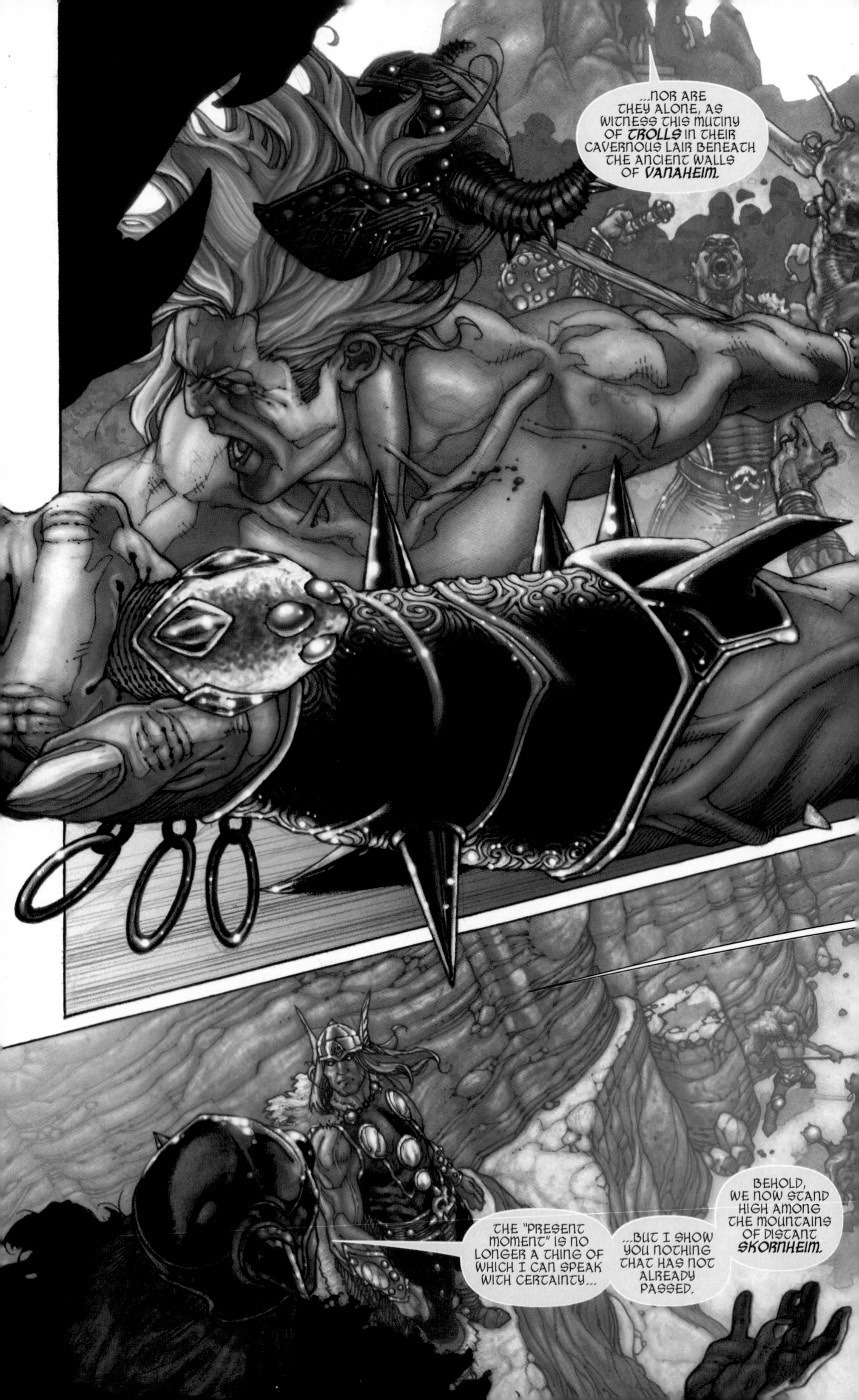
...NOR ARE THEY ALONE, AS WITNESS THIS MUTINY OF TROLLS IN THEIR CAVERNOUS LAIR BENEATH THE ANCIENT WALLS OF VANAHEIM.
BEHOLD, WE NOW STAND HIGH AMONG THE MOUNTAINS OF DISTANT SKORNHEIM.
...BUT I SHOW YOU NOTHING THAT HAS NOT ALREADY PASSED.
THE "PRESENT MOMENT" IS NO LONGER A THING OF WHICH I CAN SPEAK WITH CERTAINTY...

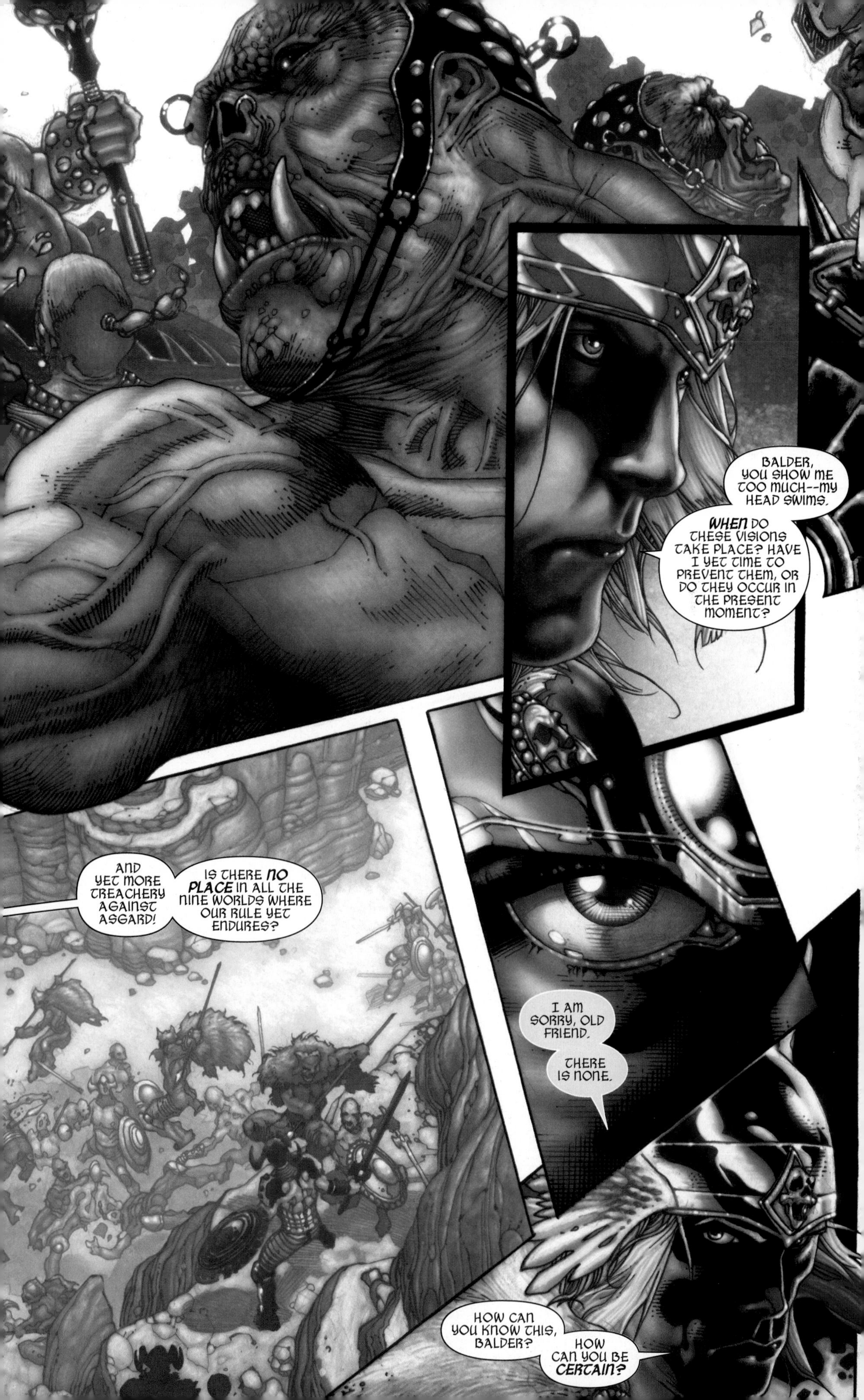

BALDER, YOU SHOW ME TOO MUCH--MY HEAD SWIMS.
WHEN DO THESE VISIONS TAKE PLACE? HAVE I YET TIME TO PREVENT THEM, OR DO THEY OCCUR IN THE PRESENT MOMENT?
AND YET MORE TREACHERY AGAINST ASGARD!
IS THERE NO PLACE IN ALL THE NINE WORLDS WHERE OUR RULE YET ENDURES?
I AM SORRY, OLD FRIEND.
THERE IS NONE.
HOW CAN YOU KNOW THIS, BALDER?
HOW CAN YOU BE CERTAIN?

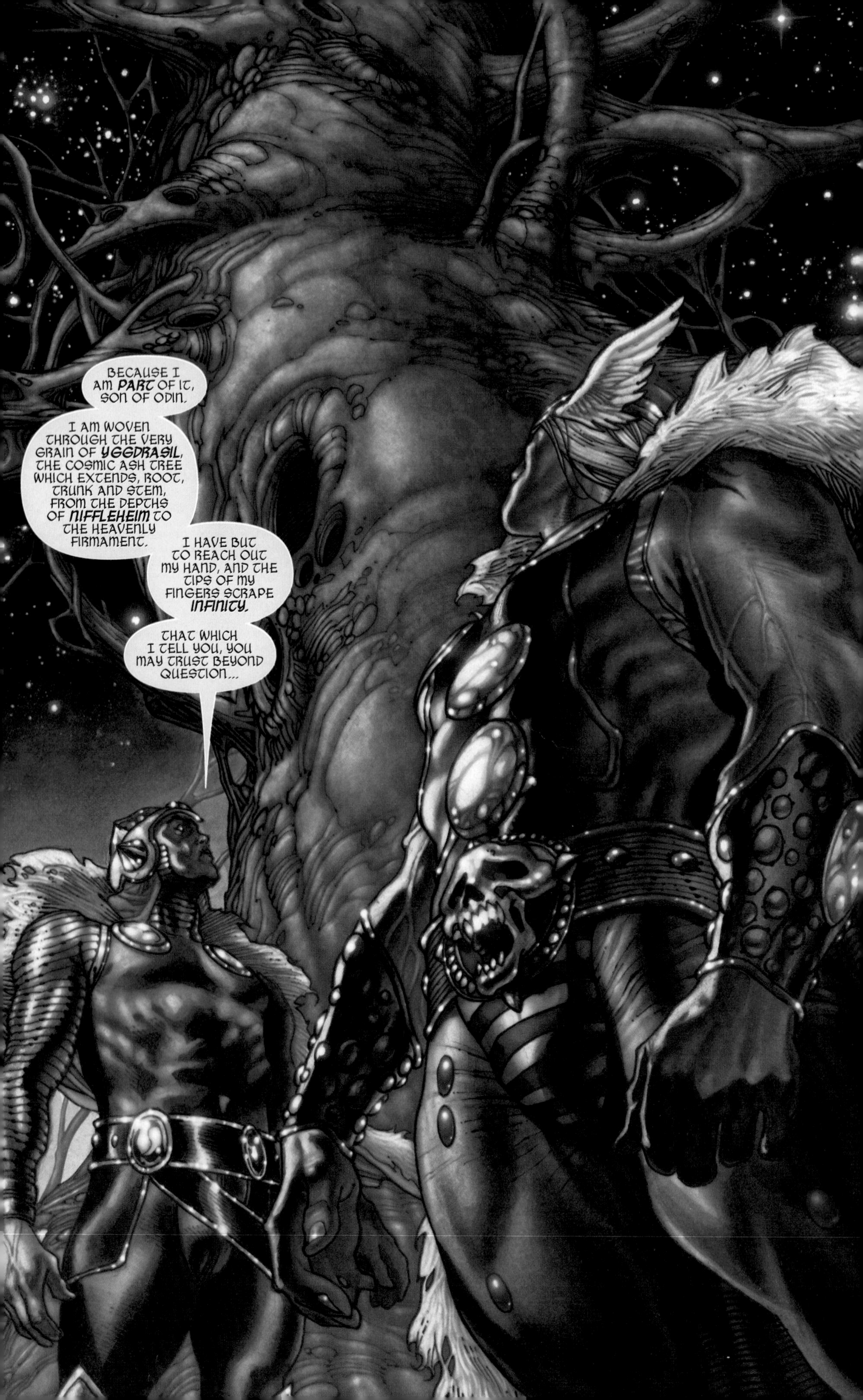
BECAUSE I AM PART OF IT, SON OF ODIN.
I AM WOVEN THROUGH THE VERY GRAIN OF YGGDRASIL, THE COSMIC ASH TREE WHICH EXTENDS, ROOT, TRUNK AND STEM, FROM THE DEPTHS OF NIFFLEHEIM TO THE HEAVENLY FIRMAMENT.
I HAVE BUT TO REACH OUT MY HAND, AND THE TIPS OF MY FINGERS SCRAPE INFINITY.
THAT WHICH I TELL YOU, YOU MAY TRUST BEYOND QUESTION...

...WERE OUR LONG *FRIENDSHIP* NOT SUFFICIENT GUARANTEE.

BALDER...

...*WHAT ARE YOU?*

I AM *LIFE.*

BUT... YOU *DIED.*

I AM DEATH AS WELL.

I AM THE *CYCLE,* THOR...

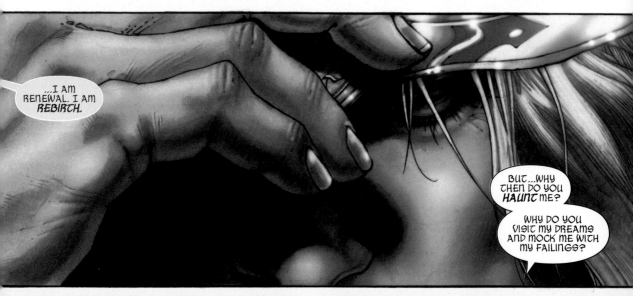

...I AM *RENEWAL.* I AM *REBIRTH.*

BUT...WHY THEN DO YOU *HAUNT* ME?

WHY DO YOU VISIT MY DREAMS AND MOCK ME WITH MY FAILINGS?

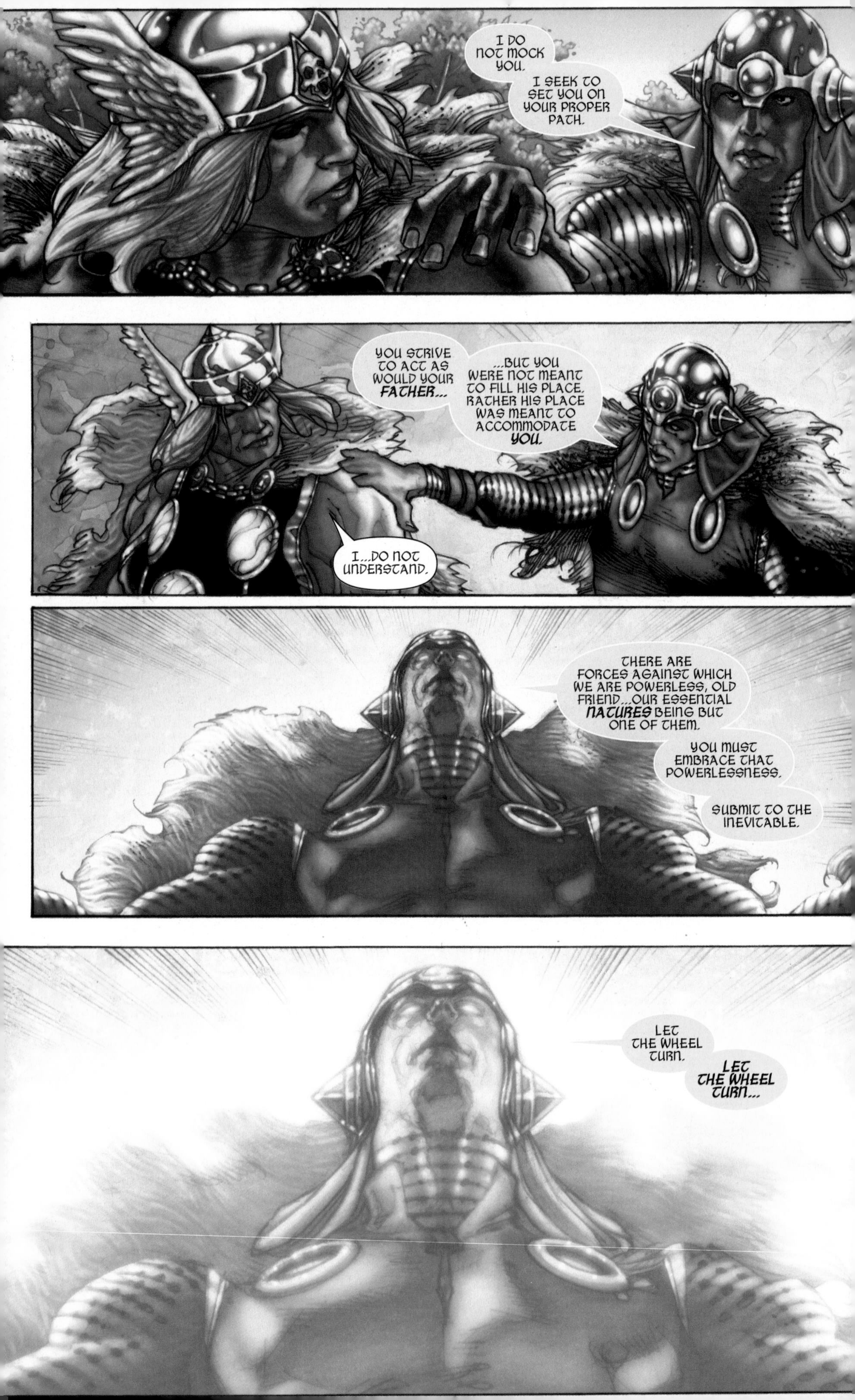
I DO NOT MOCK YOU.
I SEEK TO SET YOU ON YOUR PROPER PATH.
YOU STRIVE TO ACT AS WOULD YOUR FATHER...
...BUT YOU WERE NOT MEANT TO FILL HIS PLACE. RATHER HIS PLACE WAS MEANT TO ACCOMMODATE YOU.
I...DO NOT UNDERSTAND.
THERE ARE FORCES AGAINST WHICH WE ARE POWERLESS, OLD FRIEND...OUR ESSENTIAL NATURES BEING BUT ONE OF THEM.
YOU MUST EMBRACE THAT POWERLESSNESS.
SUBMIT TO THE INEVITABLE.
LET THE WHEEL TURN.
LET THE WHEEL TURN...

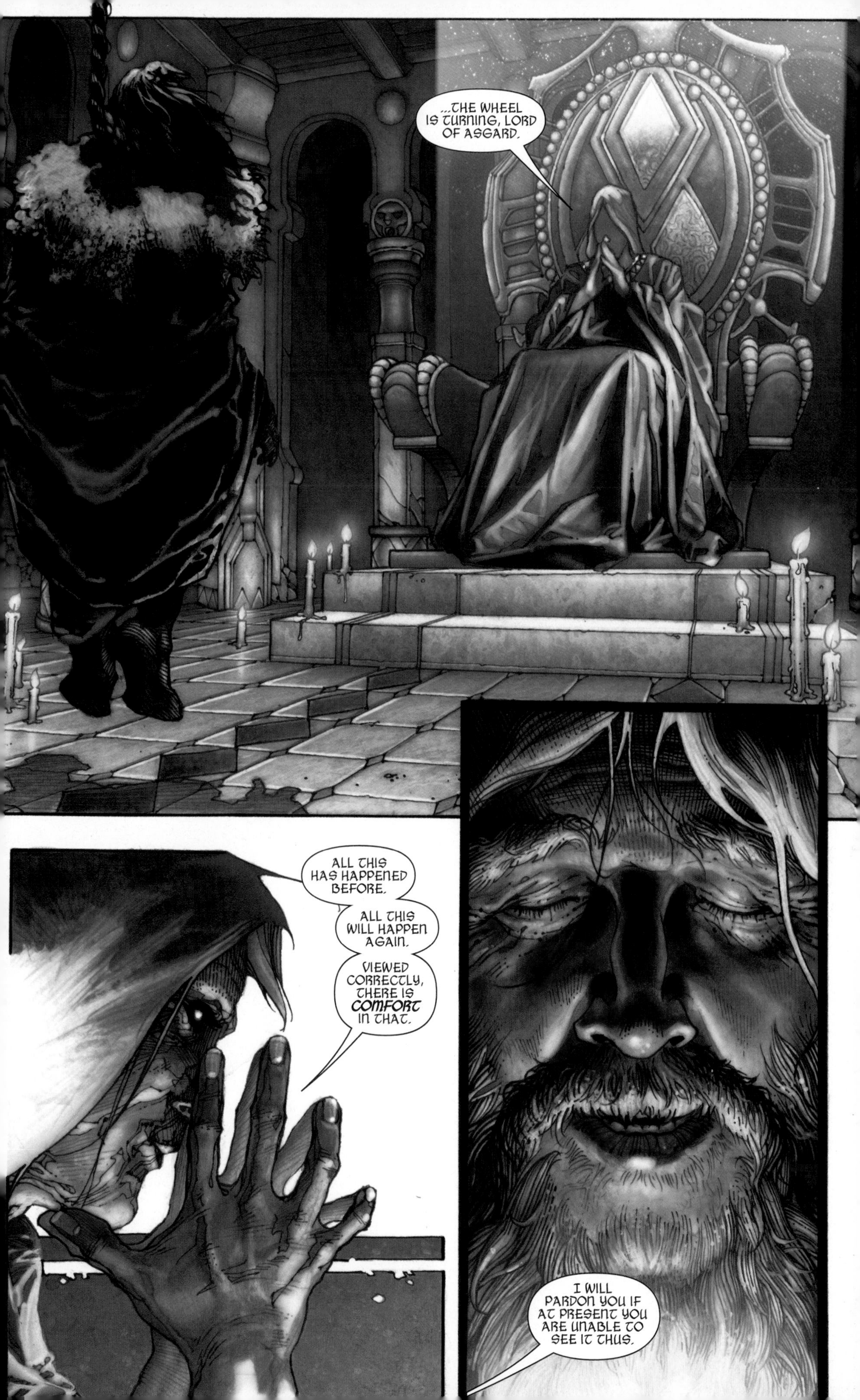
...THE WHEEL IS TURNING, LORD OF ASGARD.
ALL THIS HAS HAPPENED BEFORE.
ALL THIS WILL HAPPEN AGAIN.
VIEWED CORRECTLY, THERE IS **COMFORT** IN THAT.
I WILL PARDON YOU IF AT PRESENT YOU ARE UNABLE TO SEE IT THUS.

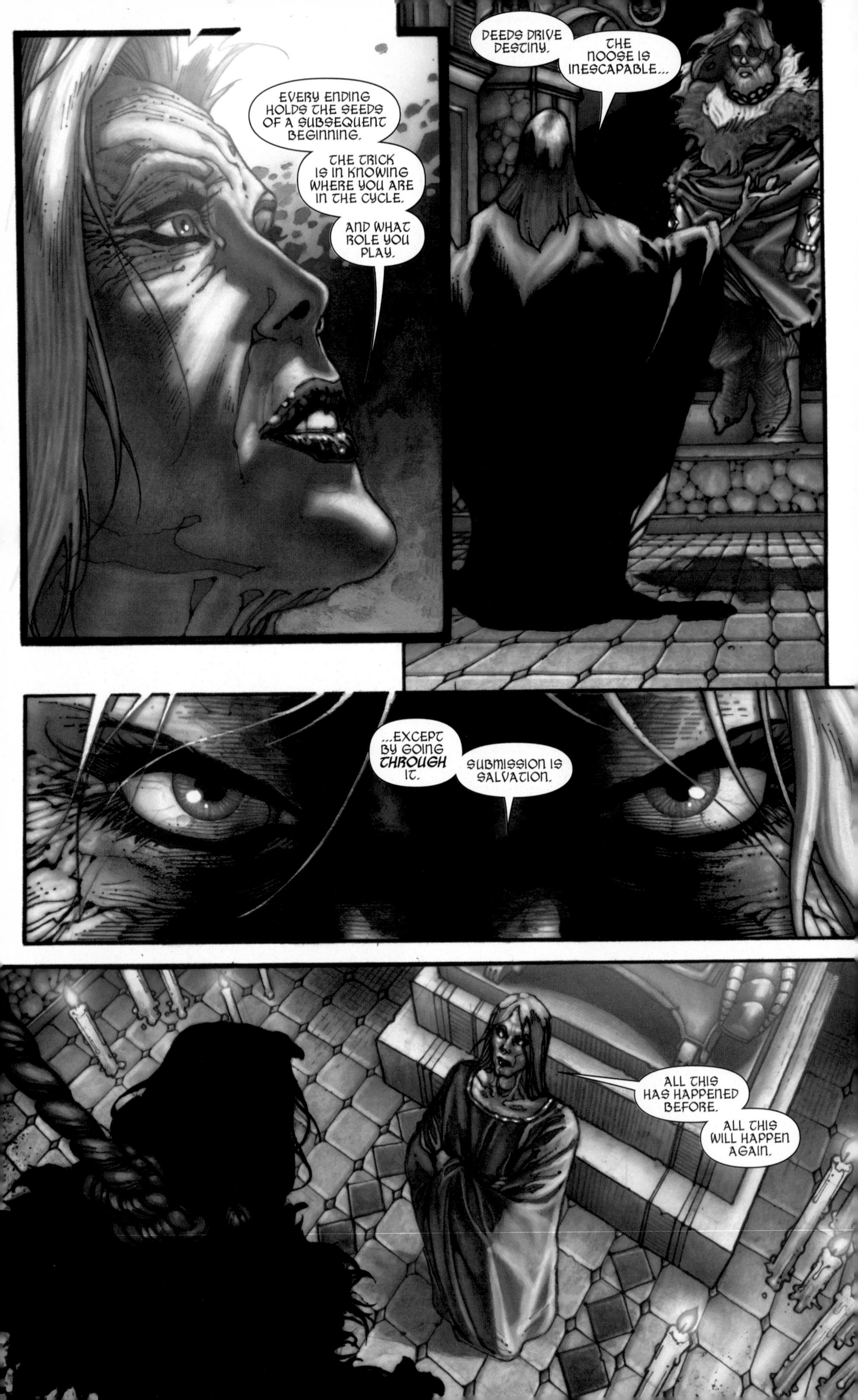
EVERY ENDING HOLDS THE SEEDS OF A SUBSEQUENT BEGINNING.
THE TRICK IS IN KNOWING WHERE YOU ARE IN THE CYCLE.
AND WHAT ROLE YOU PLAY.
DEEDS DRIVE DESTINY.
THE NOOSE IS INESCAPABLE...
...EXCEPT BY GOING **THROUGH** IT.
SUBMISSION IS SALVATION.
ALL THIS HAS HAPPENED BEFORE.
ALL THIS WILL HAPPEN AGAIN.

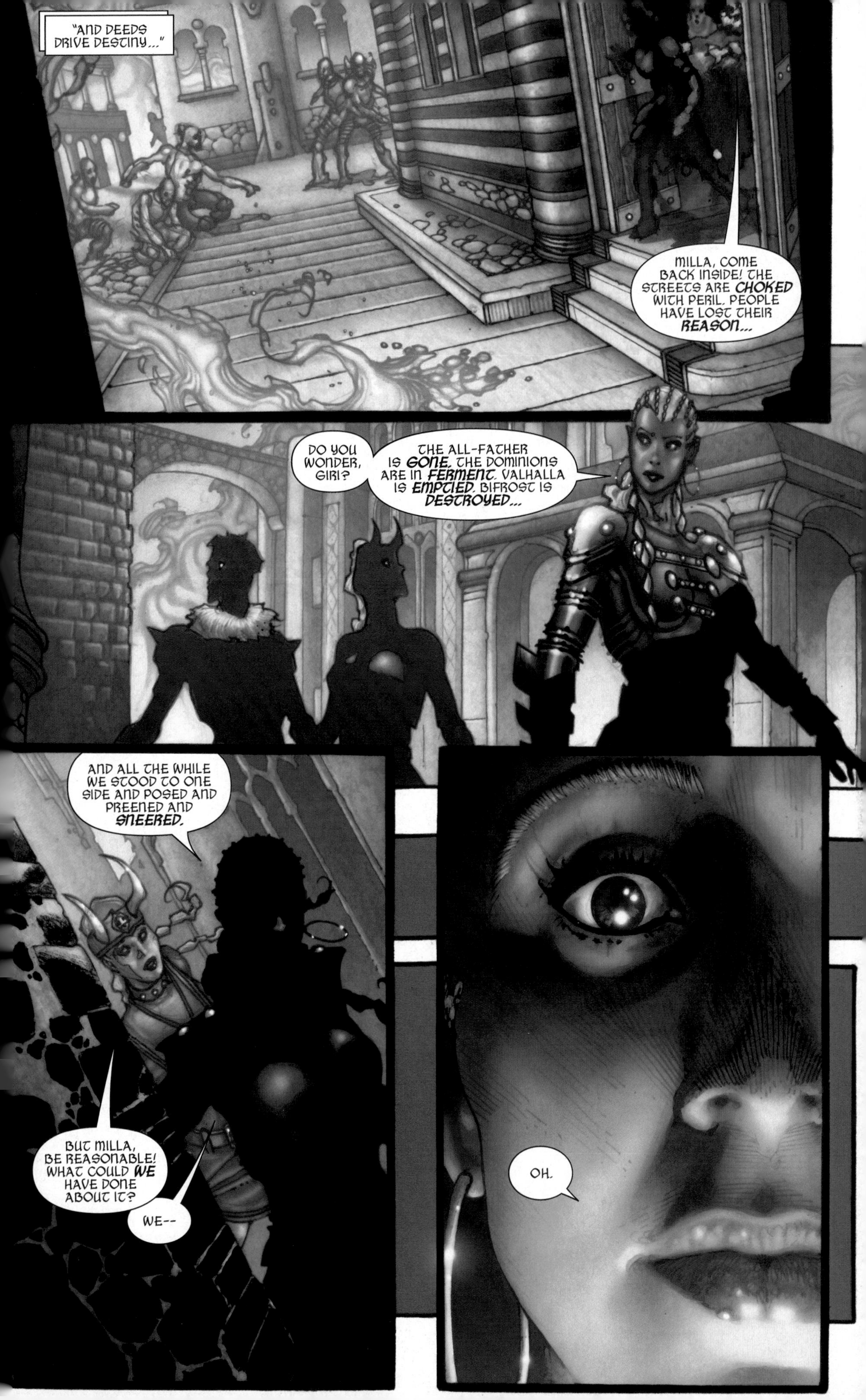
"AND DEEDS DRIVE DESTINY..."
MILLA, COME BACK INSIDE! THE STREETS ARE CHOKED WITH PERIL. PEOPLE HAVE LOST THEIR REASON...
DO YOU WONDER, GIRL?
THE ALL-FATHER IS GONE. THE DOMINIONS ARE IN FERMENT. VALHALLA IS EMPTIED. BIFROST IS DESTROYED...
AND ALL THE WHILE WE STOOD TO ONE SIDE AND POSED AND PREENED AND SNEERED.
BUT MILLA, BE REASONABLE! WHAT COULD WE HAVE DONE ABOUT IT?
WE--
OH.

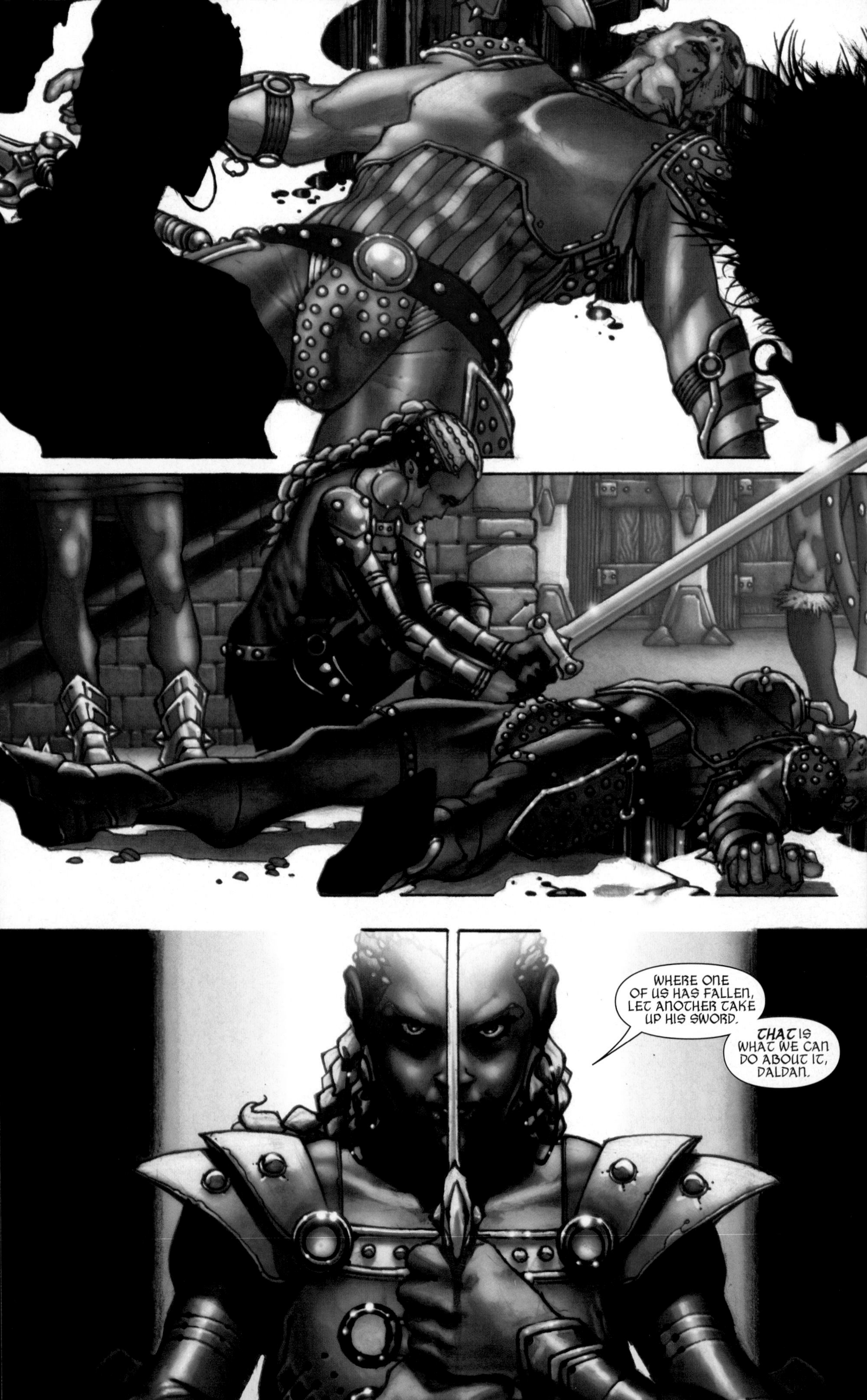
WHERE ONE OF US HAS FALLEN, LET ANOTHER TAKE UP HIS SWORD.
THAT IS WHAT WE CAN DO ABOUT IT, DALDAN.

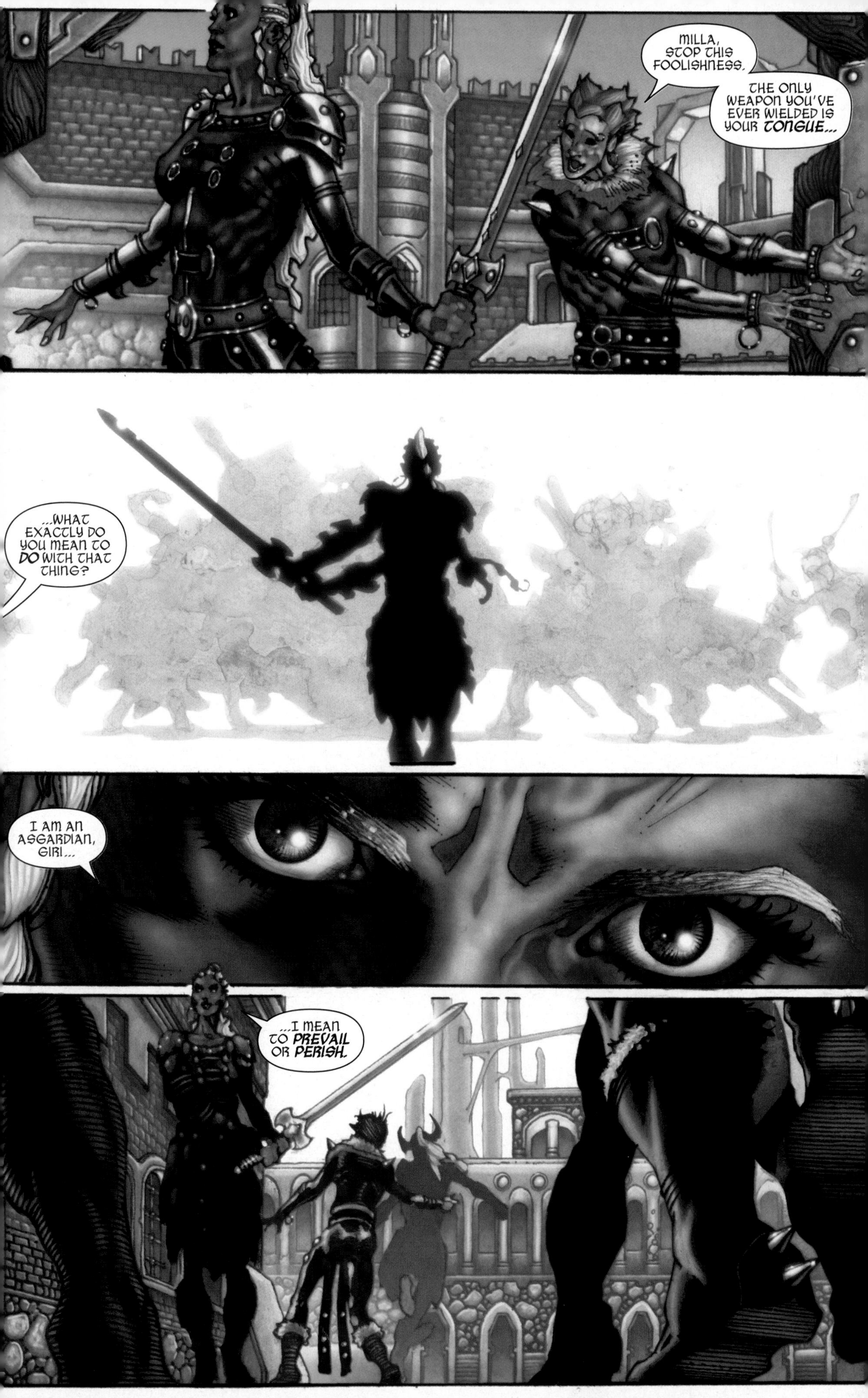
MILLA, STOP THIS FOOLISHNESS.
THE ONLY WEAPON YOU'VE EVER WIELDED IS YOUR TONGUE...
...WHAT EXACTLY DO YOU MEAN TO DO WITH THAT THING?
I AM AN ASGARDIAN, GIRL...
...I MEAN TO PREVAIL OR PERISH.

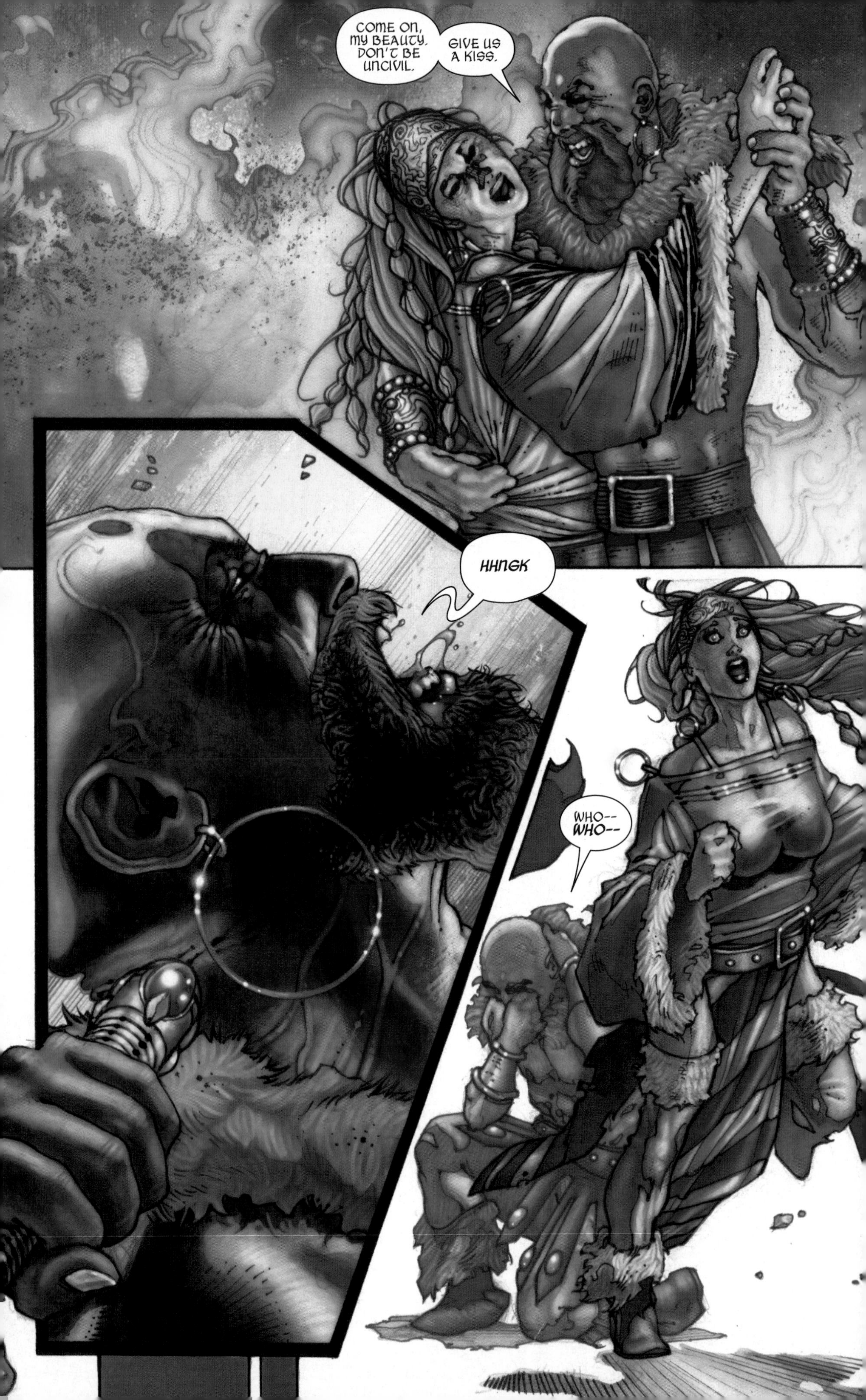
COME ON, MY BEAUTY, DON'T BE UNCIVIL.
GIVE US A KISS.
HHNGK
WHO-- WHO--

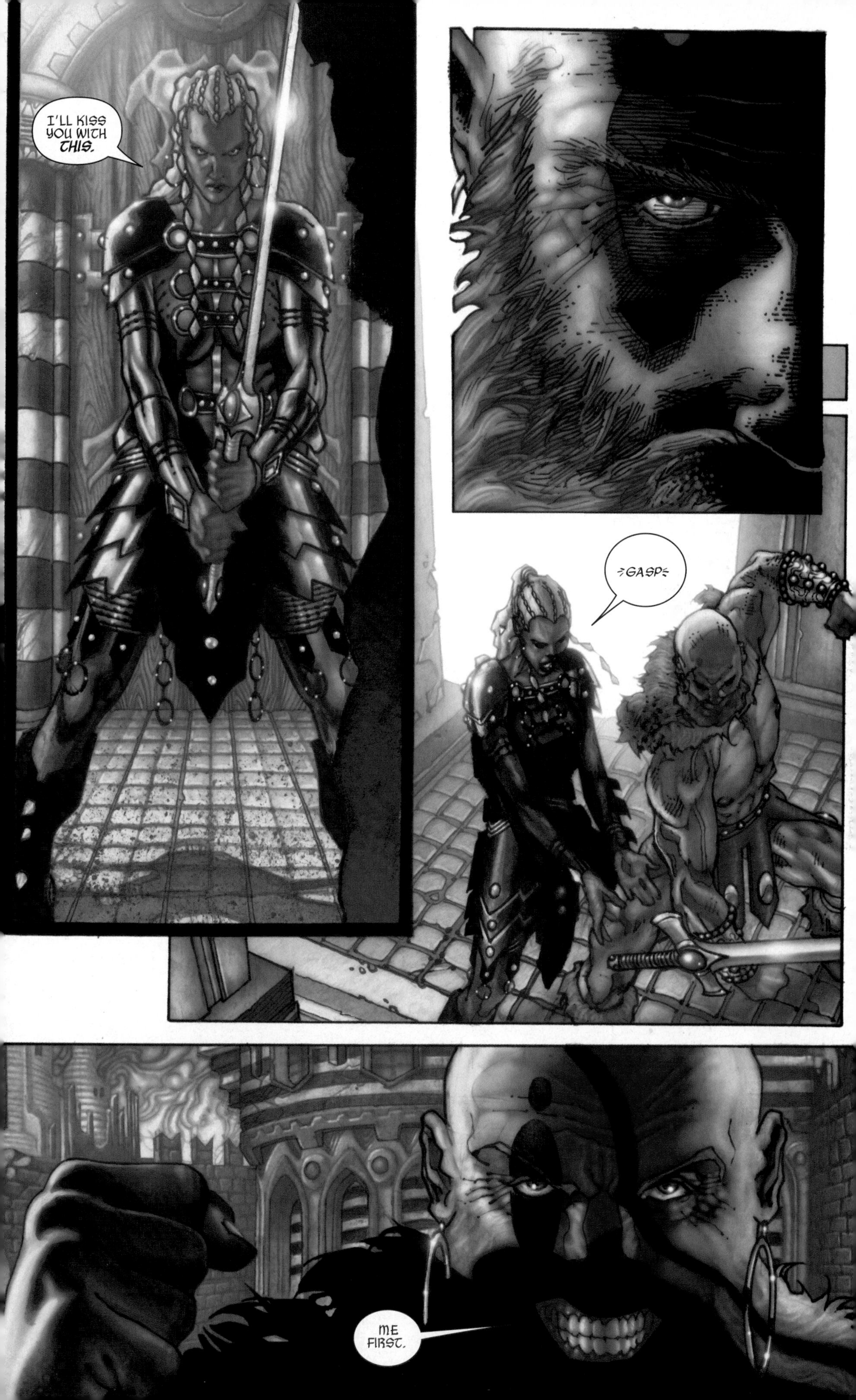
I'LL KISS YOU WITH THIS.
GASP
ME FIRST.

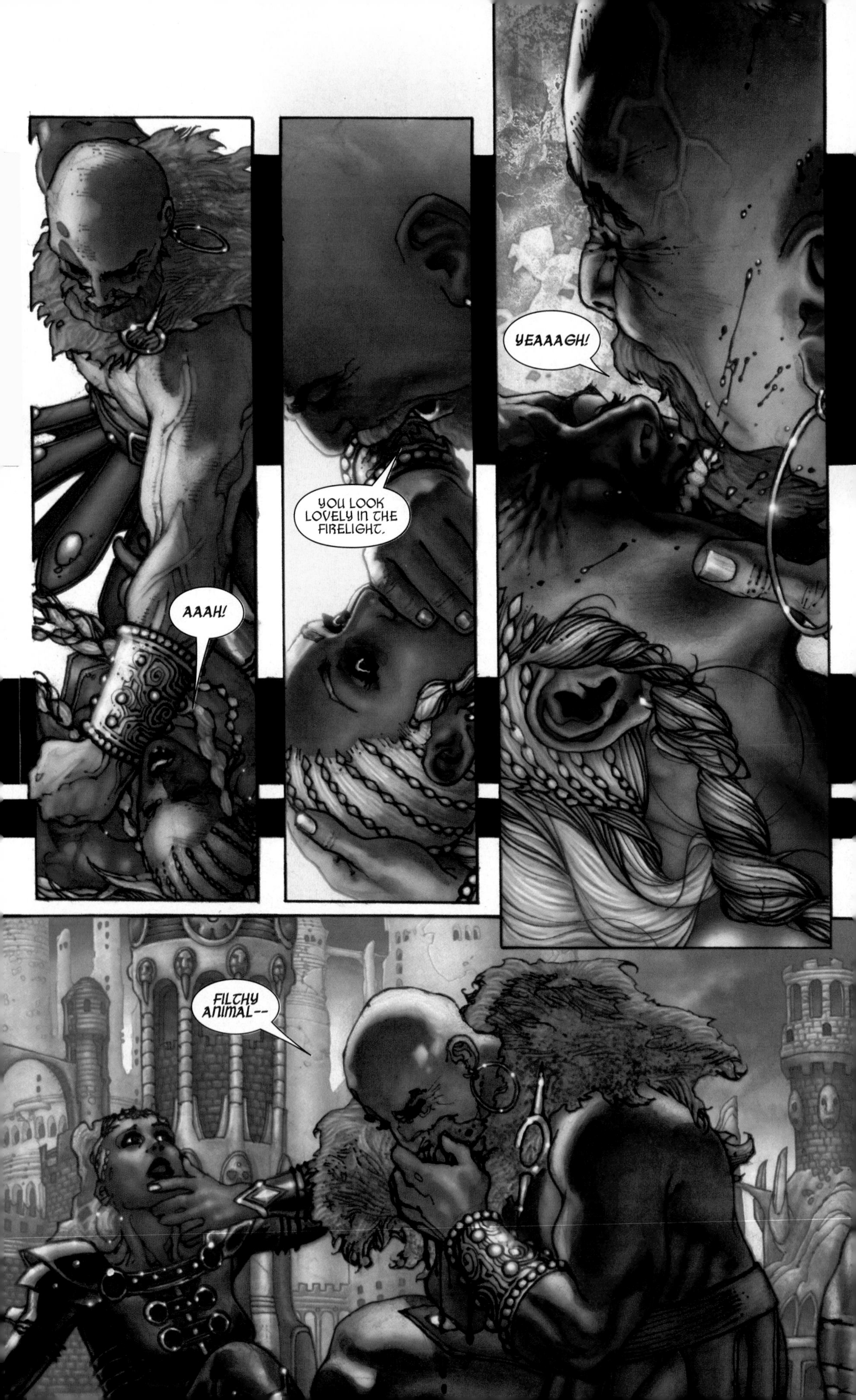
AAAH!
YOU LOOK LOVELY IN THE FIRELIGHT.
YEAAAGH!
FILTHY ANIMAL--

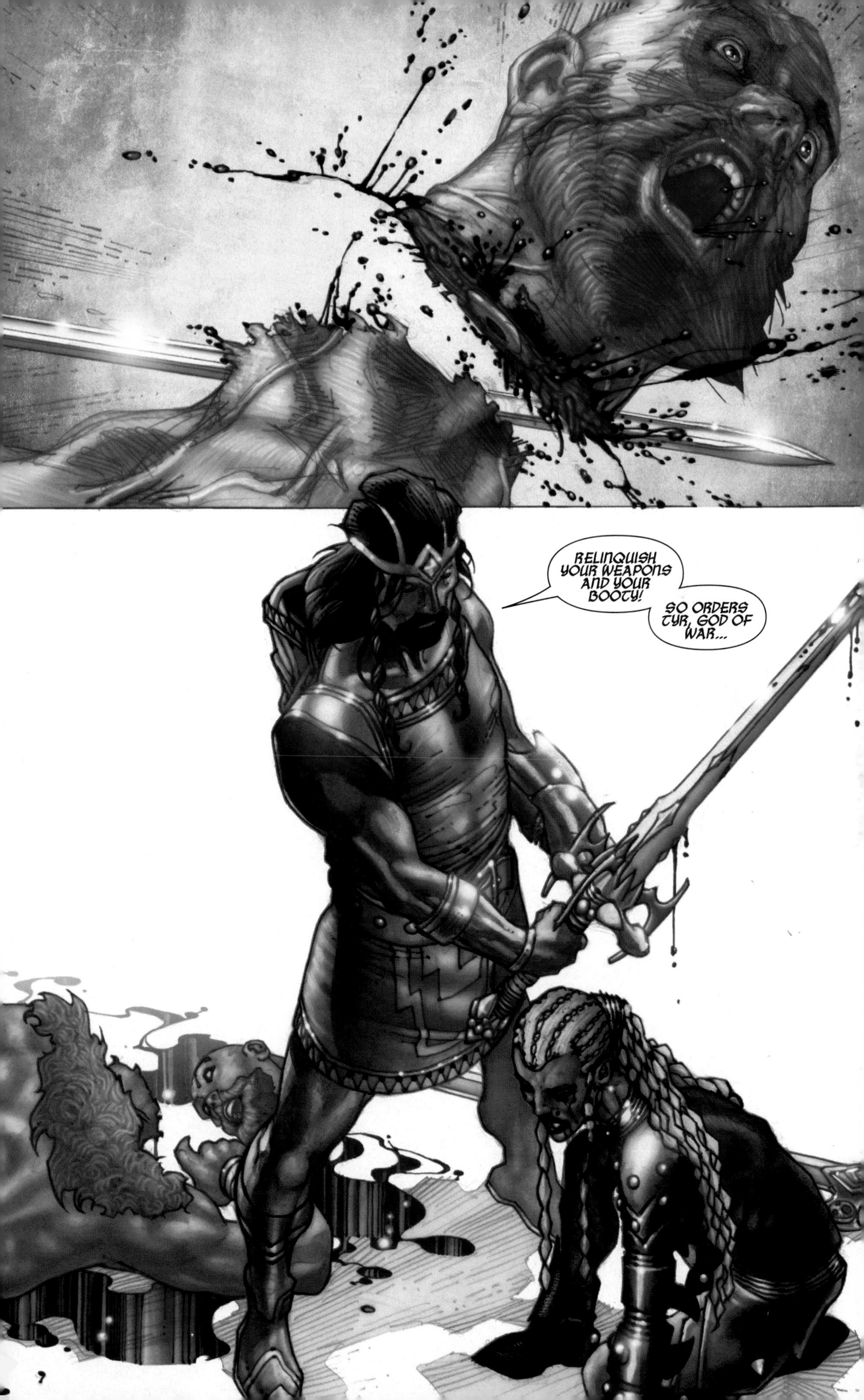
RELINQUISH YOUR WEAPONS AND YOUR BOOTY!
SO ORDERS TYR, GOD OF WAR...

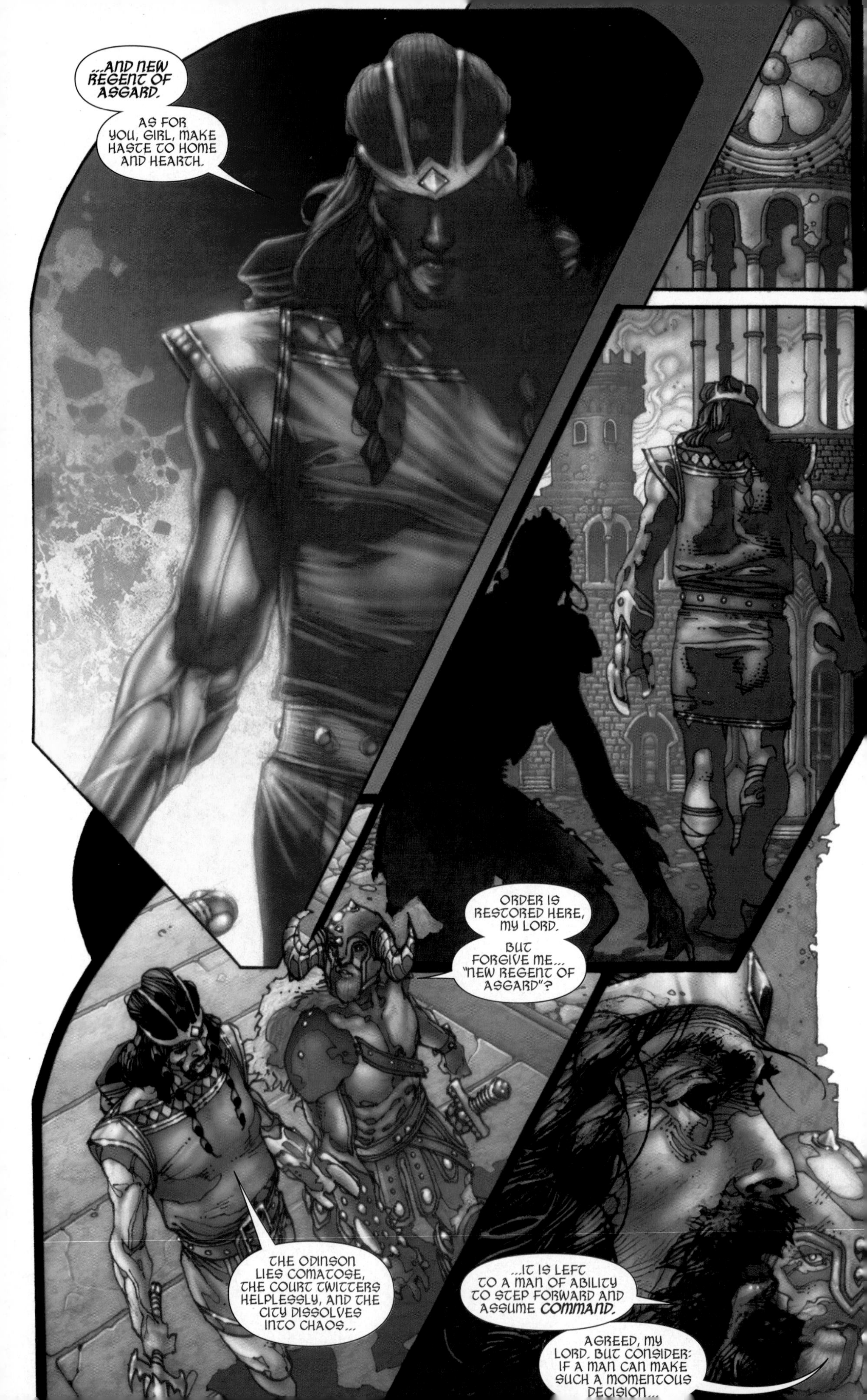
...AND NEW REGENT OF ASGARD.
AS FOR YOU, GIRL, MAKE HASTE TO HOME AND HEARTH.
ORDER IS RESTORED HERE, MY LORD.
BUT FORGIVE ME... "NEW REGENT OF ASGARD"?
THE ODINSON LIES COMATOSE, THE COURT TWITTERS HELPLESSLY, AND THE CITY DISSOLVES INTO CHAOS...
...IT IS LEFT TO A MAN OF ABILITY TO STEP FORWARD AND ASSUME COMMAND.
AGREED, MY LORD. BUT CONSIDER: IF A MAN CAN MAKE SUCH A MOMENTOUS DECISION...

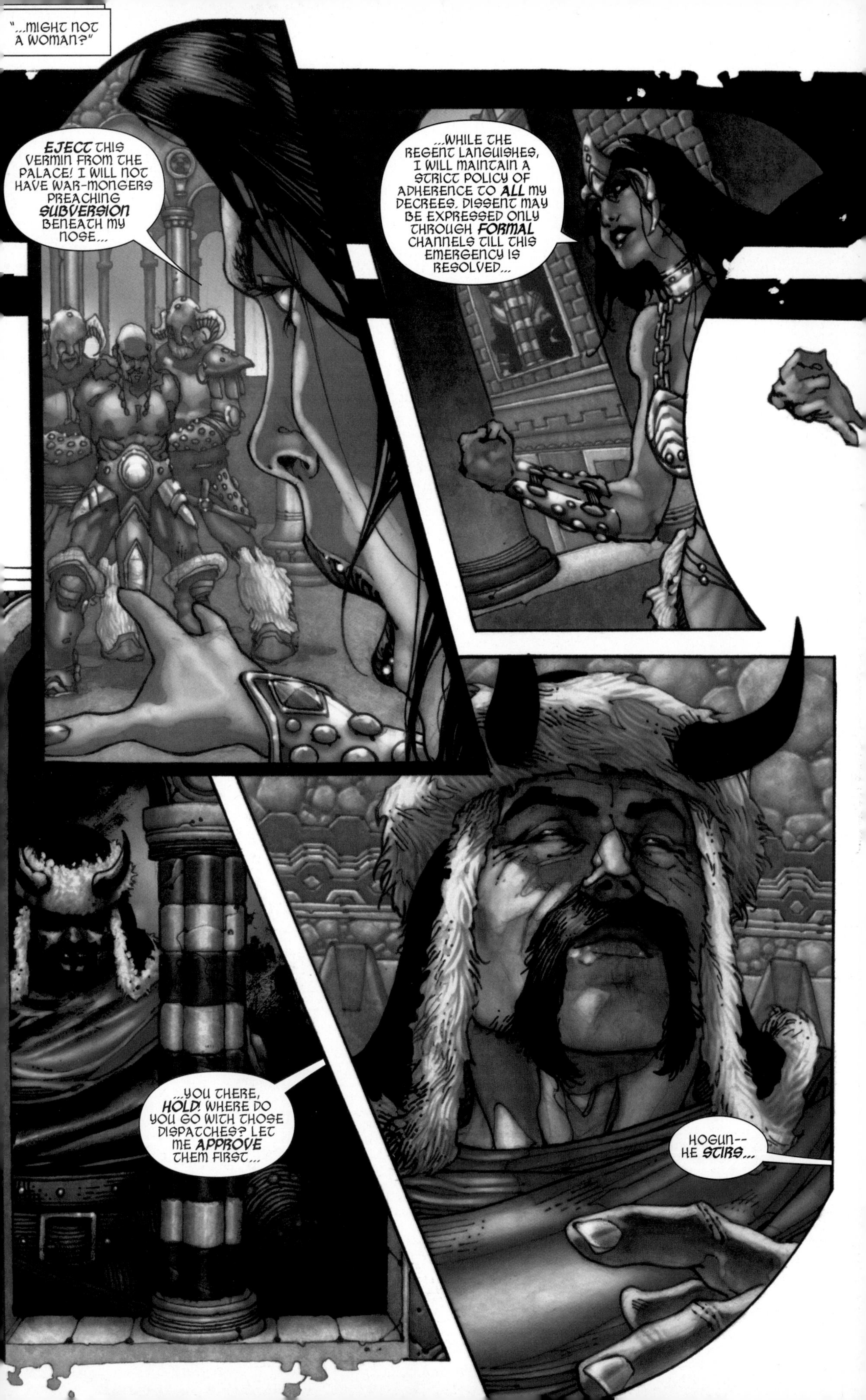
"...MIGHT NOT A WOMAN?"
EJECT THIS VERMIN FROM THE PALACE! I WILL NOT HAVE WAR-MONGERS PREACHING SUBVERSION BENEATH MY NOSE...
...WHILE THE REGENT LANGUISHES, I WILL MAINTAIN A STRICT POLICY OF ADHERENCE TO ALL MY DECREES. DISSENT MAY BE EXPRESSED ONLY THROUGH FORMAL CHANNELS TILL THIS EMERGENCY IS RESOLVED...
...YOU THERE, HOLD! WHERE DO YOU GO WITH THOSE DISPATCHES? LET ME APPROVE THEM FIRST...
HOGUN-- HE STIRS...

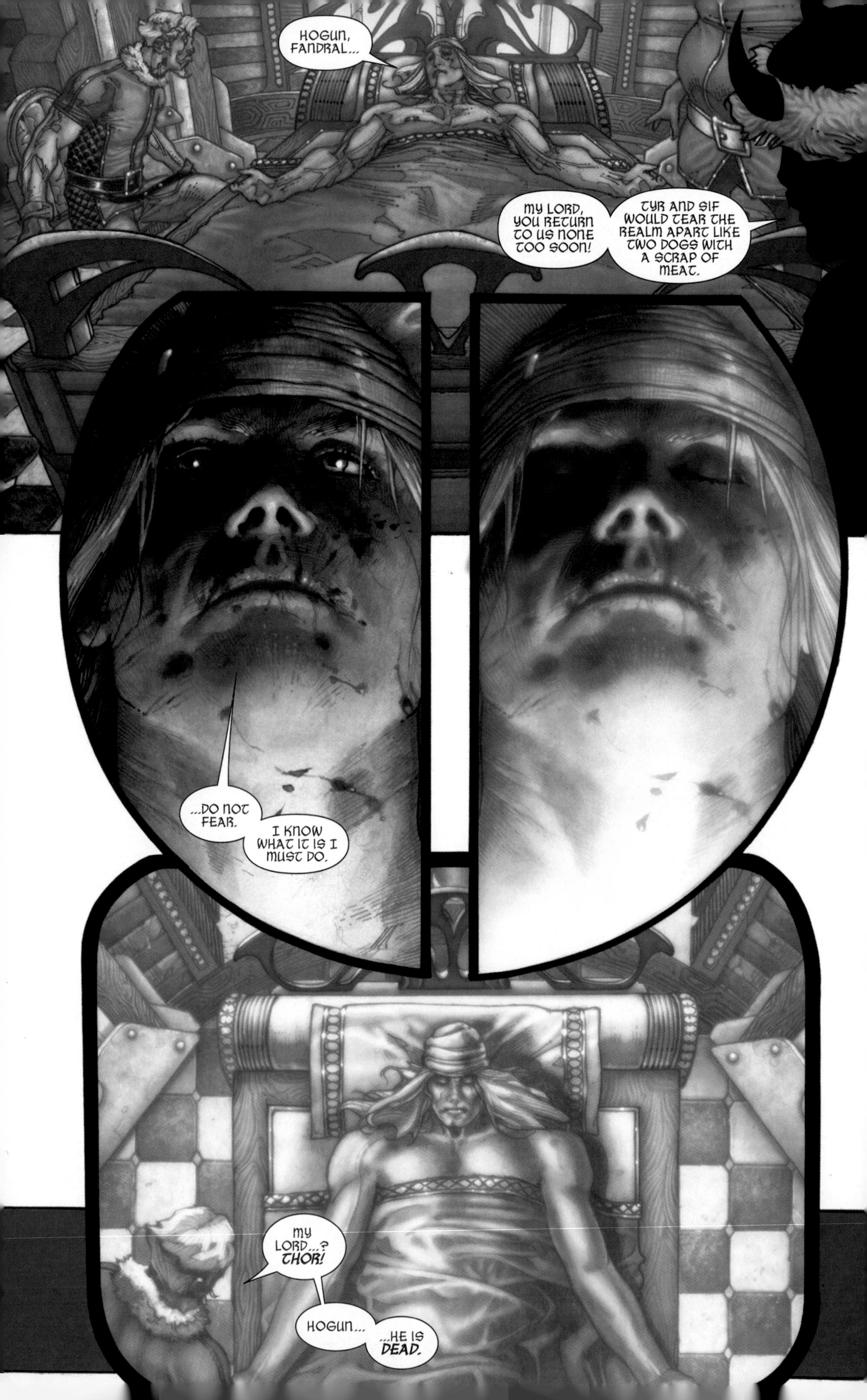
HOGUN, FANDRAL...
MY LORD, YOU RETURN TO US NONE TOO SOON!
TYR AND SIF WOULD TEAR THE REALM APART LIKE TWO DOGS WITH A SCRAP OF MEAT.
...DO NOT FEAR.
I KNOW WHAT IT IS I MUST DO.
MY LORD...? THOR!
HOGUN...
...HE IS DEAD.

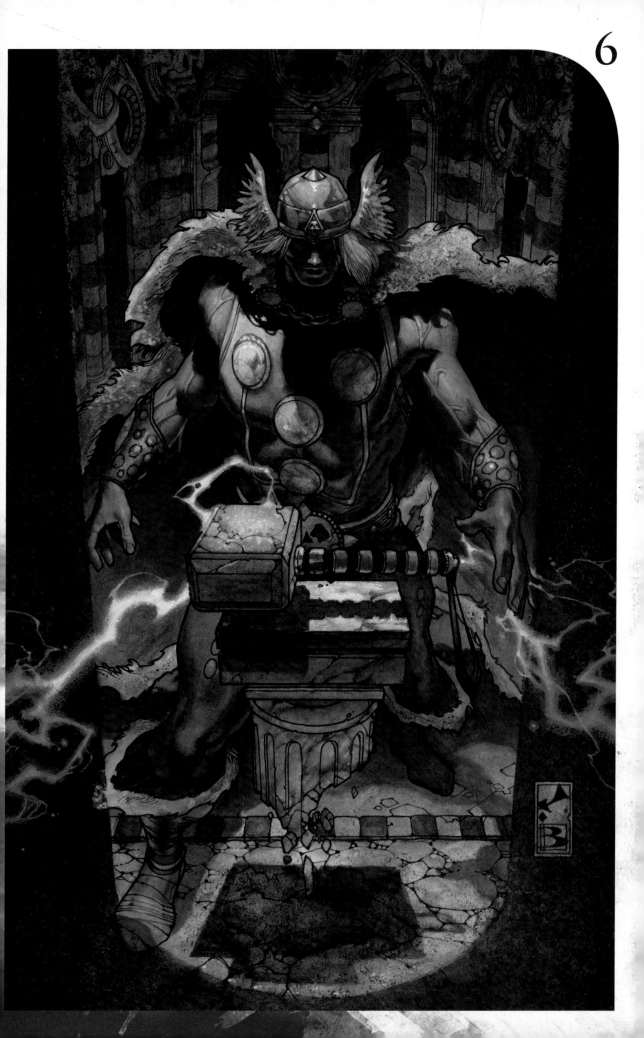

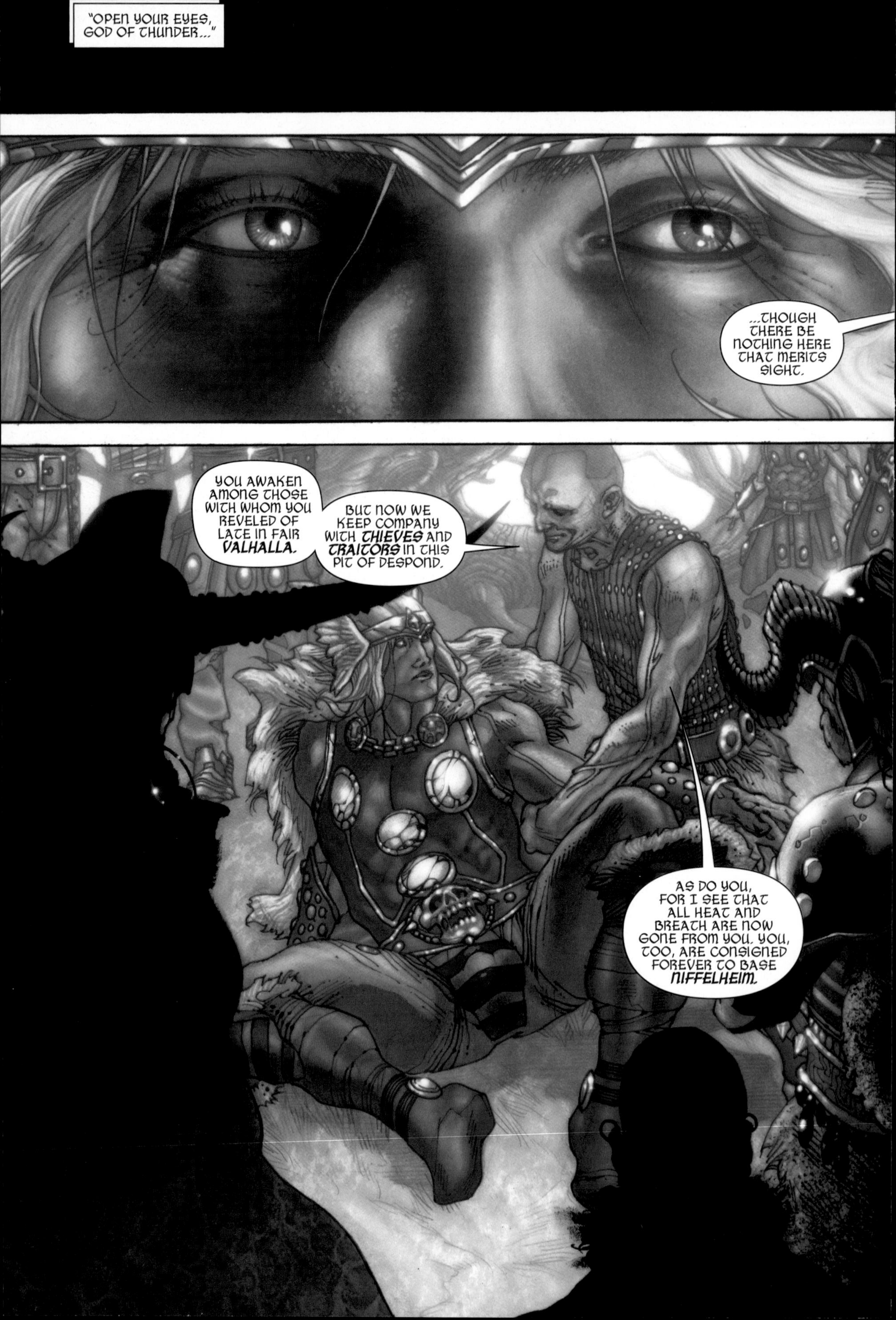
"OPEN YOUR EYES, GOD OF THUNDER..."
...THOUGH THERE BE NOTHING HERE THAT MERITS SIGHT.
YOU AWAKEN AMONG THOSE WITH WHOM YOU REVELED OF LATE IN FAIR VALHALLA.
BUT NOW WE KEEP COMPANY WITH THIEVES AND TRAITORS IN THIS PIT OF DESPOND.
AS DO YOU, FOR I SEE THAT ALL HEAT AND BREATH ARE NOW GONE FROM YOU. YOU, TOO, ARE CONSIGNED FOREVER TO BASE NIFFELHEIM.

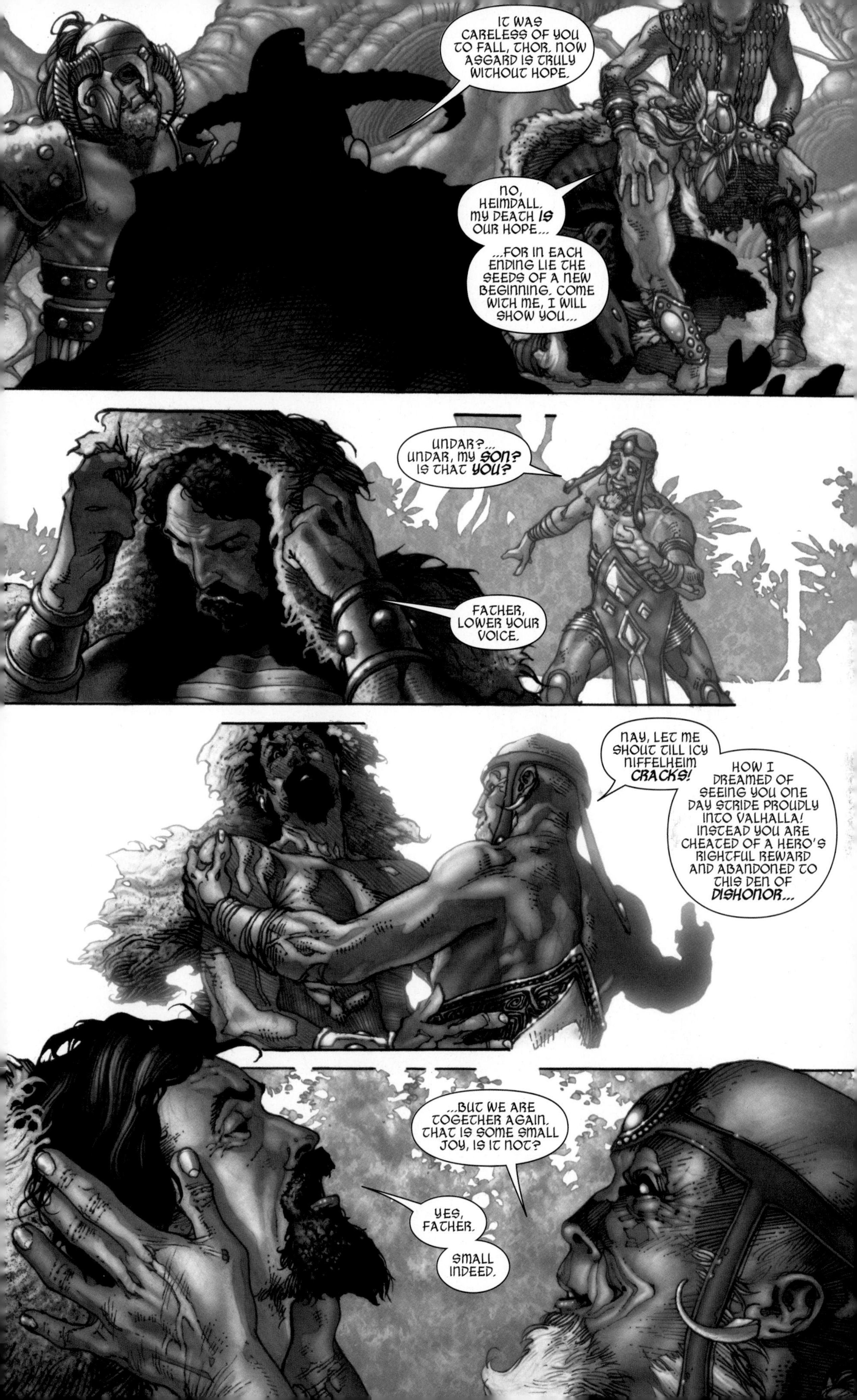
IT WAS CARELESS OF YOU TO FALL, THOR. NOW ASGARD IS TRULY WITHOUT HOPE.
NO, HEIMDALL, MY DEATH IS OUR HOPE...
...FOR IN EACH ENDING LIE THE SEEDS OF A NEW BEGINNING. COME WITH ME, I WILL SHOW YOU...
UNDAR?... UNDAR, MY SON? IS THAT YOU?
FATHER, LOWER YOUR VOICE.
NAY, LET ME SHOUT TILL ICY NIFFELHEIM CRACKS!
HOW I DREAMED OF SEEING YOU ONE DAY STRIDE PROUDLY INTO VALHALLA! INSTEAD YOU ARE CHEATED OF A HERO'S RIGHTFUL REWARD AND ABANDONED TO THIS DEN OF DISHONOR...
...BUT WE ARE TOGETHER AGAIN. THAT IS SOME SMALL JOY, IS IT NOT?
YES, FATHER.
SMALL INDEED.

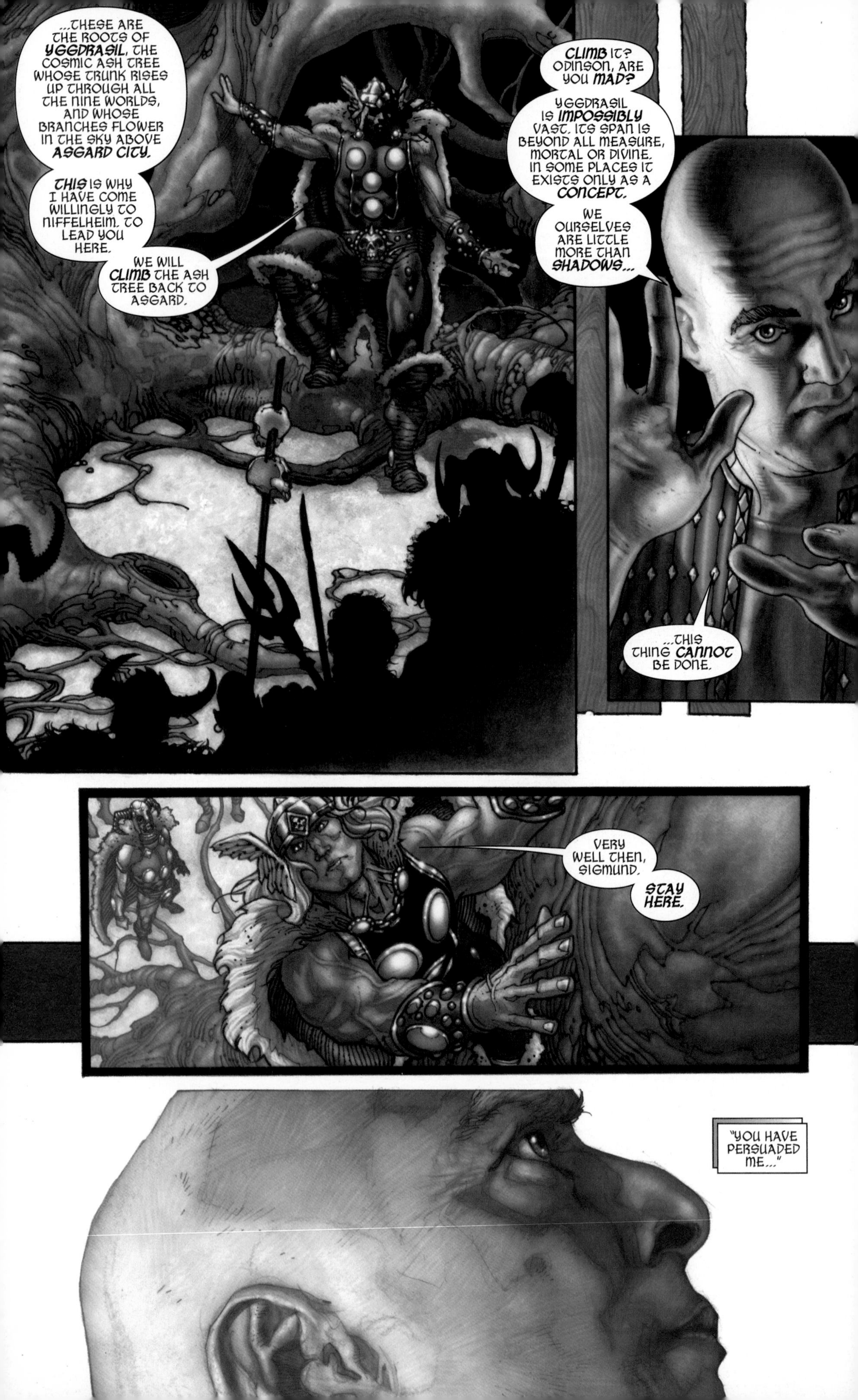
...THESE ARE THE ROOTS OF YGGDRASIL, THE COSMIC ASH TREE WHOSE TRUNK RISES UP THROUGH ALL THE NINE WORLDS, AND WHOSE BRANCHES FLOWER IN THE SKY ABOVE ASGARD CITY.
THIS IS WHY I HAVE COME WILLINGLY TO NIFFELHEIM. TO LEAD YOU HERE.
WE WILL CLIMB THE ASH TREE BACK TO ASGARD.
CLIMB IT? ODINSON, ARE YOU MAD?
YGGDRASIL IS IMPOSSIBLY VAST. ITS SPAN IS BEYOND ALL MEASURE, MORTAL OR DIVINE. IN SOME PLACES IT EXISTS ONLY AS A CONCEPT.
WE OURSELVES ARE LITTLE MORE THAN SHADOWS...
...THIS THING CANNOT BE DONE.
VERY WELL THEN, SIGMUND. STAY HERE.
"YOU HAVE PERSUADED ME..."

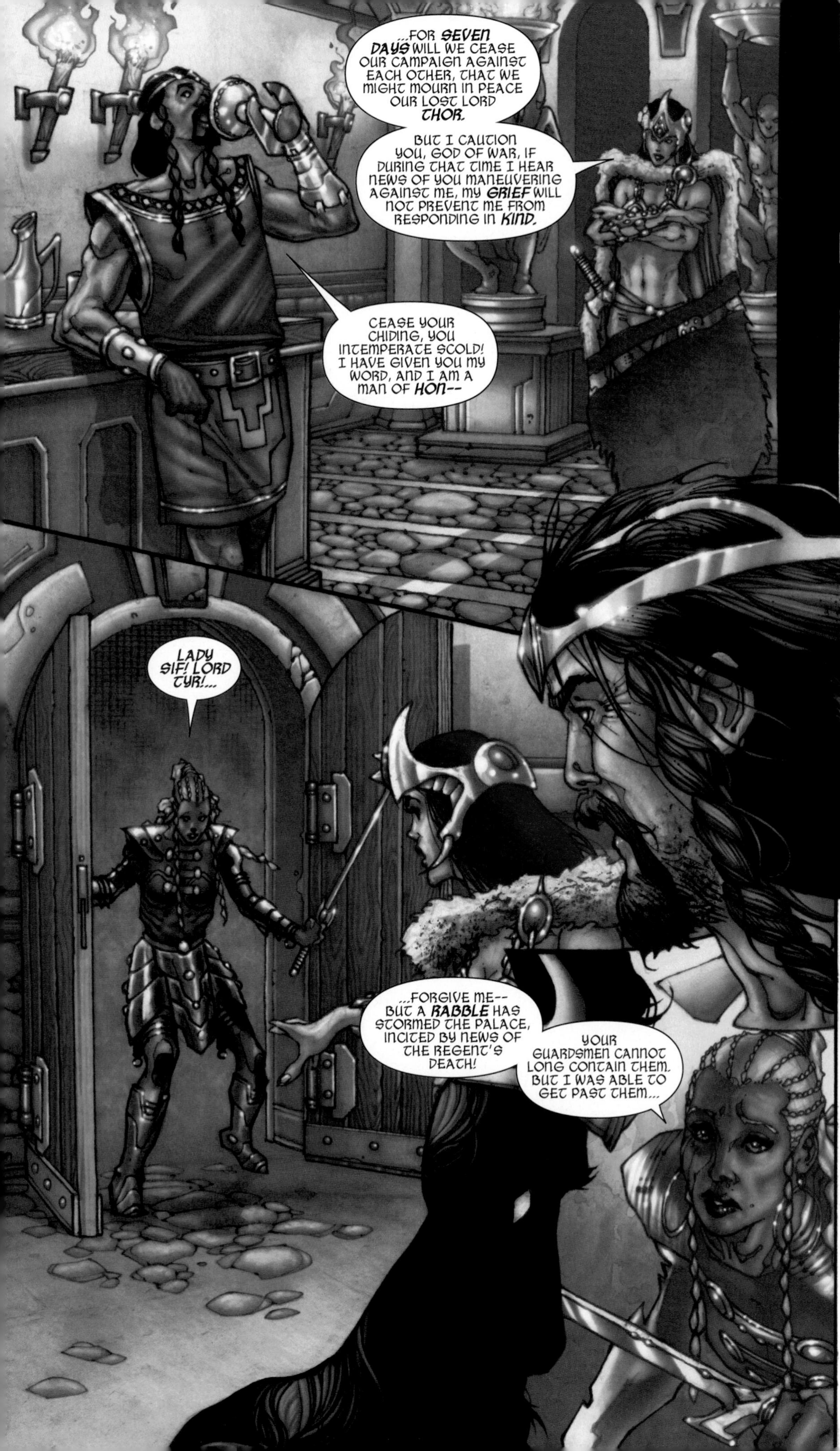
...FOR SEVEN DAYS WILL WE CEASE OUR CAMPAIGN AGAINST EACH OTHER, THAT WE MIGHT MOURN IN PEACE OUR LOST LORD THOR.
BUT I CAUTION YOU, GOD OF WAR, IF DURING THAT TIME I HEAR NEWS OF YOU MANEUVERING AGAINST ME, MY GRIEF WILL NOT PREVENT ME FROM RESPONDING IN KIND.
CEASE YOUR CHIDING, YOU INTEMPERATE SCOLD! I HAVE GIVEN YOU MY WORD, AND I AM A MAN OF HON--
LADY SIF! LORD TYR!...
...FORGIVE ME-- BUT A RABBLE HAS STORMED THE PALACE, INCITED BY NEWS OF THE REGENT'S DEATH!
YOUR GUARDSMEN CANNOT LONG CONTAIN THEM. BUT I WAS ABLE TO GET PAST THEM...

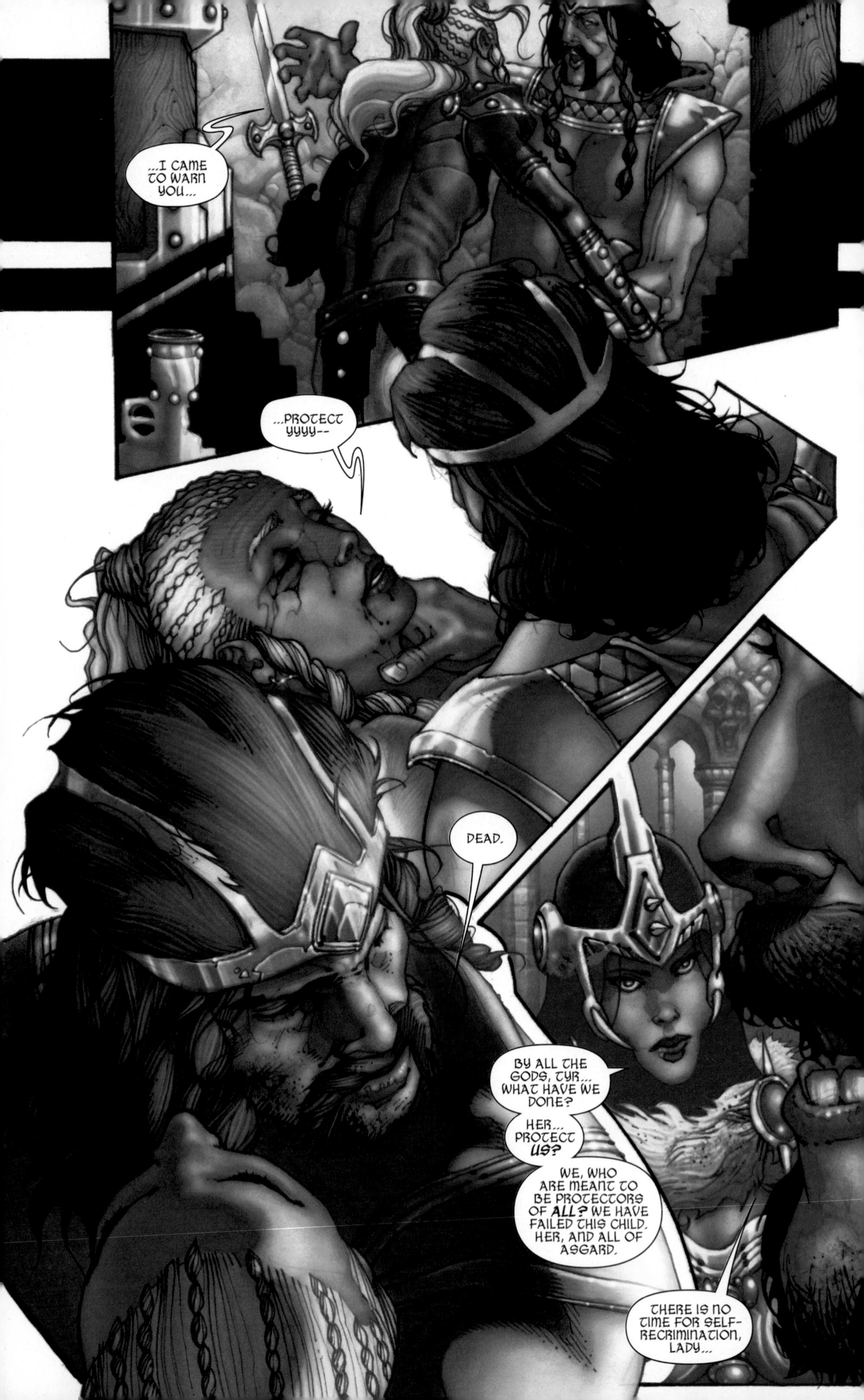
...I CAME TO WARN YOU...
...PROTECT YYYY--
DEAD.
BY ALL THE GODS, TYR... WHAT HAVE WE DONE?
HER... PROTECT US?
WE, WHO ARE MEANT TO BE PROTECTORS OF ALL? WE HAVE FAILED THIS CHILD. HER, AND ALL OF ASGARD.
THERE IS NO TIME FOR SELF-RECRIMINATION, LADY...

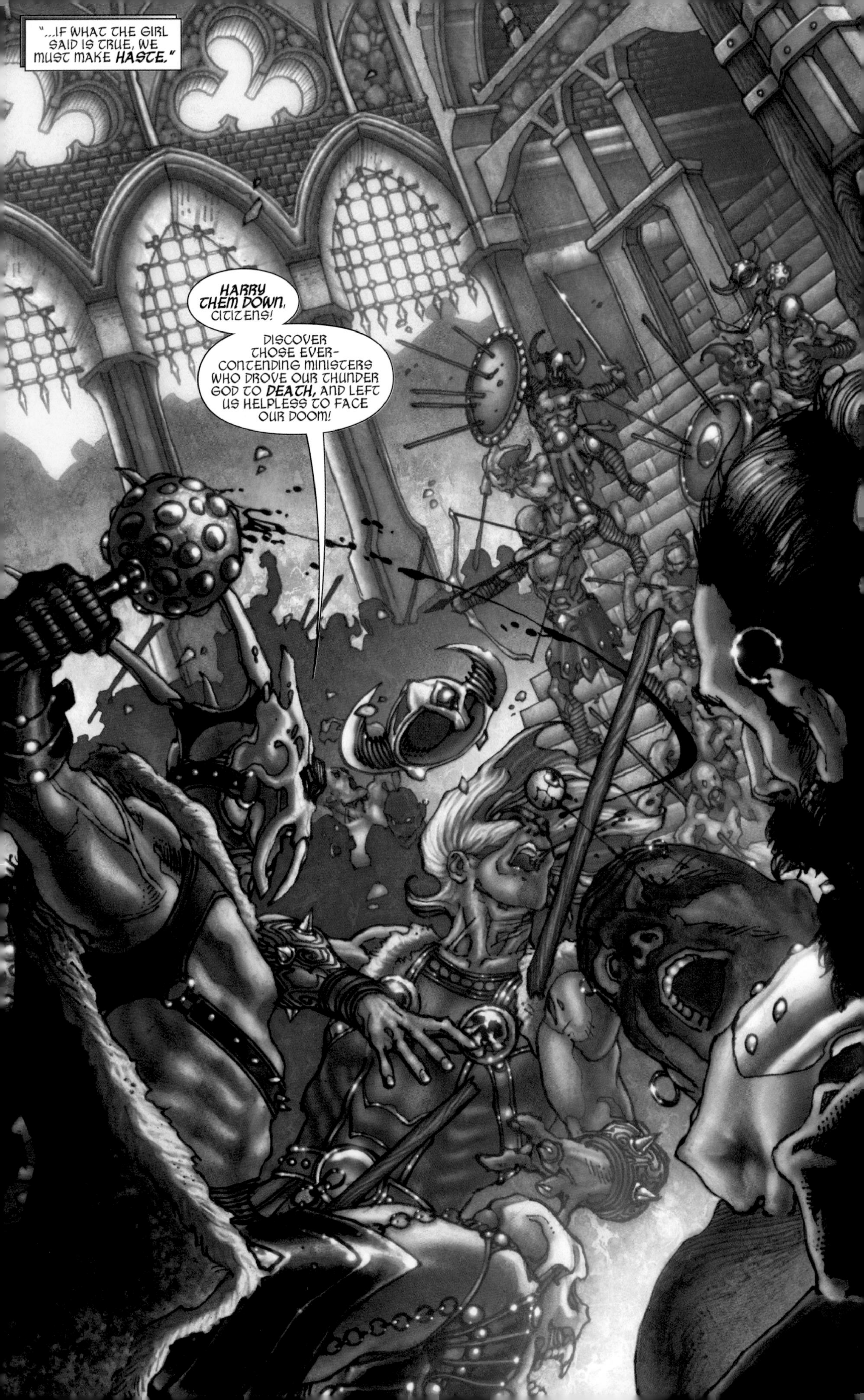
"...IF WHAT THE GIRL SAID IS TRUE, WE MUST MAKE HASTE."
HARRY THEM DOWN, CITIZENS!
DISCOVER THOSE EVER-CONTENDING MINISTERS WHO DROVE OUR THUNDER GOD TO DEATH, AND LEFT US HELPLESS TO FACE OUR DOOM!

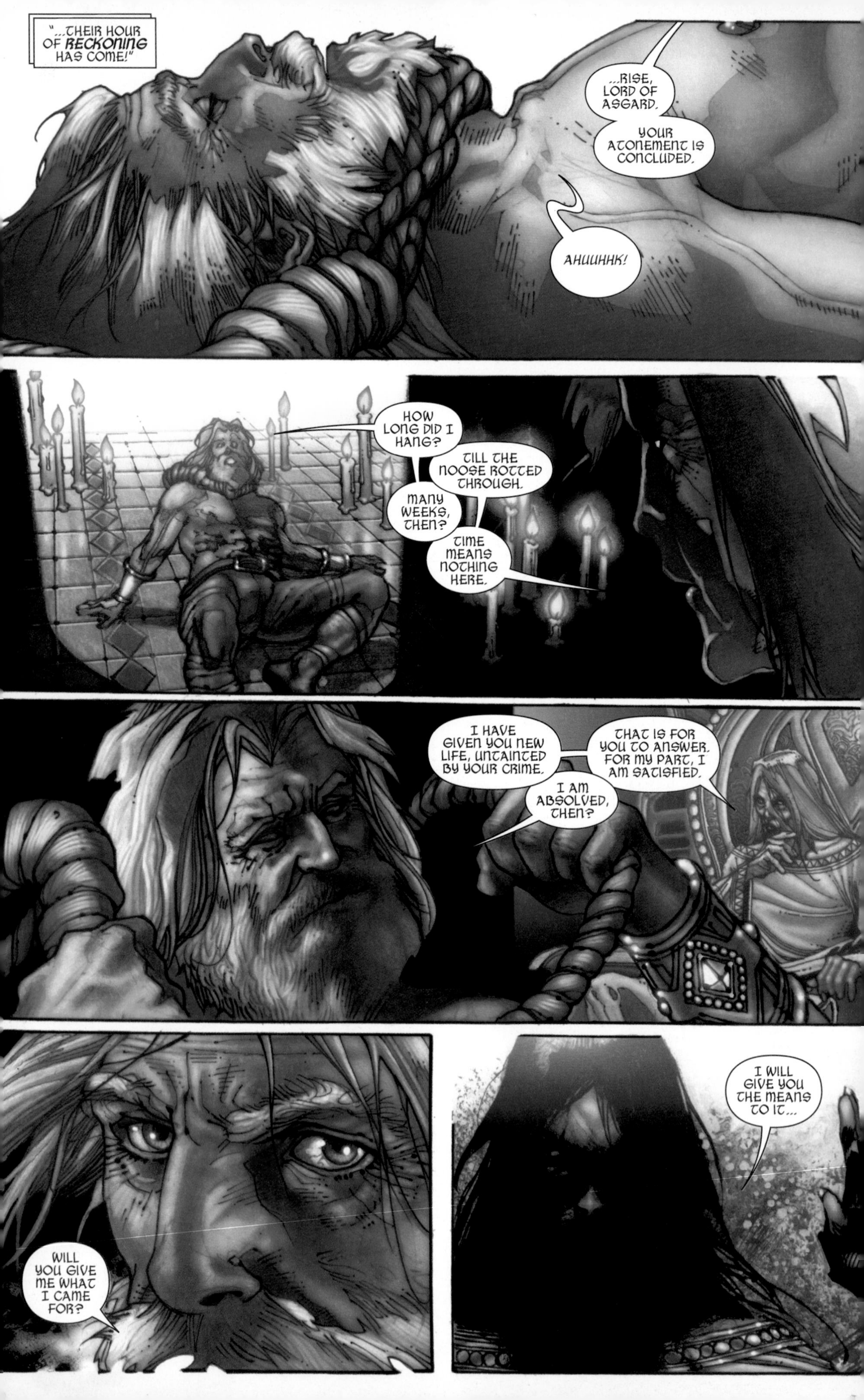
"...THEIR HOUR OF RECKONING HAS COME!"
...RISE, LORD OF ASGARD.
YOUR ATONEMENT IS CONCLUDED.
AHUUHHK!
HOW LONG DID I HANG?
TILL THE NOOSE ROTTED THROUGH.
MANY WEEKS, THEN?
TIME MEANS NOTHING HERE.
I HAVE GIVEN YOU NEW LIFE, UNTAINTED BY YOUR CRIME.
I AM ABSOLVED, THEN?
THAT IS FOR YOU TO ANSWER. FOR MY PART, I AM SATISFIED.
WILL YOU GIVE ME WHAT I CAME FOR?
I WILL GIVE YOU THE MEANS TO IT...

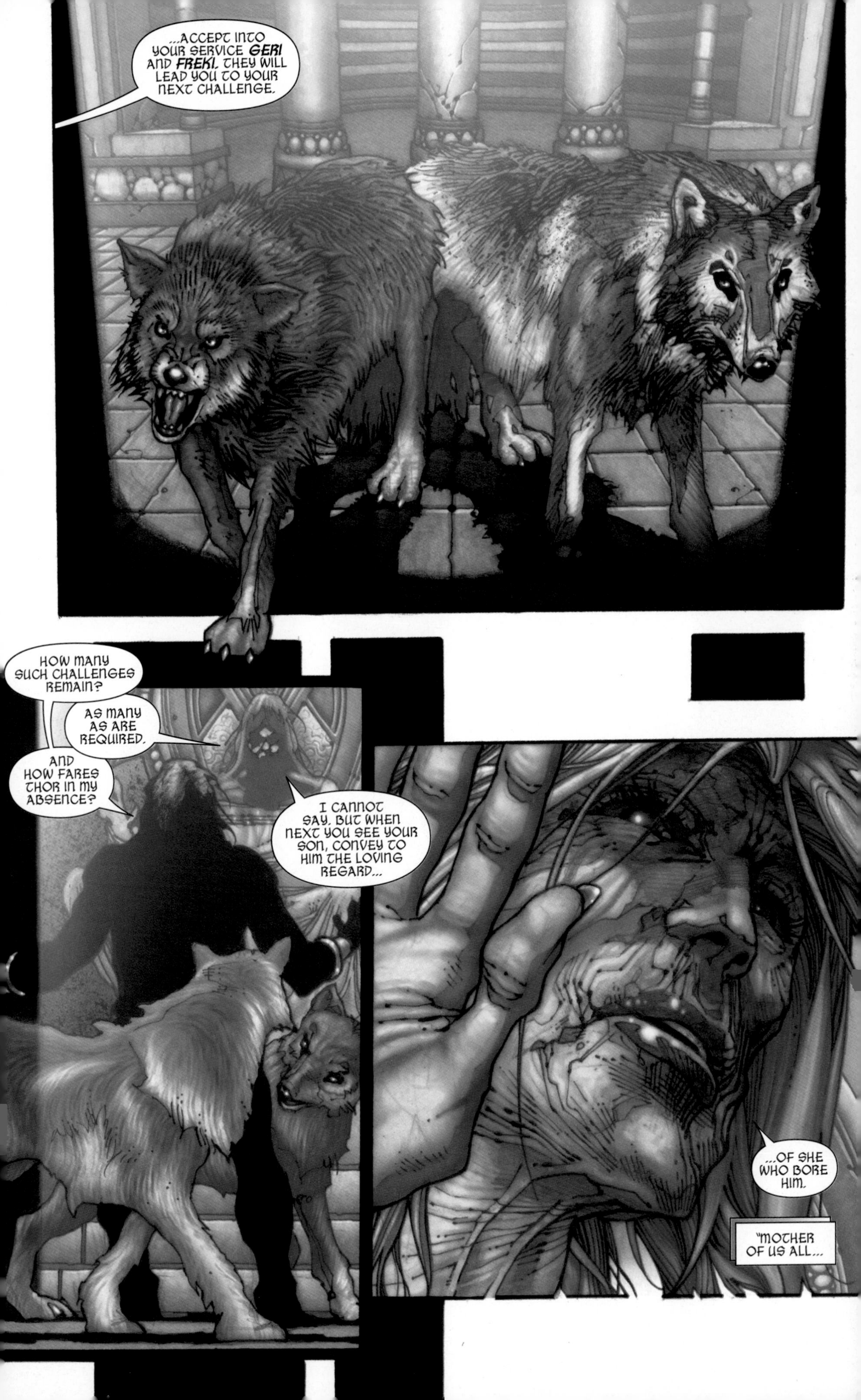

...ACCEPT INTO YOUR SERVICE GERI AND FREKI. THEY WILL LEAD YOU TO YOUR NEXT CHALLENGE.
HOW MANY SUCH CHALLENGES REMAIN?
AS MANY AS ARE REQUIRED.
AND HOW FARES THOR IN MY ABSENCE?
I CANNOT SAY. BUT WHEN NEXT YOU SEE YOUR SON, CONVEY TO HIM THE LOVING REGARD...
...OF SHE WHO BORE HIM.
"MOTHER OF US ALL...

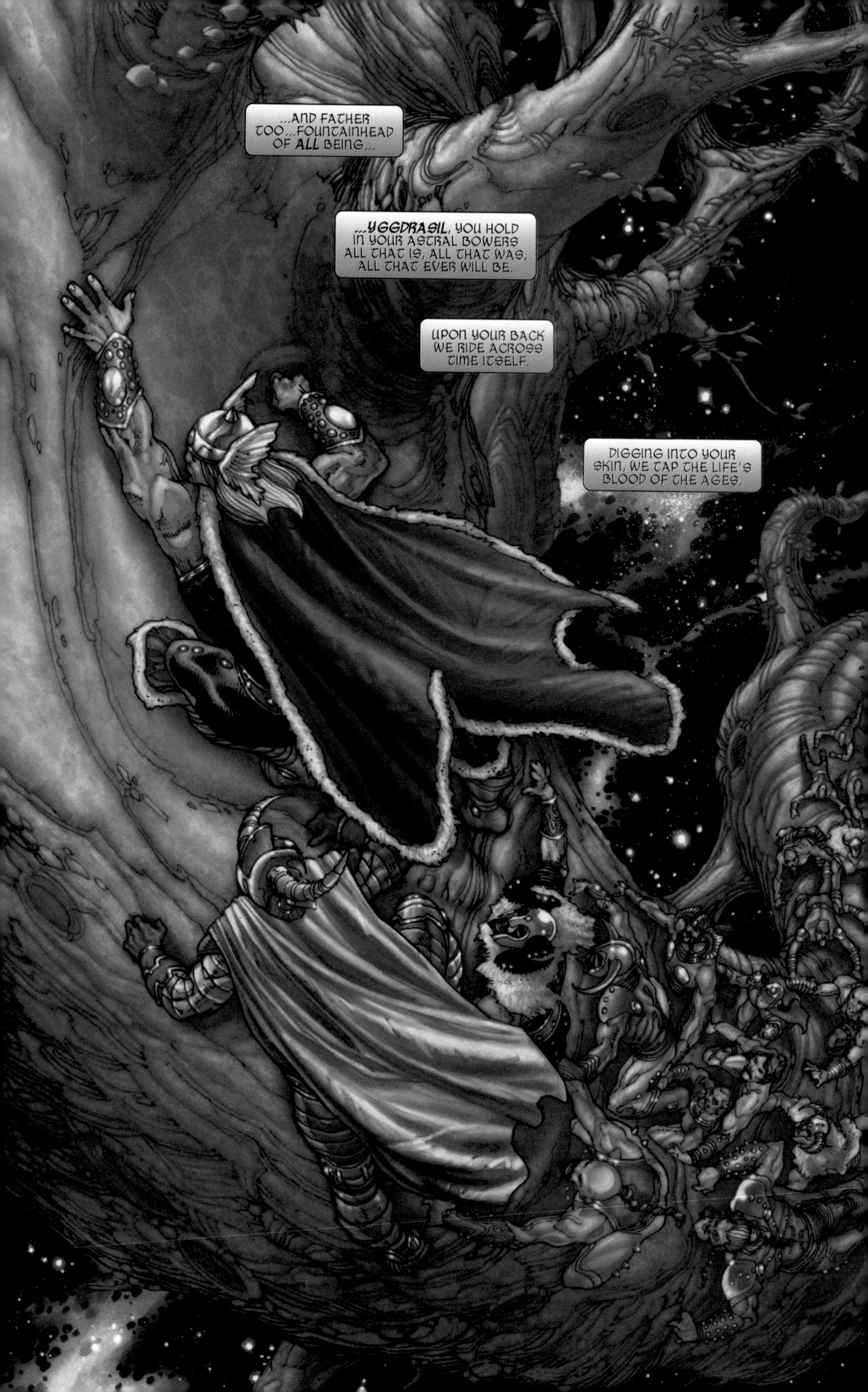
...AND FATHER TOO...FOUNTAINHEAD OF ALL BEING...
...YGGDRASIL, YOU HOLD IN YOUR ASTRAL BOWERS ALL THAT IS, ALL THAT WAS, ALL THAT EVER WILL BE.
UPON YOUR BACK WE RIDE ACROSS TIME ITSELF.
DIGGING INTO YOUR SKIN, WE TAP THE LIFE'S BLOOD OF THE AGES.

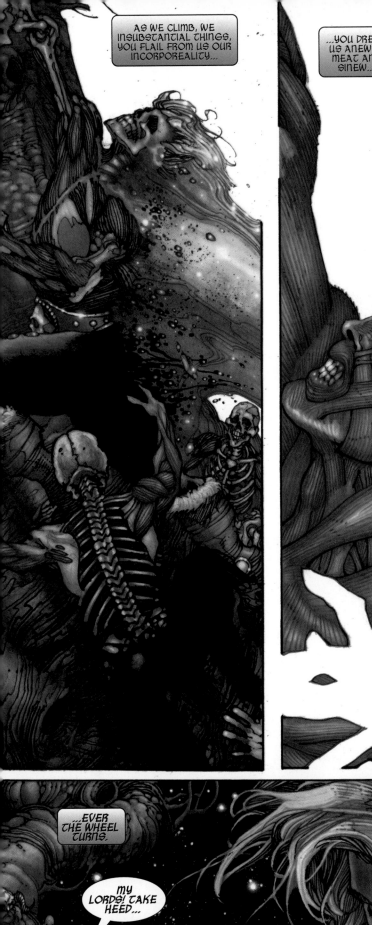

6

AS WE CLIMB, WE INSUBSTANTIAL THINGS, YOU FLAIL FROM US OUR INCORPOREALITY...

...YOU DRESS US ANEW IN MEAT AND SINEW...

...YOU REMAKE WHAT WAS UNMADE. YOU GIVE SUBSTANCE TO SPIRIT AND TEXTURE TO THOUGHT.

AND THUS THE WHEEL TURNS...

...EVER THE WHEEL TURNS.

MY LORDS! TAKE HEED...

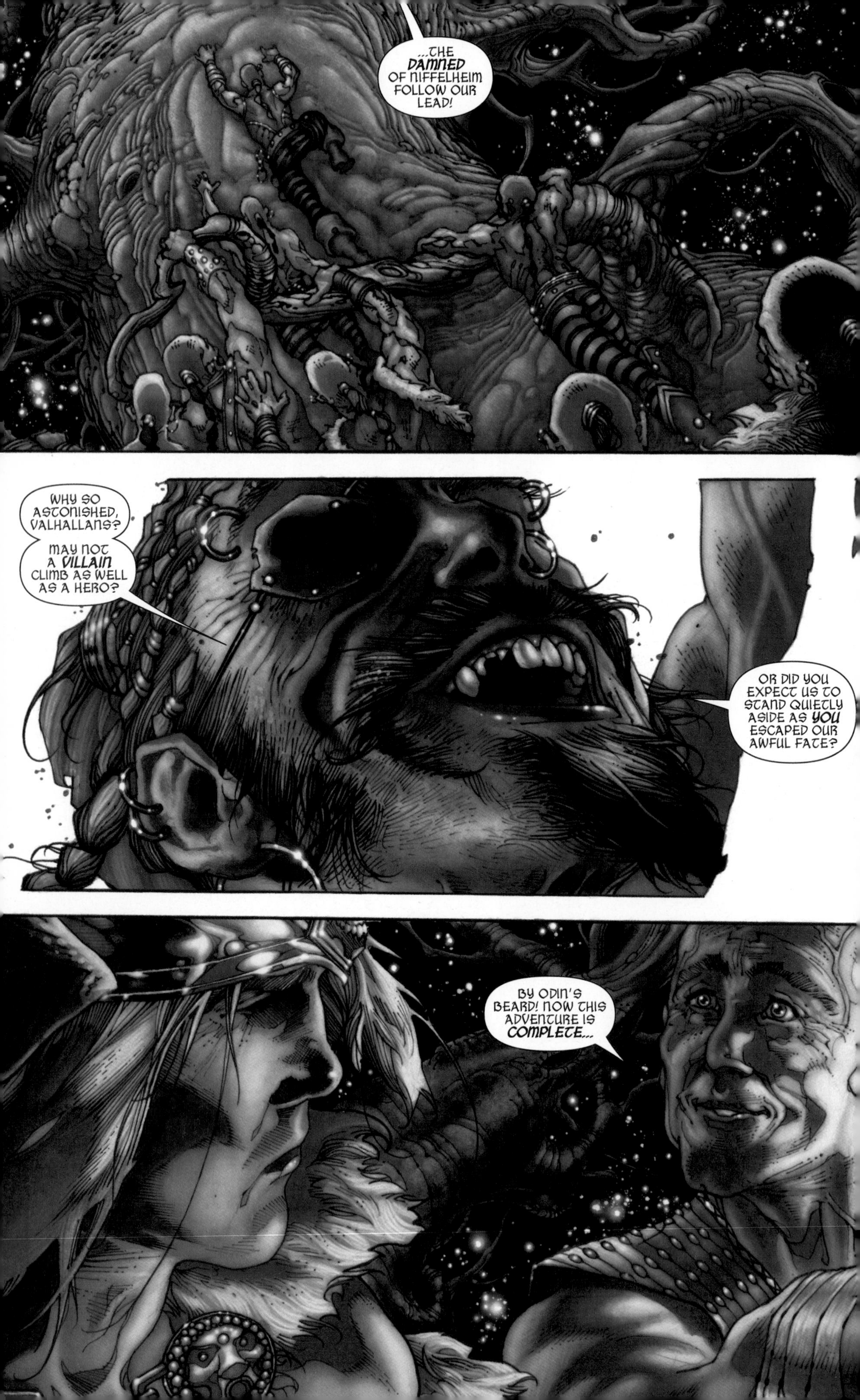
...THE DAMNED OF NIFFELHEIM FOLLOW OUR LEAD!
WHY SO ASTONISHED, VALHALLANS?
MAY NOT A VILLAIN CLIMB AS WELL AS A HERO?
OR DID YOU EXPECT US TO STAND QUIETLY ASIDE AS YOU ESCAPED OUR AWFUL FATE?
BY ODIN'S BEARD! NOW THIS ADVENTURE IS COMPLETE...

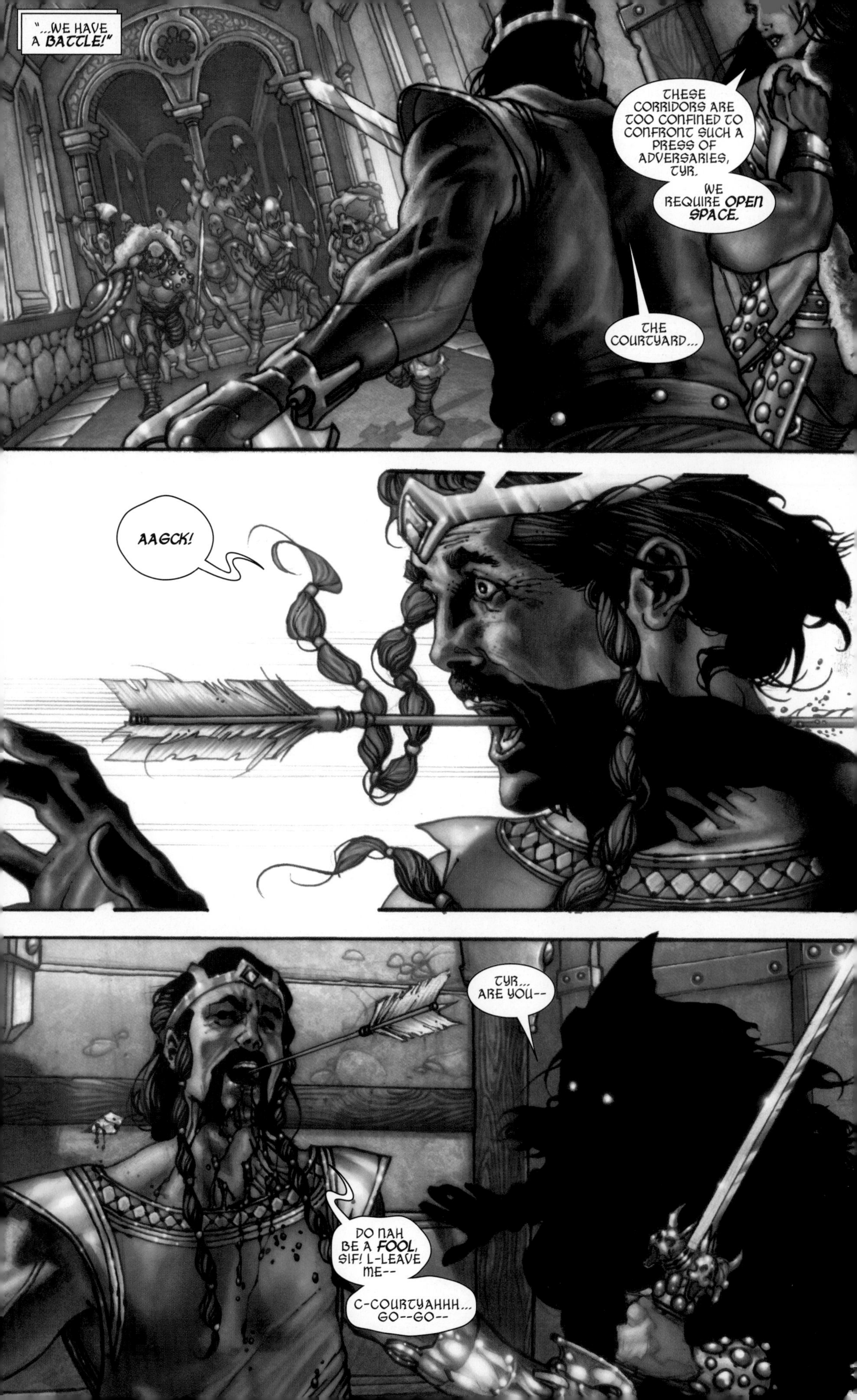
"...WE HAVE A BATTLE!"
THESE CORRIDORS ARE TOO CONFINED TO CONFRONT SUCH A PRESS OF ADVERSARIES, TYR.
WE REQUIRE OPEN SPACE.
THE COURTYARD...
AAGCK!
TYR... ARE YOU--
DO NAH BE A FOOL, SIF! L-LEAVE ME--
C-COURTYAHHH... GO--GO--

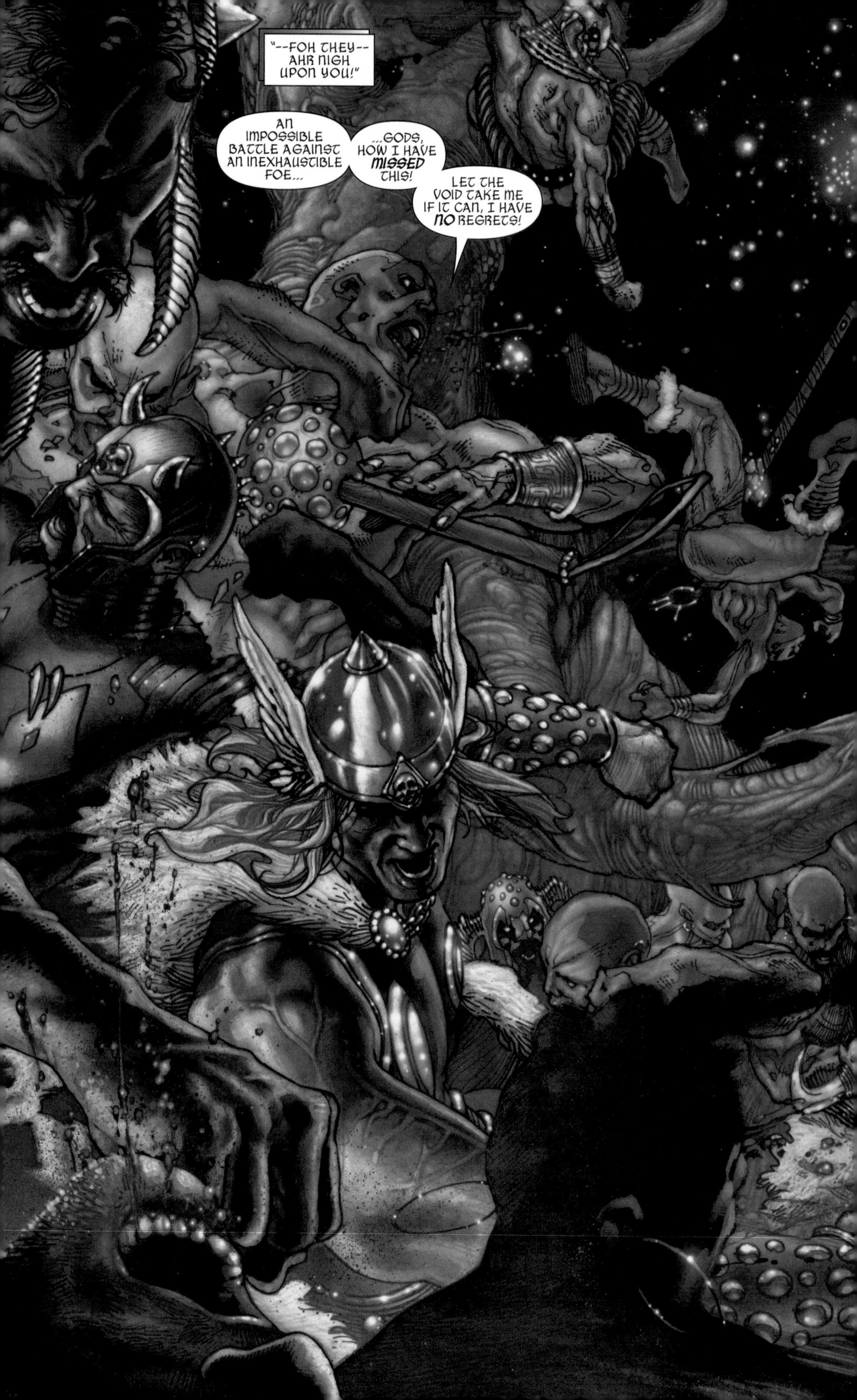
"--FOH THEY--
AHR NIGH
UPON YOU!"
AN IMPOSSIBLE BATTLE AGAINST AN INEXHAUSTIBLE FOE...
...GODS, HOW I HAVE MISSED THIS!
LET THE VOID TAKE ME IF IT CAN, I HAVE NO REGRETS!

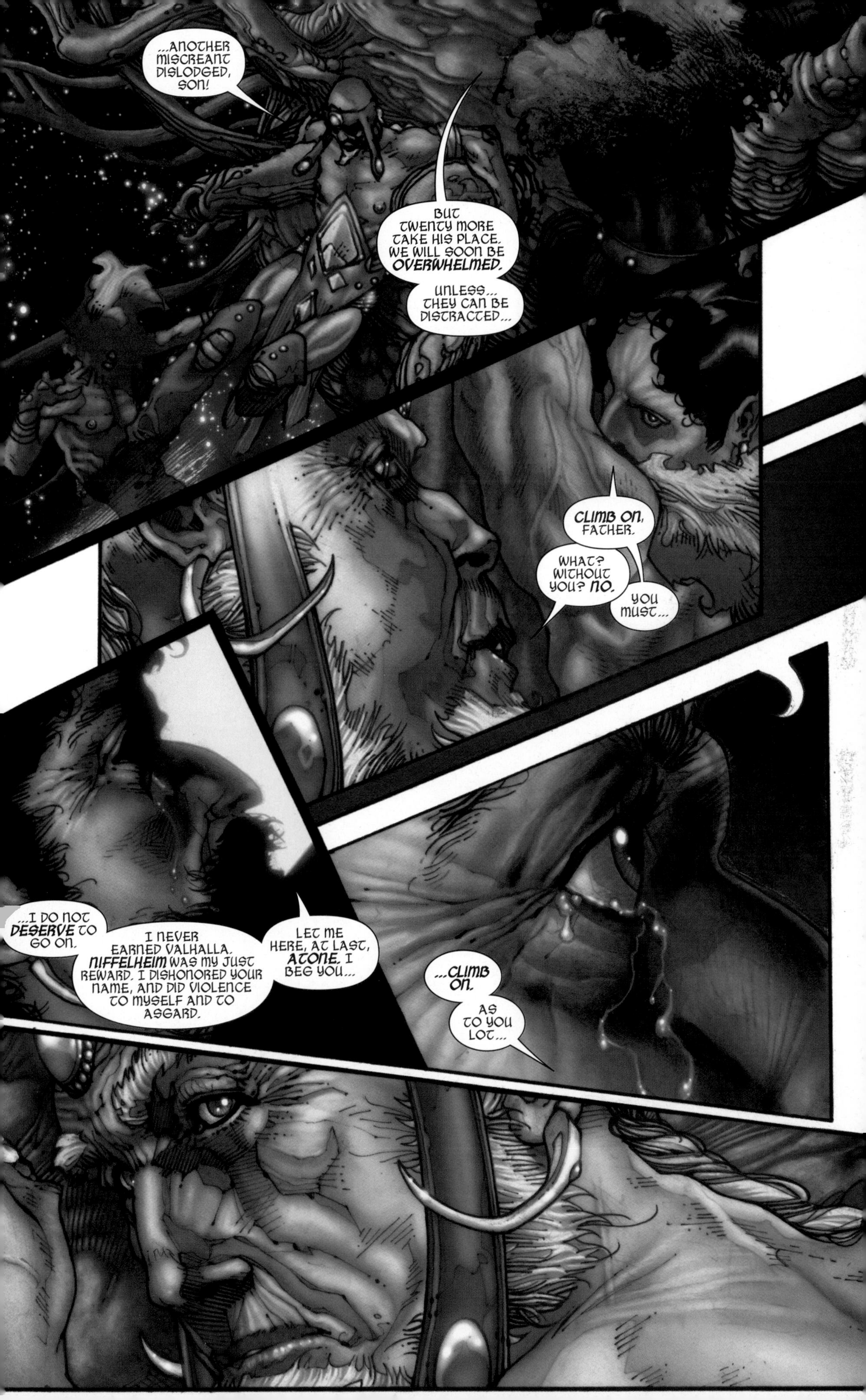
...ANOTHER MISCREANT DISLODGED, SON!
BUT TWENTY MORE TAKE HIS PLACE. WE WILL SOON BE OVERWHELMED.
UNLESS... THEY CAN BE DISTRACTED...
CLIMB ON, FATHER.
WHAT? WITHOUT YOU? NO.
YOU MUST...
...I DO NOT DESERVE TO GO ON.
I NEVER EARNED VALHALLA. NIFFELHEIM WAS MY JUST REWARD. I DISHONORED YOUR NAME, AND DID VIOLENCE TO MYSELF AND TO ASGARD.
LET ME HERE, AT LAST, ATONE. I BEG YOU...
...CLIMB ON.
AS TO YOU LOT...

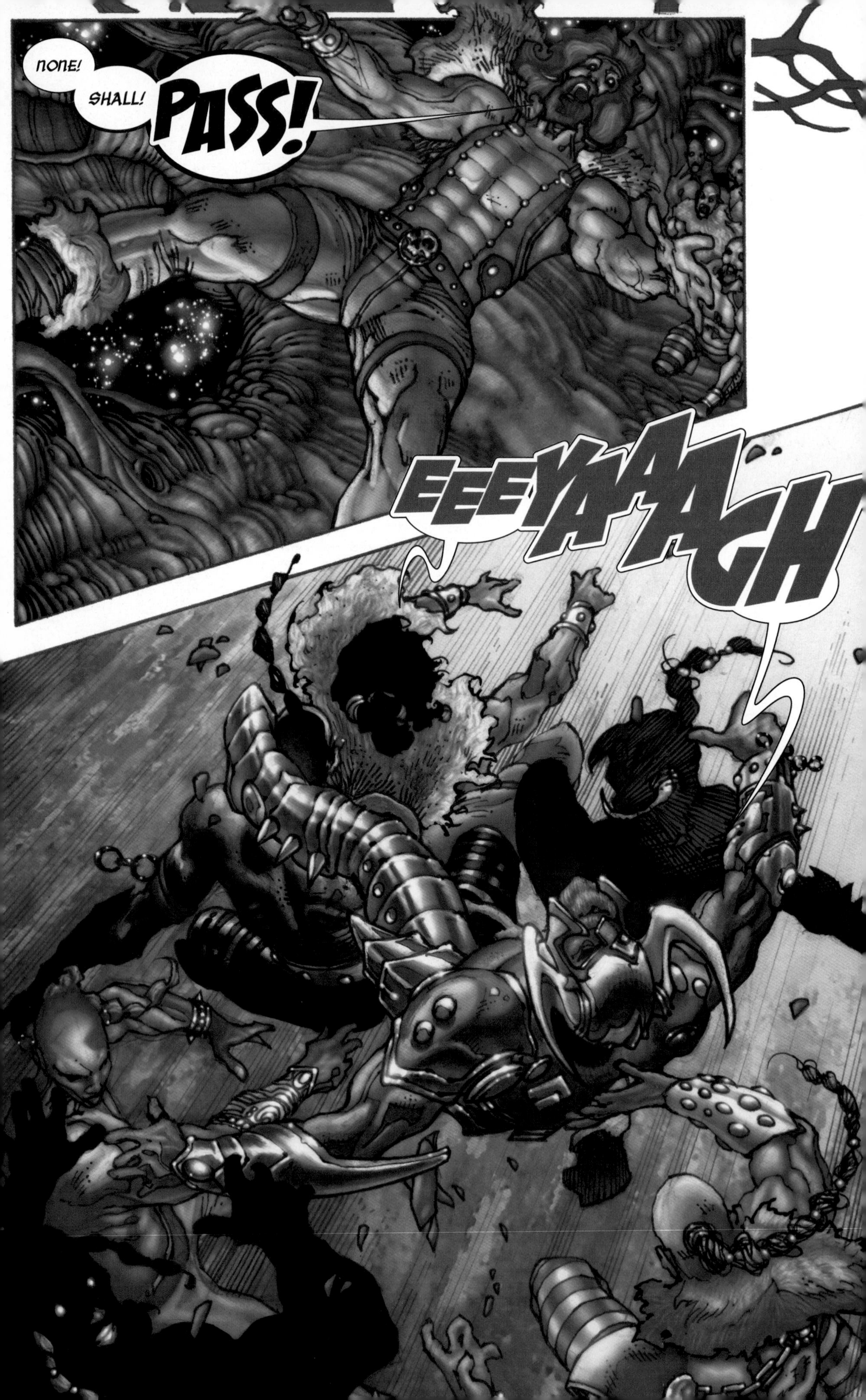
NONE!
SHALL!
PASS!
EEEYAAAAACH

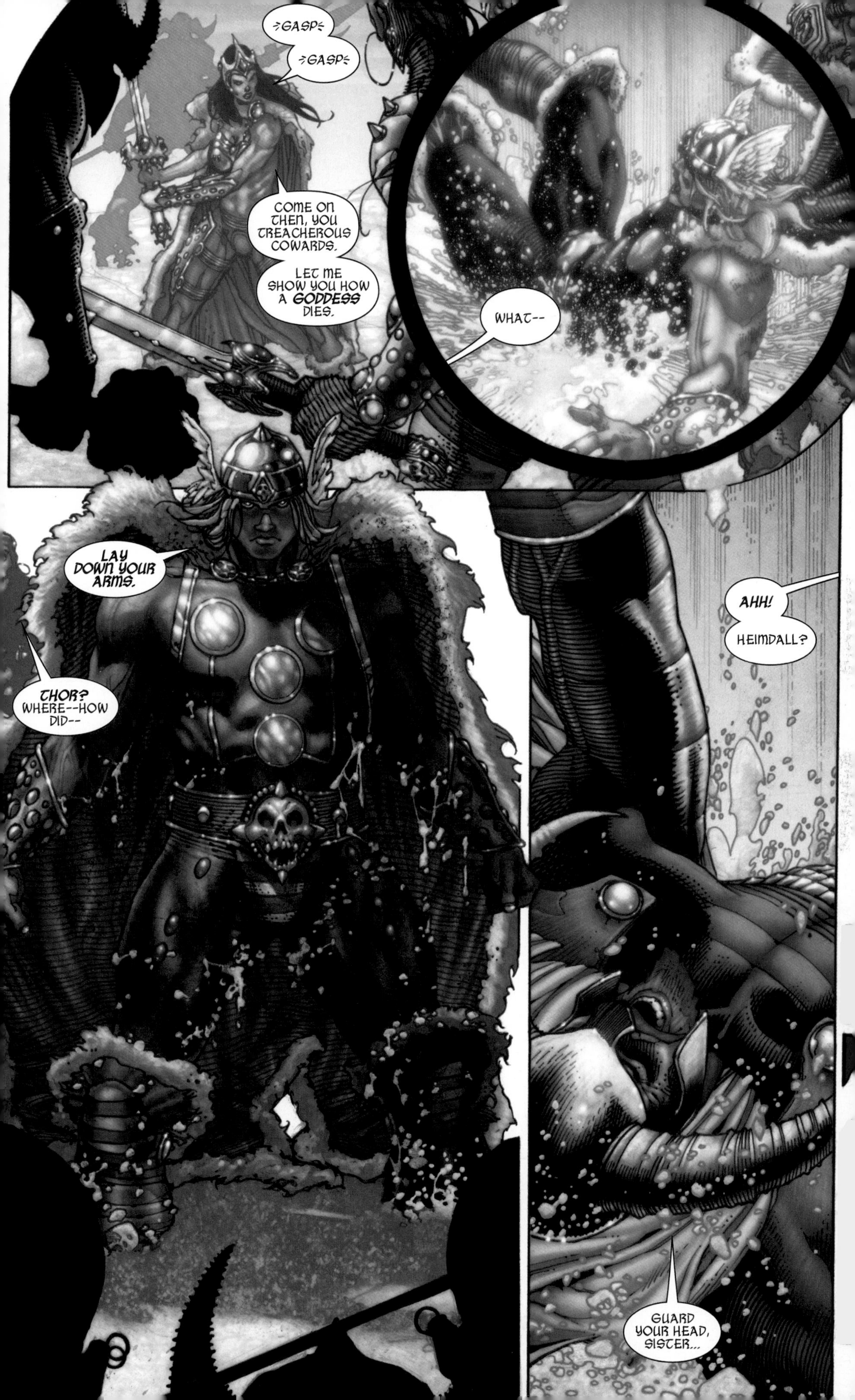

GASP
GASP
COME ON THEN, YOU TREACHEROUS COWARDS.
LET ME SHOW YOU HOW A GODDESS DIES.
WHAT--
LAY DOWN YOUR ARMS.
THOR? WHERE--HOW DID--
AHH!
HEIMDALL?
GUARD YOUR HEAD, SISTER...

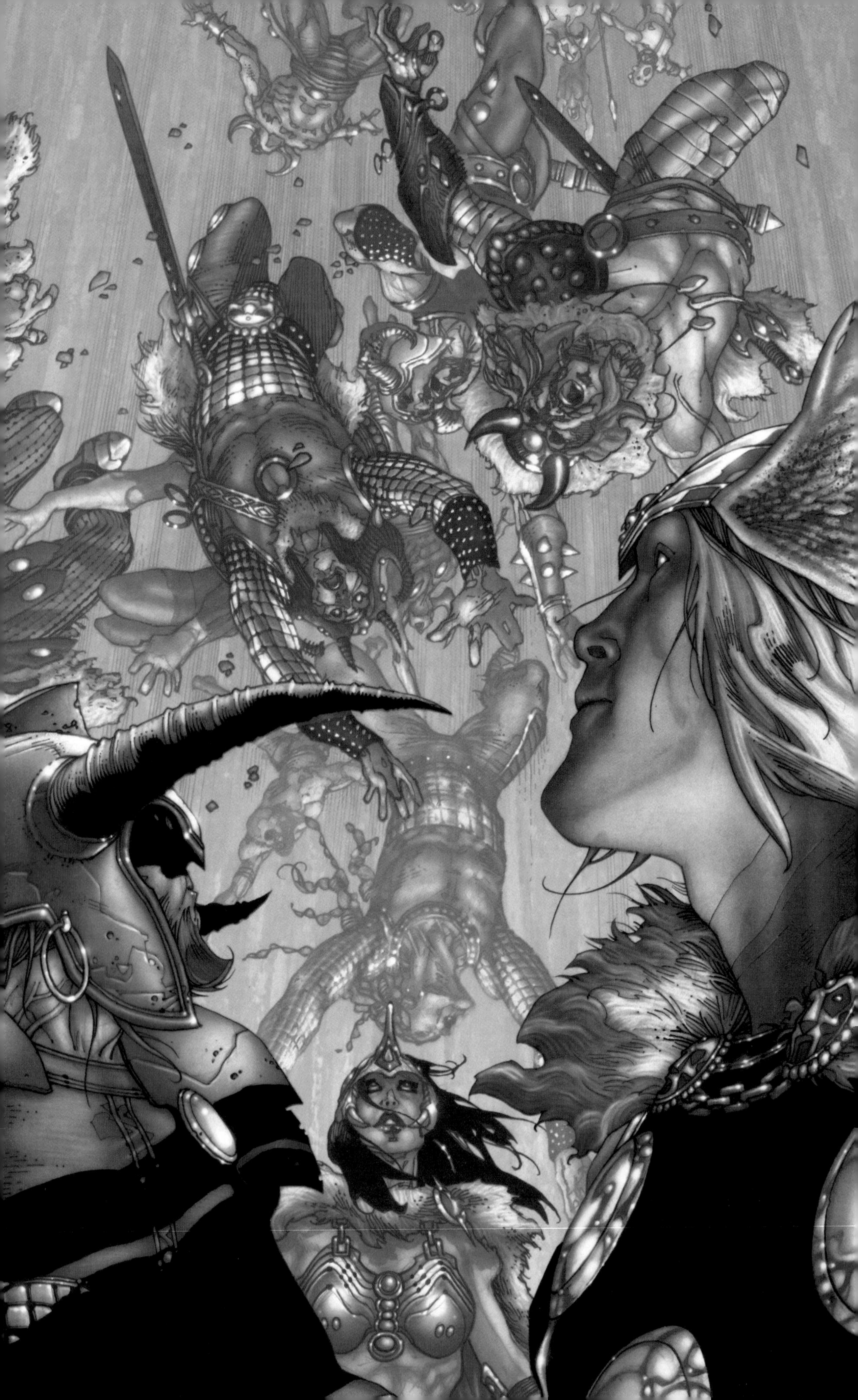

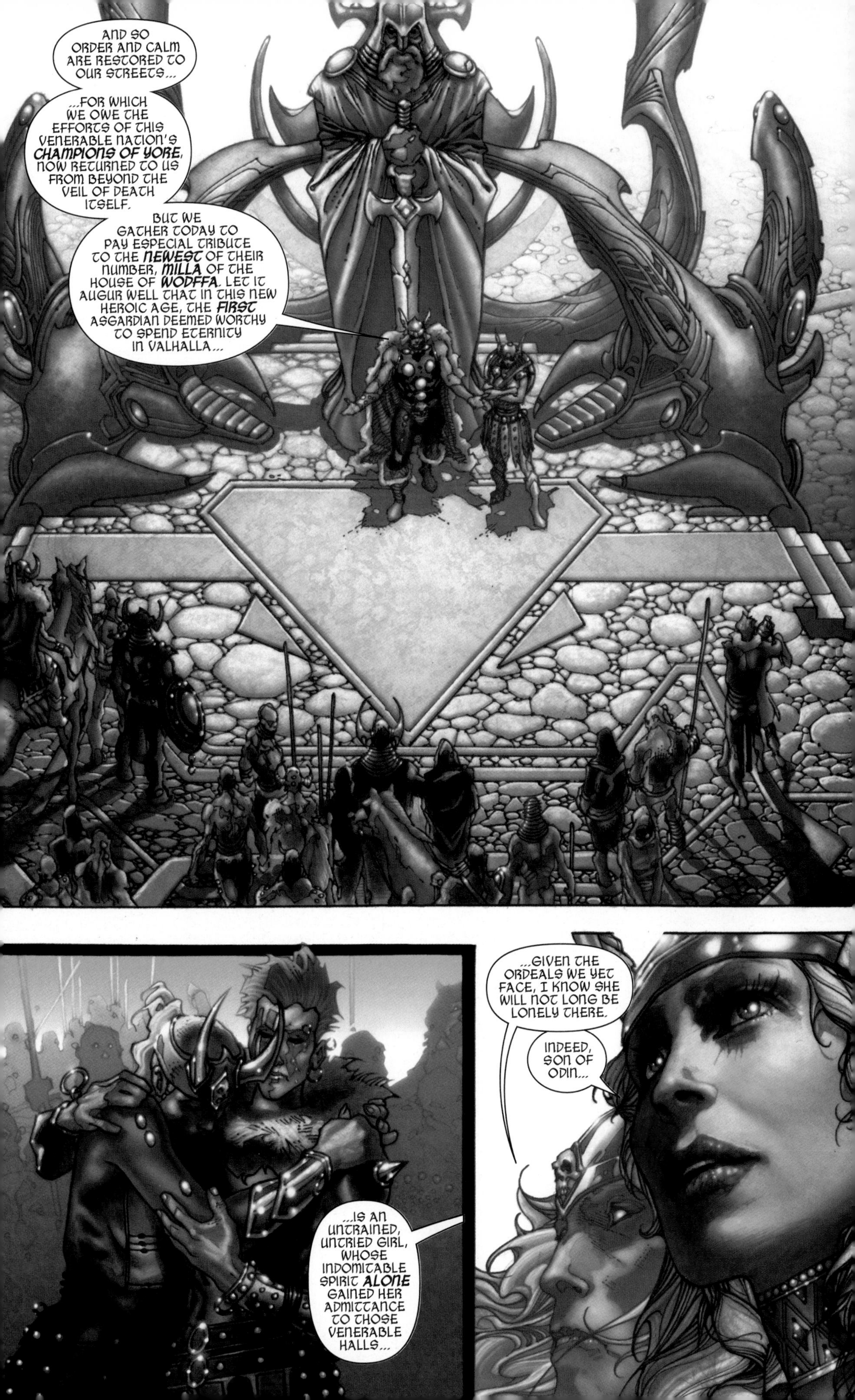
AND SO ORDER AND CALM ARE RESTORED TO OUR STREETS...
...FOR WHICH WE OWE THE EFFORTS OF THIS VENERABLE NATION'S **CHAMPIONS OF YORE**, NOW RETURNED TO US FROM BEYOND THE VEIL OF DEATH ITSELF.
BUT WE GATHER TODAY TO PAY ESPECIAL TRIBUTE TO THE **NEWEST** OF THEIR NUMBER, **MILLA** OF THE HOUSE OF **WODFFA**. LET IT AUGUR WELL THAT IN THIS NEW HEROIC AGE, THE **FIRST** ASGARDIAN DEEMED WORTHY TO SPEND ETERNITY IN VALHALLA...
...IS AN UNTRAINED, UNTRIED GIRL, WHOSE INDOMITABLE SPIRIT **ALONE** GAINED HER ADMITTANCE TO THOSE VENERABLE HALLS...
...GIVEN THE ORDEALS WE YET FACE, I KNOW SHE WILL NOT LONG BE LONELY THERE.
INDEED, SON OF ODIN...

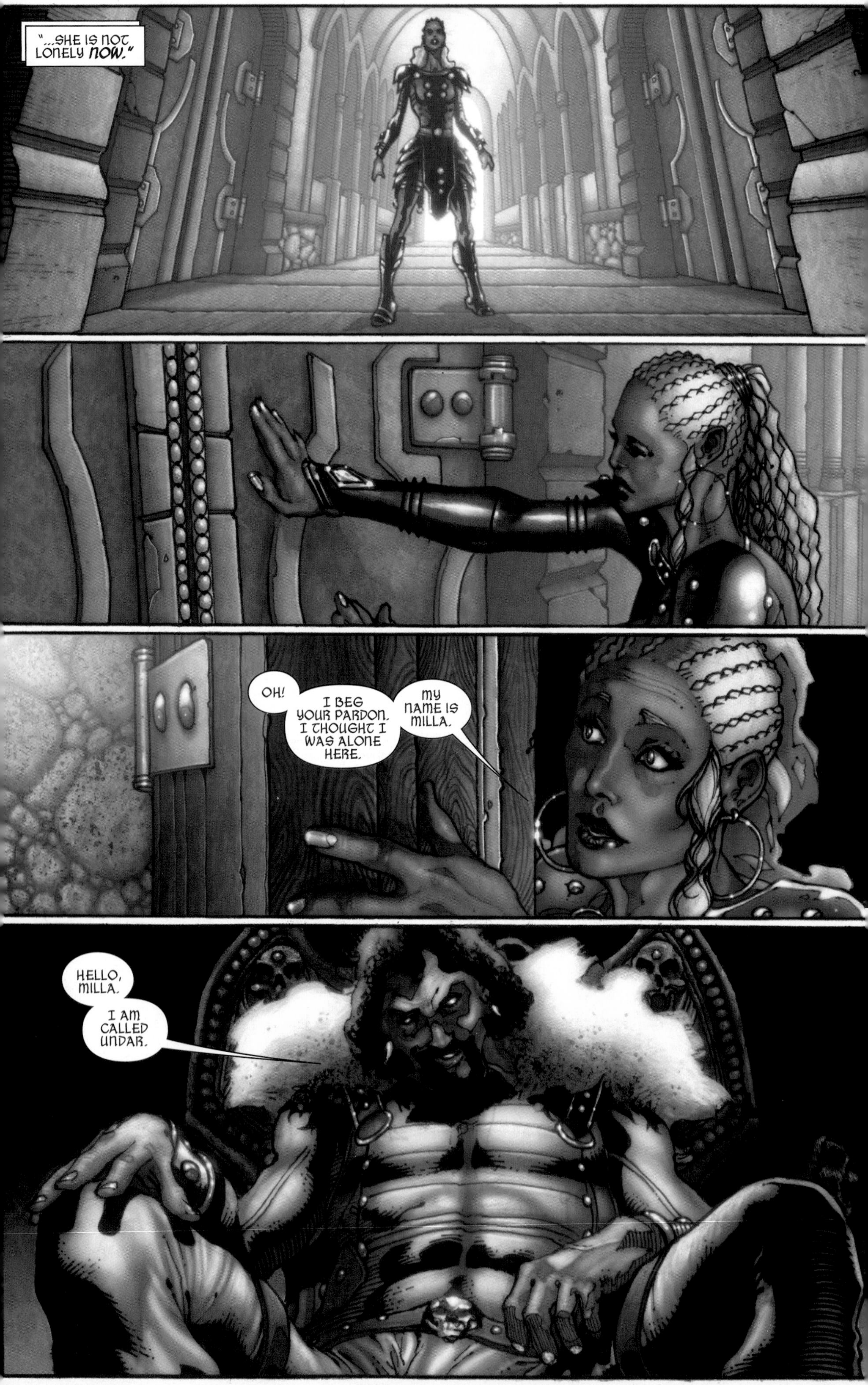
"...SHE IS NOT LONELY NOW."
OH!
I BEG YOUR PARDON. I THOUGHT I WAS ALONE HERE.
MY NAME IS MILLA.
HELLO, MILLA.
I AM CALLED UNDAR.

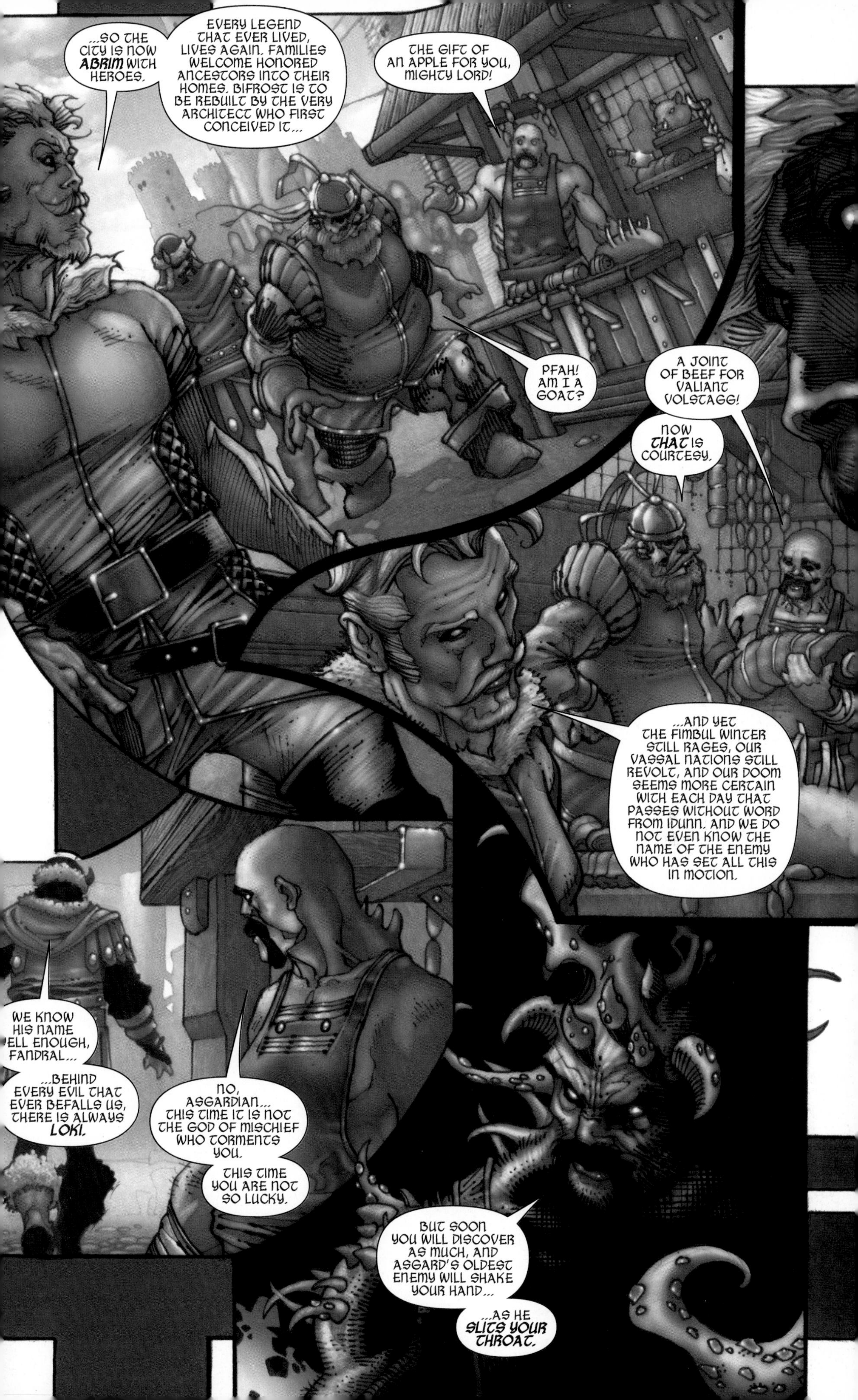
...SO THE CITY IS NOW ABRIM WITH HEROES.
EVERY LEGEND THAT EVER LIVED, LIVES AGAIN. FAMILIES WELCOME HONORED ANCESTORS INTO THEIR HOMES. BIFROST IS TO BE REBUILT BY THE VERY ARCHITECT WHO FIRST CONCEIVED IT...
THE GIFT OF AN APPLE FOR YOU, MIGHTY LORD!
PFAH! AM I A GOAT?
A JOINT OF BEEF FOR VALIANT VOLSTAGG!
NOW THAT IS COURTESY.
...AND YET THE FIMBUL WINTER STILL RAGES, OUR VASSAL NATIONS STILL REVOLT, AND OUR DOOM SEEMS MORE CERTAIN WITH EACH DAY THAT PASSES WITHOUT WORD FROM IDUNN. AND WE DO NOT EVEN KNOW THE NAME OF THE ENEMY WHO HAS SET ALL THIS IN MOTION.
WE KNOW HIS NAME WELL ENOUGH, FANDRAL...
...BEHIND EVERY EVIL THAT EVER BEFALLS US, THERE IS ALWAYS LOKI.
NO, ASGARDIAN... THIS TIME IT IS NOT THE GOD OF MISCHIEF WHO TORMENTS YOU.
THIS TIME YOU ARE NOT SO LUCKY.
BUT SOON YOU WILL DISCOVER AS MUCH, AND ASGARD'S OLDEST ENEMY WILL SHAKE YOUR HAND...
...AS HE SLITS YOUR THROAT.

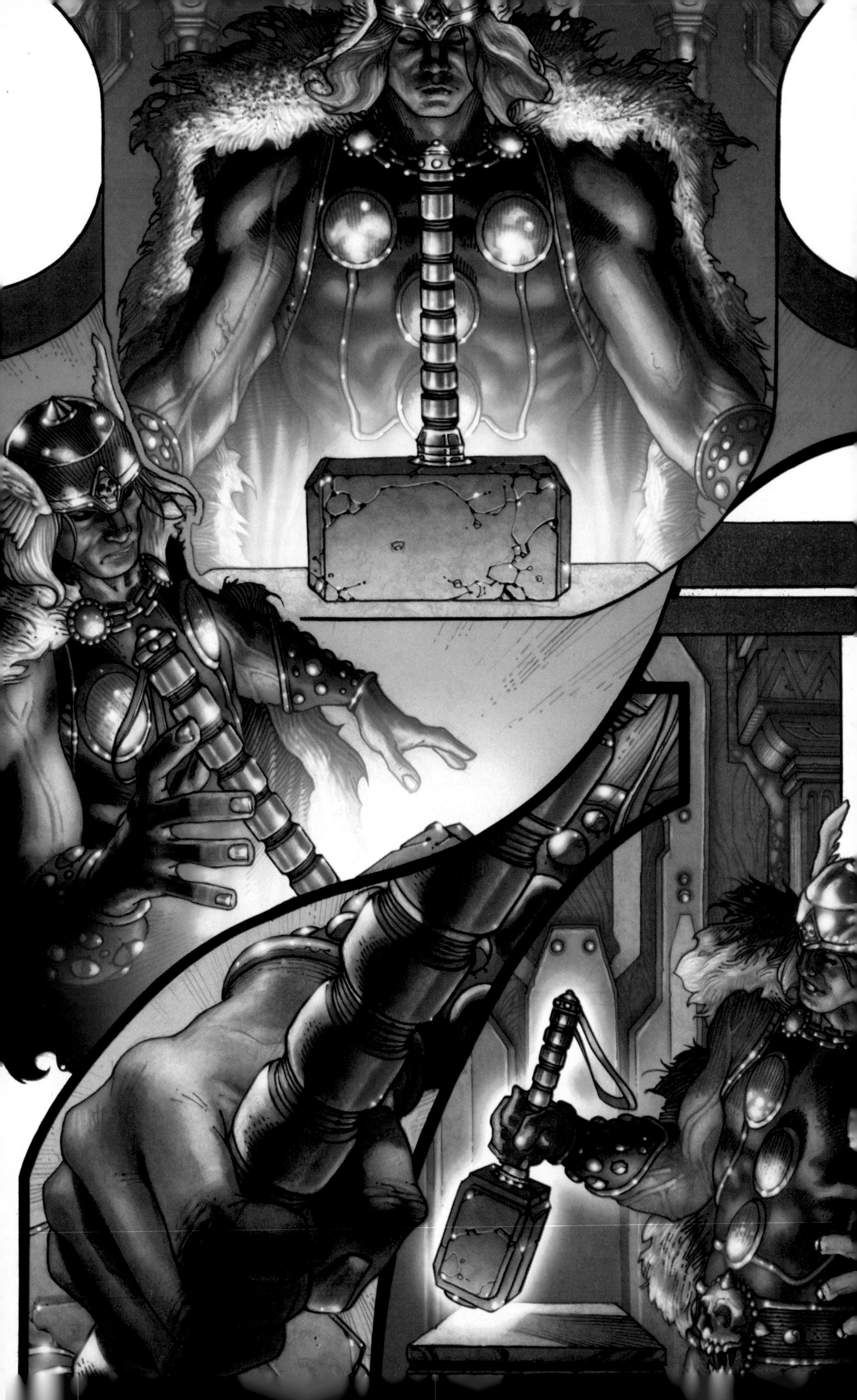

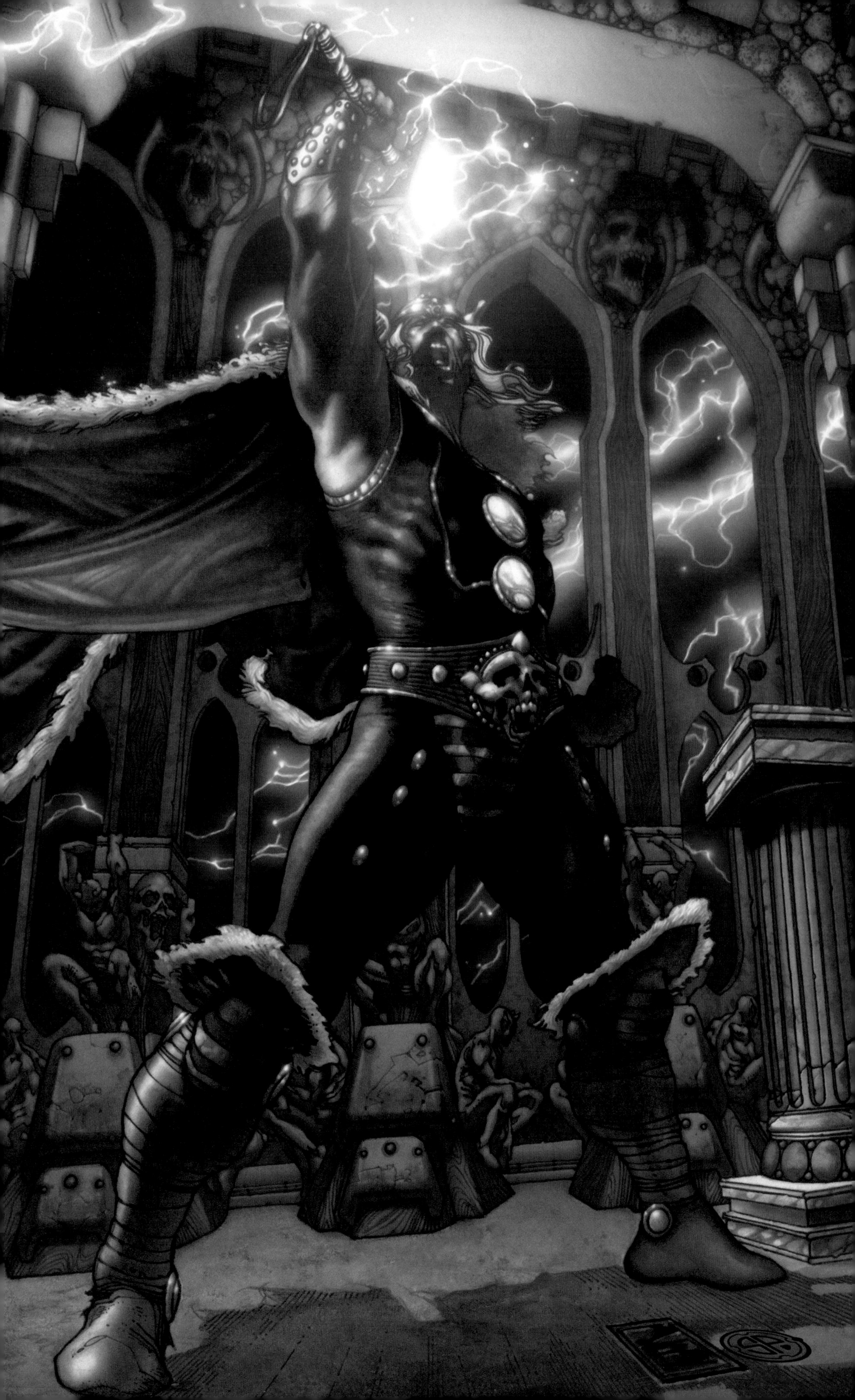

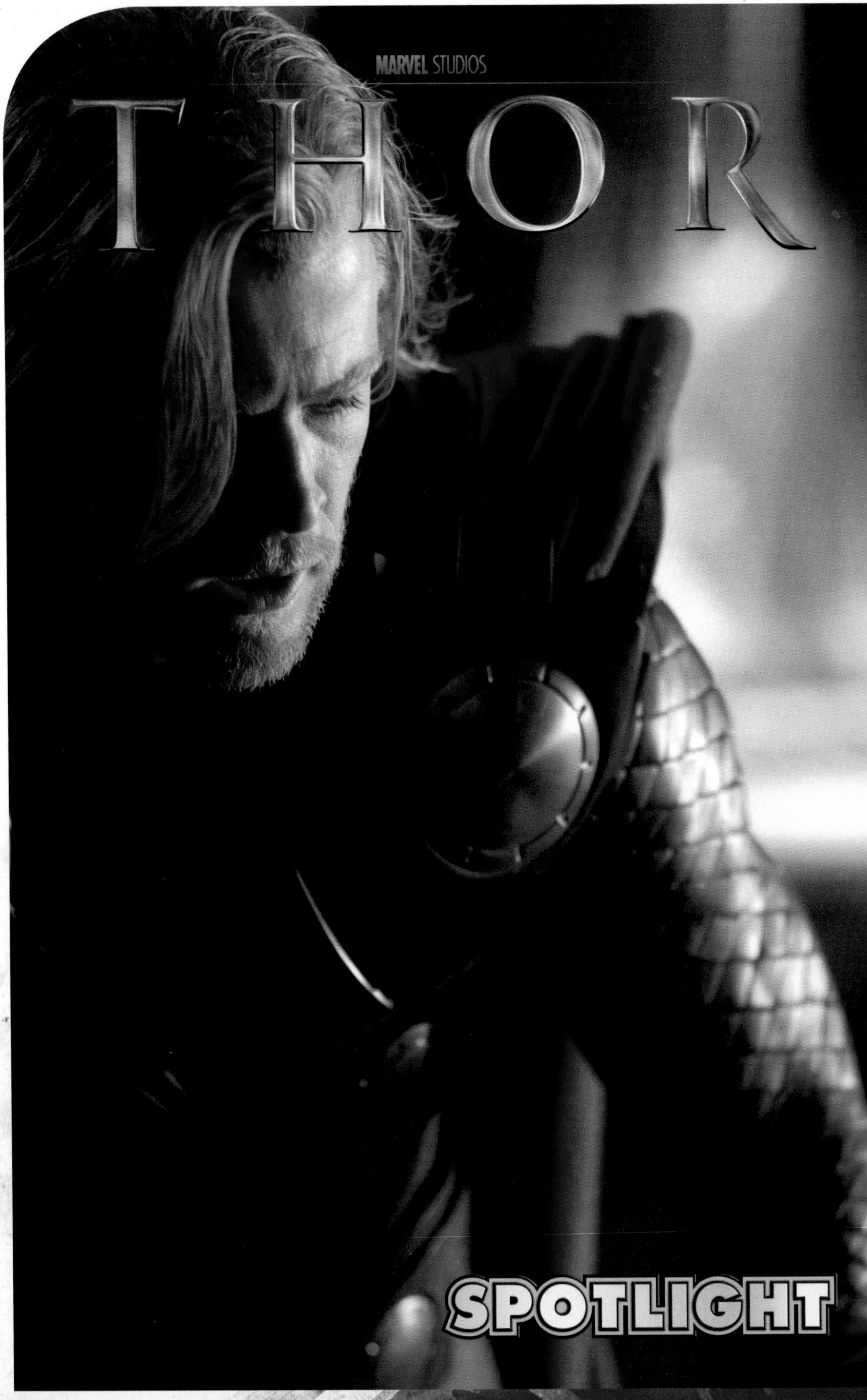
MARVEL STUDIOS
THOR
SPOTLIGHT

FOR ASGARD!

Writer Robert Rodi Has Delivered Three Astonishing Series Set in the Sometimes-Not–So-Hallowed-Halls of Asgard.

By Mike Conroy

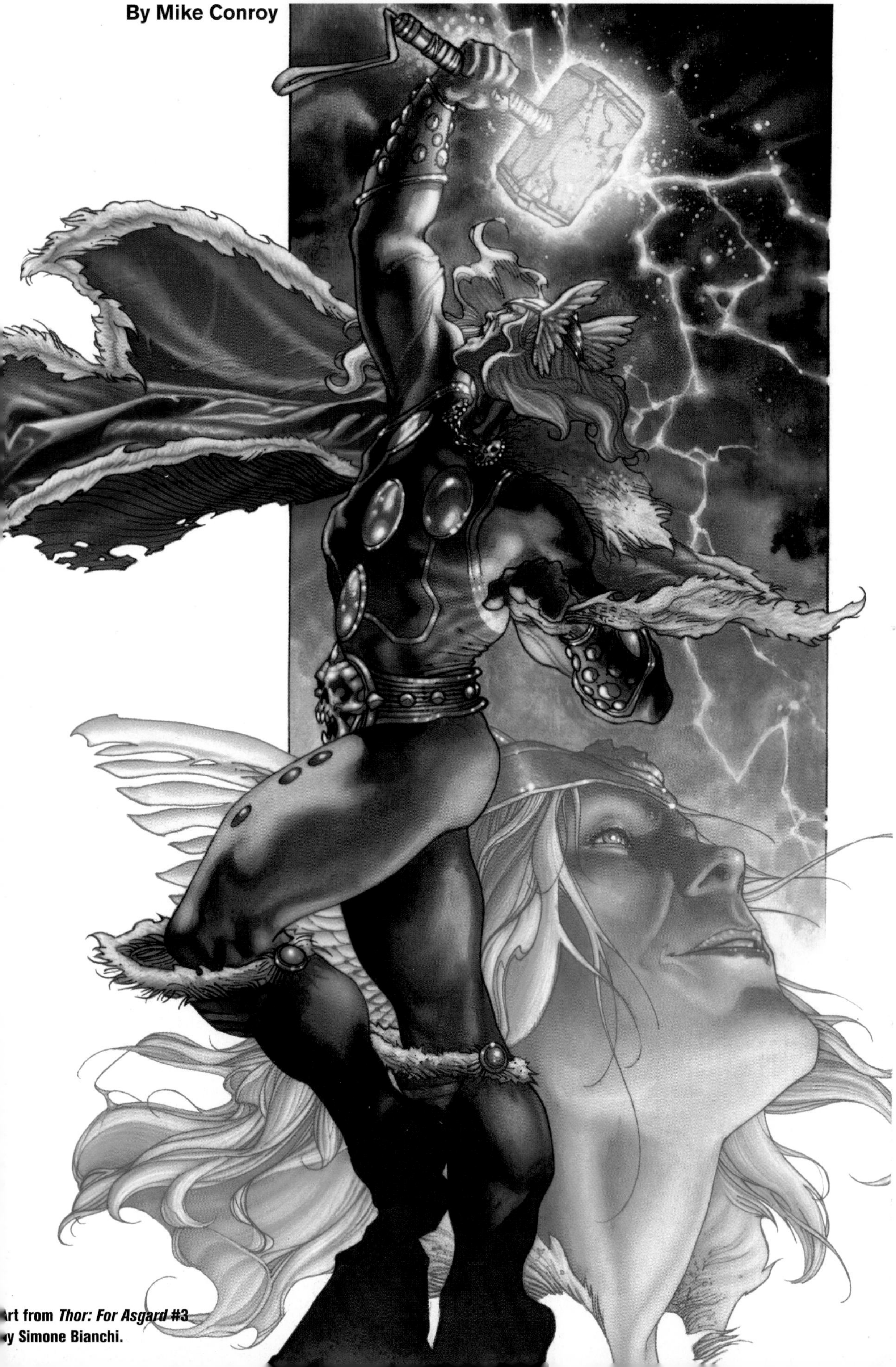

Art from *Thor: For Asgard* #3 by Simone Bianchi.

HEAVY BURDEN: The mystery of Thor's hammer provides one of *Thor: For Asgard*'s most breathtaking moments. (Art from *T:FA #1* by Bianchi.)

With his roots buried deep in Norse myth, Marvel's Thunder God is not your common super hero. There are many facets to his character, and Robert Rodi is only too happy to explore the road less travelled when it comes to chronicling his adventures.

As the *Astonishing Thor* writer put it, "I have to confess, I'm slightly more interested in Thor as a Norse god than as a super hero. If I had to choose between Thor the Asgardian and Thor the Avenger, it's door number one, thanks. And there aren't a lot of projects that spotlight that side of him, so I'm happy to help make up the balance. Fortunately, in this current market, there seems to be room for all kinds of different portrayals of the big guy, so we can all be happy."

Rodi started making up the balance back in 2004 when he wrote a *Loki* four-parter. He has, however, had an abiding fondness for ancient myths and legends. "As a kid, I had a keen interest of all world mythologies, though I learned about them mainly through movies and comics and TV. I delved into the literary sources, and other interpretations like Wagner's *Ring* cycle, much later."

Stan Lee and Jack Kirby introduced the Thunder God into the nascent Marvel Universe in 1962's *Journey into Mystery #83*. Comparing their interpretation with the Norse original, Rodi – who also wrote

> ## "...for the ancients, the gods were remote and virtually unknowable, and the myths about them served social and political functions. They weren't entertainment."
>
> – *Astonishing Thor* writer Robert Rodi

Thor: For Asgard, a 2009 six-parter – said, "Marvel's version is the Viking Thor as refracted through Stan and Jack's modern, urban point of view. You look at Kirby's Asgard; it's got a kind of burnished, sci-fi look that pulls it into the post-industrial age. And Stan added the Donald Blake identity, taming the young thunder god's arrogance by saddling him with a humble human alter-ego; again, a very modern concept – that a god could actually benefit from experiencing common humanity."

It's often said that super heroes are the 20th century's version of the ancient myths and legends. It's not a view to which the writer entirely subscribes. "I'm not sure the comparison is an apt one. For the ancients, the gods were remote and virtually unknowable, and the myths about them served social and political functions. They weren't entertainment. Super heroes, by comparison, are points of identification for readers. We're supposed to get into their skin, feel what it's like to *be* them. It's an escape, a joyride. Two thousand years ago, you might sacrifice a goat to Apollo and hope he was in a good mood that day – but with Spider-Man, you're up there with him, swinging around town, the wind whistling in your ears."

Rodi, who admits to having been a Thor fan "forever," finds much that attracts him to the Thunder God's mythos. "I love the bigness, the sprawl, the epic scale of Asgard and its denizens. I love the idea that these characters are immortal, but not immutable. They change. They're always changing. Stan and Jack's Asgardians are very different than mine, even though I'm building on what they did – just as they built on what came before them. It's a wonderful wheel of story that just keeps turning and turning, on into infinity."

Moving on to discuss Asgard's major citizens, Rodi said, "Thor's the big brother, the one everybody looks up to. He's been around for millennia, he's seen and done everything, and he knows exactly who he is and what needs to be done. The only times he suffers uncertainty or self-doubt are when he's forced

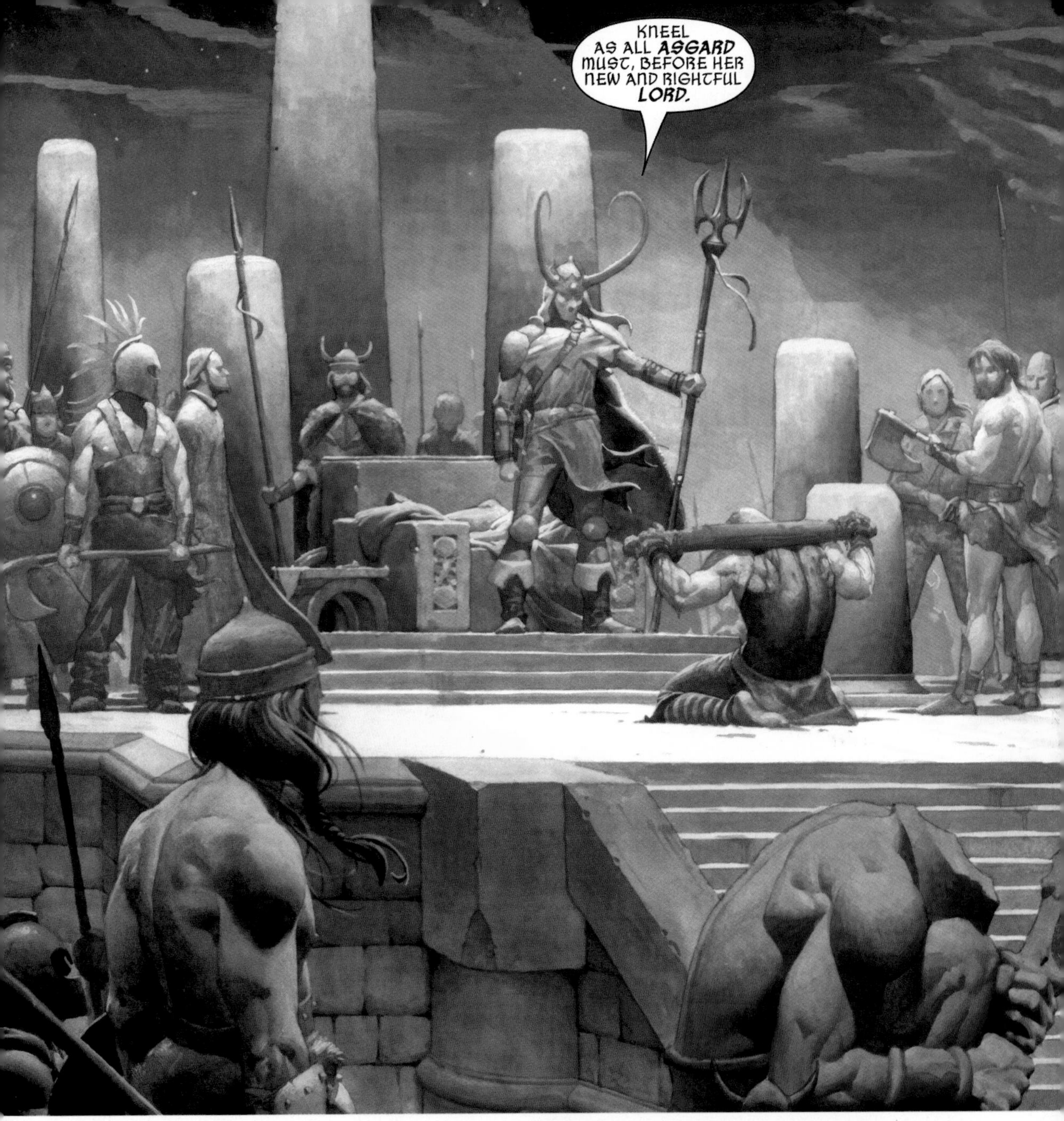
KNEEL AS ALL ASGARD MUST, BEFORE HER NEW AND RIGHTFUL LORD.

into a different role – as in *Thor: For Asgard,* where he's made to serve as regent for Odin, and he makes the mistake of trying to *be* Odin, which so undermines him he can't even lift Mjolnir anymore. But of course he gets his mojo back at the end, because he always does. He's Thor."

As for Thor's stepbrother, the Trickster God, the writer revealed his thoughts when he first discussed the *Loki* miniseries with his editor. "When Axel Alonso offered me the series, it was with the caveat that it had to be something special – something no one's done before. My immediate thought was, 'All right, then, after all these years, let's give Loki what he wants.' Instead of once again showing him trying to crush Asgard, let's start with that job already done: He's won, he's the victor, he's the new lord of the place. Odin, Thor, Balder, everyone else is in chains. It's Loki's town – which is where it all starts to unravel for him, because he doesn't really *want* to be king. He doesn't *want* to sit on a throne all day and hear

KING LOKI: The supreme ruler of Asgard lets his brother Thor know it in Robert Rodi and artist Esad Ribic's stunning *Loki*, collected in *Thor & Loki: Blood Brothers HC.*

petitions for lumber rights and sign trade agreements with Karnilla or whatever – which forces him to face what he really *did* want all those years, which is something else entirely. The idea was to turn Loki into a villain of almost Shakespearean complexity, like Macbeth or Richard III – someone you loathe. But at the same time, you're saying, 'Man, that poor, sad bugger.'"

Explaining his *Loki* was all about defining the Trickster God's character, he continued, "He starts out as the God of Mischief, then graduates to being the God of Evil – but who is he *really?* What's made him the way he is, and what keeps him going? Obviously, being taken from his real family by the man who killed his father and brought up as a lesser son in that man's court – that's got a lot to do with it.

"That's the other half of the equation," Rodi said, referring to the stepbrothers' interaction. "I wanted to

BIG EGO: Thor faces Ego, the Living Planet, in this "astonishing" art spread by artist Mike Choi in Rodi's *Astonishing Thor #1.*

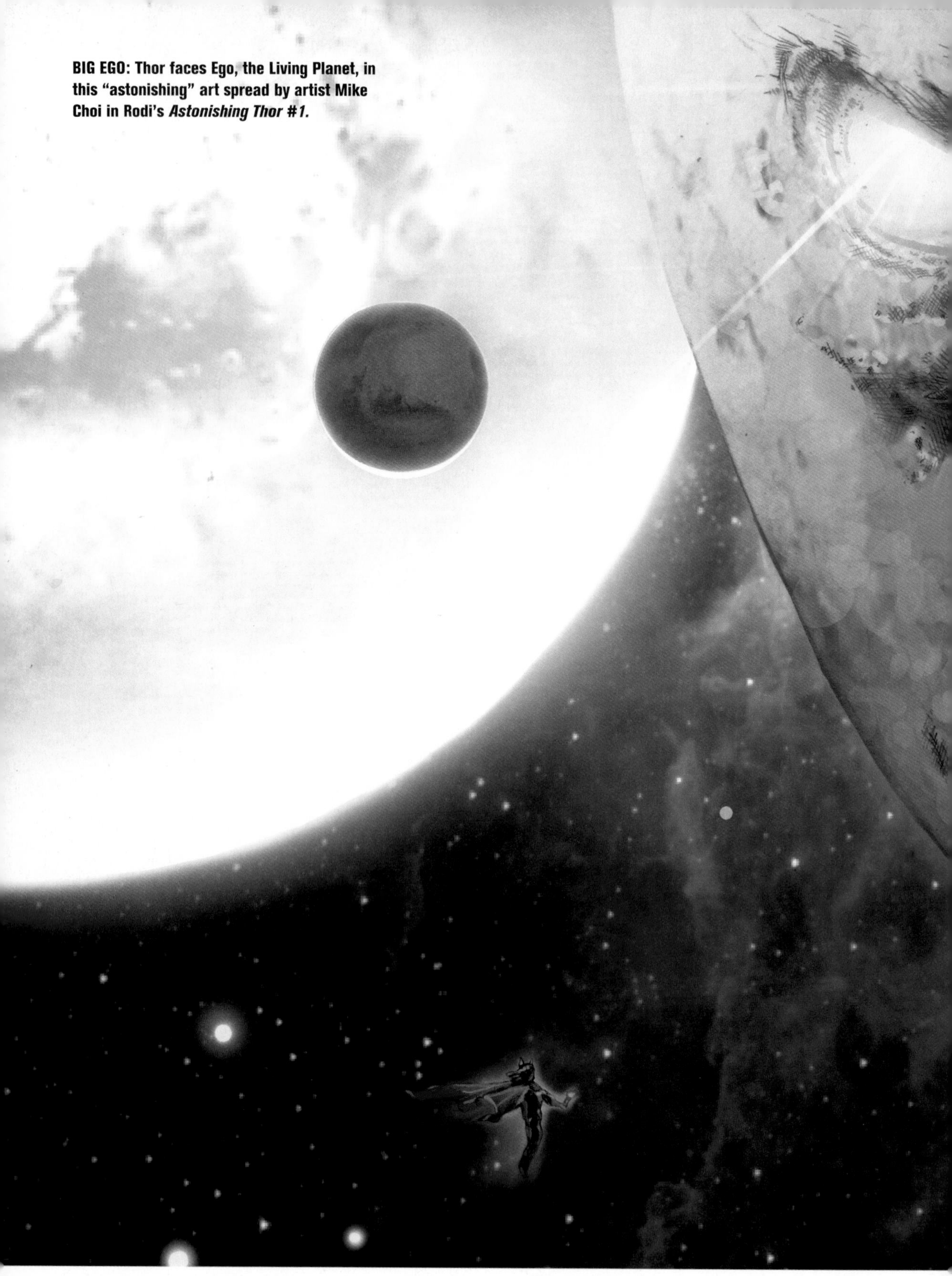

make the Thor/Loki relationship as credible as possible, so Loki's realization of how he *really* feels about Thor is at the climax of my *Loki*. Obviously, I don't want to be too specific about it, 'cause I'd prefer people go out and buy the darned book. But I'd like to think, when they read it, they'll think, 'Huh. That makes sense.'"

Then, there's Odin.

"He's the All-Father," Rodi said. "That about says it. He's the supreme symbol of divine authority, the court of final appeal. I gotta say, there have been occasional attempts to take Odin out of the series by one means or another, and it really never works without him. I do it in *For Asgard*, but with intent. Odin is off on a quest, but paradoxically that makes him more omnipresent than ever: Thor, for instance, is almost smothered by the weight of his absence."

Addressing Odin's relationship with his sons, Rodi

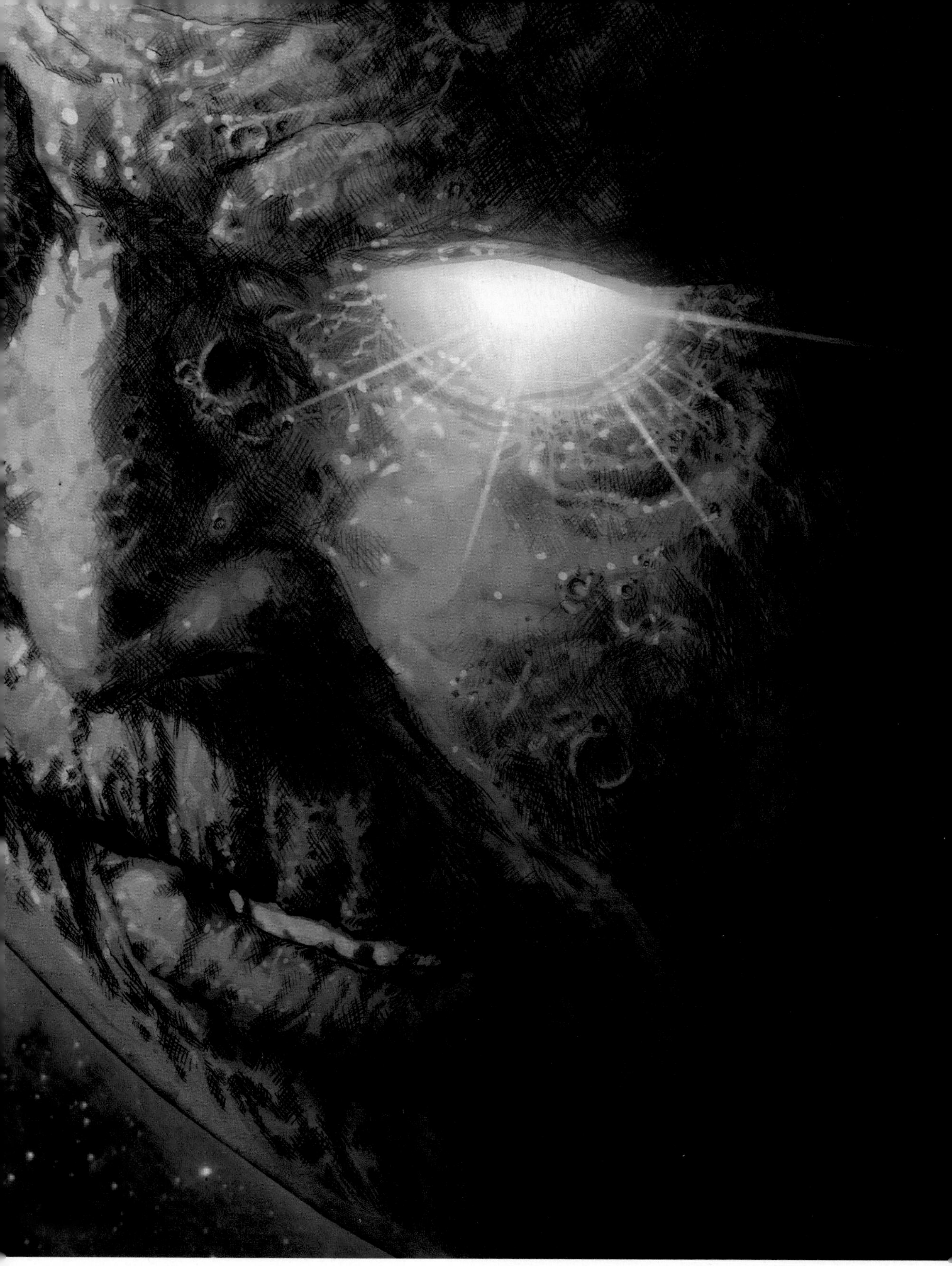

said, "That's up to each individual writer. My own idea, floated in *Loki*, is that he took the infant Loki under his wing with the specific aim of turning him evil, because that would galvanize Thor's good. Uncle Ben, he's not. But we can't judge him by the standards of humanity. He's…well, he's Odin."

Across just three series, Rodi has added much insight to the legend of Thor – but he's not finished yet. He has several ideas in the pipeline; it won't be long until he's further expanding the characters of the Thunder God and his associates, and upon the world of Asgard.

Rodi's first two forays into Asgard, Thor & Loki: Blood Brothers HC *and* Thor: For Asgard HC, *are already available from book retailers. And* Astonishing Thor, *his series with artist Mike Choi, is just getting started! Check with your comics retailer for the first fantastic issues!* •

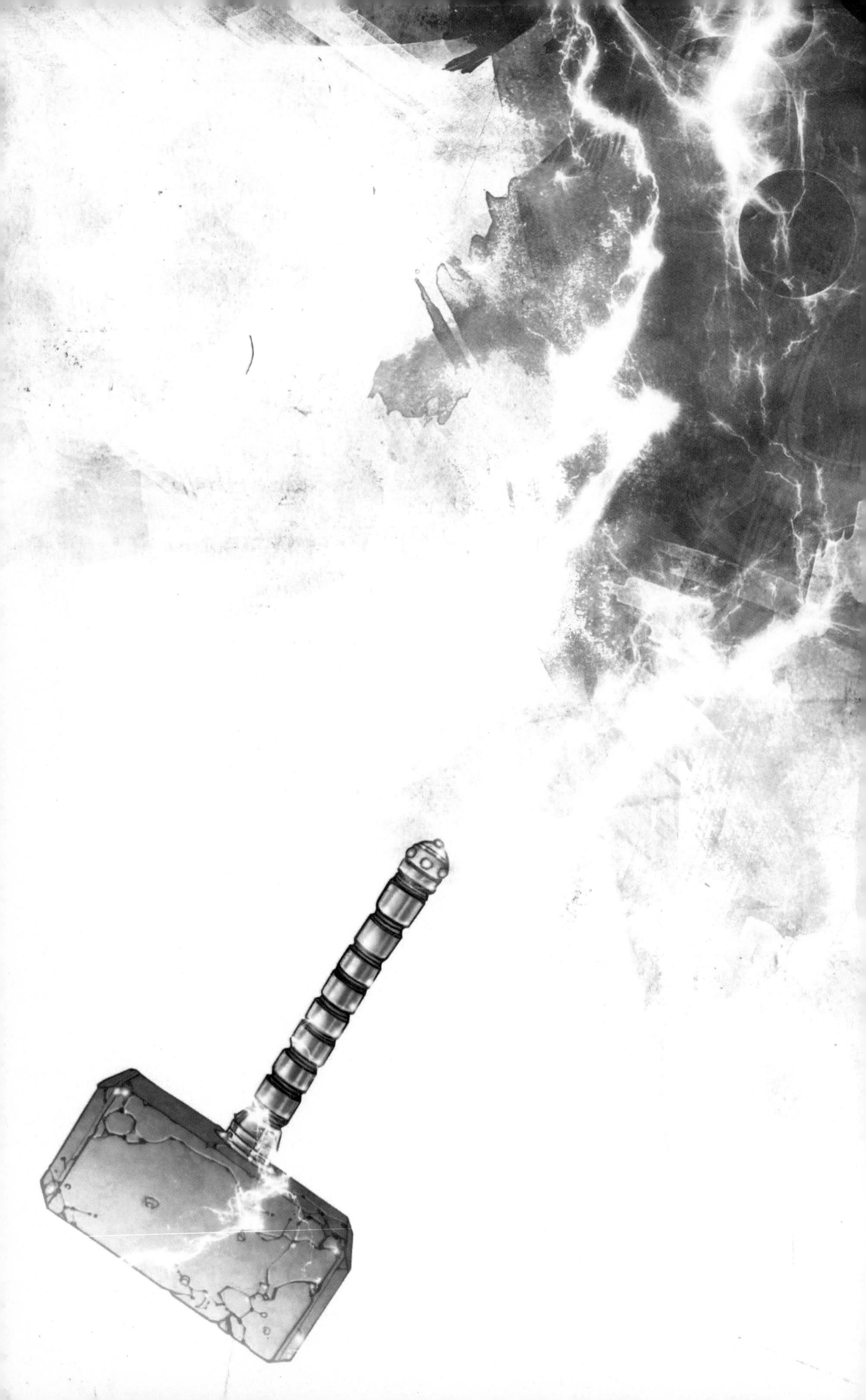